SMART
SCHOOL
LEADERS

Leading with Emotional Intelligence

Janet Patti • James Tobin

KENDALL/HUNT PUBLISHING COMPANY
4050 Westmark Drive   Dubuque, Iowa 52002

Contents

chapter **6**   **The People Side of Change   89**

chapter **7**   **The Purpose of School: Promoting Equity and Social Justice   111**

About the Authors

Writing individually is a challenging and creative process; writing with another expands and deepens this process. This book is the result of a rich collaboration. We shared ideas. We gave each other feedback. When we had a clash of opinions, we problem solved. We complimented each other's strengths. Janet depended on Jim's persistence, knowledge of the psychological aspects of leadership, and writing and editing skills. Jim relied on Janet's optimism, extensive knowledge of school leadership, and visionary perspectives. In the end, we feel richer. We completed this book and got to know each other in ways we would not have had we not collaborated. As one of us said on the final day of writing, "We lived these chapters."

Janet Patti, Ed.D. is the Coordinator of the Education Administration and Supervision Program at Hunter College of The City University of New York. Janet's research focus is on creating school culture and climate that supports academic, social and emotional learning. Central to establishing this culture are school leaders who are reflective practitioners and continual learners. The theory and practice of emotional intelligence can assist them to influence, form and sustain a school culture that promotes and supports learning.

Dr. Patti has been a teacher, counselor and administrator in the public school systems of New York City and San Diego for more than twenty-five years. She has presented seminars and lectures throughout the United States, Latin America and Spain. She is a member of the Leadership Team of the Collaborative for Academic, Social and Emotional Learning. She serves on the executive advisory board for the New York State Association for Supervision and Curriculum Development. Janet is a lead trainer for the nationally recognized *Don't Laugh At Me Program*. Her publications and grant activities promote social and emotional learning through the practice of school leadership. She is the co-author of Waging Peace in Our Schools (Beacon Press, 1996). Janet lives with her life partner, Barry Daub in New York City and can be contacted at jpatti@hunter.cuny.edu.

James Tobin, Ph.D, is a consultant who specializes in social emotional learning, conflict management and organizational change. He has worked with school systems and colleges throughout the United States and in the Netherlands. A former staff developer and Coordinator of Administrator Training for RCCP, James has trained thousands of principals, teachers, parent and student mediators in negotiation and mediation skills. He taught graduate courses in communication and critical thinking at universities such as Adelphi, Hampton and NYU. As a curriculum writer, he has created numerous reading materials for such publishers as Harcourt Brace, Macmillan, and Scholastic and written curriculums for adult learners in the workplace.

A graduate of the doctoral program in applied psychology at New York University, James is a member of the American Psychological Association and the Association for Supervision and Curriculum Development. He has been a keynote speaker at various symposiums including the International Conference on Conflict Resolution in Schools.

With Janet Patti, he conducted a three-year research project on effective school leadership, which led to the collaboration that resulted in this book. James lives with his wife and soul mate, Jean, and his son and hiking buddy, Matthew. He can be contacted at <u>jamestobin@dellmail.com</u>.

Foreword

Leadership is personal. Each organizational issue, conflict, or dilemma has its own uniqueness. Every administrative decision is set in its own context. There may be patterns among the issues and precedents for decisions but each situation requires examination, introspection and re-interpretation. That's what makes leadership interesting; and that's what makes leadership so demanding of our personal skill as well as our intellectual prowess.

I learned this lesson personally shortly after I and a group of educators founded Educators for Social Responsibility. At its beginning ESR was organized to help educators respond to children's concerns about the social and political issues surrounding them and to teach them that they can make a difference in the world. Organized by teachers and administrators in the early 1980s, we knew that children were concerned about the potential for nuclear war, about the ecological damage being done to the environment and about issues of social inequity and social justice. Many felt hopeless and helpless in the face of these issues. However, their hopelessness did not come from a lack of adequate and effective solutions, for they clearly believed that these problems had solutions. Their hopelessness came from the perception that adults could not resolve their differences so that effective solutions could be put in place. They viewed the adult world, particularly the political world, as polarized and oppositional with little demonstrated ability to find common ground. It became clear to us that young people needed to understand the tools of conflict resolution and consensus building so that they could have a greater sense of confidence in themselves and others in finding solutions to the social and political problems our world faces.

In the early years of ESR, we worked to develop curricula and provide professional development that would enable teachers to teach these lessons to their students. However, the more I learned about effective conflict resolution strategies, the more I realized the inadequacies of my own skills. My work with ESR became not only a journey in teaching conflict resolution skills to others, but in teaching myself new ways of dealing with conflict and new ways of thinking about the perspective that others may bring to conflict situations. Being confronted with one's own bad habits is never pleasant, but I felt that if I couldn't model these in my life I shouldn't be trying to teach them to others. No one ever becomes a master in conflict management or conflict resolution. We make progress, but there is always the next situation that demands that we apply what we have learned in new and creative ways.

What I learned through those years with ESR has served me well as superintendent of a medium size school district. Leadership is less about making the right decision than about making decisions that are right for those involved. Vision is critical, but developing the relationships that inspire commitment to the vision is what makes it work. Leadership is personal and relational first and strategic second. It is absolutely necessary for administrators to know where they want to take a school or district and to have a strong set of values and ideals to sustain the journey to that goal. But it is the way in which one works with others that will enable an administrator to realize his or her goals and vision.

It is for that reason that *Smart School Leaders: Leading with Emotional Intelligence* is such a valuable contribution to the field of educational administration.

As Janet and Jim point out throughout this important book, the kind of emotional intelligence that leads to successful administration *can be learned.* There are effective strategies for resolving conflicts, mediating differences, motivating others, facilitating shared leadership, and creating a sense of purpose and common vision in a school or district. However, all of these start with one's self and the willingness to continually look within, reevaluate, find new insights about one's own patterns and habits, and further refine them. In a sense, the administrative journey is not so much about the accomplishments we achieve but our own growth and development as leaders. We must become models of the continuous improvement we expect from our faculty and members of our administrative team.

The research on effective schools has shown that one important element in successful schools is the nature of the professional community within a school. Karen Seashore Louis found that successful schools possessed professionally enriching learning communities among the faculty that were characterized by reflective dialogue about practice, an openness to sharing practices with others, a collective focus on student learning, collaboration, and shared norms and values. These schools embody the qualities of an emotionally intelligent school. They handle conflict well. They support both personal and shared reflection. There is shared leadership with a sense of collective vision and mission. The administrators in these schools model the qualities of emotional intelligence that give permission to faculty members to be open to their own learning and development.

For many administrators and educators, social and emotional learning is new. It is clear to many educators that students need it but it is often less clear to us that we, too, may need to learn these skills as well. It isn't enough to build strong character education, social-emotional learning or service-learning programs for children without thinking about our social, emotional and ethical development. If we understand the importance of our own skill development, we can effectively utilize the professional development that prepares teachers to implement social-emotional learning programs and the experience of teaching these programs to nurture the development of our own self-awareness and skills.

In Hudson schools, therefore, the professional environment among the faculty is equal in importance to the instructional competence of the faculty. The challenge is less the implementation of the social-emotional programs themselves than creating an environment in which faculty can reflect on their own social-emotional skills and be open to their own growth and change. Adults often find this arena of growth more challenging because it is personal. It is as if we admit personal failure by acknowledging that we are not as good as we should be at resolving conflicts or at managing our emotions or at taking the perspective of another. However, it is vital that we make the effort, for to not do so is to deprive ourselves of a rich and fulfilling work environment and to deprive our students of the rich learning environment they deserve. Administrative leadership and modeling is critical to creating that environment, and our ability to use our emotional intelligence is the primary tool to accomplish it.

In the material that follows, Janet and Jim have provided a rich resource for school leaders that can help us build our own skills and create a school climate that supports our faculty's growth. Rarely have I found a book that so effectively weaves theory and practice into artful lessons in leadership. This work is rich with strategies, examples, living personal reflections from the field, and exercises that we can use ourselves, with our administrative teams and with our faculties. Not only have the authors placed their wealth of experience on the table for us to learn from, but they have drawn lessons from many in leadership positions about the dilemmas and challenges they have faced and how they accessed emotional intelligence to create change and growth for their faculties and their students.

As Janet and Jim eloquently detail, the path to effective leadership is through a set of social and emotional skills that are within our grasp. The key is our openness to learning and to continual self-reflection and self-renewal. They have given all of us in administration a great gift of insights, strategies and tools to achieve this. It is now up to each of us to use this work to develop the kind of emotionally intelligent leadership that can create high performing, resilient learning communities in our schools.

Hudson, Massachusetts   Sheldon Berman
July 6, 2003

1. Karen Seashore Louis and Sharon D. Kruse, *Professionalism and Community: Perspectives on Reforming Urban Schools* (Thousand Oaks, Calif.: Corwin, 1995).

Preface

"Though I do not believe that a plant will spring up where no seed has been, I have great faith in a seed. Convince me that you have a seed and I am prepared to expect wonders."

—Henry David Thoreau

Like Thoreau, we have great faith in seeds. The seed of this book is rooted in our belief that school leaders are faced with enormous challenges in this rapidly-changing, put-pressure-on-the-principal-and-superintendent era of school reform. In that seed is the kernel of truth that hard challenges are best faced if school leaders fully develop their most potentially powerful tool—themselves. In this book, we ask the reader to consider the concept of emotional intelligence and how that concept can be applied to the practice of school leadership in creating successful and caring schools. It is our contention that emotionally-smart schools are achieving, resilient, and well-led learning communities that score well on tests *and even better at life.* Though some other authors, notably Daniel Goleman, have written extensively about the connection between emotional intelligence and good schools, this book is the first to focus solely on helping aspiring and practicing school leaders become emotionally smart in their leadership.

The seeds for this book were first planted in the years we have spent in schools first as educators of young people and then as developers of teachers and administrators. In our work in schools, we observed often how well-meaning reformers forget the human element in school change. They push their programs, shift incentives here and there and leave blaming the people they left behind. We also noticed how different constituencies in a school sometimes work at cross purposes to each other even though they all have the same purpose in the end—the students' learning. Achieving that end is difficult when people do not have the communication skills, the conflict management skills or the overall "people" skills to keep on track. In this book, we will provide you with strategies for learning these skills and helping others learn them as well.

Finally, the last seed for this book germinated in our research of factors that influenced the ability of school leaders to implement a nationally-known conflict resolution program. In our three-year study, we discovered how successful leaders lead from within, developing their own inner strengths so that they could best use the resources around them. In those three years, we had an opportunity to dig deep into the thoughts and emotions of those who succeeded and those who failed. We learned their strategies and how they decided where to implement them. This research and the personal stories of many other school leaders inform this book and inspired us to write it. We targeted the book to meet the needs of aspiring school leaders veteran leaders who each day look for different ways to make a difference and for all those who have great faith in a seed.

James Tobin
Janet Patti

Acknowledgments

A successful school bears the imprint of smart caring people who come together in the interest of children. This book bears a similar imprint.

We first thank the contributors for our research–based leadership *Readings* that extend the conceptual basis for the ideas we present in this text. They are preeminent thinkers and writers from the field of educational leadership and social and emotional learning: Carmella B'hahn, Yvonne De Gaetano, Maurice Elias, Daniel Goleman, Sue Keister, Kimberley Kinsler, Marcia Knoll, Larry Leverett, Nick Michelli, Frank Moretti, Parker Palmer, Anthony Picciano, Ted Repa, and Robin Stern (see List of Contributors for more information). They willingly responded to our call to either write or share an article. We thank them so much for their ideas and their commitment to this book and to schools.

We also thank the writers of our Lessons from the Field, which are placed at the end of chapters two through ten. These gifted educational leaders were asked to write short reflections that would give you a sense of how they apply their emotional intelligence in real-life school and district settings. Their ideas enriched our book by placing the notion of *SMART* or EQ leadership into the everyday context of school communities. These writers are Sheldon Berman, Matt Bromme, Mark Gerzon, Sydell Kane, Rachel Kessler, Larry Leverett, Migdalia Maldonado-Torres, Larry Peterson, Joe Santello, Philip Santisie and Rene Townsend (more about them at the end of each lesson).

We believe our voices are clearly heard in these pages, but we are joined by other voices, some loud and some barely detected, though we can hear them whisper on certain pages. These voices belong to those whose stories we tell throughout the book to illustrate what we were trying to communicate. Some of their names we mentioned in the book. Some we did not out of respect for their wishes or for other reasons. All have made a difference in schools. They inspire us. There are many, but the names we can thank publicly include: Elaine Anderson, Mary Butz, Norma Caraballo, Emma de la Rocca, Doreen Dillon, Mae Fong, Larrie Hall, David H. Hodges, Vince Jewell, Carmen Jimenez, Scott Miller, David Mitchell, The New York City Distinguished Faculty principals, and Helen Zentner. A special note of thanks must go to Gayle Burnett, Barry Daub, Lynn Fischer, Brenda McGoldrick, Jacqui Norris and Nancy Sing-Bock whom we asked to write their stories for specific chapters because we knew that their stories best expressed what we wanted to say. The time and care they gave was considerable and most appreciated.

For both of us, this book represents decades of learning the people side of organizations. In that learning we have been fortunate to receive inspiration and support, either personally or via their writings, from a number of individuals and organizations who have helped us shape the ideas that we present in this book. Among these individuals we need to mention Richard Boyatzis, Cary Cherniss, Larry Dieringer, Morton Deutsch, Maurice Elias, Kevin Feinberg, Roger Fisher, Arthur Foresta, Dan Goleman, Linda Lantieri, Anne McKee, Tom Roderick, Peter Senge, William Ury and Roger Weissberg. Of the many organizations that align with our thinking two particularly deserve mention for our years of involvement with them: Educators for Social Responsibility and The

Leadership Team of The Collaborative for Academic, Social and Emotional Learning (CASEL).

Readings and Lessons brought words to our book but we also wanted to have something for your eyes and there again we found allies who came to our aid. We acknowledge the assistance of these allies: Shelley Berman from Hudson Public Schools; Dan Bodette from the School of Environmental Studies; CASEL staff members; Chris Burke from Hurricane Island Outward Bound; Barry Daub from the Mickey Mantle School; Larry Dieringer from Educators for Social Responsibility National; Linda Lantieri from the Resolving Conflict Creatively Program of Educators for Social Responsibility and Joan Shaughnessy, Jean Spraker and Meg Waters at Northwest Regional Educational Laboratory. The images they sent are appreciated but not as much as their generosity.

We could not write a book about emotional competencies without mentioning those in our inner circle who have shown an enormous amount of emotional skill in dealing with us as we went through this process. They supported us in ways no one else could or would. James would like to thank his son, Matthew, for letting him share stories about him with perfect strangers and for continuing to love him even though his dad was hogging the computer and missing too many readings of the Sunday comics. James would also like to tell the world that he is lucky enough to be married to the love of his life who got him through a dissertation and now this book. Janet would like to thank Barry Daub, her life partner, whose unwavering love, dedication, passion and creative "ideas" made this endeavor a reality. She would also like to thank her precious parents and her sister for instilling the inner values that guide her and for their constant love and daily supports. Writing a book and working full time is never a simple task so Janet gives special thanks to her Administrative Assistant, Catherine (Sarang) Chung, for being "Dr. Patti" throughout this project. Janet also extends her gratitude to the aspiring leaders of the Administration and Supervision Program at Hunter College who remind her daily about the need for *SMART* leadership in schools.

Finally, we would like to thank our publisher, Kendall Hunt, particularly Sue Ellen Saad for her belief in this project and our editors Billee Jo Hefel, Jenifer Chapman and Colleen Zelinsky for a million answers to relentless questions and a worthy product.

Chapter 1

Introduction

Welcome to the age of *dealing with our emotions*. We, as a society, have finally begun to recognize that our emotional selves are a critical component of who we are, how we act, who we can become, and how others respond to us. Our EQ carries as much weight, if not more, in terms of life successes than our IQ. And who is better positioned to assure that every student and every adult they come into contact with in schools develop their EQ more than you, the educational leader?

This book is about being at the forefront of school change—change in self followed by change in the people you lead. It's not specifically about one current educational focus such as how to align data to drive instruction or how to successfully implement a program in literacy or math. Yet, it is about all of them. It's about creating schools that we call *SMART* Schools—schools where everyone learns how to make full use of emotional and intellectual intelligence to accomplish goals. In the schools we discuss in this book, the assistant principals, principals, district superintendents, and other school leaders are both teachers and learners in this process of personal and organizational change. The leaders you will meet in this book are in the process of becoming the best leaders they can become. They recognize that they are the models; that their behaviors influence the culture and climate of the organizations they lead. As a result, many of those they lead work hard to develop themselves and others. Together, they create schools in which young people achieve and actively engage as citizens in a democracy. This *real change* we talk about in this book is not a function of one program or another, added school days with longer hours, or harder, high-stakes tests. It is about the deeper sustained change that occurs when everyone in the school or school district grasps the importance of developing social and emotional competencies along with intellectual ones and takes personal responsibility to insure that this happens.

Change in self is perhaps the hardest change of all. But when we are aware of our own strengths and limitations, we have the best chance of succeeding, both in trying moments and in moments of success. John Kotter, world-renowned business leader at the Harvard Business School, tells us to "see, feel and change," when we want to change paradigms. We have to show people what the problems or issues are, allow them to *feel* the need for action and compel and support them to take risks and make the change.[1] Feelings are no longer considered too "touchy-feely" for the workplace. In fact, we understand how they drive people in the workplace in many ways.

We wrote this book because in our collective experiences with leaders and teachers in schools, we have witnessed good plans gone awry because of a lack of human relations skills. Everybody talks about what the best practices are to increase student achievement and create great schools. Few, however, take the time to recognize that as professional people, we need the best practices for our behavior as well. As educators, we need to learn better ways to develop ourselves so that we don't impede the very processes we set out to improve. True, people are people, but there are tried and true practices that help us become better people. We believe that it is the responsibility of everyone working with children to be ethical, moral, civic-minded, emotionally and intellectually smart individuals who care about humankind. *We are their models. We better get it right.*

You are probably reading this book because you are pursuing a career as a school administrator, or you are a leader of a school or school district in an urban, suburban or rural community. Maybe you already consider yourself to be *emotionally intelligent* based on a lifetime of self-work directed at becoming a more integrated person in body, mind and spirit. In that case, pat yourself on the back and enjoy the additional tools this book provides for self-reflection. Maybe you are interested in the topic, care a lot about the future of our collective children and want to look at reforming schools from another lens. Perhaps you are reading this book as part of a class in education administration, or professional development in your schools or districts. Or maybe you are at your wit's end and find yourself in desperate need of something to latch onto to avoid "burning out" in work you once felt was meaningful.

Whatever the reason you have for purchasing this book, we welcome you. We believe that the key to effective leadership and successful schools in the 21st century is good people, downright smart, caring people, who excel in both IQ and EQ. This book's primary focus is to enhance your leadership abilities based on a model of emotional intelligence. In 1995, Dan Goleman paved the way to this exploration with his seminal book, *Emotional Intelligence*.[2] Across the globe, the term emotional intelligence took on great meaning. It gave license to educators to say that we *can* develop the social and emotional competencies of young people and that there are scientifically-based strategies to make this a reality. Today, many young children are learning how to develop their social and emotional competencies in tandem with academic skills in classrooms all across the country.[3] Young children are learning to communicate effectively, solve problems wisely, and control their inappropriate impulses. Many young people, in schools across this country interrupt bias and prejudice, effectively mediate difficult situations among their peers, and negotiate resolutions to their own conflicts. Others invest their time in service learning. They give back to their community in a variety of ways. In these schools, character building is at the core of the school's mission. Assuredly, these young people, who will eventually assume positions in the workplace, will possess the much-needed social skills that too many employees lack today.[4] This is the good news.

But what about the adults? The sad news—little emphasis is placed on developing these very same skills in the adults who educate our children. Where does our responsibility kick in to be real models for today's youth? Let's face it. We all know adults, many of whom teach and even lead schools, who sorely lack these very same skills. They may have gotten to their current positions because they are content smart and maybe even a cut above many others. But, are they? Empirical research leaves little doubt that IQ and other measures of cognitive ability are limited in their power to predict who will succeed. Measures of emotional intelligence, on the other hand, matter more for superior performance.[5] *SMART* schools are ones that promote social and emotional learning for adults as well as for young people.

DEVELOPING OUR EQ

What are these emotional competencies that are so critical to the success of a leader and can they be learned? A competency is defined as any measurable characteristic of a person that differentiates levels of performance in a given job, role, organization or culture. Goleman refers to these as, "learned capabilities based on emotional intelligence that result in outstanding performance at work." He divides them into two categories: personal competence and social competence (see Figure 1.1 below.) Personal competence includes two key cluster areas: *self-awareness* and *self-management*. Social Competence includes *social awareness* and *relationship management*. The "star" or outstanding leader is the person who is self aware and who consciously works at improving his or her competencies. She knows her strengths and limitations, seeks out feedback, and learns from her mistakes. As she directs her own learning, she capitalizes on her strength areas in her performance while she continuously works on strengthening her limitations. Her goal is to bridge the gap between her ideal self, the leader she wants to be and her real self, the leader she is now. EI competencies are not innate talents, but rather learned abilities.[6] If the leader is at optimal performance, so too is the prospect that her organization's performance will excel, too.

Drawing on the seminal work of Harvard professor David McClelland, Goleman, Boyatzis and McKee in their 2002 book, *Primal Leadership,* concentrate on identifying the characteristics and competencies of "star" performers. These competencies distinguish successful leaders from those who are less successful. The task for those interested in assuring excellence in leadership, then, is either to choose people who have these same competencies or help others to develop them. Recognize, it isn't easy to get people in high leadership positions to look at their own performances. Top dogs often think they are much more skilled than they actually are. Goleman and Boyatsis remind us, "Rare are those who dare to tell a commanding leader he is too harsh or let a leader know he could be more visionary or more democratic."[7] Giving feedback to the leader is doubtful, at best. Imagine a teacher or custodian walking into the principal's office to tell the principal how he really messed up when he lambasted the new teacher in the hallway the other day. Or a principal, for that matter, telling the superintendent that he disagreed with the decision to implement a certain policy that the superintendent had

Self	Other
Personal Competence	**Social Competence**
Self-Awareness	*Social Awareness*
- Emotional self-awareness	- Empathy
- Accurate self-assessment	- Service orientation
- Self-confidence	- Organizational awareness
Self-Management	*Relationship Management*
- Self-control	- Developing others
- Trustworthiness	- Influence
- Conscientiousness	- Communication
- Adaptability	- Conflict management
- Achievement drive	- Leadership
- Initiative	- Change catalyst
	- Building bonds
	- Teamwork & collaboration

FIGURE 1.1   Emotional Competence Framework
(Adapted from Goleman, D. (2001) *An EI-based theory of performance.* http://www.eiconsortium.org)

worked so hard to implement. Some things are best left unsaid. The emotionally intelligent leader recognizes this position difference, invites feedback via dialogue, focus groups, questionnaires, and 360 degree assessments. She encourages an outside coach or consultant to be her mirror of reflection into her own behavior. Over the last decade, educational leaders have applauded the concept of coaching teachers through peer evaluations and other strategies. But who coaches the leaders? Ongoing systematic, honest feedback would surely help the leader improve performance, hear some of what employees *aren't* saying, and open channels of communication that are critical to a healthy school environment.

PREPARING "NEW LEADERS"

As we write this book, there is a critical demand for quality school leaders. Many of the nation's 93,200 principals, experienced school administrators, are retiring and leaving leadership positions to novice administrators. Paradoxically, fewer candidates are applying to fill their seats.[8] While this presents a great challenge, it also presents a wonderful opportunity. The challenge is to attract and recruit strong potential leaders to fill these positions. The opportunity exits to provide them with the knowledge, skills and attitudes to lead schools with social and emotional competence.

Sadly, the aspiring school leaders we meet in most of our courses say that their school principals, or assistant principals are the furthest away from the kind of leadership we are talking about in this book. It amazes us how much we still hear about the top down leader, the autocratic leader, and the lack of good modeling that these young people need. Don't get us wrong. We know the job is tough. On a daily basis, school leaders juggle the needs and concerns of many constituencies; all the more reason why they need to have polished emotional competencies. Their responsibility is to make the tough but delicate decisions needed to promote the academic achievement of young people in a culture of safety and social and emotional health. Unlike corporate management, the product of effective school leadership is intelligent, healthy, enlightened young people who, in their own time, may become the leaders of tomorrow. Leaders who learn to lead schools with emotional intelligence will leave their imprints on society for many years to come.

Fortunately, we know many great school leaders who *are* emotionally intelligent and serve as models for the next generation of leaders. Not too long ago, we spent a day with fifty principals in New York City, talking about their emotional competencies and exploring ways to assist the new principals they mentored in the development of their EQ. Not surprisingly, these were fifty stellar principals in New York City, The Distinguished Faculty, named because of their excellent performance in leading successful schools.[9] Just hearing them speak about their passion for serving their schools and the young principals they were guiding was electric. It was as if the topic of this book was suddenly before us in the images of these *SMART* leaders bonded together in a deep emotional commitment to improving schools.

HOW TO USE THIS BOOK

In order to make the most of this book, you will need to take on the role of a reflective practitioner. Some of you may be using this book as a text to gain more knowledge about emotional intelligence in the area of school leadership. Others might be using this tool developmentally. The following overview is provided to assist you in making choices as to how to best use this text.

Target Audience

This text is designed to be used in pre-service and in-service professional development of educational leaders or by individual readers. Using reflection, skill practice, problem-based learning cases and current literature, leaders will explore, identify and improve their social and emotional competencies. They will also acquire a myriad of strategies that can assist them in bringing the theory and practice of emotional intelligence into their schools. The book can be used by university professors in educational leadership programs, local community school districts for professional development or by school leaders as self-practice or as a means of group learning with their staffs.

Chapter Design

Each of the ten chapters focuses on a different aspect of EQ school leadership. The chapters consist of three components in addition to the text:

- *Reflective questions*—We recommend that you answer the reflective questions at the end of each chapter. The questions provide opportunities for you to reflect, either alone or with colleagues, on the ideas presented in the chapter.
- *Lessons from the Field*—Lessons are anecdotal, heartfelt stories written by school leaders from across the country. The purpose of *Lessons* is to move from the theoretical into the practical so that you can see the inner thinking of practitioners in the field in relation to their use of EQ competencies. For example, you might follow a principal or superintendent making a decision about the curricular focus of a social studies program. You are made privy to a leader's reflection on how he influenced teachers to accept an impending change. You might overhear a difficult conversation between a school member and a school leader and get a chance to follow the self-talk of the leader as she resolves the conflict.
- *Notes*—Sources used in the chapters are numbered for information or quotations in the text that elaborate on a particular piece of content that may interest you. You will find corresponding notes explained at the end of the book.

Chapter Overviews

Chapter One: *Introduction* introduces you to the conceptual framework and significance of this book. It also orients the reader as to how to best use the various sections of the book. If using this book as part of a course, the problem-based learning activity provided in the Chapter One skills section can be used to frame the entire course.

Chapter Two: *The Art of Reflection* invites us on a leadership journey. The authors believe that knowing one's strengths and limitations helps to improve leadership performance. Based on the theory of emotional intelligence (Goleman, 1995), this chapter focuses on the critical competency of self-awareness which is a threshold competency for all other emotional competencies. The "star" leader can accurately self-assess and make choices about personal direction. Through embracing the inner journey, the self-reflective leader is willing to grow, learn and develop self before developing others. EQ competencies emphasized in this chapter include emotional self-awareness, accurate self-assessment and self confidence.

Chapter Three: *Am I the Model?* explores how school leaders can become models of self-directed learning while developing their EQ competencies. We look at crucial skills such as active listening, self-expression, intuitive thinking, anger management and self-regulation. This chapter discusses the importance of EQ competencies such as empathy, optimism, and trustworthiness (transparency). All of this is explored within the context of leading schools.

Chapter Four: *Embracing Conflict in Ourselves and Others* focuses on the school leader's ability to deal creatively with conflict as an essential leadership skill. In this chapter, we examine critical conflict resolution concepts and skills that we believe should be at the core of all schools. These include the ability to problem solve, negotiate, and mediate to move individuals and the organization forward to optimize learning. As part of our discussion, we provide examples of strategies that educational leaders have used to develop integrated conflict management systems in both school and district settings.

Chapter Five: *Leading Social and Emotional Learning Communities* covers the role of leadership in creating a safe and caring school culture that promotes learning. It introduces the reader to the field of social and emotional learning including character education and service learning. It paints a picture of what comprehensive social and emotional learning involves in schools. It provides specific examples of what a "peaceable" school community looks like, the values it exemplifies, and suggests strategies for implementing a similar structure in schools today. Finally, it highlights ways to address the physical, social, and emotional safety of young people through prevention and intervention in schools.

Chapter Six: *The People Side of Change* reviews the role of the leader as a change agent. In this chapter, we explore strategies that the leader can employ to optimize the learning of the adults in the organization and break resistance to change. From the situational leader to the EQ coach, the leader's ability to motivate others and use positive influence is critical to promoting change. EQ competencies such as change catalyst, developing others, initiative and influence are addressed in this chapter. Finally, it explores the process of creating a collective vision that is based on a belief that the social and emotional well-being of young people needs to be at the core of all instruction.

Chapter Seven: *The Purpose of School* invites us to consider what purpose schools serve and what that purpose means to us as leaders. It asks the question, "What do we value? What do we want our children to take with them into the future?" It explores ethical and moral decisions that the leader must make to be inclusive of all young people and adults. It asks how the leader promotes equity and social justice. It explores the critical element of the leader's role in promoting social action in young people, the school community, and the larger society. Through the use of dialogue, inquiry and consensus, the leader creates a skilled community able to share decisions and reach common ground in difficult times. EQ competencies addressed include empathy, teamwork and collaboration and optimism.

Chapter Eight: *Facilitative Leadership* views the leader of the future as one who knows how to establish a learning community based on trust, teamwork and collaboration. In this chapter, we explore the keys to creating a true community where everyone takes ownership and responsibility for the successes of children. This chapter explores the personal characteristics and strategies used by the facilitative leader as well as the school structures that need to be in place to support this kind of leadership. EQ competencies of teamwork and collaboration are central to this chapter.

Chapter Nine: *Leading the School of the Future* asks the reader to consider how leadership will change to meet the needs of future school communities. It explores ways to use the tools of technology to enhance our interpersonal and intrapersonal skills. It provides strategies for incorporating social and emotional learning with technology to promote student learning and professional development. We also highlight a number of leaders who have been at the forefront of using technology, innovative school designs, and inquiry learning to prepare their students for the digital age. EQ competencies include organizational awareness and adaptability.

Chapter 10: *Change and Renewal: The Leader's Journey* talks about the need for leaders to balance their inner lives with the demanding and complex realities of the day-to-day job. It reminds us of the toll that stress can take and offers suggestions for renewing ourselves. It also explores the need for professional renewal that balances self-development along with knowledge acquisition. EQ competencies addressed include inspirational leadership and service orientation.

Skill Building Section

Near the end of the book, you will find a series of activities that have been designed to provide you with practice in developing EQ leadership skills. These activities are grounded in the author's years of practice in facilitating intrapersonal and interpersonal skill development. After you complete a chapter, review the corresponding recommended skills. If you are an individual reader, decide which ones you want to work on by yourself, with a work group, or a colleague. If you are a course instructor or a school leader interested in developing your staff, follow the directions for using the activities with groups. We suggest that you preview the activities in advance before trying them out with a group.

Readings from Contributors

Following the Skill Building Section is a compilation of recommended *Readings* that will extend your thinking about the book's content. The carefully selected *Readings* have been provided by expert voices from the field. We asked these contributors to think about our topics and send us one of their published pieces or a new article that reflects their latest thinking about a specific aspect of the topic. The contributors represent the broad spectrum of seminal thinkers in the area of social emotional learning and leadership. We suggest that you use these readings as the basis for group discussions, dialogues and text-based discussions.

Problem-Based Learning (PBL)

Before you begin this book, we present you with an actual problem that was faced by a school superintendent in New Jersey not long ago. Whether you are working alone or with a team, we advise you to take time to reflect on this problem and jot down the major issues addressed. Focus on the "people side" of the issues. List them. Think about them. As you progress through the book, we will ask you to revisit these issues and determine if new information might help you develop possible strategies toward resolution of these issues. If you are using this book as part of a leadership development course, you should follow the steps provided in the PBL in the Chapter One skills section. This activity can be used as the thread to structure and assess your course. At the end of Chapter 10, in the *Lesson* by Larry Leverett, you will read the actual story of the superintendent who lived this reality.

Emotional Competency Inventory[10] (ECI)

The ECI is a 360-degree tool designed to assess the emotional competencies of individuals and organizations. It is based on emotional competencies identified by Dr. Daniel Goleman in *Working with Emotional Intelligence* (1998), competencies from Hay/McBer's *Generic Competency Dictionary* (1996) as well as Dr. Richard Boyatzis's *Self Assessment Questionnaire* (SAQ). We have been using this tool in our work with aspiring and current school leaders to develop the EQ competencies we believe are so critical for effective leadership. If possible, take the ECI assessment before you begin using this book. It will give you insight into your own strengths, as well as the areas that you need to develop. A special, affordable version of the instrument, the ECIU, is designed for use with university students. Participants can complete both assessments online. You can obtain more information about this tool and make arrangements for purchasing it by visiting the HayGroup website at www.haygroup.com.

IN SUMMARY

An ancient Chinese proverb says,

> *Those who want to leave an impression for one year should plant corn; those who want to leave an impression for ten years should plant a tree; but those who want to leave an impression for 100 years should educate a human being.*

This proverb reminds us of the absolute power that we have as school leaders. The learning that takes place within our school walls will be imprinted on the minds and hearts of young people for eternity. We really need the best and the brightest to run our schools. *Smart* school leaders lead with emotional intelligence—no excuses, no alibis, and no exceptions.

REFLECTIVE QUESTIONS

1. Do you believe that EQ is as important as IQ? Explain.
2. Can we direct our own learning and really change the parts of ourselves that we want to change?
3. Have you read any of Daniel Goleman's books? If so, which one did you read and what did you learn from it? If not, which book is on your reading list?
4. As you begin your studies based on *SMART SCHOOL LEADERS*, what expectations do you have about your learning process? What strategies have been helpful to you in the past in acquiring new knowledge, skills and abilities?
5. The field of educational leadership requires us to be continual learners. We cannot lead schools without staying on top of the "best practices" needed to assure that children learn. What "best practices" are already part of your active repertoire? How might this EQ learning support what you already do?
6. Think about a leader you admire. What are the qualities and competencies that this person possesses and demonstrates to others?

LESSON FROM THE FIELD

Philip Santise

We rarely get to choose when to assume the role of leadership. All too often, the challenge of leadership is thrust upon us without warning and we have to respond swiftly. A critical mistake early in one's career can be extremely difficult to overcome. We may get only one chance and the first steps are sometimes the most dangerous.

Such was my dilemma when I was offered the opportunity to serve as principal of a recently-renovated, landmark building on Manhattan's posh Upper West Side. I was a newly-appointed principal, having served as interim acting principal for two-and-a-half years in a crumbling century-old building in East Harlem. Our kids were classified as

SIE7, severely emotionally disturbed (I never liked the word "disturbed," but that was how they were labeled in the system).

The newly renovated facility was scheduled to reopen in September, and I was offered to be the principal of the building. I was thrilled to have a new home, one where I would not have to share with any other school. My excitement, however, was diminished when I found out that the community was adamantly opposed to the reopening of the building as a Special Education School. The building previously housed a number of "600 Schools," known as schools for all the "worst kids" in the system. The school's reputation was marred by complaints of vandalism, thefts, graffiti, muggings and the like. There was a sense of relief, I was told, when the building was closed three years earlier. I was about to walk into a political buzz saw.

I attended a meeting with members of the school district, community school board, officers from the neighborhood co-op boards, and other interested residents. The superintendent and her assistant began to field questions from the audience with the predictable "canned" responses. I got the sense that the community had valid concerns about the negative impact on their community. I also sensed that there was a touch of racism in their line of questions. "Where do these kids come from? How will they be coming to and from school? Will they be allowed to use our park? What do you mean disturbed? We are concerned about these kids roaming around our neighborhood."

As a new principal, my superiors did not give me much air time. The audience, I sensed, did not trust the school district officials. I felt I could respond to several of the community members' questions despite my frustration and anger. I broke protocol and addressed the group.

Effective leaders, I believe, must convey to their constituencies the core values they embrace. Given the circumstances, I had to acknowledge their concerns as legitimate, build trust and avoid promises which appeared to be patronizing. I had to express the willingness to take the heat and make decisions based on my core values and philosophy. I introduced myself and provided them with some information about my background, education and upbringing. I wanted them to know I was a New Yorker and that I shared similar kinds of experiences and values. I let them know that I intended to be there long after this meeting had ended. I would be there every day as a part of their community. We discussed the kind of programs, not students, our school would provide and the mission and philosophy of our school. "Yes, we will use the park . . . It is a public place . . . I was happy to be there in their community . . . Our children are more like yours than they are different." I asked for their support and I promised them honesty, commitment, and my best effort. My parting words were, "If you want to know who is responsible, there should be no doubt. My door is open." I would be a visible presence on their streets.

Effective leadership takes place in and out of the school. When a leader is facing political pressure to choose between his core values and the politically correct choice, one can only hope to have the courage to choose self-respect and do what is right.

Six years later, this same community is responsible for assisting us in the beautification of the school's exterior with trees, wall murals, and play areas. Donations from community organizations helped finance a series of events that led to our renaming of P811M as the Mickey Mantle School. The Mickey Mantle School is a special place for everyone in the community. Our school is used by community groups in the evenings and on weekends. General education children from the neighboring community schools now attend our extended day program. Even a universal pre-k is housed in our building. The very same coop boards who attended that first meeting in 1996 now hold their annual meetings in our school. Many of them are members of our School Advisory Board. They support the school's mission and provide political and financial guidance.

I often reflect upon those early days. A leader needs to trust that "inner sense," take risks, and know how to ride the turbulent waters when they rise.

Philip Santise has been the principal of P811M, The Mickey Mantle School, for eight years. He has been recognized as an advocate for inclusive education for children with disabilities throughout New York State.

Chapter 2

The Art of Reflection

Hannah Lutz knew that the meeting with Mary Robbins would be a challenge for her and her leadership. Everyone in a school watches the principal when a crisis occurs. They want to know how she will respond, how her actions will affect them, and what they can do in response to how she responds. In a normal day, problems for principals surface and are solved with a shuffling of schedules or a phone call to the district office but, on other days, problems explode like Mary Robbins' angry outburst at parents of students in her class.[1]

In a large school like PS 211, with nearly 1400 students and 100 people on staff, the news spread quickly though many received only small segments of the story that they quickly passed on as the whole truth. In the general office, secretaries had one story. In the teacher's room, staff members had a different tale. Parent leaders recounted their version in a tiny second floor room.

In the scope of the school's recent events, the problem between one teacher and her students' parents may not have seemed large. After all, the school had recently gone through a major renovation while school was in session. For more than a year, the dirt, dust, din and disruption had tested adults and children alike. Despite doubled-up kindergarten classes, no full gym or yard and sudden scheduling changes, the school community had come together to keep to its mission of learning. Hannah knew, however, construction had strained relationships in the school and that the way this current conflict was resolved might affect the school climate. Though this seemed to be merely a conflict between parents concerned about what was being taught and a teacher angry about having her expertise challenged, the incident was public and so took on greater meaning.

In her office, Hannah sat alone at the small conference table preparing herself for the meeting. In front of her were the notes she had written earlier. To her left the coffee and cookies she might offer to Mary to ease the tension. Silently, she sat trying to tap into what she was thinking and feeling about Mary and this situation. Later, she would say that she was aware of her own anger and frustration towards Mary based on previous attempts to problem solve with her. "Whenever she (Mary) comes in she is argumentative and whatever you say there is a comeback whether it is appropriate or not. And you want to say, 'Shut up and listen!' and it's like you've had enough."

Imagine yourself for a moment as the leader of PS 211 sitting alone in your office preparing for this meeting. What might you be feeling? Which of your beliefs and values might be wrapped up in this problem and might influence your attempts to bring this problem to some resolution?

In this chapter, we focus on the aspect of leadership that relates to self-reflection.[2] First, we present our case for a model of the principal as reflective practitioner. Second, we examine the emotional competency of self-awareness, highlighting its neuroanatomical basis and its relevance to learning and leadership. Finally, we define self-regulation and discuss how the ability to manage one's emotions energizes the leadership role.

PRINCIPAL AS LEARNER

In his book *Improving Skills from Within*, Roland Barth, a former principal and school superintendent, humorously reports:

> As learners, principals have a bad reputation. Many in my own school community wondered whether, as a principal, I was educable. Parents, teachers, students, central office personnel, and even other principals sometimes had their doubts. Sometimes so did I.[3]

Barth explains that often the perceptions of both principals themselves and the people they work with create learning roadblocks for principals. Little time, resources, or emotional support are given to the learning experiences of principals. In our own research with principals implementing the Resolving Conflict Creatively Program (RCCP) in New York City public schools, we found that most principals in our study had little support for their own learning aside from what they received from RCCP or what they could acquire themselves on their own time.[4] Gatherings of principals on the district level were primarily used as informational meetings. Questionnaires given to principals before they attended a required RCCP Workshop Series for School Leaders showed consistently that they did not believe they needed to learn the social-emotional skills they thought were important for their teachers and students to learn. According to Parker Palmer, it is discouraging and dangerous, given all the intrapersonal and interpersonal challenges that leaders face every day, that learning opportunities for leaders still concentrate on the skills to manipulate the external world rather than the skills to go inward.[5]

LEADERSHIP COMPETENCIES

Many readers might reflect on Hannah's situation as she prepares for her meeting and say, "She'll handle the situation well if she just uses her intelligence." By "intelligence," they refer to her cognitive ability. However, the concept of intelligence has expanded in recent years especially since Salovey and Mayer's introduction of a developmental model of emotional intelligence.[6] In their model they suggest that there are abilities ranging from basic psychological processes, such as recognizing one's own emotions, to more complex processes such as the ability to monitor and manage emotions in oneself and in others. These abilities constitute an important part of what Hannah will need to draw upon to deal intelligently with Mary Robbins.

Extending the work of Salovey, Mayer, and others, Daniel Goleman proposed a theory of performance that built on the EI model to predict personal effectiveness at work and in leadership.[7] Exploring the role of emotional intelligence in leadership, Goleman, Boyatzis and McKee proposed that leadership can be learned by developing a set of emotional competencies identified in great business leaders.[8] Great leaders are not strong in every competency but they typically exhibit a critical mass of strength in a number of them and generally have some skill in self-awareness, self-management, social awareness and relationship management. This suggests that EQ profiles of effective leaders may look very different from one another but that a good place to start developing one's leadership might begin with self-awareness.

SELF-AWARENESS: THE CORNERSTONE OF EMOTIONAL COMPETENCY

The Leader's Brain

How effective you are as a leader is determined to a great extent by how aware you are of what lies within you. The personal competency of self-awareness, according to Goleman, Boyatzis and McKee, consists of emotional awareness, accurate self-assessment, and self-confidence and it serves as the foundation of all socioemotional skills.

To fully understand self-awareness, it is helpful to understand how the brain works. Sparked by the invention of non-evasive brain imagery technology (e.g. functional magnetic resonance imagery), neuroscientists have found that thinking processes once thought of as the sole province of the cerebral cortex are not divorced from the emotional centers of the brain.[9] The old adage of "Leave your emotions outside the classroom door," therefore, needs to be unceremoniously deposited in the trashcan of antiquated and harmful educational beliefs. If we take a tour of our brain we see why this is so.[10] The average adult brain is a three-pound organ consisting of 100 billion cells called neurons and one trillion cells called glial cells. The neurons send and receive information in the form of electrical signals and chemical messages. The glial cells serve to keep the brain together and to provide support services to the neurons. Each neuron has a cell body and parts extending from the body called axons and dendrites. Signals that are being transmitted from a neuron leave from the axon and are received by dendrites from other neurons.

As newborns, our brains have almost as many neurons as the adult brain though the adult brain is about four times the size of its earlier version. The reason for this growth lies mostly in the tremendous growth of connections that are made among neurons. In normal development, both nature and nurture influence the extent of this growth. Think of the developing brain as a life-long connection-making system that takes in and processes information from the external and internal environments including different regions of the brain itself. Throughout life, this incredibly adaptive system creates new connections and strengthens or weakens old connections.

Emotions play a large part in this process. In the context of our everyday lives, emotions serve as signals that focus our attention, help in the process of storing memories and act as an essential ingredient in motivation. Think back to the challenge Hannah was facing at the beginning of this chapter. As she sits in her office waiting for Mary Robbins, her brain is bustling with activity. If we used the latest brain imaging technology we could get a clearer picture of just how many parts of Hannah's brain are coming into play.[11] The prefrontal cortex, of course, are activated in planning the meeting. Other parts of the cortex are also active as Hannah keeps her eyes on her notes and attunes her ears to sounds outside her door. We would also see activity in the Limbic System that consists of several areas of the brain most closely linked to emotions. This system has been the subject of research by Joseph LeDoux, who has shown that incoming sensory information is processed here even before it is processed in the cortex.[12] In Hannah's case, for example, a small almond-shaped cluster of neurons called the amygdala is processing information transmitted from the senses through the thalamus and also from emotional memories stored within it. Through its network of connections, it will communicate with the prefrontal cortex and various other parts of the brain. Most of this

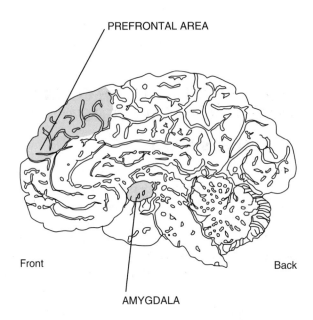

PREFRONTAL AREA

Front

Back

AMYGDALA

FIGURE 2.1   The crucial emotional regulatory circuitry runs from the prefrontal area to the amygdala, located on either side of the mid-brain as part of the limbic system.
From *Primal Leadership* by Goleman et al. Harvard Business School Publishing, 2002.

activity is beyond Hannah's awareness but the level of awareness that she does have will influence her effectiveness in the upcoming meeting.

Emotional Awareness and Accurate Self-Assessment

As his students arrive in the morning, John Scarpetto often walks through the hallways of his school holding up his right hand, palm upward, with one to five fingers extended. Today, his hand holds up three fingers.

"Good morning, boys and girls. I'm feeling a three today. How are you feeling?"

A sea of fingers rise up (none obscenely as this is an elementary school) and John assesses the emotional climate of his students as they begin the day. He knows that many of these self-assessments will be accurate because both he and his staff have taught the children lessons on developing a feelings vocabulary. The children use words and numbers to name and express the intensity of emotions that they experience. If he notices a child with only one finger up, John will either invite the child into his office for a talk or make a mental note to ask the student's teacher to be aware of the child's emotional state.

Before John's walk, he takes some time to reflect on his own emotions. He does this not only to model, or "walk the talk", a key social emotional learning skill but also because he truly believes that his own emotional awareness is essential to his success as leader. Whether he is meeting with parent leaders, supervising the lunchroom, or speaking at a faculty meeting, he knows that how he feels influences his thinking, actions, and his influence on others. John knows that the inner assessment that he takes before his walk and the climate assessment that he takes during his walk give him valuable information that he can use to make decisions and prevent problems later in the day.[13]

According to the developmental psychologist, Carolyn Saarni, one's emotional awareness begins to develop as early as the sixth month of life.[14] Before that, infants have the physical states called emotions but there is no sense of self and, therefore, no awareness that *they* are having these emotions. As they interact with others, children acquire tools such as verbal and non-verbal language enabling them to create mental representations of emotions. Labeling the emotions with words (i.e. feelings), the child becomes more adept at identifying different emotional states and communicating those states to others. As they mature, young people normally develop awareness that they can feel different emotions with different intensities about the same situation or person. Optimally, human beings develop their competency in emotional awareness to the point that they can, like John Scarpetto, use their emotions in the service of their goals. A person who possesses this competency exhibits, according to Saarni, certain characteristics:

1. A rich vocabulary of feeling words.
2. The ability to recognize and differentiate among emotions.
3. The ability to identify the physical cues (e.g. queasy stomach) that were used to appraise the type and the intensity of the emotion.
4. The ability to discern what external event or internal cognition triggered the emotion.
5. The knowledge that there are times when one might not be aware of the emotion because of unconscious dynamics or selective inattention.

This last characteristic is particularly important in developing the competency of emotional awareness. School and district leaders not cognizant that many situational and psychological factors may obscure emotional awareness are not likely to put themselves through the deliberate process of accessing their emotional state when it is essential to do so. Imagine how impaired your leadership would be if you relied only on written reports to make tough decisions. Imagine if you did not actively seek out additional information by walking through a school, speaking to key people and "getting a feel" of what is going on in the building. Thinking that you can stay comfortably in your office is analogous to believing that you are always aware of your emotions.[15] It keeps you in a safe place but it keeps you from acquiring all the important information you need to lead. Paradoxically, self-aware leaders know that they are often unaware of what they are feeling but have learned to test their thinking for any emotions hidden from awareness.[16]

Values

When there is a burning "Yes!" inside of you, it is easier to say "No" to everything else.

—A principal's remark at an RCCP Workshop for School Administrators

What do you find important in life? I (James) was asked that question on an Outward Bound Course for School Leaders after a group of fellow educators and I had spent four days steering a tiny pulling boat across Penobscot Bay to Hurricane Island in Maine. Our motley crew had learned how to work together, weathering storms and our own inexperience. The open boat was so small that we had to sleep in our sleeping bags head to foot and our only sanitary convenience was a large yellow bucket not-so-discreetly available at the stern of the boat. In those four days we had bonded as a team but now our 70-year-old expedition leader asked each of us to become aware of what values *individually* guided us in our lives. "Go find a place on the island and think about them," he suggested in the same straight-forward way he had taught us navigation and how to sail against the wind.

It was not easy to do. The values I initially wrote in my small journal were those I perceived as admirable. However, when I held them up to the course of my life I became

FIGURE 2.2
Courtesy of Hurricane Island Outward Bound School

aware that some of them were *espoused* values, or values that I wanted to possess. But they were not the ones that truly guided my life. They were not my *core* values. The more I explored what was important to me, the more emotions came to the surface, which was not surprising since our true values are emotion-laden. When we act outside our core values emotions of anger, frustration, guilt, sadness or anxiety may alert us. Conversely, when we act in step with our core values, we generally feel enthusiastic, emboldened and passionate about what we do.

As the hour we were given for reflection faded, I began to realize that some of my core values had remained constant in my life and some had changed over the years. Marrying and later becoming a parent, for example, had affected my values and, in turn, new core values impacted on how I thought and felt about work, where I live and how I viewed both the past and future.

Becoming aware of your current core values is particularly important for school leaders because the best schools are moral communities in which core values and educational practices are in alignment. When trying to create a true learning community that excels in academic, social and emotional learning, we cannot do so if we do not know what we as leaders stand for.[17] Whether we are deciding what to adopt or eliminate, what to measure or to ignore, what to fight for or against, our values influence our thinking.[18] These values can give meaning to our professional lives and keep us on course during the difficult times schools so often face. They also can be at the heart of the most intractable conflicts in a school community. For these reasons, school leaders must not only reflect on their own values but must lead others in similar reflection.[19]

Self-Confidence

In his book, *Working with Emotional Intelligence,* Daniel Goleman describes self-confidence as "an inner map of our proclivities, abilities, and deficiencies."[20] As educators, we know how powerful these inner maps are and how often students, especially in our high schools, self-destruct because of low self-confidence.

What we may not notice is how often adults in schools resist an innovation or burn out when faced with challenges because they lack the belief that they can successfully accomplish a new or difficult task. Beliefs about how capable one is to perform a certain task is often referred to as self-efficacy and, according to the social psychologist, Albert Bandura, beliefs about efficacy impact on our cognitive, motivational and emotional functioning.[21] According to Bandura, people with self-efficacy are more likely to have high aspirations, take the long view and set high standards. When faced with adversity they are better able to handle stress, to control disturbing thoughts and to use supportive relationships to maintain emotional balance.

Because self-efficacy beliefs can have such impact on a school leader's performance, it is necessary for leaders to accurately assess their efficacy beliefs especially when implementing change. Bandura suggested successful people make self-judgments that are slightly higher than what they can actually accomplish. Less successful people, on the other hand, will either make over-inflated judgments that can lead to failure or under-inflated judgments that can prevent them from even attempting change. If the leader is reflective, however, self-awareness that one is too over- or under-confident about being able to accomplish a task can lead to effective courses of action. A reflective leader might say, "I think I'm overconfident that I can bring the school constituencies to a consensus on block scheduling so I need to learn consensus-building skills or I need to bring in a facilitator." Another self-aware leader might say, "I think I'm not giving myself enough credit here. I've done a lot of consensus-building with my church and with other organizations so I think it's better if I lead this process rather than bring in an outside person."

This process of appraising one's own efficacy beliefs is not easy because it touches upon our concept of self. A basic human need is to feel competent and achieving. For school leaders, the process becomes even more difficult because the expectation placed upon them is that they have to be competent in all areas. After all, they are the "LEADER." As a result, developing an accurate picture of our efficacy beliefs is challenging and leaders will benefit if they can use their feelings as guide markers to self-understanding.

EMOTIONAL REGULATION

Mary Robbins saunters into Hannah's office, ready for a fight. Her gestures and tone of voice have triggered Hannah's anger and frustration in the past but this time Hannah keeps those feelings at an energy level she can use. Her earlier self-reflection and planning has prepared her and she is feeling proud of herself. She tells herself she can keep things under control as she invites Mary to sit down.

Mary does not make it easy. On an unconscious level, she knows what buttons to push and, as she sits down, she begins to complain. Surprisingly, Hannah does not argue with her, but instead listens intently. Not allowing her mind to be distracted by Mary's obvious attempts to take control of the meeting, Hannah continues to stay centered and actively listen. Gradually, Mary's combativeness and anxiety lessen and she discloses that she felt attacked by her students' parents and implies that she does not trust Hannah to support her in this conflict. The teacher's voice rises and she blames Hannah again for listening to the parents' complaints. In response to Mary's attacks, Hannah paraphrases what she heard and turns the attack away from her and turns to the problem of finding a solution that can work for the parents, for Mary and for herself. Hannah says that she is beginning to understand the problem from Mary's point of view and asks Mary to try stepping into her shoes to imagine the conflict from a principal's perspective.

Hesitatingly at first, Mary describes the situation as the "principal." She is annoyed and frustrated by the teacher's actions. She feels that she has to take some action. As she continues stepping out of her own entrenched position, this troubled educator gains a new perspective and discloses her feelings of anxiety about teaching a new grade and a new curriculum. She admits that the lesson that angered the parents was inappropriate but she was reluctant to reveal this to the parents or Hannah. Hannah is surprised by Mary's honesty and this new knowledge gives her a better understanding of her staff member's difficult behavior. No longer seeing each other as adversaries, Hannah and Mary use the rest of the meeting to work out a plan to help Mary become more skilled at implementing the new curriculum and communicating with parents.

Nancy Eisenberg and Qing Zhou define emotional regulation as "the process of initiating, maintaining, modulating or changing the occurrence, intensity or duration of internal feeling states and emotion-related physiological processes, often in the service of one's goals."[22] Hannah's journey to mastery of this competency was an uphill one. She knew that she had a volatile temper when thwarted by resistant or insubordinate staff members. Though the anger put teeth into her power as an administrator, Hannah knew that it also corroded her influence as a leader. Consequently, she measured the gap between her vision of a leader against her current self and made a plan for self-directed learning. She used strategies she had learned in several conflict resolution workshops to resolve simple conflicts with friends who gave her feedback afterwards. She also sought advice and feedback about her handling of conflict from trusted colleagues and an external consultant. Gradually, she found out what strategies worked best for her and practiced them until they became part of her repertoire. When she slipped, she learned from her mistakes.

If we review Hannah's meeting with Mary, we can see that Hannah engaged in a process that met Eisenberg and Zhou's definition of self-regulation. Hannah used her awareness of her emotions and the social context to formulate and implement a personal plan for modulating her anger and maintaining her empathy throughout the meeting. She was aware of the *physical cues* (e.g. dry mouth, tension in neck area) that she was experiencing and how she could use these cues to assess the intensity and duration of her different emotions. She was also aware of how situational triggers (e.g. Mary's voice) could elicit strong emotions and how these triggers were influenced by her temperament, her cultural background and past history.[23] Beyond that, Hannah had a working knowledge of which regulating strategies would most likely work in this meeting with Mary.

So let's imagine that we could place ourselves unobtrusively into Hannah's cognitive and emotional thinking as Mary walks into the office. What might we observe? We might "hear" a form of self-talk coming from Hannah exhorting herself to avoid getting emotionally hijacked by her anger.[24] She tells herself that she can keep calm and centered. She checks into her body sensations to focus on her breathing which helps her to calmly welcome Mary and invite her to describe the problem she is having. Hannah focuses on the task of listening and avoids distractions. When Mary raises her voice and Hannah responds by paraphrasing, she tells herself that she is achieving one of her goals (she might even be aware of a pleasurable emotion as serotonin levels increase). As she listens, she begins to sense that Mary is feeling frustrated about teaching in a new grade. She summons enough courage to ask Mary if her assumption is correct. Before Mary speaks a word, Hannah has her answer. A strong surge of empathy is felt and Hannah knows that something has shifted and, given time, the problem will be solved together.

For Hannah, a combination of techniques helped her to regulate her emotions. Some of them focused on reframing the appraisal of the situation ("She doesn't want to change," changed to "This is an opportunity for me to find out what's keeping her from succeeding."). Some of them focused on the physical cues (e.g. relaxation techniques) while others focused on language (e.g. avoiding words that she knew would anger herself or Mary).

These techniques helped Hannah, but there is no one best way to regulate anyone's emotions. Each person's emotional makeup represents a complex interaction of genes, temperament, personality, cultural background, familial and peer influences and individual experiences. Some people seem to be gifted in emotional intelligence and are amazingly aware of and able to use their emotions. Others work very hard to develop their abilities and still struggle everyday. It is important to remember that there are more neural pathways heading from the amygdala to the neocortex than vice versa so it is not surprising that emotions are much more likely to affect our conscious thinking than the other way around.

Nevertheless, there are a variety of cognitive strategies that have been shown to be effective in regulating the emotions.[25] Self-talk, a technique that Hannah used, is often used by athletes in combination with visual imagery to initiate performance-enhancing emotions or diminish emotions that impede success. Deep breathing exercises, meditation or progressive relaxation are particularly helpful at inducing a restful but alert physical state. Providing distractions or removing oneself from the triggering event may serve to dampen dissonant emotions. Focusing attention and recalling sensory memories can maintain and enhance resonant emotions.

SMART school leaders have a large repertoire of self-regulation strategies that fit their individual emotional makeup and can be applied to any situation. Centered by self-awareness and self-control, these leaders are able to adapt readily to change and remain open to innovative ideas and taking risks. Their authentic behavior helps them develop the trust so needed for leading others. From this foundation, the social relationships at the core of the best schools can be built.

IN SUMMARY

In this chapter, we have explored the role of the leader as a learner especially as it applies to self-understanding. It is the premise of this book that people learn to become better leaders by developing their self-knowledge and other emotional competencies. An effective school or district leader, therefore, is a continual learner. School leaders must strive to become reflective practitioners, reflecting on themselves as well as their interactions with others.

In this chapter we have presented two broad categories of emotional competencies that provide the foundation for all the rest. Both self-awareness and self-regulation are rooted in the earliest development of a person and research has found that children learn these skills first from their parents or caregivers and then from their peers. At the cornerstone of this foundation is self-awareness. Self-awareness includes an understanding of our emotions and what triggers them. It also encompasses an awareness of our values and our beliefs in our own abilities. Building upon that cornerstone is the ability to regulate emotions to achieve one's goals. School leaders who master the competency of self-regulation are better able to respond to the rapid changes in our society and to instill trust in their school communities.

REFLECTIVE QUESTIONS

1. What are your beliefs about the importance, or irrelevance, of emotions in the workplace?
2. How did you acquire these beliefs (culture, experience, etc.)? What messages or mental models guide these beliefs?
3. What feelings are the most difficult for you to regulate?
4. What events or thoughts trigger these feelings?
5. What physical cues are present when you experience these feelings?
6. How do you attempt to dampen, maintain or enhance feelings now? What strategies work the best? The least? Why do you think this is the case?
7. What can you do to improve your competency in emotional awareness and regulation in the next week? In the next month?

LESSON FROM THE FIELD

Migdalia Maldonado-Torres

I was listening to a training presentation when the following statement struck me like lightning, "You can't do it alone. This job [principal] is just too extensive for one person." I thought about the statement for a while. The presenter was on the money! If I was going to be effective in my school, I couldn't do it alone.

Three years earlier I had become the new principal of an elementary school in East Harlem, New York. The first day I reported to the school, I was greeted by a parent who stated, "Welcome to the zoo." I quickly commented, "I am here to change that."

My new school filled me with much trepidation and anxiety. It had a reputation of being a chaotic, disorderly school where students didn't learn. As I observed classes and spoke with staff, I quickly began to understand why the school had acquired that reputation. My first month I received a letter from the state "inviting" me to Albany because the school had shown "negative" improvement during the last two years. Within our district, the school had scored next to last in reading and math. I took a deep breath and knew my work was cut out for me.

My first task was to gain control of the school. Students had been allowed to roam the school at random and several staff members complained that the students had taken over the school. The school building also housed two alternative schools that were located on the upper floors of the building. The directors of the programs gave me the same complaint. One director had hired someone to sit in the middle of the hallway and keep watch. When I was introduced to this gentleman, I asked him why he was sitting in the middle of the hallway. He responded, "To keep your students from our side of the building. They run in the hallways tearing off the bulletin boards." Then, he showed me a bat. I walked away angry, outraged and determined to put him out of a job.

The situation called for a strong leader. I quickly shared my expectations for students, staff and parents. I solicited the help of those who wanted change. Few signed up for this challenge. Vision in mind, I charged ahead. The writing was on the wall.

Soon the halls echoed, "This principal meant business and she wasn't going away." Systems were set up. Law and order had to prevail in the hallways first and then the classrooms. I instituted new programs and spent endless hours speaking to parents, students, and staff members. The message was clear: "Shape up or ship out."

During the first three years, the board of education called me to sign up for school-based management. I deferred because I wasn't ready. How could I let go and share decision-making when no one had control of the school. I gingerly declined the chancellor's offer twice.

I certainly had been efficient in putting into place all the right systems in the school, but I wanted to create a culture in the school that had a sense of community. Decision-making had to be shared with the staff. To do this, I needed people to be part of the process so they could feel ownership. *I needed to change. I had to let go.* You can be efficient with things but not people. I knew I needed training, if I was going to change my leadership style.

I picked up Steven Covey's book, *The 7 Habits of Highly Effective People,* which was inspirational and made me think about managing self-first and then others. I went to a training and heard the presentation that helped me realize that solutions to problems are much more effective if they are solved by teams. It takes longer but the solutions are very productive.

After the training, I was ready to give school-based management a try. It was helpful that I had a framework to work with. The school had adopted the Accelerated

Schools Program. Although we didn't follow it to the "t," it gave the school a process of how to reach school-based management. I knew we had arrived when staff started to use such phrases as "our children" and "our school" instead of saying "these children" and "this school" The school became a vibrant place for students to learn. Parents now insisted that their children be admitted to our school.

As I reflect on the school's metamorphosis, I've learned a lot. First, *leaders must have self-awareness*. Ask yourself, "Are your actions helping or deterring your leadership?" As leader, you need to be able to step back and evaluate yourself. How do you do this in the constant buzz that surrounds the job? Watch others interacting with each other. Who are the successful teachers that are effective with their students? Observe human behavior. Leaders are not only those with positions or education. Learn from them. Visit other colleagues and ask to spend some time in their schools. Ask them to give you a tour. Watch as they interact with their staff. What qualities do they have that make them effective leaders? What qualities make them less effective? You can learn from both. Also, there are plenty of 360-degree assessment tools on the market your staff can use to provide feedback on your leadership style. But beware! This can be a very powerful tool, but it can be medicine with a bad taste. Either way it's good for you!

Second, *leaders must have the courage to change*. What good is feedback if you don't change? A true leader adapts and is ready to make hard choices including changing self. I haven't met a great leader that hasn't taken risks. You learn just as much or even more from your mistakes. If you are self-reflective and analyze your mistakes and learn from them, it makes you stronger as a leader. We tend not to analyze our successes and just take them in stride.

Finally, *leaders must be willing to learn from all situations and create situations for themselves so that they are constantly learning and evaluating*. We get so involved in our schools and organizations that we keep our nose to the grindstone. Look up and venture out of your building. Sign up for workshops. Read professional books and journals. FEED your mind. You cannot provide enriching environments for others if you are lacking. Leadership at its best is when you have self-awareness, take risks and learn from your mistakes. Be willing to learn and change.

Migdalia Maldonado-Torres, a former principal, is Director of Center for Leadership Development in District 4 of the New York City Public Schools.

Chapter 3

Am I the Model?

In many ways, the school that Nancy Sing-Bock had been assigned was an ideal one for a new principal. The school community was known for its collaborative spirit and its caring, nurturing culture. The teachers were knowledgeable about students' needs and strategies for meeting those needs. The majority of parents were supportive of the school's mission even though their struggle to make a living wage and their lack of fluency in English made involvement difficult.

On the other hand, Nancy had never been a principal before and could not be sure what to expect. The former principal, who had been the school's leader for many years, was much admired and had become the district assistant superintendent. This was no typical retirement in which the retiree was truly gone. How did staff members feel about *their* principal leaving and how did they feel about *this* person who replaced her? The situation tested Nancy's emotional competencies in dramatic ways especially now that the first anniversary of the September 11 terrorist attack was approaching. The school, PS51, was in New York City's School District Two, which was the district hardest hit by the attacks on the World Trade Center.[1]

In my first few days of being a new principal, I felt nervous in my new role. I had worked for two months during the summer, basically by myself, preparing for my school. The teachers, staff, and students were not in the building so, even though I was getting ready, it did not feel real to me that I was the principal. When school started, almost in an instant, I became the principal, because everyone thought of me as the principal. Even though I did not have the opportunity or luxury to grow into my role of a principal and what that meant, to my staff, students and parents, I was immediately transformed into the principal of PS/IS 51 because they needed a leader.

At the same time, I subtly felt the staff was watching me to pick up cues on how to approach me. Many of them felt uncertain if they would be able to continue as they always had and what my demands and expectations would be as a new principal.

Looking back, my most vivid impressions were that even though I still felt like my normal self, externally in my new role of principal, I was being transformed. I was perceived as the leader of the school and I sensed they wanted me to step into those shoes to provide them with the security and strength they needed from their leader. It seemed that externally, everyone treated and addressed me as the principal, but internally I still did not quite feel like I was the principal. For example, in the first few days, I brought curtains from home and stood on the radiator to hang them up in the office. A few people got nervous and told me to get down. I didn't know why, but I think I made them feel uncomfortable because in their head, "principals don't hang up curtains." At PS/IS51 there is a hierarchy of everyone's responsibilities, for this particular population of peo-ple, in their heads, principals don't hang up curtains.

Whether you are a first time principal in a new school or an experienced principal cel-ebrating a tenth anniversary, you are watched closely by those around you. It comes, along with a large ring of keys, with the job. Moreover, observers will be watching you through the colored spectacles of their earlier experiences with principals, both as adults and as children. Depending on the tone of voice directed at them, the words "Let's go see the principal" may still evoke a feeling of panic or pride in some staff members. De-pending on their prejudices, your staff may put you on a pedestal or in front of a target. Both places can be dangerous.

In this chapter, we focus on how school leaders, using their self awareness and self-management skills, can act in a socially-aware way that models emotionally intelligent leadership. We explore the competency of social awareness, or empathy, as it applies to both interpersonal and group communication. The importance of active listening and non-verbal communication is highlighted and strategies presented to inform readers on how to use "body language" to improve their communication skills. Communication breakdowns, however, are inevitable even in the best schools so communication road-blocks are identified and suggestions made as to how roadblocks can be either removed or avoided. Finally, we end with methods of self-directed learning that leaders can use to model what master learners do throughout their lives.

THE SCHOOL LEADER AS A MODEL

The importance of the leader as a model has been stressed by a number of writers.[2] If followers see the leader as consistently aligning her behaviors with her spoken vision of leadership, the leader will likely be viewed as a person with integrity and trustworthi-ness. By "walking the talk", she also fosters the adoption of those same behaviors by oth-ers through a process called observational learning. When leaders must intervene in the school community during a time of crisis, it is the leaders who are meaningful models who will have the moral authority to be heard. A former principal and school district leader I knew would visit schools and interrupt teachers who were verbally abusing stu-dents by gently asking them questions and listening to them rather than by shouting at the teacher to stop. This leader had a profound effect on those teachers, and by inter-vening in an assertive yet empathic manner, he emboldened others to step up as allies.[3]

But what about the leaders who are not models of what they ask from their follow-ers? How many of us have seen teachers who tell their students one thing and do the op-posite? How many of us have met (or are) principals or school superintendents who voice collaboration as a value but whose actions have no resonance with that concept? A school superintendent in New Jersey espouses the value of diversity and encourages principals to reach to people of color when his own hiring practices reflect a very different perspec-tive. A high school principal in Texas voices the importance of academics but then cuts teaching positions while leaving the athletic program untouched. An elementary school principal in Arizona stays behind her desk when meeting parents while calling for more parental involvement in a parent newsletter. What is the message in these situations?

OPTIMISM

According to research on educators' perceptions of effective school administrators, op-timism is an important characteristic to model.[4] This makes sense because optimists believe that obstacles are temporary, do not take failures personally and think that forces working against them can be contained.[5] In any school, there are bound to be crises and drawbacks and optimists tend to rise to the challenge more often than pessimists do. Principals who model this EQ competency help create a climate that fosters persistence and hopefulness.

The bad news, however, is that not every school leader is optimistic and too many schools in this country are sinking into despair. In our travels to many schools, we have visited schools mired in feelings of hopelessness and helplessness. The problems seem overwhelming, the resources are cut back and the blame game is played every day. How does anyone hold on to hope and begin to turn things around in these schools?

The good news is that optimism can be learned just like helplessness can be learned. The first step entails self-awareness. What are you feeling when an effort fails? What triggers that emotion? What are the mental scripts that you use to explain the failure and how realistic is that explanation? Are your beliefs optimistic or pessimistic? Do you say that there is nothing that you can do about the problem and there's no point in trying? Or do you say that you are convinced that you can turn these problems into challenges that can be met in creative ways?

The second step involves regulating negative feelings and beliefs, practicing new scripts and fully experiencing emotions as problems emerge. It will be difficult at first, but change will take place if you work at it. Put yourself physically in places where good things are happening in your school and, like a pearl diver, breathe deeply in that rarified air of success before returning to the muddy waters. When in the muddy waters, act and talk as if the problems will be solved. Psychologically, our minds want to believe what we say and do, so the more you act like an optimist, the more likely you will think like one.[6]

The final step is to use your social skills to develop a support group—an *Optimist's Club* (your group can invent its own name). The members are all the school's optimists and optimists-in-training who will support each other, model for others and occasionally do something a little strange to create the true sound of the optimist—laughter! Even in the most horrendous of circumstances, humor can keep hope alive (think of the movie *Life is Beautiful*) so find funny ways to celebrate even minor triumphs in your school. Put everyone on your staff in a circle and do a group massage or a group cheer. Ask everyone to dress up one day or post baby pictures on the office bulletin board. Select a Hero of the Week or have a potluck lunch for the cafeteria staff. At first, people might be resistant, but adults in our society are laughter-deprived (they laugh almost 10 times less than children do each day) so most will eventually join in happily.

COMMUNICATION

The EQ leader is aware that effective communication is the lifeblood of a caring school community. Communication enables people to teach and learn, share ideas and feelings, address needs and solve conflicts, talk about the future and remember the past and discourse with the world outside. Because of this importance, the school leader who wants to succeed needs to learn and model good communication skills.

It is useful to think of communication as a process of transferring and understanding meaning. The Indo-European origins of the word "communicate" means "shared by all" and, unless the meaning or mental pictures of those in communication are shared, there is no effective communication taking place.[7] This is an important concept, since many people understand communication to consist primarily of words either spoken or written. Yet words may be exchanged back and forth between two people with little exchange of meaning.

Communication models have been developed for a variety of processes including mass communication, group communication and interpersonal communication.[8] In this chapter, we will primarily look at interpersonal communication which conceptualizes communication as the dynamic making of meaning between a sender and receiver (see model in Figure 3.1). Let's illustrate this communication model with a short interaction between a principal, Nora, and a teacher, George. Nora has one of George's students in her office because he was fighting in the lunchroom. When Nora spots George in the hallway the sight of him evokes a whole series of connected thoughts and feelings in her mind that together make meaning. For example, Nora feels frustrated because discipline issues take up so much of her time and she is again missing her lunch. She also feels slightly surprised and pleased to see George because she thought that he had gone out for lunch. "There's George," she thinks. "I'd like him to come in to help with this." Because George is heading down the hallway she decides to encode the message into words that she delivers across both verbal and nonverbal channels. "Mr. Baxter, I need to speak to you for a moment," she shouts out and waves her hand in the air. As she calls out, a thought crosses her mind that this is his lunch period and images of angry teachers (not George) flash into her awareness. Her complex feelings of frustration and surprise "leak" into her voice. George, who did not see Nora's friendly wave, receives the verbal message along with the leaked emotions and his body tenses, the first significant feedback to Nora. George's brain filters the shout through his past experiences and, as he turns around and sees his principal, other filters of values and beliefs influence his encoding of the message. "The principal? She's upset. She called me Mr. Baxter. I was just going to do my lesson plans that she wanted. I didn't even get my lunch yet."

What feelings do you think Mr. Baxter might be feeling? What meanings might he take from Nora's message and how distorted might those meanings be? In replying to her, how will his verbal and nonverbal message be interpreted by her? You can see that there are many places throughout this communication process where meanings can get lost and relationships altered.

In this model and in the communication between Mr. Baxter and Nora, the fact that people can make sense of each other at all is amazing. At best, we can only approximate the meanings that we convey or receive. Remember the telephone game we played as kids where each person passes on a message and everyone laughs at the end when the last person says the message that has been so transformed by the line of young minds? We, as adults, still play the same game but we call it discussion, or talking on the phone or giving a direction. Unfortunately, we often get ourselves in trouble because we expect that what we communicate is clear and are certain that we understand perfectly what we are being told. What we can only be certain of, however, is that communication is not a perfect process. It is an art.

Like any art form, there are those who are gifted at it from a young age.[9] For most of us, however, we must work hard throughout our lives to master the concepts and strokes. A good place to begin is with nonverbal language, the communication channel that predominantly conveys emotion. Consider the interpersonal communication below.

You, as the supervisor, are having a coaching meeting with a new teacher, Sherry Jones, and suddenly you are aware that something has changed in your interactions. You are feeling uneasy and frustrated. What has changed? You observe that her body posture has shifted from facing you to sitting sideways and somewhat stooped. Sherry's eyes are more open as both eyelids are raised. Her eyebrows are also raised and drawn together. The mouth remains relaxed. It's then that you notice that you are pointing at her with your index finger and that you have leaned closer to her. The tension you feel around your eyes and mouth suggests to you that you are conveying annoyance or anger at her. It is a classic power movement. You are trying to make your point, but your point, both

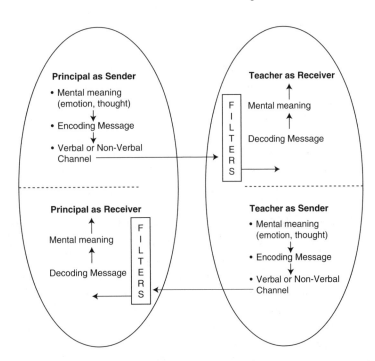

FIGURE 3.1   The Interpersonal Communication Process

literally and figuratively, is acting like a period on the end of a sentence. It is blocking the open communication you had hoped to achieve.

You put your finger down and open your palms as you sit back in your chair. Using your facial muscles, you change your expression. You monitor the tone of your voice:

> *"Sherry, I realize that I feel frustrated when you continue to focus on Ronald's mother as the only reason why he's not succeeding in school. I also realize that I was pointing my finger at you, which I apologize for, and I was wondering how **you** are feeling right now?*
>
> *"Fine," she responds but her eyes and her hand cutting the air in a chopping motion communicate something else. Apprehension has turned into another emotion.*
>
> *"I wonder if you might be feeling annoyed that I wasn't letting you finish speaking?"*
>
> *"Well, yes. I know that Ronald's mother is not the only problem. I just don't know how to handle him. And the other kids notice that he doesn't listen to me and now they are acting up. I don't know what to do and I don't want you to think that I'm not trying."*

Her face and voice says it all.

> *"I sense that you are feeling sad and maybe a little worried about how to manage your class and you don't know what you can do? Is that true?"*
>
> *"Yes."*
>
> *"So why don't we spend the rest of this meeting exploring ways we can work together to help you develop some great strategies. How does that sound?"*

The answering smile is proof enough that the problem is well on its way to being solved.

In this vignette, we can see that the principal was adept at using body language to understand the meaning of what was being communicated back and forth. With this understanding, the principal was able to shift the interaction from one heading in the wrong direction to one that could lead to a better working relationship and improved instruction in the classroom. Imagine how this meeting might have ended if the principal had not been so skilled and either had missed the nonverbal cues or had misinterpreted them. The people-smart principal or school district leader is one who knows how to "read" more than reports.

The importance of nonverbal communication in human interactions has been supported by research.[10] From the earliest age, human beings communicate nonverbally. Studies show that people use physical proximity, postures, gestures, tone of voice, rate of speech and facial expressions as cues to make meaning in their communication. At times, nonverbal cues are used to emphasize or soften a message that we are trying to convey. Other times, it may replace verbal communication entirely. In emotionally charged contexts (e.g. leadership team decision-making sessions), the amount of information communicated nonverbally may be more than 90 percent![11]

The human face, in particular, is uniquely designed to communicate and our brains seem to be hard wired by evolution to express and interpret facial communication.[12] Of the many emotions displayed on the face, six are recognized universally and, therefore, often referred to as universal or primary emotions: happiness, sadness, anger, fear, surprise and disgust. Certain groups of facial muscles are brought into action when these emotions are present and are easily identified by most people across cultures, especially if the emotion is intense. The secondary emotions, however, are harder to identify because they are often a mix of the primary emotions and, therefore, their expression, or lack of expression, is more influenced by cultural display rules.[13]

Everyone, except those with special kinds of brain damage or abnormalities, can read faces though there is a wide range of ability. Research has found that women, on average, seem to have slightly more ability to read and convey facial expression than men do.[14] More important, for the topic of social and emotional learning (SEL), is the fact that almost anyone can improve one's ability either through formal instruction or self-directed learning.

If learning how to read body language is such an important skill why is so little attention placed on learning how to do it? There are several reasons. First, our Western society places an emphasis on verbal communication. Anyone who walks into a classroom is likely to notice an overreliance on talk and literacy. Second, many people are subject to a cultural norm that says, "Don't look" when someone is experiencing strong emotions (except ironically when the person we are looking at is an actor). Another reason is that there are 3,000 different emotional signals that appear only briefly on the face.[15] Reading them can seem an overwhelming skill to master. Finally, our reluctance to spend time learning body language may partly be due to our discomfort in receiving the emotional information the human body is so well-designed to convey.

School leaders, however, need to move beyond these constraints to master nonverbal communication skills. Words are important but, if they are not consistent with one's body language, then it is unlikely that those you lead will heed what you have to say. As a leader, you will be constantly observed and, as the saying goes, actions speak louder than words. A funny example of this truth is the story of one of the greatest nonverbal communicators of all time, a man ironically who could not move his body below his waist, Franklyn Delano Roosevelt. According to legend, FDR tested out his belief in the power of nonverbal communication over words, by greeting his White House visitors one evening with a warm smile, a firm handshake and, in response to their greetings, "I'm fine, thank you, I just murdered my mother-in-law." Not one person reacted to the words. In all likelihood what they "heard" was the smile and the inviting handshake.

Active Listening

Knowing that communication is an art and that so much of communication is nonverbal, how can we improve our ability to understand the meaning that other people are trying to convey to us? We can begin by improving our ability to listen. Few of us have actually had formal training in listening skills. For many of us, our listening education consisted of observing poor role models and being told in school, "Alright, class, put your eyes on me and shut your ears to everything but the sound of my voice." Or "Just listen when I speak to you!" Listening was understood as something passive, akin to "paying attention".

Listening, however, is an active process. It is not synonymous with hearing, which is the reception of auditory stimuli. The roots of the word come from two Anglo-Saxon words meaning *hearing* and *wait in suspense*.[16] During active listening, we are receiving information with a suspense that requires engagement of our mind and body in meaning making. During active listening, we may be using any of the following skills:

1. Nonverbal Listening Responses
2. Reflecting Feelings
3. Paraphrasing
4. Clarifying Questions
5. Encouraging or Summarizing Statements

Nonverbal listening responses are behaviors that signal the speaker that you are interested in understanding what she or he has to say. In different cultures, these signals may vary. In Western culture, however, good listening means making eye contact without staring, positioning the body in an open way to the speaker (e.g. facing him, leaning slightly forward, without crossing the arms and legs), and using gestures and head nods to encourage communication. When someone walks into your office whom you need to actively listen to, move out from behind your desk and find a seating arrangement in which you can sit across from each other at eye level without any table between you if possible.

To reflect feelings means to attempt to interpret the emotions being expressed in the nonverbal and verbal communication and verbalize those interpretations to find out if you are actually perceiving their felt experience. For example, in the above communication with Sherry, the principal reflected feelings by saying *"I sense that you are feeling sad and maybe a little worried. . . ."* In emotionally charged situations, reflecting feelings is often the best strategy for defusing emotions, opening up communication, and engaging the person in collaborative problem solving. Even when your interpretation is incorrect, the other person is often so appreciative that you are really trying to understand that he will reveal his true feeling. It also happens that people will be unaware of what they are feeling until you name it for them.

Paraphrasing is the repeating back, in your own words, what you think the message is that is being sent to you. After reflecting Sherry's feelings back to her, the principal paraphrased what he had heard was Sherry's concern: *". . . how to manage your class and you don't know what you can do?"* Paraphrasing should be seen as a hypothesis you are making and, by testing it out with the speaker, you can gain better understanding. In practice, paraphrasing also gives information to speakers as to how well they are sending their message. If you use paraphrasing, you will find that people will occasionally say, "No, that's not what I meant" and then proceed to deliver their message in a different way. Sometimes they will use different words and sometimes they will use a different channel (e.g. "Let me draw you a picture.").

Clarifying questions are questions that are intended to elicit from the speaker new information that will enhance meaning. After paraphrasing Sherry, the principal asked, "Is that true?", hoping to get clarification from her. The supervisor could have also asked Sherry other clarifying questions: "Can you describe to me exactly what Ronald does that you find difficult to manage?" "I noticed that your shoulders hunched when I said that and I wonder if you can tell me what you were feeling just then?"

Encouraging and summarizing statements are useful for keeping the communication going or making sure both parties are in agreement with what has been said thus far. Encouraging statements might include statements such as "I'm glad we are talking about this" or "Can you talk more?" Summarizing might sound like "So thus far we seem to agree on three items to work on: Item one is . . ." or "Let me see if I understand what we have talked about thus far regarding your problems with the schedule change. First is . . ."

Empathy

Active listening can be seen as a manipulative strategy if the spirit of active listening is missing. And the spirit of active listening is empathy, one of the most important of the EQ competencies. Empathy can be defined as the ability to understand the perspective and feelings of another person. According to Daniel Goleman, empathy is built upon our self-awareness and self-management competencies in that we must be aware of our own feelings to tune into those of others while also being able to put aside our own emotional agendas to clearly receive the other person's emotional signals.[17] In active listening, the empathic principal seeks first to understand and then to be understood and genuinely tries to walk in the other person's shoes even if they belong to a five-year-old. During a communication workshop I led, a guidance counselor expressed cynicism about active listening because her supervisor was a master of using the techniques to patronize her when he had angered her. "Did he show you empathy?" I asked. When she said, "No", she understood the spirit of listening. If the situation calls for active listening, and at that moment you cannot be empathic, admit it and schedule another time.

Empathy, moreover, is the spirit of much more than active listening. It also provides the school leader with a social awareness that she can use to accomplish essential tasks in the life of the school. The task of assessing people's needs and designing the most effective learning experiences (e.g. mentoring, coaching, etc.) is made easier though social awareness. The ability to anticipate, recognize and meet the needs of parents and the larger community is also enhanced by empathy. Empathy also makes the school leader better able to value diversity and navigate the district politics that often ensnare socially unaware principals. In short, empathy helps us to respond to the nuances of the many social interactions that make up our school communities.

"Off" Switches to Open Communication

As you develop your empathic listening skills, be aware of how your verbal and nonverbal behaviors either open or close the communication process. Raise your awareness of the other person's body language and your own inner compass to alert you when the communication process is shutting down. The words may be still flowing, but the transfer of meaning has crashed to a halt. At these times, it is useful to stop talking and take a quick assessment of what is happening. Are you or the other person throwing an OFF switch on your communication? Just as a switch immediately turns off the flow of electricity in your office, certain behaviors will immediately turn off the flow of open communication in your relationships. In some cases, such as when dealing with a street con man, those OFF switches are extremely valuable, but far more often we use them unintentionally when the last thing we want to do is end the communication.

In Table 3.1 below, several OFF switches are listed with brief descriptions and some tips for dealing with them. This list is not exhaustive and the tips are presented as suggestions that you might try.

TABLE 3.1   "OFF" Switches to Open Communication

OFF	Description	Tips
OFF body language	Your body language or the other person's is not consistent with the meaning of your words. Another problem is that your culture's display of rules may be different than the other person's.	• If it's your body language and words, identify what you are trying to convey and then align your body and words to that meaning. • If it's the other person, express your confusion and ask them to clarify. • Make sure your body language "fits" the receiver's cultural display rules.
Too much talking	One or both of you are talking and not listening. This can happen for many reasons (e.g. strong emotions, poor skills, saving face, etc.).	• Name the problem. • You change the pattern. "Let's just slow down. Why don't you tell me again why you need this and I'll just listen."
Judging	Criticizing, diagnosing, name-calling, and giving empty praise are all examples of this OFF switch. This off switch is probably the biggest turn off to others. The person receiving it will feel judged and will either psychologically retreat or attack.	• If you're judging, stop immediately and see if communication opens. If it does not, or if the other person is judging, name the problem and agree to refrain from doing so (feel free to apologize). • Let the other person know how you feel.
Threats	Leaders can transmit threats in very subtle ways but staff members can as well e.g. "Well, I'll do it but I cannot promise that the parents will like your idea."	• Identify the feeling you are having either as the sender or receiver of the threat. • Sender—Apologize, share your feeling, ask the other person what they are feeling, and listen. • Receiver—Share your feeling and assert your willingness to problem solve with the other person if he or she agrees to work collaboratively.
Moralizing, lecturing, advising, ordering, etc.	Open communication exists between *partners* in meaning-making. Avoid words like "should and ought." People who come to you with a problem may just need to be listened to.	• Do not abuse your power. • Do not jump to giving solutions. Problem solve together. • Name the problem if you are the receiver.
HOT WORDS	Exaggerations like "always" and "never" incite. Do not label others e.g. "You're a jerk."	• Sender: Avoid using. If you do, apologize. • Receiver: Express feelings. Ask sender to clarify or stop.

Self-Expression

In opening up communication with another person, the ability to express yourself effectively is one of the most important tools you can possess in your leadership role. In the course of one school year, there will literally be tens of thousands of times that skilled self-expression will make a difference. It will make a difference between information that is understood or not, working relationships that are strengthened or not and goals that are met or somehow lost in a morass of misunderstandings and resentments.

In order to become more skillful, the foundational emotional competencies of self-awareness and self-management come into play in three important ways:

1. Self-regulation helps us to increase our self-awareness, which is essential for giving us a sense of what is important and not important for us to express. Two of your teachers have come to you with troubling news and asked for your advice. The news has triggered strong emotions in you and you are not sure what to tell them so you say, "Stop for a moment and let me think" and you take a deep breath and tell yourself to calm down. Reflecting on what you've been told and how you feel about each bit of information, you determine what is most important for you to say to your teachers.

2. Self-regulation allows us to channel the appropriate amount of emotion into our message so that our message has the best chance of being received accurately. Think of leaders whom you have known who are able to expertly express themselves and how they use emotion as part of their message. In different situations, leaders must assess various factors (who is the receiver, what is the context, etc.) and modulate their emotional expression to express themselves in authentic ways that can inform and influence.

3. Self-awareness and self-management enable us to keep our verbal and nonverbal expression consistent. When we say people are being authentic (or "real" in popular terms) we often mean that they express themselves in ways that convey what they think and feel. Sometimes, in relating to others we may find that our words are saying one thing but our voice's emotional tone or our body language is saying something different. EQ leaders "tune" their different communication channels so that they are usually on the same wavelength.

The need for an ability to fine tune one's message is most evident when you are in interpersonal situations marked by uncertainty or conflict. Because it is difficult to be in these situations, we may feel some discomfort and believe that its best to either be so aggressively blunt that you feel better (the other party, however, may feel blown away) or to avoid expressing yourself directly. The avoidance behavior may range from keeping mute to indirectly expressing ourselves using questions, jokes, offhand comments or defensive body language to "ease into" what we want to say.[18] Unfortunately, the more effective we are at aggressively or indirectly sending our message, the less effective we are at conveying the meaning of our intended message. The effects of such tactics are self-defeating since it is likely that the person receiving our blunt or indirect message will feel attacked or confused or may get the wrong message and not even know it. For leaders, especially, the effects of faulty self-expression can be disastrous.

How can leaders become more skilled in self-expression especially when they want to assert their needs and wants in these potentially difficult interpersonal situations? One of the most effective strategies was developed in the late 1970's by the psychologist and leadership expert, Thomas Gordon.[19] This strategy, known as an *I-Message,* consists of a message with three interrelated components: behavior, feelings and effects. The behavior component consists of the behavior of the other person or persons that is triggering an emotion in you. The feeling component is the feeling that comes from your self-awareness of the emotion. The tangible and concrete effects that you experience because of the other person's behavior comprise the effect component.

For example, your neighbor has been playing her new hi-amp sound system deep into the night for the past three nights and you want to let her know how you feel about it. The behavior is "playing the sound system until 3am for the past three nights." The feeling in this case may be frustration or annoyance (unless you are a night person and love the music) and the effect is that you cannot get enough sleep and you have a hard time functioning at work. In the past, you might have just kept quiet and hoped that your neighbor would stop or you might have gone over to her door, pounded on it, and screamed, "You jerk, you never think of anybody but yourself! Play that music again and I'm going to bang on this door all night."

You can easily see that the avoidance or aggressive approach could easily lead to a worsening relationship with your neighbor and still no sleep. Instead you decide to assert yourself with the following I-Message: "Rita, when you play your sound system until 3am, I feel frustrated because I can't sleep and I can't function at work the next morning." You may want to add what you want or need ("I'd like you to either turn it down or don't play it after 11pm") or you may want to try to engage Rita in problem-solving a workable solution. In any case, Rita is less likely to feel attacked and will more likely be willing to change her behavior because you have made it clear to her what your feelings are and why you are feeling them.

At first, you may have difficulty crafting I-Messages. You may have acquired the habit of giving You-Messages so it feels hard to shift gears and you may initially find that your first attempts at I-Messages are either incomplete or are disguised attacks: "I feel you never consider me (what's the feeling?) when you stay up all night (it's the loud music that bothers you) because it's no big deal to you how it affects me" (So how does it affect you in tangible ways?). It is a good idea to write your I-Message down, revise it and then rehearse it with a friend, if possible, before you deliver it. It's also a good idea to first use I-Messages with people you trust in situations that are not emotionally volatile. Think of yourself as a baseball player in Spring Training practicing a new pitch and knowing that you will make many mistakes in your delivery before you feel confident and skilled enough to use it in pressured situations. Also remember that what order you deliver the three components is not as important as bringing your ideas and feelings before the other person in order to open up the conversation and solve the problem. Finally, be aware that even an I-Message may be perceived as an attack and you may need to use a combination of active listening and assertiveness skills several times in order to open up communication.

The I-Message is also effective when the situation is positive. Let's see how it might be used in a conversation with a high school student who has often been in the principal's office for fighting and for learning new ways to handle his anger.

> **Mr. Snider:** *James, I felt so proud when I saw you stop your friends from fighting at lunch today because it showed me that our mentoring sessions on Fridays are working.*
>
> **James:** *I didn't do nothing, Mr. Snider. They would have stopped anyway.*
>
> **Mr. Snider:** *So, James, you don't think you had anything to do with Larry and Zach cooling off before they went out of control?*
>
> **James:** *Well, I did tell them to chill and I knew that Larry was about to do some hurt so I told him that I could see he was pissed.*
>
> **Mr. Snider:** *Did that help him to calm down?*
>
> **James:** *Yeah, a little. He got a look in his eye. (Laughs) I told him that he didn't want to come in here on Fridays like me.*

> **Mr. Snider:** *So I'm proud that you were able to convince Larry to calm down so that I have less work on Fridays. OK?*
>
> **James:** *Yeah, thanks.*

INTUITION AND TRANSPARENCY

Being a model for how we can relate with one another in schools requires more than skills in listening, empathy and self-expression. Let's look again at Nancy Sing-Bock's situation, which began this chapter. Nancy was new to the principalship and there were many things that she needed to learn about leading a school. Unfortunately, she did not have the luxury of a normal start to the school year as schools were mandated to do something for the first anniversary of the September 11 terrorist attack. She knew that the people in the school had strong feelings about the event. As one of her teachers, Brenda McGoldrick, recalled later:

> *Early on this summer, I began thinking about how we as a school community were going to approach and cope with the anniversary of the most tragic event of our lives. On Sept. 11, 2001 we were put to the biggest test as teachers and administrators. We amazingly managed, with little confusion and only a few spoken words, to safely get every child from pre-k through 8th grade into the arms of their parents, caretakers and loved ones. We responded in such a way that it almost looked routine. When we returned to the building 48 hours later, we looked at each other in a new light. A staff that has always had an amazing sense of community, friendship and respect was even stronger. It was an irreplaceable sense of security in such an uncertain time. How were we going to have this feeling on the anniversary when so much of the staff has been changed, including the foundation for the staff, the principal? Were we going to have the opportunity to share our feelings? Were we going to be safe? For weeks, so many questions raced through my mind, so many fears constantly lingered in my heart and mind.*

And what about Nancy?

> *I felt a lot of pressure, as I'm sure many principals did because schools were mandated to do something for September 11. I had no problem with the desire to do something meaningful with my school, but I was anxious because I did not know my community yet and was unsure of what they would want to do.*

September 11, 2002 held both promise and peril for Nancy's leadership. As the titular head of the school she now had the opportunity to be the symbolic heart of her school. Could she use her emotional competencies to make the right decision?

> *When I went to the district meeting about planning for September 11, we heard many ideas of possible activities we could do with our schools. Almost immediately, I began to think how nice it would be to do some music with the school. Music has always been an integral part of my life; my family always did a lot of music growing up, I met my husband in a chorus and continue to sing with that same chorus after 16 years. I have taught music in elementary schools, camps and day camps.*
>
> *Therefore, when I had a meeting with my staff to determine what we would want to do for the anniversary of September 11, it only seemed natural that I suggest that I would sing a few songs with my guitar. The music teacher was also excited by this and volunteered to sing with me. The staff wanted to do something brief with the entire school, and when I suggested singing, they all seemed to like that. Brenda McGoldrick, the*

resource room teacher, also volunteered to read something about why we were gathering together and explain what an anniversary is. They also wanted the ceremony done first thing in the morning. It was clear they all wanted to do something simple and meaningful for the entire school but looked to me for direction, guidance and leadership. I was reluctant to suggest singing because the staff did not know me yet. However, I was willing to take that risk and wanted to reveal and share a part of myself.

Brenda reflects:

We met as a staff, the new principal opening up the conversation. She told her story; the events she experienced (on September 11). She expressed her own feelings and ideas of how to address the day. Sighs of relief filled the room. We spoke our minds, gave suggestions and let go of our fears. But no one could come to a solid, secure decision. Nancy stepped forward and said she would be sharing her talent of singing with the school and would lead the school in songs in the schoolyard if that was what the staff wanted. Again, we looked at our new leader and sighed with relief. We now had a plan. We the staff and our students would have the opportunity to remember and reflect.

In their recounting of what happened before and during decision-making, we can see how Nancy used her EQ to guide the process. First, Nancy used intuitive decision-making when it was most appropriate. Intuitive decision-making is appropriate when there are no right answers to the problem, when the social context of the problem involves deep emotional relationships and when you are steeped in the kind of problem you are facing. While Nancy was new to the school, she was not new to the emotional milieu of a school or to the power of music to heal and to bring people together. "It only seemed *natural*" she said when the idea of using music popped into her head and that sense of feeling right when a solution surfaces is emblematic of intuitive thinking.

In recalling the meeting, Nancy gives us more insight about how EQ cultivates leadership. The fledgling principal describes how she took a risk by sharing her own story, her thoughts and feelings and her personal offer to play music for the anniversary. It was a risk for her to do so and she could have simply gone over the mandate, presented ideas from the principal's meeting or asked for ideas from staff. Her willingness to open with her own emotional memories sent a message to her staff that they could also communicate on this level if they felt safe enough. By doing this she modeled what she hoped to foster and the staff responded openly with both nonverbal ("sighs") and verbal ("ideas") language. She also displayed empathy skills by understanding the group's desire to keep the ceremony brief and by also being receptive to the desire of the music teacher and Brenda to make a more personal contribution. It was clear from Brenda's story that the staff was looking for someone to fill the large void left by a beloved principal and, on this day at least, Nancy stepped forward.

In the final part of Nancy's story, try to identify the ways that she used her self-awareness, self-management, and social awareness skills in her leadership role:

When I thought about the choice of music, my visceral feeling was that music seemed to be the right choice. Music is universal, healing, and unifying. I am finding, when you make important choices like this, you have to dig deep into your soul and go with your inner gut feelings. Deciding what to do for the September 11 anniversary involved my first group process which I needed to facilitate. As the new leader, I was a participant in the group process as it unfolded and felt I was leading it but at the same time an equal member of the process.

When the day arrived, we gathered in the schoolyard, formed a huge circle and began our ceremony. Marina, the music teacher and I sang the songs, "We Shall Overcome," "This

Land is Your Land," and "God Bless America." *As I looked around, teachers, students, custodians, kitchen help and our security officer held hands and joined us in song. Some cried, some looked solemn and sad, and others stood quietly. Brenda read a beautiful piece about why we were gathered together and why this day was called an anniversary. We lit a candle, had a minute of silence and slowly dispersed to our classrooms. Staff members and students hugged each other and I realized deep inside that we had shared a powerful time together remembering a very tragic and difficult day for all of us.*

Looking back at the personal choices I made in those first days that lead to the September 11 event, it is clear that the school came together even stronger as a community. When their principal left suddenly at the end of June, they were anxious, and apprehensive about their new principal. Taking the risk of suggesting music and singing for the school, I believe was reassuring and communicated to the community that they could continue to be the kind of school where people collaborate, share and help one another. I think the staff realized that I was the kind of leader that is not afraid to show my feelings, and willing to collaborate and listen to their feelings.

Is Nancy the kind of leader who will continue to show the courage to practice what EQ experts call transparency, which is defined as "an authentic openness to others about one's feelings, beliefs, and actions"?[20] We hope so because a transparent leader fosters integrity or a sense that the leader can be trusted. Nancy seems to know that, if she can remain authentic, others will follow. It may not be easy for Nancy to remain transparent, however, because new principals are faced with so many unexpected challenges that severely test the self-management competencies that are the bedrock of transparency. So many new principals, unprepared in their preservice education for the emotional labor of leadership, retreat behind a veneer of authority rather than risk the vulnerability of authenticity.[21] It is a fool's bargain and we suspect Nancy, with her music and her courage, will pass it by.

SELF-DIRECTED LEARNING

Perhaps the most essential characteristic that Nancy, or any school leader, can model is that of being a self-directed learner. Self-directed learning is defined as "intentionally developing or strengthening an aspect of who you are or who you want to be, or both".[22] A self-directed learner, in other words, is someone who wants to learn and is actively engaged in personal development. Imagine what it would be like to be in a school in which everyone, including the principal and the teachers, were demonstratively engaged in self-directed learning?

To be an effective self-directed learner requires an understanding of the process of self-change and the steps to achieve it. A useful model to use for this purpose is the one developed by Richard Boyatzis, Professor and Chair of the Department of Organizational Behavior at the Weatherhead School of Management at Case Western Reserve University. His model (see Figure 3.2) is based on three decades of his research on and experiences with leaders of organizations.[23]

As you can see from the model, self-directed learning is a cyclical process that involves five moments of what Boyatzis calls *discovery*. Each discovery entails a sense of discontinuity and a combination of self-awareness and a motivation to change. These five discoveries follow the following stages:

1. **The First Discovery:** *My ideal self—Who do I want to be?* In your vision of the ideal leader, what would you be like? This may seem like an easy question to answer but to really answer the question truthfully, you must first sort out what you think you

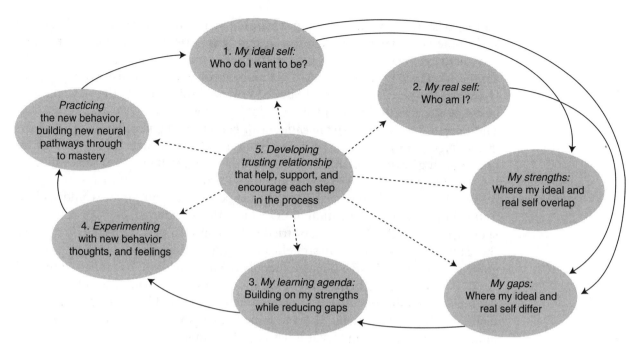

FIGURE 3.2 Boyatzis's Theory of Self-Directed Learning
(From *Primal Leadership* by Goleman et al. Harvard Business School Publishing, 2002)

ought to say as opposed to what you truly believe. In doing so it's important to use your self-awareness and to find the answer that evokes your dreams, aspirations and passion.

2. **The Second Discovery:** *My real self—Who am I? What are my strengths and gaps?* As a child, Yogi Berra, the baseball Hall of Fame catcher, was scolded by his teacher for his performance in class: "I remember a teacher asking me, 'Don't you know anything?' and I said 'I don't even suspect anything'."[24]

So, often, *we* don't suspect anything. We live our lives but don't suspect that we have lost an accurate picture of who we are as people and leaders in this time and in this place. Our natural psychological processes, developed to protect us emotionally, tend to distort incoming information to our brains so that we may see ourselves either as more like or more dissimilar to our idealized selves then to who we actually are. In our research with principals, for example, we noticed that there was often a real gap between our subjects' perceptions of themselves as collaborators and the observations of both staff members and ourselves.

This distortion may be heightened because people, especially those you lead, may not be giving you accurate feedback because it makes them very uncomfortable to do so. To break out of these informational constraints, you need to actively question your self-portrayal and seek out 360° feedback from your boss, your peers and your followers.[25] By energetically seeking out information about yourself and your performance from people who have frequent contact with you, and view you from different perspectives, you are more likely to get an accurate picture. This is especially true if you make it safe to give negative information. Getting this information will enable you to assess your leadership strengths and gaps—the gaps representing the true differences between your ideal and real selves.

3. **The Third Discovery:** *My learning agenda—Building on my strengths while reducing the gaps.* In this stage, self directed learners develop their own learning goals based

on their vision, strengths, individual learning styles, what is feasible and realistic, and a time table flexible enough to suit their own orientation to the future (e.g. I learn better if I make detailed future plans while you do better with an open-ended approach). There is no right way to plan for this discovery because everyone is different as a learner. The criteria should be how well this plan fits the way you learn best and how practical is the plan for reducing the gap.

4. **The Fourth Discovery:** *Experimenting with and practicing new behaviors, thoughts, and feelings to the point of mastery.* The brain mostly learns new habits through implicit learning, which can only be learned through repeated practice. You cannot just tell your brain to unlearn old habits and then learn new habits. If that were so, your reading of this book and your desire to be the best leader you can be would lead like a straight path to the acquisition of EQ habits. However, anyone who has learned a sport, tried to break a bad habit, or tried to learn how to play the piano, knows that the learning process is far from straight and requires prolonged time-on-task and ongoing reflection. Reflective practice literally rewires the brain by strengthening different pathways in the brain and, in some cases, even fostering the growth of new neurons. When this circuitry is strong enough the desired behavior becomes automatic and a habit. Be patient. As Seneca, the Roman philosopher said long ago, "The mind is slow in unlearning what it has been long in learning."

5. **The Fifth Discovery:** *Developing supportive and trusting relationships that make change possible.* Self-directed learning is not self-alone learning. It occurs best within a community of learners. In some school environments there may not yet exist such a community. The school leader must then find, both within and outside the school, people who will act as his support network for learning. Because optimal learning always exists in that zone between safety and risk known as challenge, a support system for leaders provides a safe harbor for experimentation while at the same time asking tough questions. Ideally, some of the people supporting school leaders should be school leaders themselves and able to understand the leader's challenges from three levels: personal, group and organizational. This support team should be there for the self-directed learner throughout the other four stages.

IN SUMMARY

Will Rogers, the humorist, once said, "Even if you're on the right track, you'll get run over if you just sit there." By reading this book you are on the right track for developing the kind of leadership that can help create a learning community, but you can't just sit there. You need to practice the EQ competencies mentioned in this chapter as well as in the other chapters. Engage the five discoveries to develop your empathy, optimism, transparency and communication skills. Seek out 360° feedback. Like Nancy Sing Bock, listen to the music of your intuitive voice. Reflect on your reflective journal and mine its resources. Are you the model? You can be if you stand up and begin heading down the track. If you do, you will find that others will follow you.

REFLECTIVE QUESTIONS

1. In this chapter, three ways are suggested for developing optimism. Which of these do you employ and when was a time that you used the method(s) successfully?
2. What mental scripts do you generally use to explain failure?

3. Look at the Interpersonal Communication Process model and think of a recent conversation you had with someone at work. What mental filters might have distorted meaning in the communication process?
4. Look at the active listening skills. Which do you regularly use at work? Which do you rarely or never use? How could you become a more active listener?
5. Which OFF switches to open communication do you tend to use when engaged in a difficult conversation?
6. How transparent are you at work? How do you assess this?

LESSON FROM THE FIELD

Joseph F. Santello

The aftermath of September 11 continues to be felt at our school almost three weeks after the event. The adage that a school is a microcosm of our society has never been more true. Staff members, like typical Americans across our country, now do things differently as well as react differently. The apprehension of what may come and the fear of uncertainty are difficult for most of us to shake.

As the principal of my school, PS 39, Oct. 2nd began like most days but shortly changed. During the outside lunch activity, four boys were accused of making ethnic slurs to a student from Pakistan. The incident also involved a physical assault on the same student. The four boys were immediately summoned to my office. Together with a teacher, the boys were interviewed and statements were taken. At first, there was denial but facts indicated that the allegations were true. Each parent was instructed to come to school to take part in a guidance intervention conference.

Although I was expected to call the report into the police department as a bias incident, I decided against it. As a father and educator, I struggled with the idea of involving the police. There are times when you're confronted with issues like this that you realize how difficult the position of principal can be. You can argue that in this situation the impact of police involvement upon these four fifth-graders would certainly impress upon them the inappropriateness of their actions. However, the flip side of the argument is that in spite of their actions they remain children. Not condoning their actions but realizing that our roles as parents and adults place the responsibility for teaching them the difference between wrong and right.

Now, don't get me wrong. I can certainly appreciate that there are behaviors that must be addressed through harsher means. And remember this is October 2, 2001, approximately three weeks after the nightmare in lower Manhattan. Those facts certainly weighed heavily on my mind. After meeting with each of the parents I was convinced that, in this case, I took the appropriate action. There was no denial and no attempts to explain away what the children had done. Instead, we formed a partnership to work together, which I firmly believe will ultimately support the direction that I took.

I think what upset me most throughout this incident was my meeting with the victim's mother. Although she was visibly upset over the actions toward her son, I believe that it is the actions of adults in our community that upset her most. She indicated that a simple walk to the deli raises her anxiety and leads to a great deal of fear and stress. When she told me that, she literally broke down. For the first time in my tenure as principal, I felt compelled to put my arms around a parent and allow her to sob openly. For me, a sick feeling quickly overcame me. As a nation, as a city and as a school community we have so much to learn about ourselves. When asked about bias all profess being free from prejudice. But is that really true? Days like this clearly indicate that the mission before us is not one to take lightly. Our actions and how students perceive our actions will remain with the children throughout their lives. If any of you feel that this is not the case you've entered the wrong profession.

Joseph Santello was the principal of PS 39 in Staten Island, New York, at the time of the World Trade Center tragedy. We asked him to reflect on the aftermath of the event and this lesson is taken from that reflection.

Chapter 4

Embracing Conflict in Ourselves and Others

I could say lots of words, but all that really mattered is how I treated my neighbors.

—Fred Rodgers, reflecting on his show, Mr. Rogers' Neighborhood

The teenagers sitting with me in a circle seemed less animated than usual. A group of middle schoolers from my town and surrounding communities, they had met with two other volunteer youth leaders and myself each Sunday morning for the past six months. They were a close knit-group, sometimes serious, sometimes silly, always laced with hormones and youthful impulsiveness. As they discussed their lives and learned skills for dealing with bullies, for interrupting prejudice and for exercising leadership, they were rarely quiet. On this day, however, they were strangely silent and subdued.

The opening Check In was about to begin. "Ok, who wants to start with the Rock," my co-facilitator asked, holding up the smooth melon-sized rock that was used to signify that the holder had the speaker's role as it was passed around the group circle. Seconds of silence passed until Dora whispered, "I'll take it."

Dora looked over at two boys who did not always respect the rule that no one can interrupt the person with the Rock. "I know that you're going to laugh at what I'm going to say," she said defensively. "But I'm feeling sad about Mr. Roger's death. I've been thinking about it since I heard. He was such an important part of my life."

I looked over at Robert and Michael ready to pounce on their sarcastic remarks or giggles. Instead, I saw them sit up from their lounge lizard cool pose and pay attention. The next speaker also revealed his sense of loss about Fred Roger's death a few days before. Each teen in turn shared their feelings about the children's show host. Each recounted a favorite memory of a puppet skit or a special show about an emotional issue that touched upon a conflict that they had grappled with as a young child.

When Michael's turn came, I fully expected him to either use humor to deflect the emotional weight of the others' memories or to pass. I feared that he would take his role as the final speaker in the circle as a chance to grandstand and ruin the emotional connection that had been created. After all, this was the person in the group who reveled in Point and Shoot video games and being "macho" to the point of sometimes intimidating others. As he took the Rock, he seemed to weigh it in his hand and then said:

Yeah, Mr. Rogers was cool. I liked the way he talked to me. He was kind of funny but you always felt he was talking to you. My Mom would yell "Mr. Roger's is on" and I would come running into my living room and sit down in front of the TV. I loved that show. I was so sad when my Mom told me he was dead . . . He was just so cool.

It was bittersweet listening to the teens' stories especially since I was in the midst of writing a book with Janet about leaders creating caring schools. On one hand, it was so hopeful knowing that these young people had felt such emotional resonance with an adult male who was smart, honest and so caring in an authentic way (he never commercialized his popularity with licensed products a la Disney). On the other hand, I was saddened because I knew from our previous meetings that the schools they lived in each weekday for almost half their waking hours did not feel like a "neighborhood." Their schools were considered excellent schools judged on academic scores but each teen, without exception, dreaded going back to school the next day. For the most part, they were high achievers but they felt very disconnected from the adults in their schools for several reasons:

- Principals and teachers were seen as more interested in getting the teens to do what they wanted than in creating self-directed learners. Consequently, the teens believed that success was determined by how well they could figure out what the teachers wanted and then give it to them even when they thought the teacher was mistaken.
- Teachers were viewed as being stressed and, as a result, overloaded them with long hours of boring homework and prep work for standardized tests.
- Bullying and cliques were seen as an accepted reality of the school. Teachers and administrators were seen as unaware of the extent of the problem and, if they acted, it was only after a blatant incident occurred and a student needed to be punished.
- Adult modeling of effective conflict resolution was rare as teen-adult conflicts were generally dealt with through the use of power thus leaving many of the teens to feel helpless. "They don't practice what they preach," one youth sighed.

In this chapter, we examine how school leaders can begin to create the kind of "neighborhoods" in their schools that resonate emotionally for both students and adults. In this neighborhood building, a great tool to possess is the willingness to embrace the inevitable conflicts that are part of everyday living and then manage those conflicts in effective ways. Specifically, we will first define conflict and dispel some of the myths that surround it. Next, we take a candid picture of how unskilled management of conflict plays out in many of our nation's schools and the costs of such destructive conflict. After that, we offer strategies that school leaders can use to prevent unnecessary conflicts and to negotiate or mediate those that do occur. Finally, we discuss some elements of how to make this learning school wide, a process that will be elaborated in subsequent chapters.

WHAT IS CONFLICT?

Conflict can be defined as "the interaction of interdependent people who perceive incompatible goals and interference from each other in achieving those goals."[1] This is a useful definition for educational leaders because it captures the dynamics of school conflict. Conflict as an *interaction of interdependent people* highlights the way that relationships in schools often play off each other in subtle ways to either sustain or resolve conflicts. Furthermore, the idea that this process involves *perceptions* is crystal clear to any school leader who ever had to mediate a dispute in which the disputants' perceptions clashed greatly though their objectives were substantially the same.

MYTHS ABOUT CONFLICT

Conflict is like water: too much causes damage to people and property; too little creates a dry, barren landscape devoid of life and color. We need water to survive; we need an appropriate level of conflict to thrive as well.

—Costatino & Merchant[2]

I have heard school leaders boast that they do not have conflicts in their school. This boast reflects certain mistaken beliefs or myths many people have about conflict. Implicit in the statement is that conflict is something negative and good leaders can somehow eradicate it (or at least not publicly admit its presence). Conflict, however, is a normal part of everyday life. It is neither bad nor good and it is, like the water mentioned in the quote above, essential for the health of a school. Each time a teacher questions a learner's naïve beliefs about the world, a conflict begins. Each time a child plays a game or a teen works on a group project, conflicts stream forth like an incoming tide. And like the tide, conflict in a school will always be present so, if leaders want to learn how to manage and use it productively, they need to recognize that "indeed, conflict *does* exist in my school."

Conflict can have either negative or positive consequences depending upon how it is perceived and handled by the people in conflict. Constructive conflict resolution is marked by what Morton Deutsch, a founder of the field of conflict resolution, calls "an effective cooperative problem-solving process in which the conflict is the mutual problem to be resolved cooperatively."[3] On the other hand, Deutsch says that destructive conflict resolution is marked by a "competitive process in which the conflicting parties are involved in a competition or struggle to determine who wins or loses." For example, if the teacher and student described in the previous paragraph perceive themselves as engaged in a caring, collaborative process of making meaning, then real learning results. If one or both perceive the interaction as a contest over ideas then the conflict runs the risk of turning destructive to learning as well as to the relationship.

Another related myth is what I call the "The Tyranny of the Ones:" There is one best way to handle conflict and there is one right solution to the conflict. I call this myth a tyranny because it limits the freedom all of us need to resolve conflicts in new and creative ways. In everyday living, there are many ways to deal well with conflict. Often there are many solutions. Tapping into their emotional competencies, EQ leaders are able to respond in the moment to whatever actions will help them and others deal with conflict creatively.

Conflict Styles

Though we can handle conflict in many ways, psychologists have observed that most of us have a tendency to act in certain ways that can be classified as conflict styles. One of the most widely-known of these classifications identifies five distinct types based on the two independent components of assertiveness and cooperativeness.[4] Assertiveness is conceptualized as the behaviors one uses to satisfy one's own needs and concerns while cooperativeness is defined as behaviors one uses to satisfy the other's needs and concerns. In Figure 4.1 you can see that the interaction of these two components results in five conflict styles:

- **Competitive**—High in assertiveness and low in cooperativeness, a person with this style tends to see conflicts as a win-lose proposition and is most interested in getting what she or he wants.

- **Accommodative**—A person with this style tends to put great value on maintaining the relationship and meeting the needs of the other person even if his or her own needs go unsatisfied.
- **Avoiding**—Unassertive and uncooperative, this person withdraws rather than deals with the conflict.
- **Compromising**—A person with this style displays some assertiveness and cooperation but tends to seek a solution that involves each person giving up something.
- **Collaborative**—High on both assertion and cooperativeness, this person actively seeks to find Win-Win solutions that will be mutually benefiting to both parties.

It is important for school leaders to realize that all these styles can be effective in certain conflict situations and disastrous in other situations. A competitive power-based style can be useful when there is an emergency and time is of the essence (e.g. there is an intruder in the building) or when you are bargaining with a vendor over the price of school supplies. This style, however, can intimidate others and harm relationships, creating a climate of fear and anger in your school if you use it extensively. An avoidant style may be the best approach when there is an explosive situation such as a case in which an emotionally-hijacked parent is threatening you and you choose to cool things down. The problem with avoidance in many school conflicts is that the problem remains unresolved and both parties may feel dissatisfied and frustrated. An accommodating style is appropriate when you believe that your concerns are not so important to you or discover that your position was incorrect and your relationship with the other person is valuable to you (e.g. A student reporter writes an article criticizing a school policy). On the other hand, if school leaders accommodate when issues are important to them and the school's mission, their credibility is undermined and their concerns not addressed.

With the last two styles, there is often confusion between the terms. People who worked through a conflict will often say, "We negotiated a win-win solution today." But when they describe their negotiation process, you realize that they reached a compromise. A compromise, by definition, means that neither party fully satisfied their interests.

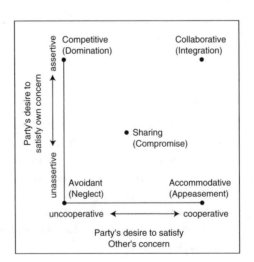

FIGURE 4.1 Five Conflict-Handling Orientations, Plotted According to Party's Desire to Satisfy Own and Other's Concerns
(Copyright © Marvin D. Dunnette with permission)

They each gave up something to gain something. A "50-50" split is a classic compromise. Compromising is an important strategy to use when collaborative problem-solving is going nowhere or there are minor disagreements and time is scarce. However, if issues are important and there is sufficient time for creating a mutually satisfying solution, then you have lost an opportunity if you do not engage in a collaborative style. As the style that combines the highest levels of assertiveness and collaborativeness it has the best chance of achieving a long-lasting solution that "enlarges the pie" and satisfies the interests of both parties.

EQ leaders are skilled at relationship management. This ability is based on the triad of self-awareness, self-management and empathy.[5] As part of self-awareness, school leaders need to be aware of their conflict style, what their beliefs are about conflict and what emotions arise in them when they are in different kinds of conflict. They must also be able to manage their emotions, remain flexible enough to adapt to the particular situation and use their interpersonal skills to achieve their goals. In trying to achieve their own goals, however, EQ leaders should also use their social awareness to understand the other person's goals, conflict style, conflict beliefs, and emotions. Using this triad leads to mutually satisfying solutions to the conflict.

SCHOOL CONFLICTS

Conflict in schools does not get much attention from the general public unless it escalates into violence. And serious violence is a big problem for many schools. According to a 2002 report from the National Center for School Statistics, there were 35 school-related homicides for the last year they had collected data.[6] The Center's findings also showed that 128,000 students 12 to 18 years old were victims in school of serious non-fatal violence such as rape, robbery and aggravated assault. In addition, between seven and nine percent of high school students reported that they had been in a fight on school property in that same year. For elementary school age children, the crimes against them are less severe but they are bullied at a higher level than older students (14 per cent of students in sixth grade versus two percent of seniors in high schools). Even more troubling are reports that, while violence in secondary schools continues to decrease, it is increasing in the youngest grades with children as young as kindergartners committing serious crimes of violence.[7]

These reports are frightening, but thankfully not all schools suffer this level of violence (with the possible exception of bullying). Moreover, most serious violence involving youth happens outside of school and schools are generally safer than their surrounding neighborhoods. The biggest threat in most schools is the everyday destructive conflict that occurs among adults and students that does not end in violence, but negatively impacts on student learning, school attendance, teacher morale, staff turnover and school climate. The biggest reducible cost in any school or organization may be unmanaged conflict with estimates of 65 percent of performance problems and 45 percent of lost management time being caused by destructive conflicts.[8] I often ask principals in my workshops to make an estimate of the costs of one day of conflicts in their schools in such areas as expended staff time, wasted opportunities for student learning, and their own involvement. I ask them to put a dollar figure on those costs. Principals are usually amazed that their calculations run into the thousands of dollars. It is clear that it is not a question of how can we can afford to teach and learn conflict resolution in our schools; it's a question of how can we afford not to do it.

RESPONSES TO CONFLICT

If conflict presents such a major problem for schools, what can schools do in response? The methods schools use typically can be viewed on a continuum between power-based approaches and interest-based approaches.[9]

POWER   INTERESTS
(Competitive)   (Collaborative)

Schools that rely on trying to deal with conflict with zero tolerance policies, discipline codes that stress control and punishment and an emphasis on such features as security guards and metal detectors can be seen as mostly power-based. Schools that rely on trying to deal with conflict with preventive instructional approaches, student generated codes of behavior and peer mediation programs can be viewed as mostly interest-based. Most schools probably use a combination of approaches depending on their philosophy of education and their current situation (e.g. a school community is moving towards a collaborative learning model but the school's location in a high crime area necessitates the use of security guards and metal detectors).

Costs of a Power-Based Approach to the Organization and to the Leader

School leaders sometimes respond to their own fears (e.g. "I don't want to be held liable") and to the fears of their constituencies by over-relying on a power-based approach. The thinking is that this is a "fearful world" and we must take control to make it safer. This fear in most schools, however, is overblown and media-induced by the old adage, "If it bleeds it leads." Unfortunately, this knee-jerk use of a power approach to conflict in a school can have several negative effects:

1. Reduction of upward communication and a decrease in accuracy ("Tell her what she wants to hear").
2. Increase in "apple polishing" and "group think" (everyone agrees with the leader and, as a result, feedback necessary for preventing bad decisions is absent).
3. Heightened competitiveness—Members of school community perceive conflict in win-lose terms. The concepts of team building and community become empty abstractions.
4. Decreased initiative and creativity—"You tell me what to do and I'll do it". "They come to me with problems that they should be able to solve themselves."
5. Increased rebellion and passive-aggressiveness.
6. Informal alliances or cliques formed to balance the scales.
7. Increased avoidance behavior—higher turnover rates, increased alienation.

For the school leader there are also many costs. The cost of enforcement is time-consuming. The stress takes a toll on one's emotional and physical health. Coercive use of power tends to diminish influence as time progresses so leaders must be continually vigilant. Such vigilance can induce feelings of alienation. I have witnessed principals barricade themselves into their offices, emerging only when a conflict has escalated to crisis proportions.

An interest-based approach to conflict also has its costs. Because it emphasizes collaborative approaches to dealing with conflict, it requires an expenditure of valuable time for working together and an outlay of resources for providing SEL skills training for the whole school community. For school leaders the costs involve a loss of control (hopefully offset by a gain in influence) and perhaps feelings of loss and uncertainty in stepping out of the traditional role of superintendent or school principal. Nevertheless, it is the approach that is most consistent with EQ Leadership.

Principled Negotiation

In their classic book, *Getting to Yes,* Roger Fisher and William Ury described a process they called principled negotiation. This process is designed to create good agreements that satisfies the parties' interests, are fair and lasting, and may even improve the parties' relationship.[10] It rests on four principles:

- Separate the people from the problem.
- Focus on interests rather than positions.
- Generate a variety of options before settling on an agreement.
- Insist that the agreement be based on objective criteria.

According to Fisher and Ury, negotiations often take the form of positional bargaining in which each person takes a position on an issue and competes with the other party to win. A parent, for example, walks in unannounced into your office and demands that you, the principal, place her child in Mrs. Hunt's class next year. Or the school board president wants you, as the superintendent, to dismantle your new diversity team. In positional bargaining, also known as distributive negotiation, parties take a competitive stance and try to secure what they want. If that stance fails, they want to at least get more than the other party. While this type of negotiating is effective in some transactions (e.g. negotiating the price of a car), it can be disastrous in school situations where the parties involved are often in ongoing relationships with each other. In the case of the scenarios above with either the parent or school board president, your relationship with both is important and a positional bargaining approach might damage that relationship no matter who "wins" their position. Too often people rush to solve a problem without taking the time to accurately define what the problem really is.[11] How many disputes have you either engaged in or witnessed in which the underlying problem at the heart of the dispute was either never explored or was quickly shoved aside in the name of placing blame? "You did this . . . you never . . . you always . . ."

A principled negotiation approach, on the other hand, asks you to see the other party as your partner, rather than adversary, in solving the problem that is underlying the conflict. By using *reframing,* or changing the way you look at the problem, you shift the focus away from the person and onto the problem. In doing so, you open the negotiation to the possibility of collaboratively generating many alternative solutions, some of which may "enlarge the pie" and enable both of you to find a solution that is mutually satisfying. These "win-win" solutions not only preserve the relationship, but also are more likely to last because both parties feel their interests are served.

The first step in principled negotiation is to identify the parties' interests regarding the issue at hand. The EQ leader uses her listening and empathy skills to uncover the underlying interest or needs that are hidden in what the other party says they want. The Japanese have a saying, "Ask why five times," and I find that is an excellent tool for finding out the interests (the other person's and my own) at the center of a dispute:

"Why do you want me to dismantle the diversity team, John?"

"I don't think it's a good idea."

"I can see that you're upset but you approved of the team last month. Can you tell me why you don't think it's a good idea now?"

"Marie, I received a call from my campaign manager and he thinks that, with all the news about harassment cases, this may not be the best time for me to sponsor this team."

"So you're concerned that your connection to the team is going to reflect badly on you?"

"That's right."

What could have been a win-lose battle framed by "I want the team" versus "I don't want the team" can now be framed differently. The problem becomes "How can we solve this problem so that I have help in thinking through diversity issues and you and your campaign do not have to fear getting hurt?" The potential for possible win-win solutions has greatly increased.

The next stage in the negotiation stage is to generate creative solutions to the problem. To do this you and the other party need to separate this invention stage from the deciding stage. This is not easy to do, but if either party judges ideas prematurely then creativity is squelched (an important fact for your teachers to consider). Therefore, it is best (especially with groups) that guidelines explicitly state that everyone will hold off judgment, try to generate as many win-win solutions as possible, not criticize each other and try to piggy-back on each others' ideas. Parties can then brainstorm for all possible solutions to the problem. Wild and creative proposals are encouraged. This is not easy for many people to do because of culture-based or idiosyncratic censors on saying the wrong or "silly" thing. Even if the seemingly "silly" idea does not solve the problem (sometimes it does), it can lead to one that does. Only after a wide variety of proposals have been made should the parties turn to the next stage of evaluating the ideas against agreed-upon criteria (e.g. the solution must be one we can realistically accomplish). Decisions based on reasonable standards make it easier for the parties to reach agreement and preserve their relationship.

Fisher and Ury were aware that parties in a negotiation are not always equal in power so they suggested that negotiators assess their *best alternative to a negotiated agreement* (BATNA) prior to a negotiation. The BATNA is the best result that you can anticipate if you did not negotiate. Without a clear sense of your BATNA, you are in effect negotiating blindly. The less powerful person in a negotiation can always fall back on his BATNA if the negotiation goes badly. Unlike the traditional "bottom line" the BATNA is not wielded like a sword to get people to sign the deal but is generally kept private. It is used to give you the feeling that you do have a viable option if the other party does not co-operate with you and this feeling bolsters your ability to negotiate well. In your preparation for the negotiation, you would also benefit by trying to assess what the other parties' BATNA might be.

Assessing Risk

To confront someone else in a conflict situation is not without risk. Even if you possess a high level of negotiating skill, you may experience a certain amount of fear or anxiety, especially if you are concerned that the other party could damage your reputation, end the relationship, or even threaten your position or your physical safety. As an educational leader you are likely to frequently face situations with parents, teachers and especially your supervisor in which you will need to accurately assess whether the benefits of confronting the other party is worth the risk. How do you judge how real the risk is when you know that any realistic evaluation of risk is made more difficult by the intrusion of past experiences and leaps of inference? What would be the consequences to you or your school if you did not act because unexamined fear kept you quiet? Is there anyway to increase our ability to realistically estimate risk so that we neither rush into a bad situation nor withdraw prematurely from a conflict that, if resolved, would benefit our school?

A practical model of risk assessment involves five steps:[12]

1. Identify the repercussions that you believe might occur if you confront the other party. List and prioritize them according to how much emotion they elicit in you.

Name the emotion that is evoked and assess how intense the feeling is on a scale of one to five with five being very intense and one being slightly discomfiting. Write this information next to the relevant repercussion.

2. Ask yourself "What is the evidence that I have that these repercussions are probable?" Have these repercussions happened to you or someone else before and was it at the hands of the person you are concerned about? Is your evidence based on direct experience or on hearsay? When you experience repercussions directly from the other person, the risk is greater. If the person did not act in any direct way to confirm your fears than the risk is probably not as great as if he had. Using a scale of 1 to 5 with 5 being highly probable and 1 being unlikely, rate the probability for each repercussion.

3. Determine how recent your evidence is and how frequently it occurred. Repercussions that happened infrequently and long ago will mean lower risk. This is especially true if the person you fear has been in conflict situations many times since the last incident and did not act in the way you fear. Write down how long it has been since there was evidence of repercussions. If there is no evidence write "0".

4. How is this current situation similar or dissimilar to past experiences with the person with whom you are in conflict? The closer the past and present situations match the higher the risk. For example, the last time the other person acted towards me in the way that I fear she was in the midst of a school audit. Is an audit or other highly stressful event occurring now?

5. Bring together all relevant information including your feelings about the situation. Ask yourself, "How realistic are my fears and concerns?" Check into your self-awareness for any feelings, beliefs or values that may be preventing you from making an accurate risk assessment. Weigh all the factors to make a realistic assessment of risk.

Let's take the example of an elementary school principal whom I coached not long ago. She was deciding whether or not to confront her superintendent regarding his rejection of her SBM team's proposal to divide her school into smaller academies. The school had 1300 students and consisted of essentially three buildings, two of which were connected and the third across the street. The proposal, created with the consultation of teachers and parents, was intended to create three different but interrelated academies, each housed in its own building. The hoped-for effect was to create smaller schools-within-a-school that would develop their own identities and have an easier time developing a sense of community. Though not conceptualized as such, it was a great plan for preventing the destructive conflicts that were exhausting the school staff.

Though the superintendent had given his approval for the democratic process that led to the proposal, he dismissed the proposal as unworkable soon after he read it (it took him two months to read it!). When Hilda first pursued the matter by pointing out how the proposal carefully delineated steps for each and every contingency, the superintendent confessed that he had been pressured by some politically-connected people from another school to reject the proposal because it might draw students from their school. He then became angry and told Hilda in no uncertain terms that not only should she not disclose this information, but that he did not want to hear another word about her proposal.

If you were Hilda, what would you do? You have a lot to gain for yourself and your school community if you could negotiate with your superintendent for his approval to allow you to create smaller schools. However, you clearly put yourself at risk if you confront him again even if you do so in the most collaborative manner. But how much of your risk is real and, how small would it have to be, for you to take the risk given the possible benefits? In assessing her risk, Hilda went through each of the steps of risk assessment and also weighed her findings against her assessment of her own skills at negotiation and her awareness of her district's political reality. Her decision was not to confront her supervisor whom she assessed as unwilling to negotiate with anyone with little political clout when being pressured by others with a lot of clout. Instead, Hilda fell back on her BATNA. She would help her school community to develop more political clout. She would also find allies by building a better relationship with the leadership of the school that was frightened by Hilda's proposal. As part of her vision, her dream of interdependent learning academies was deferred and not dead.

BREAKTHROUGH NEGOTIATION

Hilda, in her assessment of her superintendent, came to the realization that he was the kind of person who would be very hard to engage in a negotiation. Such difficult people represent a challenge to even the best negotiators but it is important to realize two things:

1. At times *we* may be seen as "difficult" especially if our "emotional triggers" have been squeezed or our conflict style rubs against the other person's style.
2. Even the most difficult person we can imagine probably has some willingness to negotiate in certain situations. Maybe you have no idea what that situation might be, but his confidants (or his mother) might know.

This means that, given the right context, many resistant people can be influenced to enter into the negotiation process if you are able to apply an effective strategy and EQ skills. One method to get difficult people to negotiate is called *breakthrough negotiation* developed by William Ury as an extension of *principled negotiation*.[13] This method involves five steps:

1. *Don't react; go to the balcony.* Step away from the scene, calm down and gain some perspective of the situation as if you were standing on the balcony looking down at the difficult person and the problem you are facing. Prepare for the negotiation by identifying interests, BATNAs, tactics the other person uses, common and disparate goals and possible opportunities for entering negotiation. In your preparation, craft an I Message, rehearse your delivery and follow up with an ally who will give you some feedback.
2. *Disarm them; step to the side.* If the other party is as difficult as you believe, they will likely react defensively when you confront them. This defensiveness may take the form of a withdrawal or an attack. Rather than reacting in kind, use your EQ skills of awareness and regulation to decrease defensiveness. Actively listen and assert several times if need be and allow interspersed moments of silence to give both of you time to reflect.
3. *Change the game: don't reject . . . reframe.* Like an Aikido expert, step to the side in the face of superior force and reframe the problem so that the other party sees you not as the problem but as a person who can help him solve mutual interests. In the case of Hilda and her boss, what possible mutual interests might they have? How might those interests be framed so that both people see that they can best meet these interests together? Ask the other person as you would a partner, "How can we look at this problem as a way to solve both our concerns?"
4. *Make it easy to say yes; build them a golden bridge.* You may still encounter resistance but don't push. In the moment, put yourself in the person's shoes and try to understand how to build a bridge from your interests to his. For example, Hilda's superintendent may be fearful of the other school's power base because his tenure is

threatened by low test scores, lack of funding, harsh news stories and turnover. If you can show that federal funding, favorable press coverage and lower student and staff turnover could possibly result from solving *our* common problems, then he might be willing to problem solve. Be aware of opportunities to expand the pie and help the other save face. Above all, be open to the other person's constructive criticisms, creative ideas, and desire not to go too fast.

5. *Make it hard to say No: bring them to their senses, not their knees.* If the other party has agreed to negotiate, you can skip this stage but what happens if they are still being difficult? You can end your attempts, but it is often better to work through this stage. Ask the other party what does she or he think will happen if we do not solve the problem? In the case of Hilda, the superintendent could answer "nothing" or admit that test scores in Hilda's school may not rise as quickly as he hoped. He might even worry about an increase in turnover and absenteeism. As a worst case scenario, he could even imagine losing Hilda, whom he admires, and having to spend time, energy and money to find a new principal. These musings could lead him to negotiation. If not, Hilda might as a last resort inform, not threaten, her boss about her BATNA: "If we can't talk about this problem, then I need to . . . (insert BATNA) so that my students, teachers and parents feel that I am working hard to remove obstacles to teaching and learning." Very often this stage will lead to negotiation because the other party dislikes these consequences more than they dislike the idea of negotiating. If revealing your BATNA does not work, you can say, "Thanks for meeting with me," then resort to your BATNA.

Criticism of Principled Negotiation

Principled negotiation is now widely accepted but it has its critics. William McCarthy, for example, agreed with a number of the model's tenets but questioned whether it adequately took into consideration the role of power in negotiation.[14] He stated that Fisher and Ury approach the issue of power through the concept of BATNA but do not provide sufficient discussion on the factors that influence the strength of the parties' BATNAs. Another criticism made by McCarthy and Freund is that negotiations in the business world have such a competitive "game-like" culture that the collaborative model of principled negotiation does not apply.[15]

William Ury answered these criticisms in a second book in which he and his coauthors divided conflict resolution processes into three types: Those which negotiated interests, those which adjudicated rights and those which test relative power.[16] Most conflicts in organizations involve interests and can be negotiated, those involving rights (e.g. some labor disputes) need to go to arbitration and power struggles need to be defused and rules put into place to govern them. Ury suggested, however, that in a well-designed conflict management system even rights and power procedures should have secondary procedures in place that loop disputants back into negotiation to lessen the costly aftermath. For example, imagine that you are a school principal and a conflict over class assignment rights brings you into a grievance hearing with one of your teachers. A well-designed dispute resolution system might have mediators available to assist you and your teacher to figure out how you will work together after the arbitrator's ruling.

Values Collisions

A power-based dispute often has at its heart a clash between deeply-held incompatible values. Because these core values are so ingrained in our sense of who we are as people, we will often defend them even when common sense suggests our mutual interests are not served by doing so. We have all experienced times in our lives when we have been in the midst of a values collision and know how it feels to dig in our heels in shaky but valued soil. All of us can relate to the tragic hero or heroine who foolishly gives up all in order to make the other person "come around to my way of thinking." Even hilarious comedies, such as Neil Simon's *The Odd Couple,* are built on non-negotiable disputes over values.

SMART school leaders are masters at detecting any core values at the heart of a dispute in their school community. They are sensitive to the strong emotions in disputants who are locked in a "do or die" struggle over what seems to be an insignificant issue. Responding to these emotions, the EQ leader engages each disputant or group in conversations that explore whether the impasse is the result of a values collision or some other factor (lack of EQ skills, hidden agendas, etc.). By using active listening and empathy, a leader uncovers values collisions and sets the stage for the process of accommodation and reconciliation.

To give you an example, let's look at a real-life Odd Couple that I encountered in a private school that is nationally known for the quality of its education. The two teachers, a shop teacher and an art teacher, shared an incredibly large space with a rich store of materials from which students created architectural and artistic masterpieces that often integrated math, literature, social studies, art and science. These teachers were gifted professionals who had created a learning environment that was pedagogically perfect except for one thing. The environment was torn by war, a war of words, of emotion-fueled body-language torpedoes, of coffee cups strategically placed to mark off hostile territory. Negotiations had failed, no prisoners were being taken and the school's staff was being recruited to join up on opposing sides.

The school's director eventually fired the art teacher to solve the problem, but in doing so created other problems. The teacher who replaced the art teacher was not as strong-willed but was also not as talented. The shop teacher was relieved to be free of the enemy but now had new enemies drawn from the old enemy's allies. Even some unaligned teachers saw the firing as premature and, fearing that their own contracts might not get renewed, began "playing it safe" both in their teaching and in their willingness to bring up school issues. Some parents lobbied to have the director removed because she deprived their children of the "best" teacher their children ever had. Clearly, the peace had not been won in this school.

What could the director have done differently? She had spoken with both teachers, had tried to arbitrate and had warned them that she was prepared to take action if they could not negotiate their dispute. What she had not done was to ask them in an inquiring way, "Why is the position you are taking here important to you?" She had not tapped into the values that these two teachers felt were being threatened. What might have happened if she had?

Scene One

Setting   *A Wednesday afternoon. A small uncrowded restaurant near the school. Toni Gibbons, the School Director, sits next to Oscar, the art teacher.*

Toni   *(Sipping a café latte): I want to thank you for spending this time with me helping me understand what's going on between you and Felix. I now have a good sense of how you are feeling and thinking about sharing the Project Room with Felix. What I'd like to understand now is why is it so important for you to be able to leave your art material out after the students leave.*

Oscar   *(Shifts in his seat and hesitates before speaking): Toni, Felix is driving me crazy! He calls me a slob, but I don't see it that way. In my head, everything is in order and, besides*

I like a little messiness. I think creative people thrive with a little mess. And I am an artist as well as a teacher. You know that. Felix does not understand me even though I try to understand him. I want to be fair, but if the room was like he wanted it to be, I couldn't breathe. I value what Felix is able to accomplish with the kids, and I value what I've learned about architecture from him, but my independence is at stake here.

Scene Two

Setting   *A Thursday afternoon. A small uncrowded restaurant near the school. Toni Gibbons, the School Director, sits next to Felix, the shop teacher.*

Toni   (*Sipping a glass of wine*): *I want to thank you for spending this time with me helping me understand what's going on between you and Oscar. I now have a good sense of how you are feeling and thinking about sharing the Project Room with Oscar. What I'd like to understand now is why is it so important for you that Oscar puts away his art materials in the closet each day after the students leave.*

Felix   (*Placing his fork down*): *Why? Wouldn't you want a clean workspace? I can't stand the mess and, quite frankly, I cannot stand Oscar anymore. He's a wonderful teacher and a genius at bringing out the artistic talents of kids you would not expect had it in them. But he has no respect for me. I need order. I admit it and that room, in my opinion, is in chaos each day. I can't live that way. You take something out; you put it away. It's simple. If you don't respect my space then you do not respect me. I do it. Why can't he?*

If you were the school director, what values did you uncover from Oscar and Felix? Which of these seem to be core values at the heart of this dispute? What follow-up questions would you ask? How would you find out more about this values collision? Which values do you share with Felix and Oscar and do your values make it harder for you to understand either disputant?

Once you have an understanding of the values at the center of a dispute, you have choices as a leader. Sometimes, you build a bridge for disputants and help them find ways to accommodate each other. Other times, you may need to make a decision that acknowledges core values and separates individuals so their values do not clash. As a last resort, you may have to dismiss one or both parties if they continue to disrespect each other and hurt the school's mission.

A respectful inquiry-based approach can also be effective in value-laden group conflicts. In their book, *SuperVision and Instructional Leadership*, Glickman, Gordon and Ross-Gordon suggest a series of steps that a school leader can use to resolve a values-based disagreement within a small group such as a leadership team.[17] The steps include:

1. Ask each contending member to state his or her position.
2. Ask each contending member to restate the other's position.
3. Ask contending members if a conflict still exists between them. If there is none, move on as a group. If a conflict still exists go to step four.
4. Ask other members if they can generate any third position that synthesizes, compromises or transcends the conflict. Find out if any ideas are acceptable to both parties.

DEALING WITH GROUP CONFLICT

Being the leader of a school or school district often requires the leader to facilitate or be a member of an ongoing working group such as a leadership team or a budget committee. As anyone knows who has ever participated in a working group, the performance of the group is greatly influenced by how conflict is perceived and acted upon by all of its members. If conflict is seen as negative or if the members lack EQ competencies, the group may either avoid dealing with all conflict or may respond with escalating destructive behavior. Either approach will undermine the collaboration, creativity and morale of the group and may lead to a downward spiral of competing factions, poor attendance, unmet goals, scapegoating, angry outbursts and "agenda sabotage," or dissolution of the group altogether.

The *SMART* leader can do much to prevent destructive conflict while promoting a productive management of the kinds of conflict (e.g. a clash of creative ideas to a problem) that can increase group performance. This flexible approach to group conflict has at its center three core values.[18] First, the people in the group need valid information to function in the group so relevant information, including emotions, has to be shared in a way that can be understood by all. Second, group members are free to make informed choices about their own objectives and the methods of achieving them based on the valid information they received. Finally, people function best when they have an internal commitment to the choices that they make.

Germinating from these core values are offshoots that act to prevent certain kinds of destructive conflict (i.e. those arising from misinformation, feelings of exclusion, etc.) while fostering interpersonal communication, intrinsic motivation, conflict resolution skills and group guidelines that turn conflict into a rich flowering of new ideas and concerted action. Within the context of a group's growth process the EQ leader must ask, and encourage others to ask, key questions:

- What do we want to accomplish here both individually and as a group?
- How is what we are doing in alignment or in conflict with our shared vision?
- Do we have all the information we need and are there any questions we need to ask?
- How will we resolve our differences here and how will we give each other the feedback we all need to do our best?
- What have we learned from this conflict and what do we need to learn in the future to improve our group process?

Ground Rules for Working Groups

One of the most effective strategies the *SMART* leader can employ to help a group prevent and manage conflict is to facilitate the group's adoption of guidelines for working together. Ideally, the group creates these guidelines. In my experience working with a variety of school groups, however, I have found that some groups have great difficulty generating effective group guidelines. Their difficulty stems from their previous group experiences that give them a group model based on values of power and dominance rather than on the core values described earlier. In these cases, I find it helpful to ask them to share their thoughts and feelings about past group experiences, then introduce a list of guidelines based on the core values that other groups have used to work collaboratively. After giving them an opportunity to discuss the guidelines, I ask them to develop their own, taking directly from the list or creating their own. By spending sufficient time on this initial process of developing guidelines, the group gets to play with the ideas and the skills that they will need to deal with conflicts throughout the life of the group.

One set of guidelines I have found extremely useful as a springboard for guideline development is the set proposed by Roger Schwartz in his book, *The Skilled Facilitator.*[19] Schwartz's guidelines support each other and address the problems groups typically face in collaboration:

1. Test assumptions and inferences.
2. Share all relevant information.

3. Focus on interests, not positions.
4. Be specific—use examples.
5. Agree on what important words mean.
6. Explain the reasons behind one's statements, questions, and actions.
7. Disagree openly with any member of the group.
8. Make statements, then invite questions and comments.
9. Jointly design ways to test agreements and solutions.
10. Discuss undiscussable issues.
11. Keep the discussion focused.
12. Do not take cheap shots or otherwise distract the group.
13. All members are expected to participate in all phases of the group.
14. Exchange relevant information with nongroup members.
15. Make decisions by consensus.
16. Do self-critiques.

Generally, groups select five or six of the above guidelines and add a few of their own such as, "All members must turn off their cell phones." At first, group members may not keep to their own guidelines. Rather than enforcing the guidelines, you might ask what is preventing them from keeping to their own agreements. After awhile, leaders emerge who take on the role of champions of the guidelines.

Undiscussables

One of the most challenging of the above guidelines to champion is also one of the most important for the health of any working group. *Discuss undiscussable issues.* According to Schwartz, every group has issues that are relevant to the group's task but that members fear they cannot discuss openly.[20] Examples of such issues in school groups might be individual members' behaviors towards others in the group, uneven performance, treatment of students or feelings about the principal's use of authority. Rather than discussing these issues directly in the group and resolving them, group members avoid them altogether or only talk about them in rumor mills outside the group. How many times have you yourself ever waited until a meeting was over before finally discussing with a fellow group member the very thing that you both wanted to say in the group for the last three meetings? Left undiscussed, these issues begin to infect the group with a virulence that can kill the spirit of the team and escalate destructive conflict.

To champion the discussion of the undiscussable, the leader needs to summon her courage and the courage of others to raise the issue and name it as an Undiscussable. As an example, you might say, "I want to bring up something I think has become an undiscussable here. How we talk about Marion when she's not here." If you are concerned about repercussions, ask for assurance that you will not be subjected to personal attacks before bringing up an issue. "I have what I believe is an undiscussable," you might say, "but before I express it I'd like some discussion on how I can be protected from reprisals if I say it openly." As a leader, you may have to be the first to step off the diving board of secrecy. You also have to be aware that your courageous act may be greeted with defensive reactions or complete denial. On the other hand, you may be the catalyst for profound soul-searching by the group resulting in a major improvement in the group's functioning and ability to resolve destructive conflicts.[21]

Acting as a Third Party

Sometimes, in your leadership role, you will want or need to get involved in a group or individual dispute in which you are not directly involved. Intervening as a third party to a conflict presents you with certain dilemmas: *Would it be better for me to stay out of this and let the parties work it out? If I do intervene, when should I go in and what role should I take? What are the best strategies to use and what skills will I need to use them?*

It is usually better to let people negotiate their own problems. However, there are times when intervention is called for. First, consider if the parties have asked for your help. Second, is there some urgency to the situation because either the conflict is escalating quickly or some essential task is not getting done because of the conflict? Third, do the parties lack the skills to work this problem out by themselves without your help? Finally, is the cost of intervening less than the cost of not intervening? The more you answer affirmatively to these questions the more you should consider intervening.

The intervention you use is dependent on what type of conflict the two parties are involved in. If it is a rights-based conflict you may want to arbitrate (i.e. act as a judge to determine right or wrong), but if it is an interests-based conflict, then the best strategy is generally mediation (i.e. acting as an impartial facilitator of cooperative problem solving between two or more disputants). Most principals have had many experiences as arbitrators but far less practice in mediation. The process of adult mediation typically involves five stages:

First contact—The parties in conflict contact you or you contact them. You listen to them to determine if you should offer your services as a mediator. You describe the mediation process and ask them if they are interested. If they both choose to accept mediation, go to the next stage. If one or both refuse, do not try to force them, but ask them to reconsider. If either party refuses, thank both for listening and end the process. At some point, you may have to arbitrate the dispute if the dispute interferes with the school's mission.

Opening meeting—This meeting is best set in a neutral place that affords privacy. During the meeting you want to set the stage, getting agreement on such guidelines as no interrupting, attack the problem not the person, respect confidentiality and try to solve the problem. After your opening statement, ask each disputant to share their point of view, then paraphrase what they say and reflect their feelings. Your purpose here is to begin to understand and reframe the problem while helping each party listen to one another.

Caucuses—Mediators often hold private caucuses at this point with each disputant (mediators of students often omit this stage). The purpose of caucuses is to provide enough emotional safety that disputants will explore with you the conflict's underlying problem. By using your EQ, you can help disputants think critically about the problem and to test their assumptions.

Joint meeting(s)—In this phase, you basically guide the disputants through collaborative problem solving to hopefully arrive at win-win solutions. If people get stuck, you may want to invite one or both to another private caucus.

Closing—After an agreement has been struck, you may want the parties to sign the agreement and schedule follow-up to evaluate how well the agreement is working.[22]

This generic mediation model is best used when there is a dispute but no "hot" emergency. As anyone knows who has ever shadowed a school principal, however, there are times when even the most far-sighted proactive leader gets blindsided by a steamroller altercation in a hall or stairway. It could be two students or even two parents who are about to start WW III. You turn the corner and there they are. Suddenly, your emotions are triggered and your EQ kicks in. Almost instantly you assess the situation and make a choice of action. In many cases you might have chosen a different course (e.g. call the security guard or police, invoke your authority, etc.) but your cooperative orientation and something you intuitively sense, tells you to try an on-the-spot-mediation that is less procedural and less safe than the generic model. The battle in this case is between two teens screaming at each other over a girl. The conflict has escalated to the point that pushing has begun and punching or worse is about to ensue.

Remembering your crisis intervention training you call out loudly, "Which one of you lost $20?" Startled, the two students turn for a moment away from each other to look at you. In that moment you stalled the conflict spiral. "I'm glad I have your attention because I don't want to see you get hurt or in trouble," you say and continue using your EQ skills to stay calm and defuse their emotions. You acknowledge their feelings and judge that the tall young man on your left is the most upset and you ask him to walk with you for a moment. You call him by name, suggest ways for him to calm himself and "step-to-the-side" when he tries to verbally intimidate you:

> *Hey, Donald (Step to the side), you're a lot bigger than me so it would be crazy for me to try to stop you from doing something you really want to do. But I know that you're smart enough to figure out a different way of solving this problem without making a bigger problem for yourself.*

Like a jazz artist, you act in the moment with Donald and the other youth to calm them down and agree to mediation. If necessary, you were ready to step out of your neutral shoes and bring out your BATNA (e.g. call the guard, inform them that they could be suspended) but you know that only once in every ten times do you have to resort to that to avert violence. You considered referring them to peer mediation or even a session with two of the adult mediation coaches, but then you realize that now is the time and you are the one. As fate would have it, there is a quiet office 12 feet behind you and you have the key! Twenty minutes later you walk out of the office—three true believers.

In this non-generic mediation, the process was similar to the more standard version, but the principal might have stepped out of the mediator's role at any moment to fall back on a power or rights-based approach to conflict. The principal did not have the luxury to end the mediation and walk away if the parties refused to cooperate. This more fluid role for the principal makes it harder for the principal to earn the trust that the mediator's traditional role affords. Therefore, principals have to work harder to develop trust-building techniques. Linda Colburn, a former housing project manager who is also a trained mediator, describes these techniques as intuition or the ability to "read the bubbles above a person's head" as if the person was a character in a comic strip.[23] She states that she was able to use nonverbal, psychological, and spiritual cues to decide whether or not her style of peacemaking was appropriate in the cases of family conflict that she inadvertently came upon while managing.

Mediation skills are useful tools for school leaders to possess but these skills can also be learned by teachers and students. Many teachers do mediations in their classrooms. More and more schools are implementing peer mediation programs. Because of this proliferation of skilled adult and student mediators, school leaders should call upon them for creative new ideas on how to make best use of their talents in resolving conflicts among adults and students.

PREVENTION OF CONFLICTS

School leaders can also do much to prevent destructive conflicts. Through individual and collaborative action, they can develop policies and procedures that create a climate in which many disputes that thwart the good intentions of many schools never arise. Focusing on the educational leader, these actions can be grouped into three categories:

1. Leader as Champion of Cooperation.

FIGURE 4.3 Peer mediators of all ages help fellow students to resolve conflicts in their schools.
(Courtesy of Resolving Conflict Creatively Program of Educators for Social Responsibility)

2. Leader as Facilitator of Communication.
3. Leader as Buffer.

Leader as Champion of Cooperation

A school oriented towards cooperation is less likely to generate destructive conflicts than one that has a competitive orientation. According to Morton Deutsch, an organization that adopts and effectively follows a cooperative model will not only resolve conflicts but also prevent conflicts fueled by misunderstanding, resentments, bias, and a lack of coordination.[23] A school leader can help generate such a cooperative spirit in a variety of ways found throughout this book, but a good place to start is with what drives most schools—the curriculum.

A school's curriculum shapes so much of the relationships in a school. A curriculum designed to feature teacher-dominated instruction and individual competition among students and teachers is one that can undermine student achievement and intrinsic motivation. In its extreme forms in which students are tracked, teachers have no input into what is taught, and incentives or disincentives are given solely on the basis of performance, a high-rate of destructive conflicts can be expected. On the other hand, curriculums that feature cooperative teaching and learning, address the needs of diverse learners, and place a greater value on the learning process are more likely to foster human interactions that elicit constructive conflict.

SMART school superintendents or principals promote the use of a cooperation-based curriculum that integrates constructive conflict into everyday learning. They encourage K-12 teachers to use the tool of constructive conflict to enhance the development of critical and creative thinking throughout the curriculum. A fourth grade teacher asks her students to form groups that represent warring factions during the American Revolution and debate what should be done with the "traitors" *if the war had ended with a British victory.* High school students are divided into the competing families in *Romeo and Juliet* and problem solve how they will resolve their costly feud in a win-win way. A seventh grade school math class questions the figures that were put out by both sides in a local union strike. Conflict creates interest and generates learning problems to be solved, giving students exciting practice fields for learning the Standards *and* the interpersonal skills that can prevent many conflicts from ever emerging.[24]

Even excellent cooperative-based curriculums, however, are ineffective if the "hidden curriculum" teaches students that power-based approaches to conflict are the best way to relate to others. By hidden curriculum, we mean what the adults in their school teach students through their actions and their policies. As one youth said in the beginning of this chapter, "They don't practice what they preach." School leaders can champion cooperation in the hidden curriculum by engaging staff members in a process of uncovering this hidden curriculum and creating an action plan that will change policies and practices so that they are congruent with the regular curriculum (more on this in Chapter Seven). This congruence, in turn, prevents conflicts that occur when students believe that the adults around them are not "walking the talk."

Leader as Facilitator of Communication

One of the most effective ways that school leaders prevent destructive conflict is by working with others to open up the communication channels in the school. So many conflicts originate because of misunderstandings. Listen to conflict stories in schools and you will hear people who act on incomplete or distorted information.

I heard that the principal said. . . .

Who knows what they are saying in the Parent's Room. . . ?

I should tell him about this but I'd better not. . . .

Why didn't you ask your teacher about this if you didn't understand. . . ?

In an environment in which communication is top-down, restricted, distorted and closed, misunderstandings are commonplace. EQ leaders, however, can open up communication in a school or school district. By sharing information readily and encouraging feedback from various sources, leaders provide a positive model especially when they honor dissenting opinions. By providing time for members of the school community to develop communication skills and meet regularly, leaders improve intergroup relations. By redefining the leader's role from the disseminator of information to a facilitator of information, they allow others to emerge as leaders.

As an example, let's look at what one elementary school principal did after the tragic events at Columbine High School. He did not see bullying as a problem in his suburban school, but realized he was making that assumption based upon limited information. After all, the principal of Columbine had been unaware of the extent of the bullying problem. With this awareness, our principal realized he needed to go beyond reports from his teachers and guidance counselor. In his next faculty meeting, he divided his staff into small groups and asked each group to draw floor plans of the school. Then he gave them red and green adhesive dots and asked them to place the green dots in areas on the floor plan where students felt safe. Next, they were asked to place red dots in areas they do not feel safe. Groups were then asked to reflect on their "maps" and think about what they know and don't know regarding their students' feelings about the safety of their school. This reflection led teachers to use the same activity in their classrooms and some led a similar activity at a Parent's Association Meeting. The resulting maps and subsequent discussions provided "bottom-up" information to the school leadership team that revealed the bullying problem was much greater than had been thought. The team also learned where in the school the problem was most striking. This information enabled the school community to develop a series of preventive measures that made the school much safer than it had been. It also convinced the principal that he needed to find other ways to open up the communication channels in his school.

Leader as Buffer

A third important way that educational leaders prevent conflict in their settings is to act as a buffer to counterproductive demands and threats from competing agencies, excessive regulations, and media hype. EQ leaders use their experience and their social awareness to block, filter and diffuse the enormous outside pressures that can easily undermine and even stonewall the promising efforts of dedicated educators. As Shelley Berman, the superintendent of Massachusetts's Hudson Public Schools, said in an interview:

> There is constant pressure on teachers to devote their time to test preparation so that students perform well on high stakes tests. This kind of pressure undermines SEL and service learning and the solid work on improving the curriculum. As the superintendent, my role is to act as the buffer to help teachers do the right thing. I am the advocate to remind teachers, parents and administrators that even though they do take time, SEL and service-learning make a valuable contribution to a positive learning climate, and they do in fact help students perform better.[25]

In schools, EQ principals interact with politicians, media, community and business leaders, and state officials to reduce pressures that, in other schools, routinely cause teachers to feel that they are jumping through hoops.[26] They use their sense of mission and organizational awareness to determine what strategy will be effective in keeping classrooms unpressured and productive. Depending on the situation, these leaders employ a wide variety of tools ranging from EQ skills to "working the system" to protect their people. A good example of an expert buffer was a principal I worked for when I was a classroom teacher in the New York City public schools. Teachers all knew that nothing or no one came into the school unless Mr. T believed it would be good for the children. What we did not know, however, was how much he protected us from the often-conflicting regulations that seemed to be spewed out daily from central and district offices whenever there was a school incident or a school scandal anywhere in the city, state or nation.

After Mr. T. retired, he shared with me his secret. When he received these problematic regulations for the first time, he would read them and then throw them all into his wastebasket. If he received the same mandate again he looked at it to assure it was not something that was, beneath the jargon, of some value to teachers. If the regulation had nothing of any inherent value, he would toss it away. "In most cases, I never received another letter because the crisis had passed in the time it took to figure out that I had not responded to the first two letters," he laughed. Mr. T. then leaned forward, obviously feeling great pleasure in his knowing defense of his teachers. "But Jim, sometimes, maybe five times out of a hundred, I would receive a third letter *and* a phone call and then I would have to choose whether to do battle or not." Such a leader makes it possible for great teaching and learning to flourish.

AN INTEGRATED CONFLICT MANAGEMENT SYSTEM

We have discussed a number of ways you and your school community might embrace and deal with conflict to serve the school's purpose. Too often, however, schools take a piecemeal approach to implementing these methods. They have a dean, an assistant principal or a guidance counselor responsible for intervening when conflict escalates and threatens order. They implement a conflict resolution program and might even support a peer mediation program. By most measures, these schools are succeeding, but the threads binding this success are fragile. Any staff turnover or sudden budget cut could break the threads, destroying their programs. In such schools, leaders and their school communities need to systematically integrate all their approaches into their day-to-day business and add processes that shift their conflict culture towards prevention. In short, they should create what is commonly called an Integrated Conflict Management System (ICMS).[27]

ICMSs are increasingly being employed in diverse organizations as a creative solution to the thorny problem of how can we best reduce dysfunctional conflicts while promoting the kinds of conflicts that sparks creativity, informs good decisions and serves to strengthen collaboration. What differentiates a system from case-by-case approaches is that a system has features that focus on both kinds of conflicts and the interactions between them in a much more proactive approach. This systems approach consists of two essential components:

1. It develops and continuously fine-tunes a dispute resolution model that acts as a guide to how disputes need to be addressed by all based upon the organization's vision.
2. It creates an environment for fostering and sustaining the model so that people are able and willing to use the model to prevent and manage their interpersonal conflicts.

In a School or District's commitment to an ICMS might be evidenced by, but not limited to:

- Authentic and ongoing advocacy by leaders from all constituencies (Administration, Staff, Parents, Students, Community). A shared vision, values and mission that is consistent with a conflict management philosophy.
- Organization-wide policies that encourage, require and supports actions that promote the prevention of unnecessary conflict, identification and management of conflict, and timely and effective resolution.
- Well-publicized and understood codes of practice that are utilized by all. For example, if a teacher-teacher conflict occurs, both parties know the procedures for settling their dispute and know the school policies (e.g. school has a conflict model) and resources (e.g. adult mediators, private meeting area) that support their efforts.
- Trustbuilding safeguards or guidelines are in place (e.g. respect for diversity, voluntary nature of negotiation or mediation, confidentiality, neutrality of mediators, and freedom from reprisal).
- Conflict management as a core competency for both adults and students.
- Ongoing assessments of effectiveness of the ICM system and individual performance.
- Clearly defined procedures for adapting the system in response to assessments.
- Sufficient resources provided for implementation including ongoing learning opportunities of a high quality.
- Stakeholder participation in each phase of creating and maintaining the system.
- Systemwide rituals that celebrate successes and enculturate newcomers.

Taking an integrated system perspective toward conflict management in your school or district may seem like juggling too many things on top of what you already do. Upon reflection, however, you might consider several key points. First, is that you probably have a number of parts of the system already in place. Second, developing diverse EQ skills in yourself and others provides you with the flexibility that is necessary to expertly juggle a variety of tasks.[28] Third, a system once set up provides a momentum that is not requiring you to be the engine. Finally, you will have more time to juggle because the system frees your school or district from the many destructive conflicts that devour so

FIGURE 4.3   A wall of student-made masks at Arlington High honors student diversity and self-expression.
(Courtesy Arlington High School, St. Paul, MN and School Improvement Program, Northwest Regional Educational Laboratory, Portland, OR. Photographer: Jean Spraker)

much of a leader's day. Once your system is in place, you will have more time for accomplishing the meaningful tasks you have on your "To Do" list. In the next chapter we highlight one such system called the *SEL Schoolhouse*.

IN SUMMARY

In this chapter, we asked you to entertain the radical idea that conflict needs to be embraced by school leaders. Like the diversity that powered the creation of the inspiring art in the photo above, conflict can energize learning and build community when human beings learn how to deal with it effectively. With that concept in mind, we asked you to reflect on the way you think about conflict and your own conflict style. In addition, we discussed organizational approaches to conflict, from power-based to interest-based, and suggested that an interest-based approach is more congruent with a caring, learning environment. Elaborating on this approach, we described several strategies for resolving individual and group destructive conflicts and for promoting constructive conflict in schools. Finally, the chapter asked you to consider the benefits of thinking systemically about dealing with conflict. In Chapter Six, you will have an opportunity to reflect further on these benefits in the context of school change.

Neither chapter nor book, however, can possibly give you the deep understanding of conflict management that you will need to effectively use the strategies described in this chapter. It is hoped, therefore, that you will avail yourself of the many experiential workshops offered by organizations like Educators for Social Responsibility and practice what you learn. Consider embracing conflict like embracing a dance partner. Learn your steps, work at them, be flexible, develop mastery and then improvise. You may step on a few toes along the way but you will feel set free. And, as you use your competencies to create the feeling of "neighborhood" in your school, you can be assured that Mr. Rogers would be proud of you.

REFLECTIVE QUESTIONS

1. On the third page of this chapter there is a quote from Costatino and Merchant. To what degree do you agree or disagree with their point of view? Why?

2. Looking at Ruble and Thomas five conflict styles, what would you say is your typical conflict style?
3. What do you like about the way you deal with conflict and what would you like to change?
4. Think of an organization that you are currently part of. Would you say it is closer to being a power-based or an interests-based organization? Explain your reasons.
5. Think of a difficult person with whom you come into contact. Use the five steps of risk assessment described in this chapter to assess the risk of confronting that person. Based on that assessment, how great is the risk? Explain your reasoning.
6. Think of a team or working group of which you are a member. Which of the guidelines suggested by Roger Schwartz would be most helpful to opening up the communication?

LESSON FROM THE FIELD

Rachel Kessler and Mark Gerzon

They were part of a small group at a principals' institute who had been asked to choose a controversial topic in education about which at least two present could disagree. It was hard choosing from a list made in the larger group of more than twenty-five red-hot conflicts confronting them. It was also difficult for most of the small groups to choose because as professional educators in the 90's, they tended to line up on the same side of the debate. Finally, this group landed on school uniforms, because there were two of them who vehemently disagreed.

With so many major issues on the list—vouchers and charter schools, school prayer, standardized testing, racism, etc.—we could not understand why this group picked school uniforms as the topic for their debate and dialogue.

We had come to the Toynton Institute to give a group of 40 principals tools for helping their communities navigate what they called "paradigm fights"—issues where conflicting belief systems were tearing the community apart. We wanted them to experience a variety of styles of discourse so that these leaders, and the communities they served, could make conscious choices about how to talk to each other to accomplish different goals.

Having covered three or four newsprint sheets with their lists of controversial issues in education, they listened to us describe the styles of discourse: verbal brawling; debate; discussion; negotiation; council; dialogue. The 90's had been a decade of verbal brawling in the U.S. Civic and political leaders were all eager to find our way to creative, respectful dialogue to resolve our conflicts. We were invited because we had discovered a useful sequence to help people do so.

Once the principals chose their controversy, we asked them to experience the costs and benefits of debate. Their small group split into two teams, lined up behind the two individuals who took opposing positions on the issue. They supported their leader in coming up with sharp, incisive, convincing arguments for their position. Then, they engaged in a debate.

In what Deborah Tannen calls "the argument culture," debating is not difficult for most of our citizens. Principals, however, are so skilled and practiced in the arts of peacemaking, protection and appeasement that this was a challenge for many of the groups. Nevertheless, it was familiar territory. When the debates were over, no one was persuaded—each side was more firmly fixed in their own positions.

This was the point where we introduced the practice of council—a time to sit in circle, to share stories from the heart about the life experiences which had shaped those positions. For council to be effective, we needed to elicit from the group a set of groundrules that could make it safe and appropriate to risk the vulnerability of telling your story.

"What conditions do we need to create here to make it safe and appropriate for you to talk about some things that matter deeply to you?" I asked. They responded: "Empathy." "Listening" "No interrupting" "No personal attacks" "No aggressive body language." "Value participation and inclusion." "Work towards understanding." "Value process and people (not just outcome)." We added two more: "the right to pass" and "fairness" so that no one could dominate the conversation.

We began the small group councils with the benefit of this tone and set of agreements suggested by the larger group. The council also provided the safety of structure: rules that required only one person to have the floor at a time and that ensured that each person had their opportunity to speak without fighting for the floor. In each group, one principal volunteered to be a timekeeper to ensure fairness. Another volunteered to be the "leader"—modeling the willingness to risk vulnerability by sharing the first story and the gift of deep listening to each person who spoke thereafter.

And we set the theme. "Tell your group something from your life story that might help them understand why you hold the position you do on this issue."

"I've never been a fan of school uniforms," said one principal, a white woman in her late forties. "I don't know why, but they just seem depressing. Instead of lots of color and individuality, it's just the boring, dead blue or gray or whatever." She paused, then looked out the window. When she turned back to the group, a tear was coursing down her cheek. "My dad used to put on his uniform every time he went away for the weekend to Army Reserves. I hated when he left. Then one time, when I was 13, he put on his uniform for a long time. He went to Vietnam and never came back. I guess I've hated uniforms ever since."

The eyes of the group shifted quickly to the African-American principal sitting to her left. It was his turn to speak next, but he waited until he was sure she had recovered her composure before he began.

"I went to a high school," he began slowly, "where there were few minority students. I think my white classmates were so uncomfortable about the race issue that they just ignored me. They weren't mean or anything; they just pretended as if I wasn't there. I guess that way they didn't have to be afraid of making some kind of mistake. Since my freshman year, I had played trumpet in the band, but I wasn't very noticeable. . . . just one of a crowd. But my junior year I competed and became drum major—you know, the guy with the baton in front of the band who sets the tempo. Suddenly, at football games and rallies, everybody noticed me in my uniform. First, the band members began to pay attention to me and then all sorts of people started saying "hi" to me in the halls. I guess it sort of went to my head, because in my senior year I decided to run for class president, and I won."

"I'm in favor of school uniforms," he concluded slowly. "I think they help create a common bond."

For a moment, the rest of the group fell silent. They knew, as I did, that both stories were true, honest and heartfelt. They also knew that they led the two speakers to precisely opposite conclusions. Without the stories "on the table," the two principals could have argued for hours about the "merits of the issue." Now that their stories were heard, *and respected,* they were able for the first time to take a fresh look.

The atmosphere in this group had shifted. Caring and open-minded respect had replaced the half-humorous, half-hostile banter around the debate. Beneath the dry brittle surface of a controversial issue ready to flare up in any school community were the tender feelings of pride and belonging, fear and loss, patriotism and grief. The meaning became more important than the outcome—the person more important than the position.

From this place of caring, curiosity and respect, a group can begin the process of inquiry and collaboration that allows them to find a constructive solution to a polarized situation.

"You cannot kill a man once he has told you his story," says a Kenyan poet. Creating the safe conditions in our schools and communities for personal stories and finding the courage to tell our own stories from the heart, leaders can develop the trust and authentic community that leads to building, rather than burning, the bridges that honor our differences but sustain our essential connections.

Rachael Kessler is the Director of the Institute for Social and Emotional Learning in Boulder, Colorado, author of The Soul of Education(2000) and co-author of Promoting Social and Emotional Learning (1997) both published by the Association for Supervision and Curriculum Development. Working with teachers, school leaders and other educational organizations, Kessler incorporates the importance of the inner life of both teachers and students into the classroom.

Mark Gerzon is the president of Mediators Foundation, a non-profit incubator of innovative projects dealing with resolving conflict and promoting cross-cultural and cross-ideological understanding. In 1997 and again in 1999, Mark was selected by the U.S. House of Representatives to design and facilitate their Bipartisan Congressional Retreats. Called an "expert in civil discourse" by the New York Times, Mark is a consultant to communities and organizations throughout the United States.

Chapter 5

Leading Social and Emotional Learning Communities

"Until I became involved in schools, I didn't understand that children need to form emotional bonds with their teachers and see healthy social relationships among the adults in their lives to function well in school."

—James Comer[1]

INTRODUCTION

The lessons of leadership come continuously, some silently and others in loudly echoed voices. We don't need a tragedy such as Columbine, September 11, the war in Iraq or the myriad of catastrophic events that have plagued our nation over the past decade to remind us that young people today, more than ever, are in need of emotional support and social skills. Whatever your current educational title: teacher, counselor, principal or superintendent, you see the struggles and hear the stories of today's youth that contribute to their lack of identity, purpose, ability to achieve and hope for a future. Too often, their words and actions reflect fear, abandonment, loss, isolation, rejection and discrimination of all kinds. You, more than any other professional, know first hand that the violence young people face has no geographic limits, no racial boundaries, and does not discriminate between genders. And no matter how hard you work, the young people who enter your doors daily come from environments that often deplete them, rather than nourish them. Our society, too often, promotes disrespect, intolerance, injustice and hate rather than respect, celebration of diversity, social justice, equity, and love.

Although the rampage of school shootings have thankfully come to a halt at the time of this writing, incidents of physical and verbal aggression among young people and between young people and adults continue to be a major cause for concern. Early and mid-adolescents in particular, faced with the onslaught of peer and adult expectations and often-negative role modeling, become the most common victims. Studies tell us that schools, especially high schools, often feed the potential for young people to fail.[2] External factors alone, such as a school's size, academic curriculum and social organization influence the decisions that young people make about staying in school. Students, especially those from poor and disadvantaged families and neighborhoods, are more likely to stay in school when they perceive their relationships and interactions with teachers and administrators as positive. And many socially-isolated students who struggle with peer rejection and bullying are often the very students who are recipients of teacher insults and bullying.

This chapter provides examples of how some educators have addressed these concerns in schools. It shares the recent efforts of educators focused on developing the social and emotional well being of young people along with their cognitive capacities. In this chapter, you will meet several school leaders who have placed the education of the mind alongside the education of the character and the heart. We begin to look at school culture in this chapter, and explore ways to create climates that are "peaceable" and conducive to learning. Several educational leaders share strategies that have helped them build a comprehensive SEL-based school wide culture. Finally, we will look at the context of school safety and the prospects that a peaceable school culture can offer to counteract bullying and other school discipline problems.

SOCIAL AND EMOTIONAL LEARNING (SEL)

Despite the pressure of accountability, educators across our nation *are* addressing the development of the social and emotional competencies of young people. In their schools, young people and adults are building environments of physical and emotional safety designed to support the communities of learners in and outside of its walls.

Over the last few decades, we have increased our awareness of ways to develop young people's prosocial skills. These skills include the ability to make sound, safe decisions, negotiate conflict and confront possibly harmful situations in non-violent ways. We have seen an ebb and flow of these and other SEL strategies as far back as the affective education movement of the 1960's. In the 70's and 80's the cooperative learning movement established the teaching of social skills within the context of the instructional paradigm. In the 80's and 90's conflict resolution, became recognized as the Fourth R.[3] Teachers began teaching young people how to resolve conflicts through curriculum-focused strategies, peer mediation and youth leadership development. From the 90's to the present date, character education, service learning and social and emotional learning have become familiar terms to educators. Informative research about the brain's ability to adapt and learn mechanisms to prevent aggressive tendencies has been integral in supporting the need for teaching direct social skill development in schools.[4]

One of the major differences between earlier movements and those of today is the focus on both preventative and comprehensive school wide approaches. SEL concepts and instruction need to reach all young people, not just those labeled "at risk." Intervention strategies are still needed for troubled young people who may be perpetrators or victims of potential bullying, or, severely at risk for other potentially harmful behaviors. But, school wide prevention efforts have the greatest chance of influencing the majority of young folks. Prevention strategies such as those we addressed in Chapter Four regarding conflict resolution need to be included in every aspect of the child's education, from kindergarten through high school. These kinds of comprehensive SEL approaches must incorporate a variety of culture enhancing strategies to support the direct teaching of pro-social skills in the classroom.

SEL concepts and pedagogy build young people's social and emotional skill base through every facet of the school day and beyond. Young people across our nation are learning how to make the right choices. They now have strategies to assert their needs in ways that they will be heard and listen to varying perspectives. They are walking away from potentially dangerous situations. They are experiencing the value of kindness and caring. They are increasing their capacities to empathize with others. Young people are speaking up against bias and are becoming allies to those hurt by individual and societal discrimination. In short, the lessons that today's youth are learning in schools that embrace SEL is how to become good people. They are developing personal characteristics such as kindness, empathy, integrity and compassion. At a time when our national media consistently report the misuse of power, squandering of wealth, dishonesty and hate, young people are being taught to become caring, contributing citizens.

This said, Eric Schaps, President of the Character Education Partnership, reminds us that character development occurs over time, and is formed in many ways. Schaps asks us to recognize that the development of character not occur in isolated, sporadic moments.

> *One way (it develops and forms) is through the exposure to actions and attitudes of others particularly those whom we have come to care about and trust. Another is through engaging in moral action, such as service to others. A third way is through open dialogue about the complexities of moral situations and alternative responses to those situations. On the other hand, there is little evidence that moralizing to children or giving them direct instruction in moral principles has much effect.[5]*

Schaps warns educators to avoid superficial approaches to character education. Too many schools display brightly covered bulletin boards that contain the moral code of the month, or the most outstanding citizen of the month, as examples of character education. In some schools, young people are taught to recite and define moral values from lists of words that are posted around the classroom. Morning announcements remind children to concentrate on the character word of the day. These external attempts at building character do not allow children to really grapple with values and morals. Outwardly impressive signs are good reminders, but they are not enough to impact the hearts and souls of young people. Real character education does just what the name implies. It provides opportunities for young people to live these values. They participate in building a caring school environment that values honesty, integrity, and other moral values. In these schools teachers use instructional strategies such as cooperative learning to advance social skills and academic learning. They use literature-rich stories to provoke discussion and dialogue about moral dilemmas. Class meetings resolve conflict or encourage decision-making. Peer leadership and involvement in school wide leadership roles promote self-efficacy. Service learning projects allow young people to give back to their community, expand their self confidence and instill pride. Dana, a high school student who has been involved with peer mediation for some time shares:

> *At first I didn't want to get involved. I thought the kids at our school would mock us, and that it could even be dangerous. But, I knew, deep inside, that I had to take a stand and do something to help my friends and other kids. Too many people just stand by and watch their friends hurt themselves with drugs, alcohol and other things. Being a bystander who watches and does nothing contributes to the problem in a way. Now, after doing this for a while, I can't imagine doing it any other way.*

Research on the impact of SEL initiatives such as Character Education, Service Learning, and programs such as Resolving Conflict Creatively, and The Responsive Classroom has become increasingly more available. In the early 90s, Dan Goleman, along with a cadre of health and school-based psychologists and school practitioners, co-founded the organization The Collaborative for Academic Social and Emotional Learning (CASEL). The primary mission of CASEL is to advance the science of SEL by studying the effects it has had on young people's academic, social and emotional development as well as on school institutions that incorporate SEL into their culture. Through CASEL's efforts we have learned a lot about what makes for effective social and emotional learning efforts within the context of schools.[6] Weissberg, Resnik, Payton and Utne-O'Brien tell us that in order to incorporate SEL into the heart of schools SEL programs:

- Are grounded in research.
- Teach students to apply social and emotional learning skills and ethical values in daily life.
- Build connections between students and their schools.
- Provide developmentally and culturally appropriate instruction.
- Help schools coordinate and unify programs.
- Enhance school performance by addressing the affective and social dimensions of academic learning.
- Involve families and communities as partners.
- Establish successful organizational supports and policies.
- Provide high-quality staff development and support.
- Incorporate continuous evaluation and improvement.

In this vein, CASEL asks us to think about integrating these efforts such that all facets of the school are working together. Figure 5.1, The Schoolhouse Model, portrays schools that utilize a variety of effective SEL programs and strategies. Both Model A and Model B provide valuable opportunities for preventative and intervention programs for young people. But, in Schoolhouse A, the SEL efforts are random and disconnected. In this school, providers such as administrators, teachers, counselors and other support service staff go their separate ways. They work well at what *they* do, but there is little or no integration about what *we* are doing. Conversely, in Schoolhouse B the practitioners offering this wealth of services provide a comprehensive, integrated service model. These folks not only talk to one another, but they share programs and strategies via small group

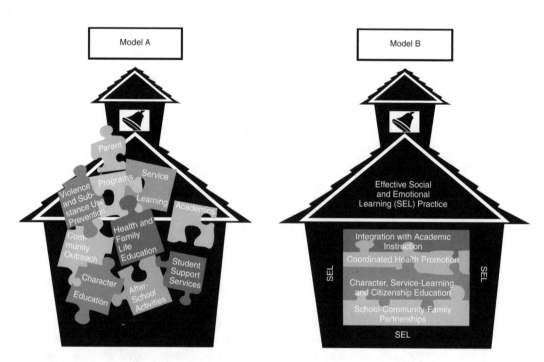

FIGURE 5.1   The SEL Schoolhouse

(**The SEL School House model is used with permission from CASEL www.casel.org** It can be found on the cover of *Safe and Sound: An Educational Leader's Guide to Evidence Based Social and Emotional Learning Programs* (CASEL 2003) the results of a three year study funded by the U.S. Department of Education's Safe and Drug Free Schools Program[7])

FIGURE 5.2   JFK Middle
(Dr. Sheldon Berman, Hudson Public Schools, 155 Apsley Street, Hudson, MA 01749 www.hudson.k12.ma)

and large staff meetings, interclass visitations and school study team meetings. They not only look at the services that individual children receive, but they also plan on methods to coordinate SEL experiences with general classroom instruction, after school programs and school-wide activities.

As we plan our integrated approach, we also need to consider the sequential development of SEL skills from early childhood to adolescence. The sooner we begin SEL instruction, the better chance we have to secure long lasting effects. Preschoolers and kindergarten children in SEL classrooms across the world are learning ways to express their feelings, be assertive in positive ways, accept other points of views and lend a helping hand to another. These efforts continue as young people approach middle and high school. Norris Haynes and Steve Marans remind us that adolescents have to[8]:

- become more aware of feelings;
- identify and name feelings;
- associate specific feelings with specific beliefs and attitudes;
- monitor changes in feelings, beliefs and attitudes.

Helping adolescents become more self-aware will provide them with the tools to deal with difficult situations. such as when they are recipients of bigoted remarks, or negative peer influence.

Research regarding the impact that SEL has on children's healthy development tells us that,

> *Children's ability to manage affective, cognitive and social behavior plays a critical role in determining both their exposure to life stress and ability to regulate responses when this occurs.*

Additionally, ample research is now available validating the impact that social and emotional learning has on academic learning and school success.[9]

Across our nation, many school districts have put SEL initiatives at the forefront of the instructional focus of their schools. They have managed to balance the academic, social and emotional well-being of the young people in their schools. Jim and I have been fortunate enough to work with a few of these dedicated visionary leaders to learn how they instituted and incorporated SEL concepts, programs and instructional strategies at the core of their school district's mission. In each of these school districts, all very different from each other, the message is clear-SEL is just as important as Reading, Writing and Arithmetic.[10]

THE HUDSON PUBLIC SCHOOLS

In 2001, The K-12 Hudson Public School District in Hudson, Massachusetts was honored as the only school district to receive the National Schools of Character awards for its exemplary work in promoting the social, ethical and academic achievement of it students. In Hudson, SEL is embedded into every aspect of the District's culture. Teacher, parent, administrator, support staff, administrative staff and parents know that character education is as important as academic achievement[11]. The mission statement of the Hudson Public School reads:

> Our goal is to promote the intellectual, ethical and social development of students through a challenging instructional program and a caring classroom and school environment.

The Hudson Public School's mission statement, grounded in research and practice, exemplifies the vision of Dr. Sheldon Berman and his staff. Clearly, its goal is to provide the children in the district with the best education needed to be successful in life. Shelley, as he is often referred to, shared that the strong beliefs and values he brings to his school organization have been influenced by his earlier experiences. Among these, his role as President of the non-profit organization Educators for Social Responsibility was instrumental:

> When I came to ESR long ago the country was dealing with the nuclear weapon crisis. As educators, we realized that people didn't have the negotiating skills and the ways of working with others to resolve conflicts effectively. Our role as educators had to be to develop those skills in young people so that they were better able to address challenging personal, social and political issues thoughtfully and peacefully. SEL accomplishes that work. It is challenging and personally demanding. In order to make the transition to peaceful resolution of conflict it takes professional development, knowledge, and a basic inclination and willingness to change on a personal level.

Shelley's commitment to creating schools that teach young people effective strategies for resolving conflict, empathizing with others and promoting civic action is evident in Hudson's initiatives. A quick glance at his budget priorities and district-wide instructional goals exhibit strong support and direction for SEL initiatives. Most of Hudson's seventeen instructional goals, like many school districts today, address academic achievement in areas such as math, literacy, technology and science development. But Hudson stands out from other places in a number of ways. In Hudson schools, teachers regularly foster democratic instructional practices such as inquiry-based learning, differentiated instruction, multiage grouping, conflict resolution, and alternative forms of assessment. They also offer a variety of SEL strategies such as character education, service learning and the establishing of a caring community. Hudson's first four instructional goals are aimed at:

1. Strengthening the integration of character education in the curriculum pre-K-12 by continuing to emphasize Hudson's core values of empathy, ethics and service.
2. Expanding and enhancing the understanding and integration of community service-learning into the curriculum.

3. Expanding the instruction of social skill and ethical development, multi-age grouping or looped classrooms, and teaching conflict resolution, peer leadership and peer mediation.
4. Increasing participation in class and school governance through class meetings, active student councils, forms of school governance that engage all students in dialogue, and the development of Responsive Schools.

In Figure 5.3 below we see an example of how Hudson's social and emotional learning initiatives translate into programs or strategies that schools can implement. Hudson uses a number of social development programs that address SEL competencies, in particular, how to increase empathy and caring. The Responsive Classroom Program is at the core of Hudson's character education efforts. Over 80 percent of Hudson's elementary and middle school teachers are trained in instructional strategies that foster a sense of community based on care and service. Second Step is used in conjunction with Responsive Classroom strategies to build social skills, such as empathy, at the elementary school level. Additionally, the Don't Laugh at Me program which focuses on anti-bullying strategies, is used in classrooms and in after-school programs to enhance Hudson's empathy development efforts.

Ethical development is at the core of each of Hudson's schools. Hudson is moving in the direction of implementing conflict resolution and peer mediation programs this year. At the middle school and high schools, there is a strong focus on developing student councils that take an active part in school life as well as participate in community projects. At Hudson High School, the school has begun its transition to a democratic governance structure. By clustering students into units of 100 to 150 students each and providing scheduled time for democratic dialogue all students engage in pertinent discussions and decision-making opportunities. Students are engaged in discussions about the quality of the food service program, disciplinary issues like smoking on campus and the very structure of the governance of the school. Last year, Hudson received several grants that opened up the dialogue around student and faculty leadership training that will impact governance decisions.

Hudson's grant initiatives have allowed them to participate in numerous areas of service-learning. Each grade has integrated a variety of service projects into the curriculum. For example, at the Hubert Kindergarten Center teachers integrate service into a thematic unit on quilts that integrates math, language arts and social studies. The quilts made by each class are donated along with a book written by students to needy mothers and young children at a homeless women's shelter. First grade teachers work

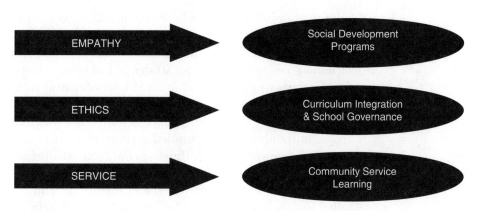

FIGURE 5.3

with the local senior center to build relationships between first graders and senior citizens. The fourth grade teachers integrate service into a year-long field science study of local wetlands and woodlands by working with students to advocate for environmental reclamation preservation, and protection of these areas. All ninth graders take an integrated English and social studies core course focused on civics in which students design projects to improve their local community. In an effort to improve their program, 15 Hudson educators participated in action research with Brandeis University to examine the impact that service-learning was having on students. Hudson also formed a parent advisory group and a youth council that empowered students to award minigrants to teachers to engage in service-learning projects. It's no wonder that all the elementary schools have received designations as Massachusetts Service-Learning Leader Schools and the middle and high school were selected as National Service-Learning Leader Schools!

Hudson Public schools clearly have found a way to balance the many functions that schools must play in the development of its youth. I asked Shelley how he has managed to put this work so front and center of everything he does in Hudson, given all the other demands he faces. He replied:

> *As a leader you always have to know the big picture and see the long term. You can't get mired in the details or the crisis of the moment. SEL sets the conditions for learning. It creates a climate in which students can do their best. But most important, it gives students skills they will need to live and work well with others and the experiences that make them effective community members and citizens. You also have to keep in mind that this is long term work; it can't be turned around in a year or even two and it wouldn't be worth it if it could be.*

Shelley provides insight into the depth of SEL work in schools.

> *Integrating SEL into the daily life of the classroom and school requires that teachers become conscious that the ways they behave and teach have as great an impact on learning as what they teach. Although most effective teachers possess the skills to resolve conflict and build a sense of community, effective SEL requires teachers to become more introspective about their practice and skill in areas of social development. This deeper level practice involves modeling and bringing it into the cluster of the classroom and school. In this way, it comes alive and is the essence of what the classroom community is about. This is personally challenging and requires learning over a longer period of time.*

Shelley shared some key strategies that he used to help move people along to embrace these changes. He recommended the following:

- Look for strategic moments where people can see the need for social skill development. Early in the development of its SEL program, Hudson had a discipline issue at the elementary level that created momentum to work on prevention via social skill instruction, positive rewards for students, and service-learning.
- Allow teachers who are excited about SEL training to share this excitement with others and put resources towards providing professional development for those interested. In Hudson, after a few teachers returned enthusiastically from Responsive Classroom training, Shelley funded seventeen teachers to attend similar trainings. This group then spread the enthusiasm until almost all elementary teachers had voluntarily participated in this five-day training program.
- Include the SEL focus as part of the evaluation of administrators [and teachers]. Shelley lets his administrators know that this is something he is passionate about and encourages them to write a few goals that they will incorporate. It has also been

incorporated into the district goals set by the school board to provide policy support for SEL.

- Hire staff that embraces the SEL values and belief system. In hiring interviews, Hudson staff make it very clear what their culture is like and what the expectations are for being part of their family. In fact, Hudson's advertisement explicitly indicates that the district is looking for teachers interested in character education and service-learning.

- Encourage newly hired staff members to get trained in SEL and encourage them to become trainers of others. Shelley believes that new, talented, teachers should be encouraged to take leadership to promote a sense of meaning and purpose and a commitment to SEL.

- Model and be active in SEL committee work. Shelley chaired committees himself. In doing so, he modeled his commitment and built relationships with staff members.

Shelley's experiences can serve us well. When leaders at the highest levels of our schools support SEL, the message of its importance rings loud and clear. Shelley's vision, passion and commitment to children are an inspiration to us all.[12]

Vignettes from Peaceable Principals

In this next section, we meet three school principals in New York City public schools who are involved in the second year of implementation of a nationally recognized SEL program, the Resolving Conflict Creatively Program, an initiative of Educator's for Social Responsibility.[13] These brief reflections will provide you with insight into (a) the ways SEL can be helpful in addressing school culture concerns, (b) some effective strategies for implementation and (c) examples of short term challenges and successes that school leaders may face in the early stages of implementation. As you read, pay close attention to each principal's thought processes, questions and actions as they began to create their peaceable schools.[14] Notice the way they think about their leadership and how they set the stage for this new learning and culture to emerge.

Ellen

Ellen, a medium-height, Caucasian woman, is the principal of Park Street Elementary School, a school of about 800 students in a low-income neighborhood in New York City. Seventy-five percent of the children in grades Pre-K through 5 are African American, twenty percent are of Latino descent and about ten percent are White ethnic or from another ethnic background. There are fifteen self-contained special education classes housed at this school.

For six years prior to becoming the principal of Park Street School, Ellen worked as a Special Education supervisor. As part of her assignment, Ellen spent one day a week at Park Street School. Ellen was not unfamiliar with the range of issues confronting this school. In fact, her previous experiences propelled Ellen to take the job of principal at Park Street School. She shares: "This was a school that was given to me because nobody else wanted it, a school that I willingly accepted because I really felt that I could make a difference."

Ellen brought in RCCP for a number of reasons. First and foremost, the aggression that children used to resolve conflicts needed to be reduced. On a scale of (1-5), five being high, Ellen rated the physical altercations between her students as a (4). There was also a substantial amount of cultural conflict in the school between children from Africa and African American students.

Ellen also brought in the program because of the teacher training it offered. She needed a cohesive, collaborative working team as she planned to move her school forward to meet high instructional standards. Ellen's teachers were used to a more dictatorial leadership style, traditional teaching methods and non-collegiality. Ellen fostered a participatory, democratic style of leadership. Using cooperative instructional strategies she increased collaboration among colleagues. She says,

> I think that you need to have people talk to you. I don't think that you can make decisions by yourself. And, if you make a decision that is truly unpopular in this school, you are only going to run into difficulty-everybody will be against you . . . Most of the teachers who were here before me were asked to simply maintain their classrooms. They were expected to keep the children quiet and in the classroom; that was it. Now we are asking teachers to look at standards, assessments, and the best practices that make for effective schools. This is a big change. Also, teachers need to learn better classroom management strategies. A lot of the teachers really don't know how to resolve conflicts and they sometimes exacerbate the problem just by the way they talk to the children.

Two years into the program, Ellen shares stories about the changes she is beginning to see in her school. Two of her most exciting pieces of news are the fifth grade youth leaders and her lunchtime teacher study teams.

> You have to see these fifth graders. They are amazing! They are helping to set the tone of the school with their leadership. They meet once a week and come up with strategies to keep the school peaceful. All the kids love them. The intergroup conflict is so much better now. What a difference!"

Later, Ellen invites us to a lunchtime teacher study group meeting. At this meeting, a teacher presents her expertise in science to a group of eight of her colleagues. Ellen whispers, "They have come a long way. A year ago, they never spoke to each other. Now, they are collaborating on a regular basis."

Donald

Packer Middle School, a tall, brick facility located in Flushing, New York, is a grade 7-9 school that serves a diverse population of approximately 811 students. Donald, a stately African American male, is a second year principal at Packer Middle School. Previously he was a K-2 elementary teacher, a middle school Special Education supervisor and an assistant principal. Students at Packer speak a variety of languages including Spanish, Chinese Korean, Russian and Farsi. At the time of this study, twelve percent of the students were identified as English Language Learners, and seventy percent of students were considered below the poverty line.

Donald brought RCCP into the school primarily because he believes steadfastly that conflict resolution is a way of life. Both children and adults need to learn effective strategies for resolving conflict and how to take more responsibility for their own actions and decisions. For David, the program served to support his belief system and vision for the school. He shares: "It helped me to know that I was going in the right direction and that I really had to follow my heart and what I felt was the appropriate thing to do."

During the first year of his participation in the program, there weren't any major violent incidents among young people in his school. Still, teachers were concerned with their safety. Donald said: "Up until now, I haven't seen us having any real problems. But increasingly, I see gang members recruiting kids. I see behaviors in here that I can't attribute to anything other than a process of gang initiation." By the second year of our study, however, some of the conflict appeared to escalate. In certain instances, students verbally threatened teachers. Donald attributed some of the problem to kids being kids, and to the unwillingness of staff to be flexible with their power and status. He explains, "Kids get angry with teachers because teachers say or do something that they disagree with, or they think those teachers are wrong." Staff members, according to Donald, are in need of better skills to de-escalate conflict with young people.

Donald reports that there are also splits in loyalty and support for his leadership style among the staff. The previous principal was much more authoritative than he is. Many teachers want him to make more of the decisions instead of taking their own responsibility. Teachers, on the other hand, want Donald to "crack the whip." According to them, kids are undisciplined. They want him to concentrate on punishing them rather than on conflict resolution. Subsequently, Donald spent his first two years improving discipline standards at his school. He recognized that this had to be done before his staff would be willing to embrace his vision.

Despite these setbacks, during the second year of implementation, Donald exhibited some hope. He smiled as he said,

> I see children who are removing other children from conflict. In their own childlike manner they are addressing it in another way. Even if it's just to say, "Come on, man, you are going to get yourself in trouble. Let's move off from here." There is movement in the right direction . . . And teachers are more collegial. There's more discussion of issues. I think that people aren't afraid to state what they think. They know that nothing is going to happen to them as a result of stating what they feel.

John

P.S. 378, a sparkling clean, older building with a large inviting playground, houses 500, K-5 students. John, an Italian American who grew up in the school's neighborhood, has been the principal of Elementary School 378 for 11 years. He talks about his school with an intimacy based on a long-term, caring relationship. PS 378 is a very stable school with a veteran staff and a small percentage of immigrant students. About half of the ethnic students fall below the state mandated poverty line. The majority of children are White ethnic and there are a growing percentage of Latin American and Asian American students.

John listens attentively when others speak to him. He is known to respond to most situations in a calm, honest manner. In his school, he often can be found outside his office either walking through the hallways or visiting classrooms. Prior to being a principal he had been a teacher, an educational evaluator, a special education administrator and an assistant principal.

John requested involvement with RCCP because he wanted to equip adults and children with social and emotional skills. He also believed the skills would help *him* learn how to deal better with situations he faces. According to John, the climate of the school was good but not great. His teachers handled most school conflict by sending notes home to the parents or by sending students to him for disciplinary action. Physical fighting seldom occurred, and most student conflicts were verbal.

Initially, John was skeptical of how worthwhile the RCCP training for principals would be but gradually he realized that what he was learning was useful. He told us,

> As the years go on, the principal's position requires that you be more of a mediator, more of a negotiator . . . That's what we are not trained enough in. Just because we are all principals, and we pass an exam, doesn't mean we can relate to people at that level. Some of my colleagues want to steer the ship the way it was steered 30 years ago.

John applied his newly improved listening skills to a conflict he was facing in his school. He invited an angry parent member to express her anger. Rather than reacting to her anger, he listened. She told him that she was angry about the way he responded to her during a recent school review process. By meeting with and listening to this parent he built the first step toward regaining trust.

In order to foster acceptance of SEL at his school, John teaches classroom lessons. He read through the teacher's manual and selected lessons related to the expression of feelings. He tells us,

> I try to relate it to what I went through in my personal life in November [the illness and death of his mother]. It [the Feelings Barometer lesson: showed the children that sometimes a −5 day is not the worst thing in your life, and that you have to be able to think in perspective. The lessons have been great and now I get emails at home from some of my students who tell me, "Mr. S. I'm having a +3 day."

The lessons had other effects. Students began coming to his office to say, "I'm having a −5 day." John helped them understand their feelings and try to create solutions to their problems. "I've never been so enlightened in my life," John confessed, speaking about how much young people want him to listen to them. John visited so many classes that eventually he was greeted regularly by whole groups of children who were communicating numbers as he walked through the hall. Teachers too loved seeing the boss teach a lesson. They interpreted his lessons as a deliberate message that said, "Hey look, if he thinks it's important, maybe it is."

Lessons Learned from Reflective School Leaders

What lessons can we take away from these three school leaders who accepted the challenge to create peaceable schools? Clearly, the vision of their schools placed SEL at the core of the school's mission. They considered SEL as a tool to help young people and adults acquire much needed skills. At their schools, they asked people to embrace new instructional methods and to improve relationships with young people. They were reflective about their own role and development in all of this. They worked hard to create teamwork and collaboration. They modeled the behaviors they wanted others to embrace. Each principal faced unique challenges in their schools and used different strategies to address them. Ellen concentrated on student and peer leadership. Donald focused on improving school wide discipline and Joe focused on direct teaching of SEL skills.

Like Ellen, Donald and John, many school leaders search for ways to create a peaceable environment in their schools. The implementation of SEL, like any change process, can be an arduous task. The rewards, however, are plentiful. Regardless of the need to increase competency in literacy and mathematics, we cannot lose sight of the fact that children learn from the words and actions of the adults in the classroom and school. What transpires in that schoolhouse forms the basis of many lessons they will draw upon for the rest of their lives. Whether our children learn the ways of bullies or the ways of peacemakers depends largely on the social and emotional competencies of that classroom teacher and the emphasis placed on SEL instruction in the classroom and school.

Learn about the many SEL research-based programs and strategies available to schools.[15] Be comforted as you pursue this goal. Policymakers, politicians and the public in general are supportive of including some form of character education, service learning, peacemaking and other social emotional learning programs into K-12 education. Remember that increasing the social and emotional skills of young people requires more than simply one program. It requires a school culture that says, "This is the way we do things here." As a leader, you must continuously weave an incredible tapestry of services for young people via classroom curricula, parent workshops, mental health services, after school programs, as well as through the modeling that adults provide. Provide children with the tools that will keep them safe. Nurture them. Educate them. Prepare them not only to cope, but to participate as skilled citizens of the democracy in which they live.

SEL TEACHING AND COACHING

One of the major concerns of teachers who embark upon the path of bringing SEL into their classrooms is how to fit this new learning into their already overcrowded school day. School leaders need to know how to help teachers acquire their new skills and learn ways to make SEL part of their active repertoire. As teachers become more comfortable with the lessons, they will be able to infuse SEL into everything they do. Skills such as communication, conflict management, decision making, perspective-taking and goal-setting can easily be incorporated into many academic content lessons. What is important to remember, however, is that SEL instruction requires sequential, skill-building opportunities. In order to assure that young people unlearn negative, patterned behaviors such as aggressive responses to conflict, teachers need to consistently teach SEL skills. Young people, in time, acquire positive new behaviors that replace their former patterned responses.

A second critical learning tool for the teacher of the SEL classroom instruction is the use of affective instructional strategies. These affective teaching strategies lay the groundwork for creating a climate of trust and safety for learning. SEL strategies may include but are not limited to the use of reflection, inquiry-based learning, problem-solving, good communication, cooperative learning, and team-building exercises. School leaders need to learn ways to coach classroom teachers in the use of these instructional strategies. The following lesson plan guide can assist administrators and teachers with infusing SEL strategies into their regular teaching instruction.

- *Setting the Stage for Learning:* Teachers begin their lesson with a "Gathering" or a "Go-around" that gets them ready for the new learning they are going to present. For example, if teaching a lesson on the types of writing, you might begin with a "Go-Around" such as, "Tell me a person to whom you recently wrote a letter." Young people might answer, "a friend, my teacher, my mother, or a politician." This is a good way to get them to learn about each other and ready to talk about the different purposes of writing.
- *Body of the Lesson:* This is the part of the lesson where the teacher presents new knowledge and concepts. Whether this lesson helps children identify the many purposes of writing, or the reasons why an airplane flies, the body of the lesson should contain opportunities for active engagement of young people. Ways to accomplish active engagement include the use of pair-shares, interviews, microlabs, fishbowls, cooperative learning groups, concentric circles and other interactive learning tools.
- *Learning Styles and Special Needs:* Teachers plan lessons geared towards multiple learning styles. They involve the primary learning modes of their students and foster the development of other modalities. Training in multiple intelligence theory and differentiated instruction can be helpful to the SEL teacher. Constructivist approaches encourage teachers to help each student progress from the knowledge they already have to the acquisition of new knowledge.
- *Time for Reflection:* Reflection is a critical part of any teaching lesson. Teachers ask young people to reflect in pairs, small groups or in their private journal. They can reflect upon their learning experiences at the end of the lesson, or even at the end of the school day. Reflection increases students' self-awareness and expands learning.

- *Practice of the New Learning:* As in all good teaching, young people need multiple opportunities in which to practice the new learning. School leaders should help teachers learn ways to build in multiple opportunities to practice affective strategies.
- *Whole Class Debrief:* Teachers who promote dialogue about the learning process increase the potential for learning in the classroom community. When a lesson ends, teachers encourage young people to share the instructional strategies and knowledge that most enhanced their learning. This process enhances students' meta cognitive processes. It also helps them recognize that the way they learn may be different from that of another class member. Whole-class debriefing helps to bring the class together as a team. It also gives the teacher a sense of the learning that has occurred.

A PEACEABLE, CARING LEARNING SCHOOL CLIMATE

Take a breath, sit back and consider for a moment the climate of this social and emotional learning community that you are aspiring to establish. What are the characteristics of such a place? What are the norms, beliefs and values of the people in this school?

Based on the work of Educators for Social Responsibility and specifically that of our late colleague and internationally recognized conflict resolution expert, William Kreidler, schools that are "peaceable" organize around six themes: communication, cooperation, appreciation of diversity, expression of feelings, decision making and conflict resolution. Teachers in their classrooms address these themes. The themes also permeate the school's culture.[16]

As a former school administrator, my colleagues and I (Janet) integrated these themes into a large comprehensive middle school in San Diego in the early to mid 90's. At the Roosevelt Middle School, teachers received training in conflict resolution and inter group relations. As leaders, we gave the message that these life lessons held an important place in the student's curricular program. They were as important to us as subjects like mathematics and literacy. We infused SEL direct skill building components into our literacy and social studies block so that all kids would get the lessons on a daily basis. Teachers of all subjects found ways to infuse the social and emotional skills embedded in the peaceable school themes.

We also recognized that curriculum is not just what is taught in classrooms. Every school institution has a *hidden curriculum* as well. How the leader models this work can be observed in (a) the way decisions are made, (b) the student activities that take place, (c) the students who are chosen to lead student government, (d) the arrangement of the furniture in the classrooms, (e) the holidays, rituals and celebrations that take place and (f) the instructional strategies that teachers employ. All are part of the curriculum that contributes to a peaceable school.

We knew that students lacked a substantial voice in our school so we looked for ways to include young people in school wide decision making. We created youth leadership teams and re-evaluated the role of student governance. We learned that while SEL programs are essential components of a peaceable school much more is needed. *All* members of the school must participate and contribute to the peaceable school culture. Many variables impact the progress of institutionalization of a peaceable school. School leaders have to inspire, influence and motivate the community members to embrace these new ways of being. Lee Bolman and Terrence Deal's leadership gifts of authorship, power, love and significance become invaluable tools to help the school community prosper and grow.[17]

Placing social and emotional learning at the forefront of a school creates a very specific, predictable climate. Organizational behaviorist, Renato Taguiri, describes the characteristics of the total environment in a school building by four dimensions: ecology, milieu, social system and culture.[18] Ecology refers to the physical and material environment of the school, the cleanliness, upkeep and design of utilization of building space. Millieu encompasses all of the social dimensions of the organization. Social system represents the administrative structure of the organization. Culture refers to the values, beliefs and norms of the people that are reflected in every aspect of the organization. As you think about establishing a peaceable climate in your school, spend some time envisioning what these dimensions might look like in your school (See the Peaceable Schools Activity in the Chapter Five Skills section.)

As the peaceable school themes became an integral part of the school culture many positive climate changes slowly emerge. At my former middle school, I watched aggressive middle school leaders transform from fighters to communicators of their needs. Instead of forming isolated cliques, they now embraced diversity. Their concerns went from worrying about "me" to caring about the safety and welfare of their schoolmates. These were exciting times for all of us. Our students were indeed waging peace in our schools. Many students became youth leaders in the school. By the eighth grade, many of this school wide group of over 100 students went on to become mediators (more about this in Chapter Seven).[19]

SEL, SAFETY, AND SOUND DISCIPLINE

Managing school discipline and safety is essential in a peaceable school environment. Creating a more democratic environment does not mean that young people and adults are not held accountable for their actions. As part of the democracy they live in, young people have to know the difference between right and wrong. They have to take part in creating the kind of climate that encourages individual and collective growth. They have to take responsibility for each other as strong, viable members of their school community. Peaceable school communities establish sound discipline procedures; consequences for serious infractions are clear.

In this final section, we share some intervention strategies that an EQ leader can use with young people who are prone to disputes and violence. We also address ways to help adults who lack skills to positively de-escalate these behaviors. Inherent in the school leader's job is the responsibility to teach young people the moral code, the "rights and wrongs", and the "do's and don'ts" that will prepare them as social beings in today's world. Consider the following:

- In every school we find young people with a varying level of social skill development. They arrive at our doors with years of experiences that teach them how to act negatively or positively in social situations. Some kids are more aggressive and some are more passive. Still others, are able to use their strong social skills to communicate negotiate and even mediate conflict for self and others.
- As a school administrator, your primary concern is insuring the safety of every young person, including those who may be perpetrators. Equally as important as physical safety is putting a process in place to teach young people and adults emotional self-control methods. Young people need skills to draw on as alternatives to habitual negative behaviors. Adults need effective means to de-escalate student conflict.
- It is never acceptable in schools, or anywhere for that matter, for a young person or adult to be a perpetrator. It is not okay to bully, malign, or physically and

psychologically violate another human being. (In a nationwide study of 16,000 young people in grades six through 10, nearly 30 percent admitted to being bullied or bullying others. Nine percent admitted they bully someone once a week.)[20]

- The zero tolerance policies of the last decade have held young people and their families accountable for serious actions. The down side of such punitive measures is that we have no clear evidence that zero-tolerance approaches that suspend and expel kids change behavior or improve school safety.[21] Furthermore, when kids leave schools so does their unresolved anger. Someone or something in their communities becomes a target of their rage.

Study after study has proven that high quality intervention and prevention programs reduce the risk of alcohol and drug abuse, early pregnancies and incidences of child abuse, and even subsequent incarceration of possible offenders. Still, many think that law enforcement alone will cure people. Punitive measures put a temporary lid on abhorrent behaviors. These behaviors, untreated, find means of expression. Troubled kids get passed down from one school to another. Many finally end up somewhere in the juvenile justice system. We are remiss, as a society, in the much-needed investment in mental health. Dr. Bernadetto Saraceno, Director of the Department of Mental Health and Substance Dependence for the World Health Organization shares, "If we can increase the treatment rate for mental illness, this contributes to decreasing the burden of mental disorders and also reduces the distress to the affected families and society in general."[22]

James Shaw in his book *Jack and Jill Why They Kill,* reveals the shocking stories of kids who committed homicide.[23] He spent four years interviewing 103 incarcerated youth who had committed heinous crimes. The book sent chills up my spine as I read the cold-blooded stories from these children's mouths. It is no surprise to learn that many of the young people Shaw studied had been bullies and victims of bullying. The US Department of Justice expects that one in four children who bully will have a criminal record before they reach the age of 30. We now know that bullying has been a factor in two-thirds of 37 school shooting incidents in our country. Shaw reaches out to parents and educators pleading that we listen to these children and see their pain early on before the damage is done. Depression is often a cause for child bullying, suicide and violent acts.

James Garbarino, noted as "a true pioneer in our understanding of the inner life of our youth," highlights the particular difficulty that aggressive boys, many who have been maltreated face. They act from their irrational beliefs about themselves and the world around them. He shares,

> They live in a different world from those of us fortunate enough to have grown up loved, accepted, and treated well. Their social maps chart the same physical territory, but it is as if they are color-blind-not because they were born that way but because their early experiences stunted their growth. . . . They learn early that power is what counts and that conventional morality often masks and justifies abuse.

Garbarino informs us that these young people need protection and moral teaching. Punitive measures, alone, will never change their moral development. We have to provide them with opportunities to develop empathy. We need to protect them from degrading, dehumanizing and desensitizing images. We need to stimulate and support the spiritual development of boys.[24] Girls do not escape these statistics either. They are increasingly involved in more violent crime. And, what's scary is that they are more likely to use knives than guns and to murder someone as a result of conflict rather than during a crime.[25]

LEADERS RISE TO THE CHALLENGE

My fiancée is an assistant principal in an incredibly, heartwarming inner city school in New York City. P811M-The Mickey Mantle School (Figure 5.4), educates and cares for a population of about 180 emotionally disturbed children, ages five through fourteen. Approximately, 90 percent of these young people are boys.[26] I continue to learn great lessons from Barry as he recounts the daily roller coaster of school events that occur when children are in emotional crises. The adults and children in this school face the same challenge as their regular education peers to meet the required academic standards so that children are successful in life. But in a school such as P811M, both adults and young people know that developing social and emotional skills is paramount to future success. One might ask, "How does a leader assure for the safety and learning of children who are often so hurt and angry?" Barry, speaking for the dedicated adults in his school tells me, with a smile, "You give them a stable, safe, consistent, secure and loving environment, with a lot of structure. You listen, and you teach. You keep expectations high and you anticipate setbacks. In a nutshell, you just love them. That's what you do."

But the staff of The Mickey Mantle School does much more. They use a comprehensive SEL approach that includes a multitude of prevention and intervention programs and strategies. These include the anti-bullying program. Don't Laugh at Me conceived and produced by Peter Yarrow of Peter, Paul and Mary; the Goldstein Social Skills program, and the Life Space Crisis Intervention program, to name a few.[27] They also utilize SEL-related software programs offered via their technology labs to build preventative skills. Additionally, the school has a strong crisis intervention program with crisis counselors and a crisis room where kids go to de-escalate and manage their anger. All this is supported by a meaningful academic program that provides children with the same opportunities as children in regular education schools.

In dealing with troubled young people, the Life Space Crisis Intervention program, in particular, offers adults a series of noteworthy strategies. In Life Space trainings, adults learn how to identify young people's irrational beliefs. They help children recognize that these beliefs no longer work for them, and work towards changing destructive behaviors. For example, a child who has a tantrum because of a pattern he developed to protect himself from his abusive parent learns that this behavior doesn't work at school and wont get him what he needs (love and acceptance). Adults learn ways to de-escalate the child and then how to move the child from crisis to a plan for change. Adults learn

FIGURE 5.4   The Mickey Mantle School, P811M New York City

how *not* to enter the "conflict cycle" with the young people by using a combination of attending, listening, observing and responding skills. Teachers learn how not to allow a troubled child to push their buttons and hijack them into irrational words or behaviors.

For less severe cases of "rule breaking," classroom teachers utilize instructional discipline and avoid punishment. Carol Leiber tells us, "Guided discipline is "present and future oriented; it focuses on the student's need to regain control, self-correct, redirect focus, or get back on the track."[28] Defiance to teachers, skipping school and name calling are socially unacceptable behaviors that are best treated by breaking old patterns and building new skills. Young people armed with arsenals of skills such as active listening, assertive language, perspective-taking, empathy-building, decision-making strategies and the ability to be an ally for another have real alternatives to violence. In-school suspension rooms are excellent places to build on these skills with designated personnel. Student support groups and small group counseling sessions help children to build bonds, gain self-confidence and release the emotional baggage that keeps them from learning. Youth leadership groups and peer mediation are proven ways to build resiliency and teach new skills.

IN SUMMARY

As we bring this chapter to a close, it might be helpful to summarize some of the strategies that school leaders can use to establish SEL in their school communities. Leaders can:

- Explore the multitude of great SEL programs and resources that are on the market. Visit the CASEL website (www.casel.org) to find out which programs would work for you.
- Work with social agencies and corporate sponsors. Bring their services and resources into your schools. Join together with other school leaders to share expenses and write grants.
- Regularly assess the emotional climate of your school. Listen carefully. Do not allow the "code of silence" to grow in your school. Identify and intervene immediately with bullies, kids and adults.
- Encourage your children to become peacemakers. Give them the hope and know-how to make a difference in their school, their homes and their communities.
- Integrate SEL into every part of the curriculum instruction in the classroom and schoolwide activities.
- Model your commitment to SEL by matching *your* behaviors to the culture you are hoping to establish.
- Attend an SEL training with members of your staff. Teach a lesson or two in classrooms, and stay to the course. This will build commitment and ownership a lot faster.
- Put aside professional development dollars for staff members to receive training and turn key the training to others at your school.
- Encourage staff members to include SEL instruction as part of their annual goals and objectives.
- Learn effective intervention strategies that will assist you and your staff to embrace even the most troubled young people.

A word of caution: Make sure your school is physically safe for learning and that the children and teachers *are* and *feel* safe. Schools with violent cultures may need to cling on to some of the more severe safety measures such as security officers, metal detectors and expulsion. But, even troubled schools would be remiss if this is all they were to do. Physical safety isn't enough. Be sure your school's climate projects social and emotional safety. Make EQ as prestigious as IQ. Remember the words of eighth grade student and former "bully" Brandon, "The lessons taught me to get respect in another way."

REFLECTIVE QUESTIONS

1. Do you believe that SEL instruction is as important as academic instruction in schools?
2. What do you know about SEL programs and instruction? What do you want to know?
3. Is the school you lead or work in a caring community, a peaceable school? Explain the reasons why or why not?
4. The principals in this chapter used a variety of leadership strategies as they began to bring SEL into their schools. Have you used any of these strategies before? What other strategies have been effective for you? What strategies might you want to try out?
5. Is your school safe? If so, what makes it safe? If not, what makes it unsafe and how could that be changed?

LESSON FROM THE FIELD

Sydell Kane

I had been a principal for five years. Things were progressing nicely. We received a few grants that created interesting opportunities for education, but I still felt a twinge of unhappiness. I reflected to see if I could discover the source of my discontent. The staff was working hard. They were starting to collaborate on their grade levels, but there wasn't a feeling of unity in the building. Although I insisted that children in special education be included in every possible activity, they were still considered a separate group. Teachers on a grade did their own thing; there were no inter grade activities. Parents worked for their child's class or on a school fundraiser, but that is where it ended. How could I make this school into a caring community? How could I promote the social and emotional learning skills I knew were critical for the children and adults at my school? I had to start at the beginning. I had to build community.

I found my opportunity one day when a teacher shared an interesting article that described a class who got involved in an international educational care giving opportunity. Classes of children sent their stuffed animals out into the world and asked the people who received the animals to write about their country and send the animal back. The staff and I toyed with the idea. We decided it would be a wonderful way to bring the school together in a "bear care" kind of way! If each class had their own teddy bear to send out into the world, this could be a great project.

The hunt for bears began. At first, when we saw the prices for teddy bears, the project looked very bleak. We didn't have hundreds of dollars to spend. Everyone searched for inexpensive bears that summer. At the beginning of August, while on vacation, I happened to go into a fabric/sewing store that had a sale on teddies. Explaining the need for and use of a large quantity of bears, the store manager gave us the bears at a special low price.

Now the work began. A committee was formed and the plan began to take shape. It began with each class receiving a ten-inch teddy bear. The class had to name it, give it a personality, make its clothing and provide a diary to take on its travels. Everyone was busy. Parents helped make clothes for the bears. We enlisted the help of relatives, friends and business associates. Travel agents and airlines were contacted. The bears were going to travel. Everyone was talking about the project. Children discussed it in the lunchroom and yard, parents talked in the streets and supermarkets and teachers compared notes in their lunchroom. Relatives called to ask if they could be included too.

It was decided that the bears should have a bag just in case people gave them souvenirs. Each night a different student was able to take the bear home, share it with the family and bond with it. Parents, grandparents and siblings became part of the activities. Finally, it was time for the bears to leave. We held a school-wide party to bid the bears farewell. Bears were dressed in their travel finery. With tears and delight students talked about their bears. Everyone had a chance to participate. There was no special education or general education, no kindergartners or sixth graders, just children and teddy bears. The district superintendent and several community people came to add their good wishes and fond good-byes. Suddenly the school felt like one big family starting out on an exciting venture.

Soon these soft cuddly travelers were packed in valises, carry-on-luggage, overnight cases, shopping bags and briefcases. They were spotted on planes, buses, trains and cruise ships. While the children learned geography, problem solving, reading, mathematics, writing and social studies, all the constituencies in the school community began to bond into one large caring family.

Instructions had been sent out with each bear asking travelers to send back a photo or postcard and make an entry in the bear's diary. If they wished, they could place a small souvenir or memento in the teddy bear's backpack. Then the traveler was asked to give the bear to another traveler to take elsewhere and continue the cycle. The school was jumping. A giant map went up in the hallway to plot each mascot's travels. Letters, postcards and news about the bears were posted on bulletin boards, read over the PA system and put into a newsletter. Some were included in the PTA monthly Bulletin. We heard reports of bears sitting next to the pilot in an airplane visiting far away places. Bears were seen in Hungary, Florida, Crete, Bangladesh, California, Vietnam, Israel, St. Maarten, Disney World and Japan. They enjoyed cruising in the Caribbean as well as the Aegean Sea. They even enjoyed a soda in a bar in Milan.

The changes in our school's culture soon became evident. If a class couldn't get a parent for a trip, another parent from a different class would volunteer to go along. Parents became more interested in serving on the School Leadership Team, working around the school and helping out. Teachers from different grades and programs began to work together on projects of mutual interest. The school started to get publicity. Two airlines, TWA and Singapore Airlines wrote about the project in their in flight magazines along with several local newspapers. Alumni from all over the world, reading about the school's program, sent letters. A Canadian local newspaper became interested and put pictures of the project on the front page of its weekly. All of this promoted a wonderful feeling of pride and achievement in the entire school community and its extended family. Needless to say, the wealth of educational opportunities made the teddy bear venture a great success. But the real success was the bonding that developed. This continued and grew in subsequent years. Of course, it needed to be continually nurtured, but it was easy once the ties were there.

I learned a great lesson about the importance of teamwork and the collaboration of staff, parents and children. Our teddy bear project created an understanding of differences; it helped us build empathy and brought us together as a caring school community. The lesson really came home to me one day, in particular, during a school assembly. One of our Down Syndrome children was chosen to participate in the color guard along with other children. He was obviously frightened and not sure of what to do. Another student went to him and whispered, "Don't be afraid. Hold my hand. I'll take care of you." And she did. From then on, I made sure that whatever we did, we made it a school wide endeavor. That way, everyone felt part of the big picture.

Sydell Kane is a retired principal and Adjunct Faculty member at Hunter College. She served over eleven years as a New York City elementary school principal.

(Courtesy of Resolving Conflict Creatively Program of Educators for Social Responsibility)

Chapter 6

The People Side of Change

You know, I took all the required courses in school to get my certification to become a principal and I even feel pretty confident about instruction and what kids need to learn. I thought I was ready, but no one ever told me that once I became a principal I would have to be everybody's mother and father. Everyone seems to need my attention and approval. This high school has 3,500 young people in it and over 200 staff members. I need to do a tap dance to meet everybody's needs. My job is to make sure that the kids are learning. But, it seems that without dealing with everyone's needs, I can't get the kind of learning going that I know needs to happen.

Today, for example, I got in two hours before everybody else so I could plan out my day and get some work done. I'm never sure what emergency will take place, what teachers are going to call in sick. I always have Plan B ready. Today was quiet. I did my morning rounds, visited classrooms. I saw some wonderful teaching going on. But there were a couple of classrooms that caused me to shiver. I wonder how Ms. C ever got a teaching credential? I know I have my work cut out with her. How am I going to change the way things are done in that classroom? . . . I had a meeting with the union representative at 9:00. We have a better relationship this year. I worked hard at it, but I still can't get her to support all the changes I want to make in staffing. Then at 10:00, Mrs. D, my key parent, came to see me. I'm really angry with her. She wants the ninth graders to wear team jackets even though we worked long and hard as a school to keep them out of here, after the gang threats we had. It's not that I'm not open, but this is a real safety issue. At 11:00, I had my meeting with Tomás, my new paraprofessional, been here three months. Great guy, but he comes in late twice a week. I've given him a bunch of chances to right the record, but he keeps screwing up, and his brother is on the school board. So, I'm trying to work with him, but nothing seems to change his behavior. I am definitely going to have to start writing him up.

The superintendent wants me to make a difference in this school. That's why she placed me here. I had a pretty good track record at my other school, although it was a lot smaller. I've been here two years now and the changes are coming slowly. The kids are great, but they need so much. So much of what I can do depends on my staff. No one person could do this job. 1 have friends who run companies. They tell me I'm crazy for doing what I do. But I love my work. Dealing with kids is the greatest, and in many ways so difficult. They could never imagine running a business in the way I have to run the school. I tell them my stories: Imagine that on a daily basis, one of your employees bursts out crying because the stress of the job is getting to him, or one of your employee's mother comes in to reprimand you because he hasn't been treated well, or didn't get promoted at the last promotion time. Or even yet, the Director on the fifth floor above you arrives at your door complaining that your employees were misbehaving and acting rudely on their floor? . . . On a more serious note, imagine having to call in the paramedics because your employee is suicidal or the psychologist because one of your employees came in with bruises all over her body? Or what about the employee who went to bed hungry because there was no food on the table . . . and then imagine on top of all of this, you receive a call from your boss saying that on the last performance assessment, your 4th level division did not substantially improve and what were you going to do about it? My friends tell me they wouldn't take my job for all the money in the world. I'm not complaining, I love my work; but there aren't enough hands or hearts to efficiently run a school operation today to meet the demands of the stuff our young people are bringing to school, as well as the adults that are teaching them.

—Interview with Peter, high school principal

Like Peter, school leaders across our nation are struggling to do their best for the young people they serve. The wise, caring school leader aspires to create change in the school that will hopefully bring student success. Far too often, however, changes are imposed on them by national, state and local mandates or arise from sudden crises. Far less often, school leaders are free to make changes that they know are just plain good for kids.

These are uncertain times. The No Child Left Behind Act mandates that schools make steady gains in reading and math test results so that by 2013-2014 all students will meet state defined proficiency levels.[1] While discussions continue about who should best run our schools, corporate executives or instructional leaders, children and teachers in their classrooms grapple with the effects of funding cuts, school violence, social changes, intolerance to diversity and, in some cities, threats of terrorism. Added to the teacher's already overcrowded agenda is the urgency to develop young people's ability to cope with these and other uncertainties. Leading schools today require a sharp set of skills. Today's school principal cannot get by with mediocrity. He has to be a genius at the craft of leading. Too much is at stake.

Peter, a case in point, is moving at a pace faster than most of us could ever imagine. He, like many other principals has become an artisan of multitasking. What the public doesn't understand about "increasing academic achievement" in schools is that this cannot be done without tending to all of the needs he describes, and more. Though some may disagree, schools are not corporate ventures. The profit margin of school is the success of children. To create this success in children, the principal has to improve learning conditions in the whole school. Teachers, school custodian, secretary, parents, the school's leadership team, teacher assistants, school nurse and others need to improve their performance. In a service organization such as public education, it isn't enough to "sharpen the saw" of just the teachers. You have to assure that everyone has the well being of children first and foremost, and that they are performing at their best.

This chapter speaks to the "people" side of change-faced daily by the school leader. While keeping the ship moving, how does the principal get optimal performance from his crew? And, how does he equip himself with the tools and strategies needed to do this? Throughout this book, we have referred to the star performer as one who has the emotional intelligence that propels him forward to recognize and improve the limitations in self and others. Peter and other school leaders have to put the systems in place to support the legal and technical changes incurred by legislative mandates and guidelines. But these changes will not flow without the inspiration, creativity and commitment of the people in the organization, As Goleman says, "Beyond technical expertise, the change catalyst needs a host of other emotional competencies. . . . In addition to high levels of self-confidence, effective change leaders have high levels of influence, commitment, motivation, initiative, and optimism, as well as an instinct for organizational politics.[2]

In this chapter, we are concerned with the change process. We explore the concept of "visioning" as it relates to driving change. We observe how the leader sets the tone for building relationships with others. We spend time reflecting on the style of the leader that best motivates others to top performance. As we talk about change, we remind ourselves of the importance of such EI competencies as influence, inspiration and developing others. Finally, we talk about ways to sustain change over time.

As you read this chapter, ask yourself, "How do I, as principal, lead the transformation of others in my school? What can I learn as an EQ leader that will help me develop others to be the best that they can be? We talk a lot about what leaders need to do to drive change; but we rarely teach leaders how to increase their own abilities to be able to motivate others, inspire and *be* that catalyst for change.

SYSTEMS CHANGE AS PEOPLE CHANGE

Over the past twenty years we have learned a lot about change. Hall and Hord's work in the change process has helped us to anticipate certain aspects of change. Planning tools such as their Innovation Configuration Map (IC), help us think about the steps needed for effective implementation of a change event. It gives direction to the change process by asking us to reflect on the changes we hope to see in the long haul.[3] Change is a complex, interconnected process at every level, be it individual change or organizational systemic change. No deep change happens overnight; no change is the same. Michael Fullan, Dean of the Ontario Institute for Studies in Education of the University of Toronto reminds us, "Every situation will have degrees of uniqueness in its history and makeup which will cause unpredictable difference to emerge.[4]" And few changes are sustained without complex knowledge about change and commitment to it over time.

John Kotter, expert on leadership at the Harvard Business School, in his book *The Heart of Change* agrees that the most challenging part of instituting change is changing the behavior of people.[5] He outlines a few strategies for bringing in the change. Begin by "creating a sense of urgency" for others. Make the change relevant. Explore the need. Why do teachers need this math program or that set of materials? Choose a strong, leading team whose members are respected by others. They will create the buy-in you desire. As I reflect on the process of implementing school wide conflict resolution in my former school, the urgency was the increase in school violence. Everyone agreed that this had to improve. But it was the commitment and dedication of a few lead teachers that made the difference in the staff's acceptance of the change. Elaine, a much-respected teacher, led the implementation process. She taught lessons in her class and invited others in to observe her new teaching strategies and the positive effects they were having on her students. She even volunteered to teach in interested teachers' classrooms. Her enthusiasm was so contagious that it encouraged many staff members to sign up for the district-provided workshops. Within two years, teams of teachers were leading this innovation over all three tracks of our multi-track, year-round school. Close to 75 teachers were trained in conflict resolution and teaching its principles in their classes.[6] In my present role as coordinator of the Education Administration Program at Hunter College, I have been implementing substantive changes in the program's content and in our teaching pedagogy. The urgency caused by the shortage of quality school principals in New York City Public schools has helped me to push forth substantive changes in a meaningful and expedient manner.

The Language of Vision

Leaders need to have a vision; that's a fact. Unfortunately, little is actually done to develop the educational leader's vision of how to lead a school. Sadly, many leaders just "shoot from the hip" and hope that what they envision their schools to be will happen. Others have a deep intuitive sense of what they want their schools to look like. Still others, have thought long and hard about their vision. They utilize the language of that vision to drive the changes they hope to see in their schools.

When my colleagues and I set out to change the school culture and climate we had a clear vision in mind. We wanted to change our school culture at a fundamental level by addressing issues of inequality, racism and ways to manage conflict. Before we began our school transformation process, we had deep conversations about the changes we wanted to see in our school. We knew where we wanted to end up and learned how to move this vision forward as we went along. By the fourth year of implementation, what started with three administrators' vision became the school's vision. Soon, kids and adults were speaking the language of our vision that included conflict resolution, anti-bias work and violence prevention. Visible representations of this language were evident throughout the school. New kids and teachers were informed by others that this is what we were about. This common language was a critical part of the change process. Everybody spoke it, even if they didn't fully believe in it.

In my present role, my vision includes impacting the field of educational leadership in New York City by creating an educational preparation program of excellence. In this program we develop the emotional competencies of future and current leaders along with their organizational and instructional skills. Excellence in administrative preparation means that what we teach prospective leaders is aligned with the "real needs" of practicing administrators in urban schools. Those actually doing the job inform what we teach our students. Now, into our fifth year, the language of our vision is being translated into reality. It can increasingly be seen in all aspects of our program.

A vision provides us with directionality. It serves to guide us as we put the structures in place for long-term change. Sadly, because school leaders are so pressured to show results, many ignore this process. They lack a real vision for their schools and young people's learning. And those that do have a strong vision, often defer it to concentrate on having students pass and excel on standardized tests. While it is true that we are in a high accountability period in education, we have an immense responsibility as leaders to inspire our staffs. We want them to embrace change and go beyond the mandates to the heart of what prepares our children for their future.

Vision's Path

As you form your vision, you have to consider technological and scientific breakthroughs, political trends and economic forces and social, cultural, and personal mores. You can't create a vision in a tunnel. You need to know what's going on around you and what the realities are of supporting your vision along the way.

Next, you have to begin with the vision you hope to see. Be the change you envision. We cannot separate who we are as people from whom we are as leaders. If I believe in peace in the world and nonviolent conflict resolution as a means to resolving differences this will be a fundamental value of my school. Educators, often more reactive rather than proactive, miss the critical link between the personal and professional path. As a result, they often get where they never knew they were going. Fortunately, for many of us, the intuitive process kicks in and lends a guiding hand. We haven't all wandered too aimlessly through life. But, as adults and leaders, we need to be more in tune with the kind of school we envision leading.

Once your vision is clear, you move from your dream state to the reality. Ask yourself, "Is this vision inclusive of the community members who live and work here? Does my vision take into consideration the political, economic and social realities of the staff, families and children?" I may hope for a truly democratic school where adults and children alike have a voice and equal partnership in the school. The reality, however, of the children and families in this community may be that they long for direct leadership and support. I have experienced school communities that after years of laissez faire leadership have recruited more authoritarian and even autocratic leaders. This being the case, you can still get to your vision. Meet the community's prominent needs first, and then move the culture in your desired direction.

Once your vision is established, you need to model it. You have to create structures that support the vision and create safe places that allow others to dialogue about it. Finally, you have to constantly reflect on and renew your vision. Peter Senge's first discipline, personal mastery, says we must "continually clarify and deepen our personal vision."[7] If I believe that schools should be truly democratic, then, I must hold onto that vision, at all times. As I make my way through the daily realities that may detain this progress, I must honor the "creative tension" that results. This is the heart of the change process. The leader has to hold onto that vision, create the desire for this to become a collective vision and empower each and every person with the tools to move through this tension to that desired state. It's the leader's job to keep up the momentum to embrace that vision. Other innovations will come their way and tempt them to pull back. But, if the leader loses interest, so will their staff. Twelve years later, for example, the principal and lead teachers of my former middle school tell every new teacher who joins the staff that conflict resolution is a critical part of the school's culture. New staff members have to attend a three-day training that will prepare them for teaching and modeling these principles.

Planning and Implementing School Wide Change

At the systems level of change, every organization is complex and different; each encounters its own challenges and methods for implementing change. The slogan, "change is a process, not an event," remains a helpful adage as we propel forward to create change in our schools.[8] Inherent in this change process is the tension caused by conflict, an inevitable element that can help or hinder the process.

Ironically, I still remember the multitudes of setbacks I encountered as the change agent responsible for institutionalizing the conflict resolution program at my middle school. The school was rife with conflict! My principal and friend, Vince, kept reminding me to roll with the changes, hold onto my vision and be patient. Change wasn't going to happen overnight. He was right. By year five we were over the hump and could claim conflict resolution as part of who we were, but we still had a long way to go to have the majority of staff on board.

Substantive change takes time; it could take from seven to 10 years. And we know that we can count on periods in which we feel as if we are stuck without movement. We may even regress to where we once were. In the early 90's, Michael Fullan helped us to understand this "implementation dip," that lull in performance and confidence as one encounters an innovation that requires new skills and new understandings.[9] Hall and Hord tell us, "As individuals struggle to make the change "work" they go through the valley, or dip, of difficulties before they reach the top and emerge at a higher level."[10]

As we plan for change, it is critical to remember that schools are communities of people who are being asked to embrace organizational changes. Each person has her own "needs" and individual "wants" that she hopes for as the change occurs. Fullan reminds us, "Leading in a culture of change means creating a culture (not just a structure) of change. It does not mean adopting innovations, one after another; it does mean producing the capacity to seek, critically assess and selectively incorporate new ideas and practices-all the time, inside the organization as well as outside it."[11] Fullan calls this practice "reculturing." This process involves changing norms, beliefs and actions of the people in the school or district. Relationship-building is critical to this process. Leaders need to understand the dynamics of the groups in the school as well as individual needs and positions. At the personal level, change is extremely complex. Personal change requires self-awareness and self-confidence; it means being able to admit insecurities and seek out ways to strengthen them. It involves fear and anxiety and risk-taking. And it requires a strong leader who is a trusted coach to facilitate the process.

Addressing Resistance

Resistance is endemic to change. Think about the last time someone asked you to change a behavior. Start with something small like leaving the cap off of the toothpaste in the morning. You probably developed this habit over time and rarely thought twice about it. Not so your life partner who hates seeing the gooey toothpaste on the sink that drips out of the tube! So, she asks you to change this habit. At first, you probably feel righteous. "Why should I? I live here too." Then, you think about it and realize that it's such a small thing and you could change to make her happy. So, you try hard to remember to replace the cap. You do great for a few days and then you forget again. If you're lucky, your partner didn't catch your slip up.

In other words, changing long-embedded habits is not easy. It takes practice and commitment. Now, take this to a deeper, more meaningful part of yourself. Imagine that you are a teacher who has traditionally taught your students using whole class methodology. You dabbled with grouping for instruction over the years and never could embrace it. Your students have been fairly successful. Now, you are being asked to embrace differentiated instruction. Your principal is relentlessly leading this charge in your school. You feel angry, unappreciated, unrecognized and compelled to change. You don't believe that this new method of teaching will be worth its salt. So, you resist. You don't go to the meetings. You manage to be sick on staff development days . . . Get the scenario?

Sometimes resistance comes from deep-seated beliefs rather than abilities. Being open to the diversity of the group and inviting the different perspectives into the conversation can often promote better and more effective strategies for change than were originally considered. Remember, conflict appropriately addressed, can promote growth and bring about unimagined positive consequences. Critical to helping someone through this process is a highly-skilled, emotionally intelligent leader who knows when and how to validate, support, question and probe.

> *In a study of over 100 managers and white-collar workers Robert Baron (1990) found that negative or critical feedback was considered a greater source of conflict and frustration than disputes over power, mistrust or personality struggles. Those who were ineptly criticized felt discouraged, demoralized and demotivated.*"[12]

Constructive criticism, or negative feedback, is much easier to be heard when a trusting relationship exists between you and the listener. It also helps when previously decided upon ground rules have been set. Think about it. When you know that you haven't lived up to your own expectation, or that of someone you respect, you don't feel good inside. You are more willing to listen and even change the behavior in question. Position power can often get in the way of delivering feedback. If there is an obvious difference of power in the relationship, (teacher/student or principal/teacher) the recipient needs to know that this is not driving the negative feedback. Nobody wants to be told what to do, and no body likes to be motivated to change by fear.

A good way to start a feedback conversation is with something like, "I would like to give you some feedback about X. Is this a good time?" This starts off the conversation with a deference to the receiver and usually creates a willingness to listen. Once the recipient is willing to listen the following tips can be helpful:[13]

- Ask the person to reflect on the situation first and self assess. "I wonder if you can tell me how you think you did leading the assembly the other day?"
- Describe the situation from your point of view, as you observed it. Be explicit. Talk about exactly what you observed. "I noticed that the children were laughing and not listening to the presenter."
- Offer specific information that the listener can recall or envision and let the listener know how the behavior you are referring to made you feel. Helpful words could be, "I'm concerned about . . . I'm uncomfortable with . . . I'm confused when. . . .
- Invite the recipient to comment on how he sees the situation and to provide more information that clarifies.
- State your hopes and expectations and invite the recipient to give his.
- Set a timeline for the change you hope to see.
- Summarize what you both have discussed and the next steps that will take place.

Remember, feedback can also be given when the person exhibits a behavior that you appreciate. Don't give false praise, but look for those moments when you can affirm the person for a job well done. Even in the above conversation, it would serve you well to offer truthful, positive comments about other behaviors you may have observed in that particular moment. This helps to remove the focus on the negative behavior and allows the person to avoid internalizing that all behaviors were unacceptable.

Choosing a Leadership Style—Ellen, Donald, and John

Your role as school leader is critical to the change process. What approach do you take in working with teachers, parents and young people? Does the style of leadership you use make a difference in the outcomes you have reached? Does it help you to be more directive and more controlling, or more open and democratic in nature? What works? Is there really a difference?

The study of organizational behavior has taught us a lot about effective leadership, in particular, about leadership behaviors that can produce desired results. We have come a long way since the early 1900's when leaders expected workers to produce the quality and quantity needed for the mass assembly line. Accuracy and precision of parts and products were the predominant concerns of the times. We learned a lot from the study of social systems. Mayo's Hawthorne studies at the Western Electric Plant in the 1930's helped us to look at the relational aspects of workers. We learned about the positive effects involving them in dialogue about their performance had on production.

McGregor's work in the 1960's with Theory X and Theory Y helped us to think that maybe we needed to look at the relationship between leader and follower. We began to link leadership behaviors with expected performance results. Edward Deming's work in Japan, long since prominent in the United States and utilized by school districts (TQM), informed us about the process that promotes quality products via quality performance. Deming's 14 principles shed light on many key leadership strategies such as creating ownership among the workers in the organization and the process of continual learning. The early work of James McGregor Burns in transformational leadership still holds a prominent place in the study of leadership. The "transformational leader" aims to develop others in the organization to reach their full capacity so that everyone is functioning at optimal performance.[14]

But how does the leader motivate others to work at their best capacity? Almost a century has passed since the classic study by Lewin, Lippit and White which looked at the impact different styles of adult leadership, democratic, laissez faire or authoritative, had on the performance and behavior of children in the classroom.[15] Years and numerous studies later we find that there is a time and a place for every style. Hersey and Blanchard's work in Situational Leadership informed us that varying one's leadership style based on the needs of the follower's readiness and ability levels would produce more effective, long lasting results. When the leader knows his staff, he can determine the most appropriate leadership style to assure higher performance.[16]

In the recent book, *Primal Leadership*, Goleman, Boyatzis and McKee revisited the critical aspects of leadership styles. Of the six styles that describe leaders, four of these styles visionary, coaching, affiliative and democratic directly increase performance. Two of the others, while sometimes useful, were found to hinder performance-pacesetting and commanding. These findings are based on a study, conducted by the HayGroup, of almost 4,000 executives from a variety of fields across the globe. What is particularly compelling about these findings is that leaders who used styles with a positive emotional impact experienced better financial returns than those who did not. The leader's positive leadership style impacted the climate of the organization and ultimately their performance. Of all the styles, one stood out to produce the top results, the visionary style.[17] The visionary leader:

> *Articulates where a group is going, sets people free to innovate, experiment and take calculated risks. They know the big picture and how a given job fits in and the sense that everyone is working toward shared goals builds team commitment: People feel pride in belonging to their organization. [A visionary leader] gives people clarity; they understand what's expected of them.*

For a moment, think of a leader who served as a mentor for you somewhere along your professional growth path. What qualities did this person possess? What did that leader do to help you (a) want to develop in certain areas, (b) guide you along the way, (c) provide you with strategies, skills and the feedback that you needed, and (d) let go when you no longer needed their assistance? Now, think for a moment about your staff. Concentrate on one person in particular whom you may be working to develop. What seems to be working? What presents a challenge? Put yourself in the shoes of this person. What might this person be thinking about the quality of your assistance? What might be needed that you aren't doing? Ask the person to share his thoughts. You just might find out helpful information that will encourage you to use a different approach and a different style of interaction.

Let's return to the three principals we met in Chapter Four, Ellen, Donald and John. What styles did they use to lead the changes in their schools? What can we learn from their experiences that might help us refine our own skills? Jim and I used the Hersey and Blanchard LEAD 360 assessment tool to get answers to these questions.[18]

Ellen

Our first impression of Ellen, a two-year principal at the time of this study, was that she was observant, warm and a very "take-charge" leader. Ellen indicated that her leadership style was more collaborative and participatory and that she saw herself more as a facilitator than a manager or a visionary leader. She says, "I think one of the things that I do best is listen. I'm capable of listening to people and not being judgmental. If I want to be judgmental I'll stop myself and say, 'Forget this, you're really out of the court.' . . . You have to take a step back, and think about what you are going to say to [people]. It's a real hard thing to do." When asked to describe Ellen's leadership qualities, her teachers chime in, "She's fair. She involves everyone in decisions but makes the final decision when necessary. She delegates. And, she knows instruction."

One veteran teacher speaks about Ellen's ability to rekindle her interest in teaching. Ellen pulled her out of the classroom and put her in a teacher leadership position. With tears in her eyes the teacher shared, "It was her belief in me that caused me not to retire." The two other teachers agreed that Ellen encourages each and every one of her staff members to find their own strengths. Ellen is on her way to becoming a transformational leader. She brings the best out in her people.

The Hersey and Blanchard LEAD 360-degree Situational Leadership assessment confirmed Ellen's self-analysis. Ellen's predominant style is that of *selling,* a style often effectively used with staff members who are unable (unskilled) but willing or confident to learn. These folks need lots of professional development opportunities and encouragement from the leader. Ellen's secondary style is *participating,* a style used with followers who are able (skilled) but lacking in maturity. We use this style with those who are unwilling or insecure about learning. These staff members are capable of running with an innovation but they need encouragement and support to take leadership. Ellen is aware that her staff members are at different levels of readiness and ability to learn. She uses various strategies to get them involved and provide support.

Ellen spends her days modeling and providing teachers with opportunities for instructional growth. She has had to create a desire for them to *want* to do this. She even started a Collaborative Teaching Model for new teachers last year. This year 20 teachers were involved in this weekly lunchtime sharing of ideas and strategies. Ellen doesn't consciously adjust her leadership style. She recognizes, however, that she has to do this to get good results. Goleman, Boyatzis and McKee might define her style as affiliative or democratic. Although she doesn't really see herself in this way, we think she is certainly on the road to becoming a visionary leader.

Donald

Donald, whose style is mostly facilitative in a system that wants him to be more top-down, shares the following, "Given the traditional structure of the public school system, truly democratic schools may be rare, at best . . . They want me to make the decisions here. They just aren't used to taking the lead."

Donald defined himself as an active listener who used win-win negotiation, mediation, team building, community building, coaching, facilitating interaction meetings and prejudice reduction. He considered himself to have a high problem-solving ability especially with controversial issues and dealing with emotional trauma. He tells us, "Leaders need to know and be sensitive to the elements and implications of conflict resolution. They have to become aware of how their behavior facilitates positive or negative conflict. They need to know how to get past no."

Based on the data from the Situational Leadership analysis, Donald is a participatory leader. Folks who loved being included by Donald saw him as facilitative, a listener, supportive and comforting. Those who needed coaching received it. Donald delegates appropriately to staff members who are willing and able to take on new challenges. His shortcomings were that he tried to be participatory with folks who wanted him to just delegate. They saw him as patronizing them and not trusting them. Donald also incorrectly used his participatory approach with staff members who weren't willing or able to accomplish his objectives. These folks needed more direct leadership. He spent time rewarding them in the hope that they would improve. Instead, this kept them somewhat dependent on him and only fostered more non-performance.

Donald believes that all staff members have the ability to make their own decisions. He says, "I ask them how they want to see something resolved. I try to find a common issue, resolve it or deal with the discipline. But it doesn't always work this way. Staff members want him to make more decisions. One teacher says, "I would like to see a tight, structured school. You know, consistency and consequences." But another teacher says, "He is caring and gentle. He can listen. He takes no offense to criticism."

By year three of our study, Donald reflects, "I think I have to be more directive when there are situations that are not going exactly the right way. But for those who are working and doing what they are supposed to be doing I treat them the same. When a problem comes up and they haven't resolved it on their own and it blows up, I have to take the rein. That's all there is to it." Donald who is usually more facilitative is learning to be more directive in certain situations. No matter how skilled he is, sometimes others aren't. At times, he needs to step out of his comfort zone and use another approach to spark their learning. In *Primal Leadership* terms, we see Donald as a democratic and affiliative leader who is learning to vary his style over time.

John

Our third leader, John sees himself as mostly an organizational manager and in some respects a visionary. In making school decisions he likes to get input from people and then make the final decision. On certain issues, however, such as safety, school procedures and communications between teachers and parents, John used a direct, telling style. On instructional issues in the classroom, he defers to his teachers' strengths.

John's teachers perceived his leadership in similar ways but they emphasized his participatory style more than his direct style. They reported that he is open to their ideas, that he takes times to listen to different perspectives and that he is very generous with support. John has an open door policy. On the LEAD 360 instrument, John scored highest in two situational leadership styles, participatory and selling. Clearly, John is a fixer. He uses the selling style in the hope to fix everyone, get him or her to learn. He does engage in telling, or as he calls it "demanding" behavior and he tends not to delegate. John is more like our affiliative and democratic leader. He uses a commanding style as well and has been consciously reflecting on ways to incorporate other styles, as needed.

Our study results also taught us that the principals, like many managers, tend to use a style of leadership that is most comfortable to them rather than using the style of leadership that might promote better performance by those they lead. While all three principals saw themselves as participatory in nature we found that over the three years they spent more time selling or trying to get buy in for one program or another. Constant federal, state and local mandates were being imposed on them and propelled them to juggle multiple balls. Like Peter, our high school principal, whom we met in the beginning of this chapter, these three elementary school principals have adapted a style that seems to work for them.

While most principals had moderate style adaptability, none of them were experts at modifying their leadership style based on the needs of the constituents. In other words, they used the same leadership approaches with the new teacher who was just learning how to teach effectively as they did with the seasoned teacher who was a master teacher. All principals, some more than others, would benefit from learning ways to adapt their style, which might, ultimately, enhance implementation of any innovation. Of course, if we want principals to do this, we have to provide them with opportunities to be reflective about themselves and their staffs. Plagued by daily managerial dilemmas these principals, like so many others, pushed forward and mostly used a style they were comfortable with in the hope that people would come along.

Interestingly enough, these principals' results are no different than the majority of results found for leaders in a variety of fields across North America.[19] While CEOs predominately use style four (delegating) and style one (directing), middle managers such as school principals mostly use style two (selling) and style three (participatory). Principals are constantly trying to move people to a readiness place so that they can delegate to them. But the question remains, "to whom will they delegate?" Unlike CEO's in the corporate world, schools are not structured in a way such that administrative teams can be delegated to easily.

As you continue on your leadership path, think about the style you are using with others. Ask a colleague to give you feedback. Ask the question, "Could I have done it differently?" Seek to understand who needs more guidance and who can be counted on to get the job done with little direction. Take the Emotional Competency Inventory (ECI) to assess your emotional intelligence. Look into other leadership inventories that will provide you will data for your own improvement. Chart a course for your personal development and help others develop theirs. One simple rule of thumb is the following: At the end of the day, when you finally get that hour alone, take out your journal and think about the people you interacted with today. "What did you say? What did they say and do? What promoted their performance? What can you do differently tomorrow?"

Lessons Learned in Implementing Change

As you move your vision into reality you will need to draw upon a number of your EQ leadership competencies. Be adaptable. If you are too comfortable with your style, it could be that you need to force yourself to be a little uncomfortable. This could really help you to provide better leadership for someone who needs a different style than you are accustomed to use. Be aware of the personal resources you have to draw on. Defer to others who have the skills that you don't. Be willing to put your vision on hold at times until others can embrace it. Learn about what motivates others to want to change.

My colleague, Tony, who led the search committee that hired me reminds me, "We hired you because your style is so different from mine. I didn't want to hire somebody just like me. That wouldn't help the program!" At first I was shocked. But he was right. We balance each other so well; each of us is good at what the other is not. So, we have to have the self-awareness to know who we are and what we can and can't do, and the willingness and humility to seek out what will better the organization. This may entail individual change and letting go of certain long held beliefs and actions. You have to be adaptable and willing to grow. Leaders have to make a "commitment to the truth," as Senge puts it, and ask the question, "How do I change my underlying beliefs?"[20] Then the leader has to model these beliefs and inspire and motivate others to join him on this path.

Leaders of change have to know that their way of doing things isn't always the best way to get things done. I can still remember the mistakes I made when I was trying to make a difference in the rate of student discipline and behavior problems at my middle school. I was unstoppable. I was determined to really change my 1500 student body such that every child would receive conflict resolution and every teacher would *want* to teach the lessons. Boy was I surprised when I discovered that some folks were *never* going to teach them, didn't believe that young people should learn how to resolve conflict and were even bad mouthing me to their friends! I tried everything including teaching the lessons myself in the hope that they would model. Fat chance. They were correcting their lesson plans while I was teaching for them.

I learned a lot since those times, from my colleagues and friends. My dear friend, Arthur Foresta, Director of The New Visions Principal Mentoring Program in New York

City, and former principal of a democratic school, is a great example of EQ at its best. In speaking of changing his school culture he shares,

> Even though I wanted a democratic school where we were all working collectively towards the goal, I still wanted it my way; it took a lot for me to step back and let the staff do it their way instead of mine. Eventually, they did come around to my vision, but it took a few years longer than I wanted it to. That was hard, but the change was lasting.[21]

Another critical component of implementing change is knowing something about what motivates others to learn. While the goal is to get folks to a place of readiness for self-directed learning, the path from here to there is not so simple. Once you have an understanding of how and why people make the choices they do you have a better chance of influencing them to change.

LEADERS AS MOTIVATORS

The school leader is the primary person responsible for motivating the adults in the organization to perform optimally on the job. At every school, we all know those staff members whom we just can't seem to bring on board. For one reason or another, they don't want to be a team player. There are others, who are motivated but need so much instructional support. No matter what you try, you just don't see the improvement happening.

Historically, psychologists and organizational behaviorists have delved into the human psyche to discover what mechanisms motivate some individuals and some groups to be more successful than others. We have learned a lot about ways to motivate others from theorists such as Maslow whose hierarchy of needs postulated in the 1950's continues to guide us in considering people's human motivations. We know that people need to have food on the table, heat in the winter and a place to live before we can expect them to perform their best on a job. We also recognize that we all have the human need to self-actualize, to maximize our potential and to be something in the grand scheme of the world we live in. This drive compels many of us forward to reach our highest potential.[22]

The ongoing debate exists in education as to the benefits of intrinsic and extrinsic motivation to motivate children to achieve. That same debate exists in the field of management. Frederick Herzberg's early work with motivators and hygiene factors informed us that while hygiene factors such as pay, schedules, and work conditions are important, they will pale in relation to motivators such as a personal sense of accomplishment, increased responsibility and factors that promote personal growth and development. Sadly enough, while Herzberg popularized his theory in the 1950's and 60's, many organizational systems today, including education, still use praise and punishment. They dangle tangible job rewards such as bonuses and pay increases to produce job satisfaction. These strategies may get folks to accept the job, but do they get higher performance? Herzberg thinks not, and we agree with him.[23]

Traditionally, schools have been structured in ways that have attempted to motivate employees as well as children through rewards and punishment (extrinsic motivation). We know, through years of motivation studies, that it is through intrinsic motivation that we get the most long lasting performance results. While not considered a major motivational theory, Glasser's Control Theory has been helpful to teachers in motivating their children. It can also help leaders understand the needs of adults. Glasser's Control Theory helps adults see that the only way we can really evoke change in others is to help them recognize they are being driven by their own internal system. Each individual alone has real control over his own actions. Everything we do in life is purposeful. We try to fulfill basic needs such as the need to survive, the need to belong, the need to gain power, the need to be free and the need to have fun.[24]

I can recall a time when a staff member at my school was furious because a student had drawn a picture of her on top of his paper during class. Needless to say, the picture was not too kind. Howe had painted the teacher as a rather plump woman with horns! The teacher wanted Howe punished. She wanted me to throw the book at him. Truthfully, I was at a loss. "Okay, he had been disrespectful, but seventh grade boys can sometimes be that way, not grounds for suspension." When I met with the staff member I confronted her. "What was really going on here? Was this about Howe or was this about you?" In the end, she admitted that she was embarrassed, hurt and angry. Her need for survival had been threatened. She was also clearly in a power struggle with Howe. She was overweight and was feeling insecure about this. Following our discussion, the staff member had a private discussion with Howe during which time she explained how his actions made her feel. He apologized and the relationship was healed. From this moment on, this wonderful teacher was more aware of her own emotional hijacking and used her emotional self-control and conflict management skills to handle conflict situations with her students.

Based on sixteen years of research on intrinsic motivation, organizational psychologist Kenneth Thomas, has found that people are motivated to self manage their work because of four sets of intrinsic rewards.[25] They make emotional judgments about their work involvement based on the following motivators:

- A Sense of Meaningfulness: You sense that this work will be worth your time and energy and that the purpose of your efforts has meaning in the larger scheme of things.
- A Sense of Choice: You feel that you have some choice in how and when the work is done and that you can use your own judgment to act upon your own understanding of the work.
- A Sense of Competence: You sense that you are doing well in the accomplishment of the work.
- A Sense of Progress: You feel that the work is moving forward and you can tell that your efforts are meeting with success.

But how do school leaders promote these motivators in their schools? They motivate by encouraging all members of the school community to reflect on the value of what they do. They motivate by insuring that all have opportunities for exercising self-initiative and challenging work. They motivate by making it safe for feedback and self-assessment. They motivate by calling upon all to be cheerleaders for one another. Finally, they motivate by calling upon their own power of self-motivation.

The kind of motivation we are talking about is not an easy task, especially in schools that have traditionally used top down evaluation models to determine performance. District-driven evaluation checklists often still rate teachers' effectiveness in the classroom. Dialogue about performance is kept to a minimum. In fact, the entire process of teacher performance evaluation is often adversarial in nature. Teachers fear the evaluation process. Administrators feel their hands are tied because of union protections. This kind of process often depletes rather than builds. Using a performance driven approach doesn't get leaders the mileage they need. They ask the staff member to conform to the leader's vision of ideal performance instead of what the staff member's vision is of his ideal teaching performance.

Goleman, Boyatzis and McKee take another approach to motivation. They see real sustainable change as that which is prompted by one's own desire to change along with one's own performance plan for self-change. In Chapter Three, Jim shared "the five discoveries" of the self-directed learning model proposed by Boyatzis. These are designed to help an individual with the process of self-change. Using a self directed approach, the motivation to change comes from seeing the gap between one's ideal and real self. The developmental work is focused on bridging the gap between the two.

Self-directed learning is derived from the work of the late Harvard psychologist, David McClelland, whose life work focused on studying motivation based on achievement drive. McClelland believed that the need to achieve is a distinct human motive that could be distinguished from other human motives. Achievement-oriented people, according to McClelland, are driven by their own personal achievement, more than reward or success. They get their "high" from solving difficult problems. These folks like constructive criticism because it helps them perform better. These types thrive on thinking of a better solution and better ways of doing things. These risk takers don't gamble; instead they plan calculated risks. They are realistic about what they can and cannot do. McClelland believed that one could promote performance through identification with these achievement-oriented competencies exhibited by top executives, those designated as the best and the brightest. His thinking was that an organization should either select people who exhibited these competencies or help others to develop them.[26]

At the Weatherhead School of Management at Case Western Reserve University, Richard Boyatzis put McClelland's work into practice.[27]

After several weeks of assessment, feedback, and reflection, the students in Weatherhead's MBA program list their personal and career goals. Then, the instructors help them to break the goals into sub goals and action steps. They challenge the students to provide a rationale for each goal and to indicate how they and others will be able to tell when they have accomplished it. Students ultimately must state their goals in terms of an outcome that is specific and concrete, personally meaningful, affirmatively stated, realistic and tied to a time frame.

Boyatzis began working with EI competency development in the late 80's. In speaking of Boyatzis' work, Cary Cherniss and Dan Goleman share,

A series of longitudinal studies under way at the Weatherhead School of Management of Case Western Reserve University has shown that over two to five years people can change on these competencies. MBA students averaging twenty-seven years old at entry into the program, showed dramatic changes on videotaped and audio taped behavioral samples and questionnaire measures of these competencies. In the graduating classes of 1992-95 there was a statistically significant improvement on 71% (five out of seven) of the competencies in the Self-Management cluster, 100% of the competencies in the Social Awareness cluster and 50% of the competencies in the Social Skills or Relationship Management cluster.[28]

Developing Others

If you have made mistakes . . . there is always another chance for you. You may have a fresh start at any moment you choose, for this thing we call "failure" is not the falling down, but the staying down.

—Mary Pickford

In trying to motivate others to engage in self-directed learning we need to create safe environments where a learning agenda can be set between staff member and leader. It would be wonderful if your staff could use a tool such as the Emotional Competency Inventory. Gaining their 360-degree feedback results of their emotional competencies could help them set their EI learning goal with you, along with their instructional goals. Goleman, Boyatzis and Mckee tell us that in order to help people change long time embedded habits they need to (a) bring bad habits into awareness; (b) consciously practice a better way; and (c) rehearse the new behavior until it becomes automatic. Your job, as leader, is to model this same emotionally intelligent behavior and then to provide coaching experiences for your staff members. In schools today, we have finally embraced the need for teachers to have mentors to help them with instructional practices. We also need to provide mentors to develop their EI competencies. In the long run, improving their emotional intelligence will result in their improved performance. Ultimately, the children will reap the benefits.

As you reflect on your leadership, have you set up conditions that enable people to make choices and develop trust? Can they exercise initiative and creativity? Do they have the information and resources they need to "own" their work? Do you provide the learning opportunities, feedback, and appropriate level of challenge that will help your people to feel competent? Are there methods in place to set goals, assess progress in significant ways, solve problems when obstacles appear, and celebrate successes?

A great source to consider when thinking about ways to inspire and motivate your staff, is the guidelines for learners from The American Psychological Association.[29] These principles hold fast for both young learners and adults alike, whether we are talking about promoting knowledge, skills or attitudinal changes. They take into consideration metacognitive, cognitive and affective principles of learning. Do you remember what Peter said at the beginning of this chapter? He felt as if he were the parent for each member of his staff, a role he didn't bargain for but, nevertheless, embraced. Peter could be helped by gaining some skills in developing some of the folks who appear to be exhausting him in the opening scenario. Let's look at an example of how Peter, and you, could use the competency of "developing others" in the daily life of the school. Shanda, an instructionally strong third grade teacher, continuously raves about how well her students are doing on the standardized tests and every test, for that matter. True, she is very good at pedagogy and particularly gifted in teaching literacy. As principal, you are ecstatic with the outcomes you see in her children, however, not so her teaching colleagues. Shanda's assured nature and high performance intimidates the others who feel incompetent, unfavored and even fearful that their children do not do as well. You would love to be able to use Shanda as a staff developer so that others could learn some of her strategies, but she is not liked or respected by others. At meetings, whenever Shanda speaks up, eyes and heads roll. So what do you do?

First, how would you define the problem? Clearly, there are several problem areas in this scenario. Shanda, while an excellent classroom teacher, lacks an awareness of social cues and the importance of teamwork and collaboration. In general, her relationship management skills need work. The "other" teachers are also problematic. They probably need some strong mentoring in instructional pedagogy and maybe even content. They lack self-confidence and the self management skills needed to improve themselves so as not be offended by Shanda's behaviors. But, for our purposes, let's focus on Shanda's development.

Many leaders would probably avoid the problem with Shanda by not addressing it and letting the chips fall where they may. Others might tell Shanda that she needs to "watch her talk because others are getting jealous." They might tell the "others" something like, "Oh, that's how Shanda is. She doesn't mean anything by it." They might say something more aggressive like, "Why don't you grow up and learn something from her?" A great way to put fuel on the fire and add to the dysfunction that already exits at this school!

The emotionally intelligent leader recognizes that everyone in this scenario needs development. The leader sets a plan to address this and provide opportunities for growth

TABLE 6.1   American Psychological Association Learning Principles

The learning of complex subject matter is most effective when it is an intentional process of constructing meaning from information and experience.
The successful learner, over time and with support and instructional guidance, can create meaningful coherent representations of knowledge.
The successful learner can link new information with existing knowledge in meaningful ways.
The successful learner can create and use a repertoire of thinking and reasoning strategies to achieve complex learning goals.
Higher order strategies for selecting and monitoring mental operations facilitate creative and critical thinking.
Learning is influenced by environmental factors including culture, technology, and instructional practices.
What and how much is learned is influenced by the learner's motivation. Motivation to learn, in turn, is influenced by the individuals emotional states, beliefs, interests and goals, and habits of thinking.
The learner's creativity, higher order thinking, and natural curiosity all contribute to motivation to learn. Intrinsic motivation is stimulated by tasks of optimal novelty and difficulty, relevant to personal interests, and providing for personal choice and control.
Acquisition of complex knowledge and skills requires extended learner effort and guided practice. Without learners' motivation to learn, the willingness to exert this effort is unlikely without coercion.
As individuals develop, there are different opportunities and constraints for learning. Learning is most effective when differential development within and across physical, intellectual, emotional, and social domains is taken into account.
Learning is influenced by social interactions, interpersonal relations, and communication with others.
Learners have different strategies, approaches, and capabilities for learning that are a function of prior experience and heredity.
Learning is most effective when differences in learners' linguistic, cultural, and social backgrounds are taken into account.
Selling appropriately high and challenging standards and assessing the learner as well as learning progress—including diagnostic, process, and outcome assessment—are integral parts of the learning process.

with Shanda and the "others" in most need. Shanda may be unaware of her effect on others and even the fact that she has great potential for leadership. In conversation with her, you both might agree that she work on her "teamwork" skills and her need to share her accomplishments with others. Shanda also needs to pick up on social cues. Her "accurate self-assessment" is probably out of whack. You might help her to display more "empathy" in meetings by asking clarifying questions to gain more information about "others" needs, rather than just spouting off what "she" does to get improved instruction. You could encourage Shanda to attend training in communication or diversity skill awareness so that she improves her own skills. Finally, you might ask Shanda to keep a journal of her interactions with others at meetings and in other settings, over a several week period of time. You could then meet with her to ask her to share her awareness with you. As you begin to see change, you might assign her to mentor one other teacher who is willing to work with Shanda. In this way, she could begin to learn how to better collaborate, while she provides teaching expertise to another, her area of strength.

You are probably saying to yourself, "Alright, I can do this with Shanda, but I can't do this with everyone in the school. They all have their issues!" Right. You are not a personal therapist nor are you a pastor or spiritual leader. But, you are the school's leader. And when *you* become transparent enough so that your staff sees and understands *your* objective-that everyone be the best that they can be-others will be more willing to acknowledge their limitations and work at improving them.

Self-Efficacy Revisited

Remember our earlier discussion about self-efficacy? Bandura tells us "perceived self-efficacy is defined as peoples' beliefs about their capabilities to produce designated levels of performance that exercise influence over events that affect their lives." Staff members with heightened self-efficacy will be able to take on more difficult tasks and challenges and rise above them. Conversely, those who are riddled in self-talk about their personal limitations will be very reluctant to take on new challenges. Bandura provides us with some development tools to increase self-efficacy. These include guided mastery experiences, instructive social models and effective social persuasion with successive reinforcers.[30]

Mastery experiences allow staff members to feel as if they have gained a sense of control over their perceived abilities. As educators, we learned to do this early on with children. For a low-performing child we provide one-on-one tutoring and peer mentoring. We assign leadership roles and employ a multitude of other strategies that help the child build his competencies and belief in his ability. The same is true for staff members with low self-efficacy. With these employees we need to first establish a relationship of trust. Then we need to provide clear directives and examples that they can follow. Steps need to be simple and repeatable. Feedback and support will increase the desire to try new strategies.

Earlier we spoke about the critical nature of modeling and learning from observation. In developing efficacy for new teachers, provide them with excellent role models such as a master teacher. Create that "coaching" relationship. While modeling by observation is fruitful, the teacher as learner needs guided practice to try out these new strategies. The teacher also requires immediate supportive feedback. These opportunities need to be consistent and long-term for success to occur. Bandura calls this "resiliency through practice." What about the reluctant, jaded, seasoned teacher who is low in self-belief? Same thing. The difficulty here is to find a place of willingness to learn. Maybe you can set up opportunities for him to work with a trusted colleague who is moving forward and developing strength. You could have him attend a conference or training program. You might even provide opportunities for this person to serve as a mentor in an area of strength. Perhaps, you might even need to change *your* leadership style to work with him.

Next, perhaps the simplest venue we can utilize is that of "social persuasion." An honest display of confidence can go a long way with staff members who lack belief in their own abilities. Support them by setting up as many opportunities for success as possible so they can affirm their belief in self. Finally, remember that groups demonstrate collective efficacy too. The more your staff members believe they are valued, the more they will work collectively towards their goals.

As you strive to develop the knowledge, skills and dispositions of the people you work with, take a good look at each and every one of them. Talk to them about their needs. Design a growth plan that is specific to each of them. The word will get out that your organization is focused on self-directed learning. So, be sure that, as leader, you model this for everyone else.

Inspiration and Influence

There's no way around it. In order to catalyze change, a leader has to be an expert at inspiring and influencing others. Goleman reminds us that leadership is the ability to articulate and arouse enthusiasm for a shared vision and mission. He says, "Step forward to lead as needed, regardless of position; guide the performance of others while holding them accountable; and, lead by example."[31] "Forcing" change upon others just doesn't work. You'll get what you want in the short run, but the changes will show only on the surface. This is often a challenge to the school administrator because the daily demands take up so much of the job and accountability is so high. Yet, we need to remember that "the leader is the key source of the organization's emotional tone. The excitement emanating from a leader can move an entire group in that direction."[32] So much of the job of the school leader is about relationship management, inspiring, influencing and developing others. Remember Peter's story? Not a minute of his day was about paper-pushing. It was all about interactions with others.

Think about any great leader who has inspired you. Sometimes we talk about their gifts as charisma. Inspiration, however, does not require charisma, although this person may have that quality as well. It's that passion and commitment to their belief that draws others. In our business of education who would argue with someone who models a belief in what is right for children? Someone who accomplishes this not by dictating or commanding, but by *living* that belief? The great ones, Ghandi, Martin Luther King and Mother Theresa are our best examples of this *servant leadership*. But there are many others right there among you who possess these same characteristics in varying degrees. These are the folks with that twinkle in their eyes, with a positive solution for every challenge who have a respect for human dignity and individual worth. These are the ones that others like being around and who adults and children alike trust and respect.

I can still remember listening to the conversations with Debbie Meier, educator, author and McArthur Fellow while "cabbing" to school in the early 70's. It was Debbie's belief and drive that began the first elementary school that led to the establishment of many high performing alternative schools of choice in District 4, Manhattan. Debbie talked incessantly about what she envisioned for Central Park East Elementary School, the challenges she faced and the steps she was taking to change this school around. As a young teacher, I was privy to these powerful conversations. I saw, heard and felt her passion. Those critical moments inspired me so intensely that they continue to drive my personal vision about education today. I doubt Debbie realized the impact she was having on me in those moments. She was then and continues to be an inspirational leader for educators across our nation and world.[33]

Can we learn how to inspire and influence others to follow the vision we know is intuitively right for our schools? It begins with awareness and it happens with action. Above all, it has to be part of who you are and what you believe in. As a school leader, you have to believe your vision is attainable, and that you have the ability to make a difference in the lives of young people. Knowledge of motivation theory and how adults learn are helpful tools to take on this journey. Maybe you need to do some reading about self-directed learning, adult learning theory, or organizational politics. Perhaps you haven't read anything about the change process in awhile. Buy a book. Go to a seminar. Do some of the exercises in this book. Self-renewal on all levels is a critical part of the process. If I'm not good to me, I can't be there for anybody else.

SUSTAINING CHANGE IN SELF AND OTHERS

We need to look at this process of change as a dual process, one of developing self and developing others. Critical to your leadership is your ability to be reflective throughout the process and willing to learn, grow, adapt and try something new. It's not okay to just want others to do this. You have to use every ounce of your emotional intelligence to lead people to their desired change. The best and most lasting changes that occur are those that help people transform themselves. I always tell my students, "Unless you can look in the mirror and see your own flaws, you aren't ready to be a leader." Without this, the change cannot be sustained.

In the research Jim and I did with principals, it became clear that all eyes were on the leader. If the leader believed in the change and modeled it, the culture of the school reflected or was in the process of mirroring the desired change. If the principal had little or no clue about how the change was being implemented, than the culture did not reflect the change. Some leaders will spend a lot of time creating the vision, building consensus and adopting a new curriculum, or teaching method. But then when it comes to the painstaking task of implementing the change, they drop the ball. When this happens, the intended change paradigm falls short. Too often, leaders trust that teachers will continue to develop the new tools on their own. Teachers will often attend an initial professional development session, receive their materials but may never pick up the materials again. With any new innovation, teachers need ongoing support, check-ins and study teams to talk about the new learning and build confidence and expertise. But, time, money, and, too often, poor leadership allows these opportunities for growth to fail. The leader as change agent, needs to have the vision, the ability to develop that vision and the ongoing commitment and strategies to enforce the implementation of that vision. If they can't, they need to appoint someone else who they know will carry the change forward for them.

On the other hand, you don't want to breathe all over the implemented change. Michael Fullan, says, "Living on the edge of chaos means getting used to a certain degree of uncertainty."[34] You can't micromanage a change. You'll die wanting it to happen your way and the change will die with you. Trust that you've done your job. The goal is to insure that the change will survive long after you may be gone. So, let it develop with the organization's flair and creativity. And of course, expect conflict. Change doesn't happen in a neat little package. You would be a pretty scary leader if the change you wanted looked exactly the way you envisioned. Allow diversity to embellish, squish, and reframe some of the initial design. Remember the adage that conflict brings opportunities for growth and change. Be surprised. Step back. Being a parent to change will cause more resistance than you can imagine. As Meg Wheatley says, "If you're interested in creating sustainable growth, sustainable productivity, sustainable morale, you can't do that through autocracy. . . . If you're trying to create a healthy organization, one that can sustain itself over time, simply legislating and dictating behavior and outcomes doesn't work at all."[35]

Finally, we would be remiss if we did not spend a moment recognizing that life in and of itself is a constant change process. People are consistently being put upon by every force there is to rethink, rework and reclaim themselves in the midst of turbulent times. People can be very fragile and even frightened when too much change forces them out of a comfort zone. Honor their process. We force change down people's throats today without giving them a chance to breathe. If it's harming children, then by all means, charge ahead. If not, take a deep breath and remain optimistic that all of your efforts will eventually take hold.

SUMMARY

In this chapter, we looked at the people side of school leaders and of those they hope will embrace the changes they champion. We recognized that central to being catalysts for changes are the EI competencies that support us as we lead the way. Leaders of change like master magicians often need another "mesmerizing card game," another "tool in the tool chest," to convince their audience and hold their attention. They know exactly what steps to take to inspire and influence their constituencies. But unlike the magic show that beckons us on through dazzlement and surprise, the leader of school change inspires and influences by guiding others every step of the way. EQ leaders not only show their own vulnerability but they support and develop others who may be uneasy or even fearful of change. The change we want in others requires an open heart, a transparent and ethical way of being, and a clearly defined picture of the future that leaders see for the young people they serve. The words of John Lennon and Paul McCartney say it best:

REFLECTIVE QUESTIONS

1. How do you handle change? Do you go with the flow? Are you adaptable? Does it take time for you to shift your position? What helps?
2. The situational leadership model describes our predominant styles as telling, selling, participating or delegating? How would you describe your predominant style? Are you able to adjust your leadership style according to the needs of others?
3. Are you able to recognize resistance in others? How do you handle their resistance?
4. Lots of leaders can lead but fewer leaders have the gift of helping others to develop and grow. Does this come easily for you, or is it difficult? What are the ways that you try to develop others? What strategies do you use?
5. Think of a leader who inspired you. What about that leader inspired you? What effect did this leader have on your life?

LESSON FROM THE FIELD

Rene Townsend

Our Board of Education gave us a mandate to change all 13 elementary and three middle schools from traditional to multi-track, year-round education calendars—and to do it in just over one year. We had been building a school a year, but simply could not keep up with the number of new youngsters coming to our district. As a result, our Board directed staff to create a new approach to "housing" students. With no money beyond the current building program, our options were limited, so we offered various versions of multi-track, year-round calendars from which the board selected one. We needed a minimum of two years to implement this enormous change. The Board gave us one. How would we ever do this in a quality way? But upon reflection, I knew there was no choice. Our students simply needed more space.

Thinking about the multiple tasks we needed to complete was overwhelming. Quite frankly, I had some moments of quiet panic. Not only was I worried about my own ability to lead people through this change, I was concerned about the workload I would ask of an already over-extended leadership team at the district office and at each school. I had no choice but to draw on my inner strength, stay focused on the students and staff I served, and meet the expectations of my employer. The fact was, board members were sensitive to what they were asking, but they wanted students in better conditions as quickly as possible—and, so did I.

I rose to the task and knew my fellow educators would too. We always found a way to do what must be done. I believed that we had two major considerations: how to frame the task to fully engage all stakeholders, and how to communicate effectively and efficiently throughout the process. I had been superintendent for two years at the time this change came. We had established a culture that was positive and trusting, but this would test it. Perhaps it was naïve, but I thought I might be able to use this challenge to strengthen our team and the culture.

FRAMING THE TASK

Our calendar change could have been viewed as a purely mechanical task. After all, we were moving teachers, students, furniture, bus, maintenance, food schedules and more. But while the mechanical things were driving us, we were working with people, both big and little. I constantly reminded myself and others that education is about dealing with the mind and heart, not "things."

I knew that we could buckle under the pressure because of the size and demands of this job, or we could use it as an opportunity to analyze systems in all areas of our district through a new lens. When confronting new challenges we can sigh and wonder how we will get it all done, or we can frame the challenge in ways that appeal to our higher selves and lift people up to do their best work.

We thought about the district's basic mission first—that of educating our students to high standards. So, we approached this system from a student-oriented point of view, that is, "If we are going to have to do things differently, how can we do them better so that students will benefit?" The defining question we asked of others and ourselves about every potential decision was, "What will be best for our students?" Adults often make decisions that meet their needs, not because they are selfish, but because change creates anxiety. I knew that if we could reduce the sense of risk we could break through resistance. We looked for the least radical options available. Big challenges mean stepping way outside our comfort zone and staying focused on the impact on students.

COMMUNICATION

Converting our schools to this new multi-track, year round system was, in essence, creating three schools out of each existing school. It meant setting up new structures and systems. We needed a variety of advisory committees each representing all stakeholders. The first thing was to gather the leadership team together along with leaders of our employee associations and parent leaders. We invited their suggestions about the committee structure they thought would work and then about who should be on each committee. We ran articles in school newsletters and the local newspaper, inviting community members who were interested to call and join us. Although we didn't get much response from the general community, the few who responded made wonderful contributions. They viewed the fact that we had asked positively. To ensure a full range of views, we encouraged "critics" to join the committees; often those who are opposed offer important insights that might not have been considered otherwise.

As each committee began their work, I met with them to share our focus on students and clarify their task and timeline. I shared with them our charge: every recommended change had to explicitly spell out how it would be the best one for our students. All were reminded of the importance of their role as key communicators to all their constituents. Word of mouth as well as written communication was critical to success of the process.

We made communication of each group's progress a priority and a way to keep all of us positively headed in the same direction. In each piece of internal and external written communication, we highlighted facts, timelines, meeting dates, opportunities for input, decisions, and impacts on students and families. I modeled this through my own internal newsletter to staff, through a few columns for the local newspaper, and by offering to speak at community service clubs and organizations. We were committed to honest communication, not a "schmooze" job. Not every decision made the district better in educating our students. We openly informed staff, parents and the public about what we were able to do—and not do. Framing our task on what is best for students, and ensuring on-going internal and external communications, allowed us to accomplish a major change in an effective manner.

I was proud and sometimes just simply amazed at what we had accomplished. I felt good about framing the issue around what was most important and was humbled by the collective strength of the team in making it happen. In the final analysis, we made the shift smoothly, and never lost our focus on why we exist—for our students.

Dr. Rene Townsend is a partner in Leadership Associates, a superintendent search firm, an associate in the consulting firm, Innovative Strategies, and an instructor and coordinator in the Educational Leadership program at California State University, San Marcos. She is the former Superintendent of the Coronado and Vista Unified School Districts, both in San Diego County, California.

Chapter 7

The Purpose of School: Promoting Equity and Social Justice

It is often in the clash of irreconcilable ideas that we can learn how to test or revise ideas, or invent new ones.

—Deborah Meier, 1995

Not too long ago I (Janet) attended a powerful week-long institute offered by *Facing History and Ourselves,* a non-profit organization designed to provide middle and high school educators with content and curriculum that connects human behavior with the events of history.[1] This training broadened my awareness of the meaning of democracy. It opened my eyes to the inequities and tragedies that have historically devastated people who are different. It propelled me forward to be more of a voice for equity and social justice.

The Facing History pedagogical approach uses a case study to explore how a new democracy established after World War I in Germany collapsed and led to the rise of Hitler. Through factual stories grounded in historical events we learn how such evils as racism, anti-Semitism, homophobia, sexism and violence were allowed to happen then, and continue to be perpetrated in today's world. We learn how often members of a society, consciously or unconsciously, have oppressed others. Forty-eight years-old, at the time of this training, I had never really thought about the conditions that existed and allowed Hitler to rise, and wield such destructive power. Growing up as a white, middle-class woman in an all girls' Catholic school, I learned about Hitler and the genocide of the Jewish people. I was never taught anything about how the Holocaust came to be. I had never questioned why many nations of the world, including my home, the United States, had not acted immediately to stop Hitler in his tracks. I had not heard of the term *ethnic cleansing,* [a term that refers to the conscious annihilation of people thought to be inferior because of race, skin color, and other physical manifestation], nor could I imagine that the term would still hold meaning today in places such as Kosovo and Rwanda.[2]

I have long since recognized that I have been at an advantage because of my white skin color and the middle class status given to me by my second-generation, Italian-American father. My working class father labored in the *rag* business (as the manufacturing of women's clothing was called) to provide me with the gifts I have been given. I have never known poverty. I have never experienced hatred or been oppressed for my race, my ethnicity, my religion or my sexual orientation. Like too many women, however, I have been oppressed because of my gender. I have struggled to overcome inappropriate and at times violent male domination both personally and professionally.

As a lifelong educator, I have dedicated my work to making the world safer for our children. I continue to be committed to creating safe and caring schools. Such schools teach adults and children about the inequities and injustices that come with individual and institutional racism, sexism, heterosexism, and other forms of oppression. In my eyes, after parents, only the school possesses the incredible power to shape the body, minds, hearts and spirits of our youth. Increasingly, I recognize the critical role that I play. As an educator, I am able to break down stereotypes, challenge racist, classist and sexist attitudes. I can empower others to prepare our children to live lives that acknowledge and promote equal access for all human beings. As teachers and leaders, we have the opportunity and obligation to equip young people with the skills that prepare them to question the way things are and to challenge them with dignity and respect. For the good of humankind, our children need to be taught to care and participate in actions that promote the social well-being of not only their North American brothers and sisters, but also their global family. Our youth deserve to be informed early on about the paths to promoting equity and social justice. They need to be expected to be part of the solution to creating a just world.

While my early education grounded me in academics and taught me the value of caring for others, it did little to challenge me to become an active contributor to our society. It has been my critical questioning and search for understanding as an adult that has taught me to view the world through multiple lenses. Today's youth, are growing up in a multicultural world that *requires* them to have knowledge and skills to question, problem solve, listen to diverse perspectives, make decisions and act as socially responsible participants in our democracy.

This chapter explores the purpose of schools in a democracy. It asks you to rethink the question, "As an educational leader, what do I value?" "What do I want our children to take with them into the future?" What is the leader's role in developing a social conscience in our youth? It provides a perspective of what the teaching of social justice, equity and social responsibility looks like in today's schools. It acknowledges the imbalances of power that exist in our society and talks about ways to address these in schools. It asks you as an EQ leader to reflect on strategies for increasing empathy and intercultural sensitivity in all members of the school. Finally, it offers suggestions that will help a skilled community reach common ground during difficult times.

WHAT DID YOU LEARN AT SCHOOL TODAY?

Before you read any further, stop for a moment and ask yourself, "What do I most want young people to learn in schools today? Take a pencil and jot these ideas down, right here:

_____

_____

It might be interesting to inquire of others around you what they think young people should learn before you even read this chapter. When Jim and I ask this question across the nation to thousands of educators, the responses are unanimous. They include comments such as to respect self and others, to care, to believe in themselves, to honor diversity and to be self-motivated. Equally important as the teaching of math and literacy is the teaching of the social and emotional skills such as how to get along with others.

A momentary visit to the beginnings of American schools reminds us that the purpose of schools in the early 1800s (primarily owned and run by religious and private groups) was to teach "Protestant ethics, non-partisan patriotism, instruction in American English, norms of punctuality, achievement, competitiveness, fair play, merit and respect for adult authority." As schools became more centralized and public education compulsory, the focus of schools shifted towards the development of the nation's intellectual capital by providing a sound basic education rooted in academics.[3] Over 200 years later, the debate continues as to what should be the purpose of schools.[4] While the consensus of many Americans is that schools should teach children the basics of reading and writing, those who are hiring our graduates ask for more. They want employees who can think, make informed decisions, get along with others, be flexible and creative and able to adapt to and lead in our quickly changing technological world.

Many believe that schools today should assure that young people learn the much-needed skills to actually participate in a democracy. In the high-stakes testing climate of schools today, how can we encourage young people to dialogue about sensitive topics such as prejudice, discrimination and other social injustices? A good place to spark such conversations around difficult issues is by reading one of the many provocative readings in the Facing History Resource guide titled, "What did you learn at school today?" This reading is set in The Weimer Republic in post World War I democratic Germany, in the 1920s. It was here, in Weimer, that the new government officials wrote their constitution and created a democracy. But Germany's loss and the newly-imposed political sanctions they faced angered many Germans. They had fought long and hard and now had to concede too much power and ways of being. Unrest stirred. By 1921, Hitler had formed the National Socialist German Workers Party. This Party and other political groups began to fight against much of the post-war imposed changes. As all of these events were developing, school life continued as it had always been. Schools taught that there was a natural God-given order to things and a hierarchical distribution of power. The newly imposed democratic ways did not seep broadly into the minds and hearts of young children. The following paragraph from the above-mentioned reading allows us to see into the mind of one German high school student named Klaus:

> *There was a great deal of control over my life and that of my friends from the school and from parents. But somehow, we all felt this was necessary; so that we could get through that Arbiter [high stakes exam], get into a good university, and be free. We lived for the future. We had to think very little, take almost no initiative; our days were charted out for us. It seems strange that with bloody street fights almost every weekend, groups of brown-shirted men singing aggressive songs on Saturday mornings as they marched to their training grounds, political assassinations on the front pages of the papers regularly, we never felt threatened, never afraid of anything but failure in school.[5]*

Failure in school, pass the tests, violence around me . . . I can't help but shiver at the remarkable similarity between some of what goes on in many American schools today and schools in Klaus' day. Schools in a democracy should promote critical thinking and help young people to question the events that are happening around them. While our nation strives to close the educational gap between children with privilege and children in need, I worry that the way we are going about this could just be all wrong. While "what is" isn't working in much of our public education system, I worry about the group think that can occur by promoting cultural literacy and standardization of learning for all children in schools. Knowledge is indeed power. We must be sure that our children have access to both. But, there are many paths through which we can access this knowledge. While our children must learn to read and write, they must also be able to think independently. If affirmed for who they are, they will challenge mediocrity, speak up against injustice and question the status quo, when necessary.

Ironically, the public pressure that demands that we *leave no child behind* can too easily ignore the need to develop the social, emotional moral and ethical development of our youth. We must be careful not to extol nationalistic views without the encouragement of the expression of differences. We must not promote academic learning at the expense of developing the hearts and social behaviors of our children. We must open the doors to our children's questions, promote debate and give them the social skills that will lead to the development of great minds and caring people. Their critical thinking will help them bridge the gap between the past and now. As informed citizens, they will actively seek to address the problems in their present day local, national and international environments.

THE TIMES THEY ARE A CHANGING

Gary Marx, Professor Emeritus from M.I.T invites us to consider a number of challenges that will alter the way we envision school in the upcoming years. First, the number of our nation's older generation has surpassed the number of young people. While our nation's schools continue to grow, the large majority of its teaching force is on the verge of retirement. School systems across the country are already grappling with ways to fill the shoes of those who are leaving, teachers and school principals alike. By 2030, the Baby Boom generation will be between 66 and 84 years of age. They will be drawing upon their social security benefits. It is imperative that today's educated young people secure good paying jobs that add to the supply of available revenue for this generation and those that follow.

A second shift is that our nation's traditionally minority populations are increasingly becoming the majority. Shortly after 2050 the white majority will shrink to below 50 percent of the US population. We will be a nation of minorities, although the power structures will not adequately resemble these changes. Issues of class and education will further separate us out as majority and minority. The gap between the "haves" and the "have-nots" will continue to widen.

Another trend to consider is the fact that "knowledge" and "relationships" are becoming the new basis for wealth. Those who have sharp skills in managing themselves and others will be at the forefront of change. People will want to know more and be included in decision-making discussions. In schools, as we continue to stress the high-stakes performance of our children, the parents of those who are not succeeding will demand personal explanations and appropriate services for their children. The Millennial Generation, children born in 1983 and beyond will use their knowledge and relationship skills to demand solutions to an accumulation of problems and injustices. This is the population of people who will be in positions of national and world leadership. Their moral and ethical calling will be to right the wrongs and deal with injustices.

We will continue to move through the age of information and technology. Nanotechnology, technology at the molecular level, will drive the economy of the future. Schools will be pressured to adequately prepare children for the current times. Young people will arrive at classroom doors with more information than most teachers have [see more of this in Chapter Nine]. Given this change in the dissemination of the knowledge structure, schools will have to consider teaching more across disciplines, incorporating multiple intelligences and making a commitment to prepare students as intellectual entrepreneurs. Scientific discoveries and societal realities will force widespread ethical choices. It will be incumbent upon schools to help young people to problem solve and explore solutions to ethical dilemmas.[6]

In short, we better start rethinking our business of schools now. We need to find ways to give young folks the skills to work within the framework of a democracy. More voices will be at the table and higher demands will be placed on what we are teaching our children.

TEACHING AND LEARNING FOR DEMOCRACY

Teaching to impart democratic values is not widely at the forefront of the schools' purpose. From the enactment of Brown v. Board of Education of Topeka in the 1950s to the present day No Child Left Behind legislation, we have embraced the realization that schools do not serve *all* children. Legislators and politicians continue to impose a number of measures to try to create equal opportunity for all children. While positive changes have been made in this direction, they are not enough. The real issues of social justice and democracy receive fancy band-aids. Real change that can create more inclusive schools for our global community never quite makes the cut. Multicultural education, while recognized to make a difference in the way we interact with and instruct diverse populations is still questioned. Bilingual education has taken a back door to the "All English" movement. The number of children of color in Special Education classes across our nation is on the rise.[7]

Deborah Meier, educator, activist and author known for her successful work at Central Park East in New York City tells us,

> *Children grow up and the kind of habits of mind they bring to both the workplace and the polling place will determine our common fate. It's quite possible that American society can develop a viable economy that ignores the fate of vast number of its citizens, one not dependent upon a universally well-educated public. But only at a cost to democracy itself. Schools dependent upon private clienteles-schools that can get rid of unwanted kids of troublemaker families, exclude on the basis of this or that set of beliefs, and toss aside the "losers"—not only can avoid the democratic arts of compromise and tolerance but also implicitly foster lessons about the power of money and privilege, a lesson already only too well known by every adolescent in America. In schools that are public, citizens are joined by right, not by privilege.*[8]

Teaching for democracy matters. In order to promote the teaching and learning of democratic practices, we need to provide teachers with appropriate professional development. First, school leaders have to have deeper inquiry-based conversations with their staffs. The leader's vision of a democratic school needs to be embraced by everyone. Through ongoing dialogue, leader and staff can come to a place of agreement as to how to take that vision into practice. Second, professional development opportunities need to provide new skills. Here, initial conversations extend to intensive discussion about practice. Instructional practices incorporate the use of critical strategies such as cooperative learning, debate, dialogic inquiry, Socratic seminars and decision-making models. Teachers learn how to build on students prior knowledge as they construct meaning from classroom lessons and life. Lessons carefully blend cognitive knowledge with affective strategies to foster acquisition of the new learning. Young people actively engage in learning rather than remain silent and compliant. Their voices, freely expressed, reflect investigation of facts, critical thinking and well-formed opinions.

Third, when teachers feel comfortable and safe they are willing to take risks. Making mistakes is part of everyone's learning process. Novice teachers, often receptive to new learning, may lack the teaching expertise for effective implementation. Seasoned teachers may make attempts to use more collaborative forms of instruction, but may be restricted by more patterned authoritarian approaches. Both novice and seasoned teachers, may be challenged by democratic practices such as sharing the "rulemaking" with their students. They may believe that the teacher sets the rules and children are expected to follow. Alfie Kohn reminds us:

> *Some educators reject rewards and punishments, believing, as I do, that a child may act in the desired way only in order to receive the former or avoid the latter. These educators want students to be self-disciplined, to internalize good values so that they no longer need outside inducements. But even this goal in not ambitious enough. The self-disciplined student may not be an autonomous decision maker if the values have been established and imposed from outside, by the adults. Accepting someone else's expectations is very different from developing one's own (and fashioning reasons for them). Creating a classroom whose objective is for students to internalize good behavior or good values begs the question of what we mean by "good." Moreover, it may amount to trying to direct students by remote control.[9]*

As leader, your task is to help teachers feel safe enough to experiment with "new ways of being" such as classroom management in which young people are part of the discussion, rather than the recipients of the "teacher's rules." Your encouragement and support are critical ingredients. Make the resources and professional supports available for them to expand their repertoires. Create school schedules that allow teachers to work together to build their lessons and share their expertise and ideas. Form study groups at lunch time like Principal Ellen did in Chapter Five. Free a teacher up so that he can observe his colleague teach a lesson. Remember, in order to learn democracy we have to practice democracy. Recognize that, at times, cultural norms are such that democratic practices can be seen by children and adults as "time for play," and "not so serious business," or even as inappropriate subject matter for schools to address. Advise your teachers how to go about democratizing classrooms at the pace that both their students and your school community can accept. At times, you may even be challenged to defend their actions to community members and district officials who distrust the new methods they are utilizing. They need your support as they teach children our history of democratic practices that challenges the status quo and urges their involvement in social action.

When Jim's son, Matthew, was in the fourth grade, he and his classmates studied about the Japanese internment in United States camps during World War II. Many of the Japanese-American children at the time were taken out of schools and placed with their families in internment camps. The fourth graders conducted research, read stories and culminated their learning by writing a play based on their research. Their play told the stories of the children who were sent to the camps and the reactions of their classmates who watched them leave. They prepared to perform their play in a school assembly but were stopped along the way by the school's principal. Jim, a parent in the community, questioned the principal regarding her reasons. She explained that another parent complained about the nature of the play. This parent felt that it showed America in a negative light. She didn't want her child exposed to this. Jim expressed to the principal that he wanted his child, Matthew, to be exposed to many points of views, to question motives, challenge actions and form his own opinions. Despite Jim's attempts, the principal stood firm and the play did not go on. This school leader's actions dampened the children's creativity, freedom of speech and critical thinking, and excitement about learning. In telling me the story about his son and his courageous teacher, Jim, a teacher himself for many years, said:

> *Teachers often say they want their students to learn how to think for themselves and to stand up for their convictions yet they seldom encourage students to challenge them about what they are teaching. They evaluate children all the time but do not often invite young people to give them feedback on their teaching. How can we empower students to grow*

up and change the world if we, the adults in their lives, do not give students the power to change us?

An EQ leader should welcome constructive controversy as a pathway to a democratic school.

Lessons that Matter

In this section, we provide a few examples of how to foster democratic teaching and learning in schools. In early childhood, the teacher is well-positioned to start the thinking process of abstract concepts such as peace, justice and freedom. This will set the stage for later, more profound, moral reasoning. In Jack Sloan's class, he and his students use a "sharing circle" to talk about things that matter to them. They read stories about characters who have fought for justice such as Martin Luther King, Ghandi and Nelson Mandela. They have many conversations about how each young person in their class makes a difference by helping others, sharing resources and becoming allies for someone who is being mistreated.

Today, Jack encourages the children to share an object such as a favorite book, a cuddly blanket, a piece of artwork, a special photograph or an event like a visit to a special friend's house or the loss of a pet or family member. He wants them to go beyond the concept of just liking something to understanding that some things hold a deeper "meaning" to them. Imagine, for a moment, five-year-old Jon, who brings in a picture that he drew of a man on top of a fire engine. When Jon introduces his artwork to his classmates, he says, "I like this drawing because it is a bright red fire engine." Jack then helps Jon to invite his peers to ask him questions about his artwork, and hopefully help him to extend the reasons why the red fire engine matters to him.

Initially, the children might ask things like, "Jon, do you like fire engines? Do you like the color red? Who is the man on the fire engine? Have you ever been on a fire engine?" Through conscious questioning strategies, Sloan encourages Jon to discover what has meaning to him. "Jon, you said you like your drawing because you like fire engines. Why do you like fire engines?" Jon replies, "because they are fast." . . . "Ah, so they are fast," the teacher paraphrases. "Yeah," Jon continues, "and my daddy drives them." "Oh, so your daddy is a fireman and he drives a fire engine?" "Yeah," Jon continues as he looks wide-eyed at the group, "He saves people." Jack Sloan, using a questioning tone, now paraphrases for Jon and his peers, "So, you like fire engines because your daddy is a fireman? You are proud of your daddy because he saves people? Saving people matters to you?" Jon, shakes his head and smiles.

This format of the sharing circle deepens the child's ability to think and feel about what and why certain things have meaning to them. When five year old Carla has her turn, she says, "This book is special to me because mommy reads it to me every night." Carla is more able to immediately attach the object and the reason why it matters for her. Jack Sloan might extend her thinking further by asking, "Carla, how do you feel when mommy reads to you?" Possible answers could include that she feels warm or special or loved. As one child is sharing, other five year olds listen to the different perspectives and values of their peers. Of course, they will want to chime in with their own stories about *their* mommy reading to them too, but the teacher helps them to listen to Carla's perspective. When the next child takes his turn, the teacher asks him to paraphrase what mattered for Jon and Carla today, before he introduces his sharing object. In this way, the teacher highlights that each of us have different ideas about "things that matter."

Small children could also share events that had meaning for them because they had positive or negative emotions attached to them. A child who shares, "I don't like it when they call me names," lets the group know that he has been hurt and that being treated peacefully and respectfully matters for him. Another child might speak up in support of a classmate who was criticized or hurt, letting the group know that mean behaviors are not appropriate or just. Through these and other teaching strategies, young children can learn that everyone's voice matters. They are learning perspective-taking, building empathy and participating in dialogic inquiry, at a very basic level.

Young children are not beyond taking social action that they themselves initiate. In one school where Jim was consulting, a young second grade teacher was asking her students about current events. One child blurted out that she had heard that a six-year-old had killed someone with a gun. The teacher was shocked that a number of her students knew about this tragedy and momentarily did not know what to say. Another student asked, "How did he learn how to shoot a gun?" and another child answered, "He saw it on TV." The teacher then asked her class how many children have seen violence on TV and most raised their hands. One little girl, however, boasted that she changes the channel when she sees anything violent. An excited discussion followed and many of the children said that they too would follow the girl's lead and change the channel.

The excitement of the children's spontaneous action soon was channeled into learning. The children interviewed other classes and took a survey of watching violence on TV. They read books about TV and wrote news stories based on their research. Finally, they started a campaign in the school to *Change the Channel* and transformed their classroom into an exhibition for their campaign. They invited each class to visit and learn about TV and about their social action. The local news found out about these young activists and a local TV station broadcast their story. The reporter interviewed the proud little girl who started it all. It is likely that she did not change the channel on that show!

In early and middle adolescence, democratic practices become expected by young people who learn that their voices are acknowledged and their thoughts and opinions are valued. Karin, a bright young Native American eighth grader studies the course of events of her native tribe throughout history. As a Lakota, she experiences much joy and pride in her family and ancestral history, but also much pain. As part of their integrated unit in American History and literature, Karin's class reads *Bury My Heart at Wounded Knee* by Dee Brown.[10] After a heartfelt discussion with her teacher, she decides on the focus of her presentation and subsequent dialogue that will follow. She and her small group of six students research the history of the Lakota people and facilitate a dialogue based on this book.

Using the "fishbowl" strategy, she sits with her small group in the center of a class circle. Karin precedes the book discussion with a more feelings-based introduction. She shares, "As a Lakota female, the events of my ancestors hold a lot of meaning for me. I feel very strongly about my people and my culture. I hope you will understand why after this presentation." She then reads a powerful short paragraph from one of the few survivors of the Wounded Knee massacre. She follows this passage by asking her small group to respond to the question, "What did you think of when I was reading that story? How did what I just read make you feel? What questions did it make you think of?" The students respond revealing the horror, shock and anger elicited by the paragraph. They then raise questions such as, "Why did the United States lead such a bloody battle? How did they let this happen?" They risk asking Karin, "Weren't the Native Americans at fault at all?" She asks her fishbowl peers to use their texts to explain the events that precipitated this battle. The group of six responds adding insights to the political, social and economic factors that promoted the oppression of the Lakota people, and eventually led to the well-known battle at Wounded Knee. Young folks in the larger circle, take notes and prepare questions that they will later ask their peers.

What skills did Karin possess in order to lead her group? What does Karin learn as she partakes in this activity? What about the others in the fishbowl? And the larger group? Both Karin and her peer facilitators learn a multitude of skills both in preparing for and leading this activity. They decided on the material to be covered, read it and outlined their focus. They had to distribute leadership for gathering the appropriate research and for preparing the presentation. They tested their facts for accuracy and thought about provocative questions that would stimulate the discussion. They researched answers to questions that might arise, or places to go for further discussions. They also worked together and trusted that each person would contribute their part to the whole.

What about the larger groups of students? They had to listen to different perspectives, ask clarifying questions, agree to disagree, problem solve and make judgments based on factual information and literature. They also had to trust in their classmates to obtain the information. All students also heard a personal perspective from a student who represents the background of the group studied. Not only are the young people in this scenario gathering and disseminating facts, but they are using those facts to dialogue with their peers and form their own perspectives. These older children are learning how to reason morally. They are forming their opinions about the events that have occurred, in this case, the events at Wounded Knee.

Berkowitz and Gibbs conducted a noteworthy study designed to measure ways we can move someone out of their own perspective towards accepting the perspective of others.[11] They identified a mode of moral discussion called transitive discussion, which is "reasoning that operates on the reasoning of another." In this form of discussion, each person engages the reasoning of the other person with her own reasoning. Then, she makes her own consecutive assertions. Their data revealed that a type of behavior called "operations" required that the person operate on or transform another's reasoning. This is done through clarification, refinement, extension, contradiction, integration finding common ground, or comparative critique. These operational techniques showed significant development in moral reasoning from pretest to posttest. In other words, being active participants in a dialogic inquiry-based process can help us to embrace other's perspectives and develop the ability to think morally and ethically about difficult situations.

In our work with Educators for Social Responsibility over the years, we have used a process developed by Peter Elbow to help others see beyond their own perspective and into that of another person. It is based on a concept called methodological belief.[12] Elbow developed this process while teaching writing to his students. He wanted to enlarge their vision and distract them from the overuse of critical thinking or what he calls *methodological doubt*. Students learn to consciously question hypotheses, find inconsistencies, and raise doubt about a situation or dilemma. On the other hand, "*Methodological belief,* is the equally systematic disciplined and conscious attempt to BELIEVE everything—to believe all hypotheses, premises and inferences, no matter how unlikely or repellent they seem—in order to find virtues or strengths we might otherwise miss." We have used Elbow's Believing game in our work to help workshop participants and classroom students suspend judgment and listen to differencing perspectives as they try to reach resolution in difficult situations. This powerful technique allows others to see beyond their own clouded lens that is often covered with years of their own experiences, point of view and prejudices. The intention is to help them risk listening to someone who outwardly appears to be one hundred and eighty degrees opposite to their own beliefs. Elbow tells us, "The believing game encourages what may be the most valuable intellectual or wisdom-generated mental event, namely, the act of seeing the strength in the other fellow's position and the weakness in one's own." As school leaders and teachers we may possess some very critical and judgmental points of view. Differing beliefs in effective in-structional approaches, for example, can cause anger and resentment to develop. The be-lieving game needs to be played on a regular basis to help the adults in schools bring flexibility and wisdom to their practice rather than pride, indifference and unwillingness to change. *[Play the Believing Game in the Chapter 6 Skills Section.]*

In our thirty plus years in education, Jim and I have seen too few schools that en-courage young people to develop such high level skills as those described above. While we do teach our young people about civics and democracy, we don't often teach them how to live democratically. But, in those schools that do, such as The Hudson Public Schools (described in the previous chapter) empowered students struggle with moral dilemmas, take on new perspectives and pursue social action. And the students in Hud-son are not the only ones learning how to put democracy into action. On March 5, 2003, thousands of high school students joined college students in a march to protest the then impending war with Iraq. Whether you agree with their position or not, you can value their exercise of their citizenship. Not since the Vietnam War era of the 1960s had our youth publicly risked having their voices heard.

Critical to our thinking about teaching and learning in a democracy, is the reality that many of our children face because of race, class, and other inequitable conditions. Youth who face poverty, violence and discrimination on a daily basis may feel less effi-cacious. Schools who nurture the hearts and minds of these young people must take into account the economic and political reality they face. We need to help young people gather all the tools they need: excellent reading skills, mathematical ability, higher level critical thinking and problem solving skills, and well-developed social and emotional competencies. It is the moral responsibility of schools to inform and prepare these young people to access knowledge that will allow them to shape the course of history, instead of letting it shape them.

Institutions of higher learning have to prepare teachers to think and espouse demo-cratic values. Our teacher education pedagogy needs to be replete with democratic prac-tices. The Lesley College Masters Program in Curriculum and Conflict Resolution in Cambridge, Massachusetts is one such rich program that models and teaches democratic practices.[13] In the School of Education at Hunter College of the City of New York, we strive to best prepare our educators to uphold the morals and values we are discussing in this chapter. Though social justice rests at the center of our vision of how we frame learning for our students, we have little guarantee that our aspiring educators will be able to transfer this knowledge into their classrooms in schools, too often, void of such purpose.

Democratic and Just Schools

Democratic schools are collective communities that work together to assure that the process and the outcomes of education are ethical and just. In speaking of her work at Central Park East elementary school and secondary school, Debbie Meier shared her staffs' ideas regarding democratic schools:

> *We saw schools as examples of the possibilities of democratic community and what we meant by this was continuously under debate and review. It wasn't simply a question of governance structures and certainly not a matter of extending the vote to four year olds. Although classroom life could certainly include more participation by children in deci-sions than traditional schools allowed, we saw it as even more critical that the school life of adults be democratic. It seemed unlikely that we could foster values of community in our classrooms unless the adults in the school had significant rights over their own work-*

place. For us, democracy implied that people should have a voice not only in their own individual work but in the work of others, as well. Finally we saw collaboration and mutual respect among staff, parents, student and the larger community as a part of what we meant by calling our experiment democratic.[14]

The staffs at Central Park East primary and secondary schools were committed to continual learning. They wanted to make the school the best that it could be for the children it served. Two-thirds of the African-American and Latino young people from a lower socioeconomic neighborhood in New York City's East Harlem went on to college. This success tells us that the continual learning process they were involved in worked for their kids. Dewey would remind us that Meier's school was a learning laboratory in which practices were tried and retried. Experimentation was rich. Decisions were shared as appropriate. The commitment to communal values and goals were clearly the driving force for continued change and improvement.

Carl Glickman has been passionate about the study of democratic schools for many years.[15] His recent work in identifying Great American schools reports his findings from a study of 20 such schools. He conducted interviews, made site visits and looked at data in each of these schools. In his review he chose schools who met the following criteria:

- Had a history of 10-30 years of sustained consistent reform that was consistent with the school's initial core values;
- Followed progressive education which he describes as that which utilizes activity-based and participatory learning, team structures, links between school and community, performance based assessment and inclusive heterogeneous placement of students;
- Cooperated under the governance of a school district with the same funding and student enrollment conditions as other schools in the district;
- Had documented student results better than those of comparable schools on a wide range of measures, including student test scores, student performances and demonstrations, success in later life, lower dropout rates and parent and student satisfaction.

Glickman was also careful to be sure that his schools represented the multiple geographic and ethnic diversities in the US. Reporting his findings, he tells us:

In all schools three components were consistent: there was a covenant of beliefs, a governance structure for school wide decisions and an action research process for continual internal study. The covenant of beliefs was developed by all members of the school community and covered broad beliefs related to areas such as teaching pedagogy, curriculum development, professional development, grouping practices, use of school space and more. The strong governance structure for making decisions in these schools allowed them to come together as a group to resolve conflicts and move forward. Action research processes informed them as they developed and changed along the way.

Leaders of these schools were willing to modify their beliefs in light of the group's commitment to their core values. Glickman expresses that these leaders like many others had to face the opposition of those who disagreed with their motives for one reason or another. But, he says, "If the school has begun by laying a solid foundation of common beliefs, leaders have the moral authority to support the school's vision of education."[16]

Glickman cites an example of a middle school in the Midwestern United States that had a poor record of student achievement. A few staff members did not want to use the agreed upon performance-based assessment process. They wanted to work with more flexible schedules. The guidance counselor, who led the opposition to this movement, kept sabotaging the proposed changes. The principal ultimately removed him from his assignment and even began full procedures for dismissal. Glickman's principal responded to the needs of his community. He behaved in an ethical manner and basically advised the uncooperative naysayer out of the business of his school. He took action for the betterment of the whole. This is the kind of commitment to the common beliefs that is needed to create trust and move a staff forward towards exemplary practices.

Christine Sleeter reminds us that schools that are democratic are also "just."[17] They work to reduce or eliminate gaps in student achievement that correlate with group membership such as social class, gender or race. Social justice work stems from many larger bodies of knowledge including anthropology, race and ethnic studies, developmental and social psychology, and the historical studies of groups throughout time. Through a focus on social justice issues, students develop empathy and even altruistic behaviors that can help move a society forward. School teachings concentrate on fostering positive intergroup relations. They explore the meaning of prejudice and discrimination, the role of power and privilege, as it affects individuals and institutionalizes racism and oppression. Students learn the tools to analyze, evaluate and transform individual and systemic threats to social injustices. In the context of these schools, young people think and feel about their own cultural lens, and how discrimination and marginalization of groups promote powerlessness and often violence.

Sleeter prompts us to think more deeply about the ways in which we as leaders are responsible to produce schools that provide young people equal access to school resources. One school should not succeed, and another fail because of accessibility to high performing teachers, adequate facilities and research driven curricula. The Coleman Report had largely attributed school success or failure to socioeconomic status.[18] The effective schools movement of the 80's and 90's sought to equalize these differences and discover within school differences that contributed to excellence. Schools that were effective were said to have:

- a clear mission
- high expectations for success
- a principal who was a strong instructional leader
- frequently monitored student progress
- many opportunities for time on task
- a safe and orderly environment and
- strong home-school relations

One study conducted by Reyes, Scribner and Scribner (1999) looked at eight schools along the Texas-Mexico border that were serving primarily low-income Hispanic students and demonstrated high achievement. These schools were characterized by:

- high involvement of community and families with a shared decision making body in which parents participated;
- collaborative governance and leadership with a more facilitative leadership and a common vision and mission;
- use of a "culturally responsive pedagogy. Teachers had high expectations for children's achievement. They built upon the children's home knowledge and learning, used higher order thinking and constructed knowledge from these; and
- use of "advocacy-oriented" assessments to assign grades or describe achievement levels. Assessment was used to improve performance not just provide outcome measures of success or failures.[19]

We now have a knowledge base that supports teaching and learning practices that make a difference for children, especially children of color. As leaders, you must also find ways to initiate this dialogue among the adults and young people in your school to assure that the scales are balanced and that justice is upheld.

The Power Lens: Individual and Collective Work

As we strive to give all children the opportunities to be successful in schools and ultimately in society, we have to equalize the power-sharing playing field. The way it stands right now, kids of color and kids from families with low socioeconomic status are not part of the culture of power in our country. This said, it is even more incumbent upon us to find ways to provide these young people the much-needed basic skills, democratic social skills and emotional competencies within the fabric of a just and caring school. Lisa Delpitt tells us that students and adults need to know both the explicit and the implicit rules of power as they try to create a more just society. She speaks of five aspects of power dynamics that are at play in our schools and classrooms every day. It is the job of the school leader to know these, embrace them and educate others in the school about there existence and effects on young people. These are:

1. Issues of power are enacted in the classrooms (teachers/students and students and students.)
2. There are codes or rules for participating in power, a culture of power (These include ways of being, dressing, behaving, etc.)
3. The rules of the culture of power are a reflection of the rules of the culture of those who have power.
4. Being told the rules of the culture of power helps others who are not in the group acquire power.
5. Those with power are least aware of it and often not even aware that they have it.[20]

Recognizing the power imbalance that so many of our children face in their daily lives, Lynn Fischer, a colleague and friend, suggests the use of a reflective tool that she calls the "power lens." This useful model helps young people evaluate their own personal and collective powers. It helps them to honestly see where they are in the larger power structure. It puts the diversity discussion on the table and lifts the taboo of talking about issues of privilege and differences. This allows trust to build in the classroom and opportunities to help young people build the tools they need to lead successful lives. Fischer's power lens also helps young people practice identifying and cultivating their innate powers. In working with a fifth grade class she asked them, "What powers could never be taken from you?" One by one, using the lens, the children responded with statements such as, "The power to love, learn, communicate with my soul, and determine who I will become; think for myself, listen and make choices." They began to find ways to express that innate power. Fifth graders enlisted as peer mediators or volunteered to be team leaders. High school students became mentors and coaches for younger students. Lynn believes that young people need to recognize and draw upon their innate powers in order to become effective change agents within existing social systems. It gives them another tool with which to maneuver the inequities that exist.[21]

Once the safety has been established, young people can learn from hearing each other's stories about experiences that have impacted their individual perspectives. Some of us are members of dominant cultural groups. Some of us have inherited a legacy of oppression. Lynn shares, "As we share our stories we see ourselves not as victims or perpetrators but as active players within the social systems that help to determine the circumstances of our lives." I can remember doing this very activity with The Young Ambassadors at my school (described later in this chapter). After many months of working together we held a retreat that was dedicated to expelling the myths of individual and group differences. Our goal was to build community through individual and group storytelling. The healing that occurred that weekend was amazing! That group of young people came together as a community rich in diversity and established a common ground of authentic communication.

Finally, adults also need the safety to feel they have an equal seat at the table. In many of the classrooms across our nation the very adults who are working with children have spent a lifetime grappling with these same inequities. As leaders of schools, no matter what our own cultural and racial identity we need to address these issues. When there is a common language that acknowledges that there are differences in the rules people play to be successful in life, all members of all groups learn how to play the game. Even in a multicultural school environment, talk about racial, gender, sexual identity and ethnic differences can go unspoken. It's important to remember that silence does not imply harmony. Too often, inside the hearts and minds of children and adults, these power imbalances are taking their toll.

An emotionally intelligent leader structures her leadership to increase empathy between those who are different. She also promotes the richness of the diversity in the organization. If the school's culture squelches individual differences, the leader has to find ways to get those voices heard. Communication and conflict resolution skills have to be so strong that they can help others in the organization listen, question and collaborate together to improve the culture and performance of young people. Experience tells me that leaders often have to name these differences outright. And, they have to encourage others to do the same. When I saw any hint of intolerance of differences in my school, whether among adults, or adults and children or among children themselves, I called it. Putting the unspoken on the table allowed us to use the information collectively for positive change. I learned that the only way that I could open up the conversation about differences was to admit that I was a learner; I encouraged others to see themselves as learners too. I let it be known that I had to ask a lot of questions and assure that all groups were being heard. This was not easy work. It would have been so much simpler to just put a top on it all and let it simmer. But, a pot of simmering water will eventually boil over, or burn the pan! The only way that you can assure that the school provides a safe place for everyone to develop and learn from one another is by directly working with the issues as they arise.

YOUTH IN ACTION: TOMORROW'S LEADERS

In this next section, we will talk about what leaders can do to increase social responsibility among the youth in their schools. We will look at ways to help young people develop empathy and expand moral values and beliefs into moral and social action. Building on the research of theorists Kohlberg, Damon, Erickson and Gilligan, we need to think about the causes that compel someone to go out on a limb for another. Why did many people open their homes during the Holocaust and save lives, while others slammed their doors shut? Why did people risk their lives in transporting Black slaves from the South through the Underground Railroad while others reported them and gloated in seeing them lynched? During the German occupation of France, at Le Chambon, a small town in south central France, the entire community risked their lives as they actively hid Jews from all over Europe. When the war was over and Madame Trocme, the wife of the local minister, was asked why they made such a risky decision she replied, "There was no decision to make. The issue was: Do you think we are all brothers or not? Do you think it is unjust to turn Jews in or not? Then, let us try to help!"[22]

Thomas Lickona, psychologist and education professor tells us that moral action is a component of character. It puts into action our knowledge about what is right and wrong, and our feelings about "how much we care about being honest, fair and decent towards others." He tell us that in order to take moral action, we need to have skills to act, the will to mobilize and a developed habit of acting in a moral way.[23]

To accomplish the dual goal of developing civic responsibility and moral action of youth, increasingly more schools are integrating service learning projects into the heart of the school's culture. Service-learning is a teaching strategy which integrates youth service into core academic curriculum. When competently utilized, it provides students with opportunities to learn real world application of their studies, and take an active role in solving community problems. Approximately one-third of public elementary and secondary schools, more than thirteen million students use service-learning in their programs. The benefits of such program efforts include improved academic learning, civic responsibility, and social and career development. Service-learning efforts have documented increases in student attendance, school engagement, self-efficacy, greater relations with adults and other students, and a wider acceptance of cultural diversity. One study of high school students who participated in service learning activities reported that students were more likely to vote in national elections fifteen years after their participation in service learning programs.[24]

In Chapter Five, we shared some of the wonderful service learning projects of Shelley Berman's young people. In this section, we share stories of young people who have taken leadership to create safety, a nonviolent culture and an appreciation of diversity in their schools.

Lessons Learned from Youth

In the book *Waging Peace in Our Schools* that I co-authored with Linda Lantieri, I spoke about the work my colleagues and I did at Roosevelt Middle School in California to increase self-efficacy and develop moral action in our middle school students.[25] Prompted by the increasing separation of young people by ethnicity, status and gang participation we set about to infuse The Resolving Conflict Creatively Program into the school. The three-to-five year plan was to have a school with fully integrated conflict resolution visible in every classroom and every aspect of the school and community.

A near violent gang-related incident during lunch one day caused us to move even more quickly. My colleagues and I brought together a group of school leaders to help us figure out what we could do to change this increasingly violent culture. Fear and instinct told us that we adults could not change the culture of this school alone. We needed the young people. I can still remember the exact moment when about ten adults and young people sat around the table in Principal Jewell's office. At the table sat Stan and Tommy, bright, eighth-grade, African American boys who were negatively influencing the younger African American children towards violent behavior; Manny and Cesar, two Latino boys who led the Vista Home boy contingency, and Joey, a White ethnic student, who identified with the growing white supremacists movement. We invited the students to help us create a peaceful school environment rather than participate in the violence that was brewing. We agreed that we were all losing and we wanted a win-win solution. The students suggested the names of other leaders to invite into the group. Overall, we selected students with leadership skills from all groups by gender, ability, race, status in the school and academic performance. No group was excluded. We named these student leaders "The Young Ambassadors."

From this moment on, began the most incredible experience I have witnessed in turning around a culture of a school. The key factor was a critical mass of young people equipped with the very beliefs and skills we had hoped all adults and children would possess over time. These included a belief in nonviolence and an understanding of the negative impact of discrimination and exclusion; finely tuned caring communication skills that included active listening and assertive language; the conscious use of negotiation and mediation strategies in place of aggressive or passive behavior; and, a commitment to social action that focused on making the school a safe place for all.

We began to develop this critical mass of advocates by teaching in depth skills in conflict resolution to our core group of 12 young leaders. We met once a week during lunch time and later in the year organized a three-day retreat. The time we committed together allowed for the establishment of trust among these youth leaders and between adults and youth leaders. The sessions provoked deep feelings stimulated through the use of dialogue in small and whole groups. We taught "perspective taking skills, active listening" and "I messages." We told stories of pain and hopelessness. We expressed our fears and hopes for the future. We shared the pains of oppression and discrimination and the joys of achievement and power used to help others. We planned the approach we would take to bring other youth into our fold and to get more young people involved.

Within about two months, rumors were abounding on campus that these Young Ambassadors were afoot and that they were the school's "chosen ones." Since some of these chosen few also had aggressive tendencies, they caught the attention of students and teachers alike. The students were not sure of what to make of this experiment. In the past, Stan, Manny and Lanitra used to live in my office for breaking the rules. Now, they were being extolled as school leaders. This seemed like a cool thing. The teachers, on the other hand, were skeptical. How could we honor these potentially violent kids with a position of status in the school. We were, they believed, too lax.

Many believed our experiment was doomed to failure, but we were determined to make it work. We knew weekly meetings were not enough to change deep-seated negative behaviors of the troubled youth leaders. As assistant principal, I created special contracts with these more at-risk leaders. I followed them to assure they were doing their school work. I contacted their families and got them to cooperate with us. The school counselors and I spent countless hours doing one-on-one and group counseling with the kids who needed it. I became a visible force on the campus. I followed kids on the playground, into the bathrooms and wherever they gathered. I watched their interactions with other kids. I held them accountable. When they broke the rules I came down hard, but short of violent acts, there was always a chance for them to regain their position of status.

The next step was to create the school wide visible recognition. We bought and they designed their tee shirts. We asked them to wear them to our weekly meetings. At first, they refused. "We aren't going to look like a bunch of elementary school children walking around here with these tee shirts. They'll laugh at us. They'll never believe in what we are doing. Twelve of us are not enough. We need 30 of us, 100 of us." We begged them to be patient. We knew they were right, but we weren't there yet. So, we bought the tee shirts and they put them on. I remember that first day they walked the campus with those black and red Young Ambassador shirts. The bulletin announcement that morning went something like this:

> *Attention Roosevelt Students: The Administration wants to let you know that you will see on campus today our twelve Young Ambassadors. These are the young people who have dared to make a difference at our school. These kids believe that we can do things differently. They want to be champions for peace instead of violence. They are looking for others of you who want to "walk the talk" of nonviolence. If you are interested in becoming a Young Ambassador, you will have to follow their steps. Let us know of your interest. But, first, you have to "walk the talk." We have to believe that you care.*

I can still remember the fear in these courageous young leaders that day as they struggled to uphold our cause and model what they had learned in our private sessions over the preceding three months. I was so proud of them. At the end of the day they were flying high. They came rushing to tell our lead teacher, Elaine, and me the stories of the many positive events of the day; the number of times they spoke up and stopped possible altercations. They were glowing. They had made a difference already, and they knew it.

This was the beginning of a movement in that school that swelled from twelve courageous soldiers to one hundred. From our efforts at Roosevelt, the model was replicated in the school district of some 25,000 young people. Young Ambassadors became a common district name. It still is. The culture of Roosevelt changed drastically with the help and service of these young people. As assistant principal, my role changed drastically too. In time, I no longer spent my days with a multitude of fights and interventions. So many occurrences were stopped by the words and actions of our Young Ambassadors. At times, when it was safe, they intervened themselves. Other times they sent us notes and warned us of possible dangerous situations. But the role of the Young Ambassador blossomed into so much more. These young people became true leaders of the school. Soon they were

- leading Unity days at the school;
- teaching lessons in classrooms at the sixth grade level and at the elementary schools;
- building peace quilts in the school;
- becoming mediators {They attended an advanced three-day training}
- speaking at public events, on youth panels and at local and national conferences;
- arranging peace marches in the district;
- cleaning graffiti on weekends;
- developing and performing Public Service Announcements on their local cable stations for peace; and
- writing grants to support our efforts and more.

I watched our campus change from a place of potential violence to a place that promoted peace. Once threatening, "wanna-be" gang members lost their importance. The new role models were our Young Ambassadors. Teachers, reluctant to empower young people, called for them to diffuse potential fights and sent their students to mediation.

I learned a tremendous amount from this experience with these young people. First and foremost, I learned that when you respect young people and allow expression of their voice, you build their trust. With trust, you can build self-efficacy and have the chance to turn around even the most wounded young person. Through the stories of the children, I learned about the inequities they suffered due to racial, class and cultural differences. We learned as a group, adults and young people together, how to make inroads into changing these power dynamics.

Our united actions led to numerous activities that made our mission loud and clear. We organized multicultural fairs and monthly activities led by students, such as women's history fairs, dance concerts, and ethnic celebrations. Every winter, celebration of just Christmas was replaced by the school wide study and coordinated planning of winter festivities of numerous cultures. Throughout the year, students organized daily lunch time activities that celebrated our unique school cultures. I knew we were getting our message across when a sixth grade Chinese boy came to the office one day and said, "Excuse me, Ms. Patti, but I know we have been having cultural events at lunch time, and I noticed that we haven't had enough Asian activities. I wonder if I could organize a Marshall Arts performance at lunch?" "Great," I said to him. "I'll tell one of the Young Ambassadors to meet with you about the details." Our new focus was not confined to activities and events. We organized committees to ensure that our curriculum reached all children. We recruited parents of diverse ethnic backgrounds to be more present in our schools. We organized adult/student leadership meetings to address issues of concern regarding student needs. These were joyous and celebratory times. As I write this book, I wonder what career paths these Young Ambassadors have chosen. I wonder what they would say about these early experiences. I wonder if they know they remain my heroines and heroes to this day. They taught me how the power of one can become the power of many.

Many young people across our country are performing similar acts of service. They are making inroads towards creating cultures of peace. Gregory Thomas, former Director of School Safety and Planning for the 1200 New York City public schools recently shared a story with me and my students about incredible youth leaders in the Brownsville section of Brooklyn. As a response to the school administration's and students' reports that weapons and student bullying were the school's major offenses, students and adults together conducted research to uncover the depth of the problem. Survey results indicated that students were bringing knives, box cutters, and other weapons to protect themselves on the way to and from school. Students with police officers identified the sites where bullying most occurred in and outside of school. School community members, police and local politicians worked with the students to write grants. They raised money to support their efforts to change the violent culture and insure safety and peace.

The young people became known as the *Brownsville Youth for Peace*. They instituted a number of changes at Junior High School 275. They drafted a peace pledge that all students signed. They went out into the community to create an awareness of their needs for a peaceful school. They continued to raise funds. They instituted weekend events such as basketball tournaments, music jams, and role play discussions that addressed youth issues. They even implemented a highly successful reward program for students who bought into their new agenda. The changes at the school soon became evident. Teachers and students felt safer, inside and outside of their school. Many of the twenty students who began the original Brownsville Youth for Peace program, have since graduated. They continue to speak at local and national peace forums, work at violence reduction in their local communities and come back to speak to the fledgling Brownsville Youths for Peace at J.H.S. 275.[26]

As Sheldon Berman reminds us, "Educating for social responsibility helps young people understand that their lives are intimately connected to the well-being of others and to the social and political world around them, that they make a difference in their daily lives by their choices and values in the world that can enable them to live with meaning, integrity and responsibility."[27]

STRATEGIES FOR REACHING COMMON GROUND

In Chapter Four, Jim addressed ways leaders can set the tone for establishing a school culture that promotes nonviolent conflict resolution at its core. The EQ leader uses strategies such as high-level communication skills, problem solving, consensus building, negotiation and mediation and dialogic inquiry. The EQ school leader recognizes that schools are service organizations and service is inherent in his role.

When conflict and disagreement arise, the school leader does not close the door. Conflict avoided will smolder and burn up the school. When there are strong differences of opinions, the root of the disagreement often goes deep. Conflict may be attached to long held beliefs, often based on religion, gender, race and ethnic differences and the power imbalances that come with these. At times, someone's response stems from painful early experiences that have created a history of mistrust. The role of the school leader is to help bring others through these hard times, reestablish trust and create common goals. And even receptive and emotionally intelligent school leaders have to suspend judgments, expand their perspectives and be willing to do and say things differently. As we think about creating just communities that promote a belief in reaching common ground, the following points may be useful:

1. Establish and review community group norms that demonstrate the ways adults and young people will behave in the school. Post these around buildings in classrooms and on walls. Use them before difficult meetings, at parent meetings before student or adult mediations. Incorporate these ways of being into your school curriculum. Create acknowledgement systems for those who model these ways of being.
2. Recognize, early on, that there are a variety of power relationships in every school. The more you understand these and work to navigate them the more everyone will feel they have a place at the table. This will give you more support as you seek to implement your vision.
3. Build trust. It is impossible to move any agenda forward without a trusting community. Find ways to become more transparent yourself so that you are trusted. Help others to feel safe enough to do the same.
4. Acknowledge and promote intercultural understanding. Employ multicultural education methodologies in your school. Let this lens permeate everything you do. Provide opportunities for adults and young people to honor themselves and others. Promote the safety for people to ask questions and learn from one another. Encourage storytelling and celebration as a means to promote unity. Explore ways to make practices relevant to the variety of cultural groups in your school. Educate yourself and others.
5. Enlist diverse voices to examine school policies for the purpose of inclusiveness and modify policies to reflect this. Bring in the experts when needed. If you cannot suspend your frame of reference in a given situation, you may need to utilize the strengths of someone else. Someone outside of the organization can help build bridges.
6. Put the structures in place for the staff to problem solve and negotiate about curriculum matters and about the way they communicate, act, and adhere to the school's mission. Promote conflict resolution practices and reflection of emotional intelligence competencies for all students and adults. Educate and promote dialogue and dynamic inquiry at every opportunity. Professional development in these areas will create a common language for the entire community of learners.
7. Learn how to effectively use consensus-building skills. These skills can be extremely effective in bringing your staff together about critical directions that you want to move ahead with as a school. Remember, you can't mandate that people embrace deeper core values such as a belief in equity and celebration of diversity.
8. Understand that reconciliation and forgiveness are often needed where lots of hurt and damage have been done. This cannot be handled in the short run. It will involve an ongoing commitment to rebuilding a relationship that has been severed. This is, perhaps, the hardest work of all.

IN SUMMARY

In this chapter we have asked you to explore your values and beliefs as to the purpose of schools in a democracy. We have talked about the skills we hope to instill in our children, those that will prepare them to be active participants in their future. As educators we *can* and *must* teach young people ways to be socially responsible, so that they will be able to take a stand for equity and social justice. This said, we recognize that there are inequities that run deep, power structures that restrain us all. We need to give voice to these discriminatory practices and create structures in our schools and communities that counter them wherever possible. The emotionally intelligent leader bears the responsibility of increasing empathy and intercultural sensitivity in all members of the school. Finally, we have offered a few thinking points that can help a skilled community reach common ground during difficult times.

In closing this chapter it feels appropriate to share with you a letter that one principal sends to his teachers on the first day of school each year. May it kindle in you the hope and righteous indignation to move forward and build a school of young people and adults who know "what matters."

Dear Teacher:

I am a survivor of a concentration camp. My eyes saw what no man should witness:
Gas chambers built by learned engineers.
Children poisoned by educated physicians.
Infants killed by trained nurses.
Women and babies shot and burned by high school and college graduates.
So I am suspicious of education.
My request is: Help your students become human. Your efforts must never produce learned monsters, skilled psychopaths, educated Eichmanns.
Reading, writing and arithmetic are important only if they serve to make our children more human.[28]

REFLECTIVE QUESTIONS

1. Are there events from your background, gender, ethnicity, race, sexual orientation or abilities that challenge you in your personal and professional life? Are there EQ competencies that can help you to make sense of these and use them as strengths rather than limitations in your day-to-day lives?
2. In your school, does everyone have a "voice at the table?" What steps do you take to assure that everyone is included in your school's vision and mission?
3. As a leader, what messages do you give to others that reflect your vision of the school's purpose?
4. In what ways do the behaviors of the young people and adults in your school reflect their understanding and application of your school's vision?
5. When you think of your school in light of the reading in this chapter, "where do you see your school now, and where do you hope to see it in three years from now?"

LESSON FROM THE FIELD

Matt Bromme

One of the most difficult situations for a leader to address is how to navigate the turbulent waters when a conflict exists in the organization and/or in the community the leader serves. As educators, we are faced with conflicts that can become crises just by the manner in which they are dealt with at their embryonic stage. If we believe that educating children is a moral commitment, then how we address a conflict and bring it to closure serves as a model for moral leadership. As the Americans who were portrayed in Kennedy's, *Profiles in Courage,* leaders must choose a moral decision even when that decision may be a career ending decision.

An example of this is when I was faced with a conflict with parents in one of our schools. The extremely volatile issue was over the rights of students with special needs to attend an appropriate educational environment within the classrooms of students who did not have special needs. I believed that based on research, and the prior experience of several of our schools, the philosophy of least restricted environment was and still remains the most appropriate instructional program for all of the children we serve.

During the late spring and summer, one of our higher performing schools was selected and key people and I carefully planned to begin the inclusion program. We followed the same pattern as we had in the other schools where we introduced inclusion. We first met with the service providers of the children who were to be brought into the school, as well as the school and community school district staff. We carefully identified the students who would benefit from this model of instruction as well as identified the teachers at the school who would embrace the inclusion model.

In this particular situation, the conflicts arose when the parents of the children who did not have special needs learned that their children were to be part of the inclusion program. This higher performing school was chosen as an inclusion site for autistic children. It was to be a partnership between the school community, the providers of the special needs students and the community at large.

I scheduled a meeting at the school for the different groups who were involved in the issue. Students with and without special needs were invited. Parents with children who had special needs and select parents of children without special needs were also asked to attend as well as the professional staff. Since the leadership of the Parents' Association had been involved and aware of this new program, I believed that all of the necessary members of the community had been educated about the program. However, the Parents' Association quickly turned this into a conflict. Members of the Association started to make demands that were outside the scope of a Parents' Association and violated the rights of the children. The parents demanded to meet the students, have knowledge of the students' handicapping conditions, and ask questions about the children while the children and their parents were present at a meeting. This was the same Parents' Association that had rejected the opportunity of securing a gifted program because it meant that students from outside their school zone would have the opportunity to attend the school.

The Parents' Association's demands on the newly-appointed, five-months-in-the-position Principal ended with a threat. They would place an advertisement in the local newspaper advertising a meeting to be held at the school to discuss and debate the merits of this issue. Knowing that some of the school's staff lived in the neighborhood, I believed that there would be staff members working with parents to defeat the plan. I also knew that five of the nine local Community School Board members were elected from that part of the community.

The Principal needed to know that I was going to support her in her efforts to ensure an appropriate education for the students at her school—no matter what stand she took. She supported the program, hosted the meetings and hand picked the teachers. Her concern was living with the adversarial situation in her first full year as Principal. As Superintendent, I decided to take a stand that I knew was ethically correct, but politically incorrect. The inclusion model would be instituted. I informed the Principal that she should relay my decision to the Parents' Association. I then informed my School Board of my decision.

Although we had followed the educational textbook on communications, a very passionate segment of the community decided to oppose our plan. I truly believed their opposition was based on all of the wrong social and educational reasons. It would have been much easier for me to capitulate to this group of parents. I would have won peace with the local media and political leadership. There would have been no threats of letters, emails, and protests to prevent "those children" from attending school with "our children."

Leaders need to decide how to handle conflict. While my initial tone is that of collegiality and full disclosure on all issues, there comes a time when for the benefit of the children we serve, we must as leaders take a strong stand and make the right decision. It may mean that a particular conflict will escalate. It may mean that you will lose personal associations. In the long run, however, you will gain respect and have fewer conflicts as time moves forward.

All leaders must remember that at the end of the day we must take the ethical and moral position that is best for the sake of all children. We must have the courage to serve our children well. This is the only accolade that counts.

Matthew Bromme presently serves as Senior Operations Manager of Zoning and Student Choice for the New York City Department of Education. He was a Superintendent of Community School District 27 in New York City for five years and a school principal for over thirteen years.

Chapter 8

Facilitative Leadership

A Leader is best
When people barely know he exists . . .
When his work is done,
His aim fulfilled.
They will say:
We did it ourselves.

—LaoTzu

As a principal who was appointed two years ago to "shake things up" at the local high school, Ronald Bass knew what was expected of him by his superintendent. After assuming leadership, he worked tirelessly to restructure and improve the school. Now the superintendent proposed the introduction of block scheduling as the answer to teachers' complaints that they had too little time to teach in the constructivist way that reflected the school's shared vision. Bass liked the idea but, rather than promoting the idea as the answer to the problem, he thought that this was an excellent opportunity to develop the leadership potential of a staff ready for the challenge.

"You have said that your problem is not having enough time to meet with students, to plan together with colleagues and to engage in interdisciplinary learning activities in your classrooms," Bass told them. "I'd like you to select a committee that will explore this problem, generate possible solutions from all members of the school community, and then help us to decide on which action to take."

Bass gave the selected committee release time in order to interview students, parents and staff members to get a clearer picture of the problem. In addition, he gave them access to the Internet and a little travel money to explore how other high schools had solved the problem. Meeting with them regularly, he refrained from managing their efforts and stayed in the role of a coach, helping them to reflect on what they were doing and their future plans. As a final step, the committee presented their report with recommendations to the full faculty and representatives from the parents and students. After engaging in dialogue and making some small changes, the plan was agreed upon using a consensus approach.[1]

The situational leader we met in Chapter Six was able to delegate to a follower who demonstrated readiness. Yet, are there situations, as in the case of Ronald Bass' school, in which the most appropriate strategy is to go beyond delegation? In some schools, are there teachers or other members of the school community who might work together, expanding the traditional concept of school leadership to become leaders themselves? If so, what is the role of the school principal? How will the organizational culture and policies of the school and the school district have to change to enable this expansion of leadership? What are the benefits and the drawbacks of such changes and how do these ultimately impact on students' academic and social-emotional learning?

In this chapter we first explore the concept of facilitative leadership and the facilitative leader. Next, we examine how an understanding of group dynamics and team learning is an essential aspect of the facilitative leader's knowledge base. We then apply this information and systemic thinking strategies to the notion of school based management, presenting the challenges inherent in the creation of effective self-directed teams. Fourth, we address the largest stumbling block to shared leadership strategies—the issue of accountability. Finally, we broaden our exploration of facilitative leadership to look at the possibilities and pitfalls of distributing leadership throughout the school of the future.

FACILITATIVE LEADERSHIP

Facilitative leadership is defined as "the behaviors that enhance the collective ability of a school to adapt, solve problems, and improve performance."[2] A facilitative leader, therefore, is someone who helps others to develop into leaders. That role can be adopted by a number of people in a school but research suggests that the school principal can be an influential facilitative leader.[3]

The role of the facilitative leader was not widely promoted until the late 1970's when a number of businesses, trying to adapt to a rapidly changing world that demanded creative solutions to problems, restructured their organizations to take advantage of self-managed teams.[4] The reported success of these changes persuaded some school systems to develop the model of school based management. It was thought that bringing together leaders from the school's core constituencies to plan would result in better decision-making and improved student performance. In a number of states and in many big cities, school systems were mandated to quickly develop leadership teams often consisting of the principal, several teachers, and a few parents.

The notion of leadership teams is now widespread. Many corporations, government agencies, and school systems are finding that the old "factory model" of isolated workers doing individual tasks does not work well anymore. Even in real factories, like the Ford and Saturn auto plants, teams of workers are revolutionizing the way things are done, working together to generate ideas for changing work systems, taking the initiative to shut down the assembly line to avoid costly mistakes.

Though teams make such a difference in our lives, most of us grow up with little formal education in group theory. From our own first-hand experiences on various kinds of teams, we may have wondered why certain patterns of behavior emerge on all teams even though the makeup of those teams and their tasks are so different. We may have noticed that some teams perform better than others do even though the individuals on non-performing teams may be just as talented. In our own work, we may have found ourselves or others acting in unexpected ways when interacting in a group situation. It is also likely that we all have had intense emotional experiences, both positive and negative, while pursuing a team goal. These experiences and others help us to construct our own implicit theories of groups in general and teams specifically.

GROUP DYNAMICS

Though the literature about groups goes back to the ancient past, the scientific study of groups began in the late 1920's.[5] Elton Mayo, for example, conducted the earliest studies of group behavior in the workplace, from 1927 through the early thirties. The researchers were interested in investigating how conditions at work such as working hours, rest breaks, and levels of lighting affected fatigue and performance of workers at Western Electric's Hawthorne plant in Chicago. Unexpectedly, however, they discovered that productivity was more influenced by group variables than by external factors. In one experiment, for example, researchers decreased light in a work area expecting performance to be impaired but productivity increased because the cohesive work group responded to the poor conditions by working harder.

By the mid-1930's the knowledge of groups was being advanced by such investigators as Mustafa Sherif, Joseph Moreno and Kurt Lewin. Lewin was especially influential as he was the first to popularize the term *group dynamics* and establish the first research organization to study group dynamics. Though investigators over the subsequent years have come from a variety of perspectives (e.g. psychology, education, business, anthropology and sociology) there appears to be a common set of four assumptions that underlie their work.[6] First, they believe that groups are a natural human phenomenon that exists in every culture. Second, there is an assumption that groups mobilize powerful forces that can greatly influence individuals. Third, they hold that groups can produce both good and bad results. Finally, there is the proposition that a deep understanding of group dynamics can enable people to enhance the positive effects of groups.

A group can be defined as two or more individuals, interacting and interdependent, who come together to achieve certain objectives. At work there are two basic groups: *the formal* and the *informal*. The formal group is defined by the organization. The informal group is a group that is not formally structured or defined by the organization and is usually formed to attain an objective, like getting the workload done, or for social reasons. In your school, you probably belong to many formal and informal groups. How would you describe those groups?

Group development is a dynamic process characterized by continual change but there is strong evidence that this process follows a pattern of stages (see Figure 8.1)[7]. The first stage is *forming*. This stage is marked by uncertainty about the group's purpose, structure, and leadership. Members of new groups, faced with a new situation and new people, often seek to find the answers to key questions. What am I going to be doing here? How are we going to do things? What is the leader going to be like and what will other group members expect of me? The second stage, called *storming*, is the stage in which group members struggle with their new group identity. It is at this stage that conflicts, passed over or denied in the forming stage, often surface. Much of this conflict results from issues concerning control: a need to belong to the group versus a need to be independent. The task of this stage is for the group to determine how it will be led.

If the group is able to work through the storming stage, the group enters the *norming* stage in which the group establishes norms. Norms are acceptable standards of behavior that are shared by the group's members. Some norms may be formalized, as in school codes of conduct, but most are informal norms that influence people at work without even being spoken or written.

For example, where people sit in a faculty conference, what teachers discuss or do not discuss with parents and how principals intervene in staff conflicts may be guided by unspoken norms. Often a norm becomes explicit only when it is broken (e.g. a person gets on the elevator and stares at you).[8] Can you think of a common informal norm that people in your school might observe?

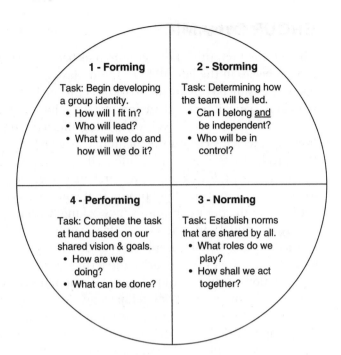

FIGURE 8.1 Team Development Cycle

Performing is the fourth stage and this is when the group, or team, is operating on all cylinders. Most of the group's energy is directed toward the tasks at hand because group members understand their roles and responsibilities, and they feel a strong group identity and cohesiveness. Some organizations or supervisors expect this level of productivity from their teams as soon as the teams are formed. The more successful approach is to be aware of the need of groups to attend to the previous three stages first and to facilitate that process. Performance is then more likely to follow. The supervisor who disregards group dynamics will meet all kinds of resistance and wind up blaming either individuals or the group for a lack of performance.

For work groups that are not permanent but formed for a specific task, there is a fifth stage called the *adjourning* stage. The task of this stage is to prepare for the ending of the group.

In looking at the model, you might assume that stages flow easily into each other and that, once a group reaches the performing stage, it remains there. In real life, however, the process is much less uniform. There is usually a progression through the stages but even high-performing teams may revert back to an earlier stage in response to change or a crisis. Another group might be performing one week and a new member enters and it shifts to a forming or storming stage. A working group seems to be headed toward the performing stage but finds itself stuck because it neglected to develop clear guidelines for dealing with conflict at the norming stage. The key for group members and leaders is to recognize the group's stage and to know how to deal with the tasks of that stage.

Team Performance

A team is defined as a group of individuals who are dependent on each other and share a common purpose. What are some of the factors that researchers have shown affects team performance? These can be divided into four interacting categories:

1. The conditions in the organization to which the team belongs. The structure, regulations, resources, evaluation and reward system, the organizational culture, the physical work setting, and the mission of the organization are all conditions that can impact on performance.
2. Group member resources. The abilities and personalities of group members can either enhance or impede the group's ability to function effectively.
3. Group variables. Formal leadership, roles, norms, group size, group diversity, and group cohesiveness are examples of group variables.
4. Group tasks. Some tasks are simple and some complex.

In any organization, there are urgent tasks that are performed more effectively by a group headed by a strong single leader than by a team. This is especially true if that "team" is what Katzenbach and Smith calls a *pseudo-team,* which is a team in name only. However, given time and conditions conducive to teams, teams will greatly outperform individuals and single-leader groups on many tasks.[9] The highest performing teams are those whose members are deeply committed to one another's personal growth and success in addition to meeting all the other criteria of a true team.

In her review of the literature, Kelley Folkerts noted that research has found a significant relationship between emotional intelligence and performance on work teams.[10] Self-awareness, self-regulation, self-efficacy, communication skills, and the ability to negotiate were central to team performance. Without these competencies, individuals who become members of work teams often have difficulty dealing with the conflicts that are normal in group problem solving and planning and, as a result, become emotionally segregated and blame others for their difficulties.

Conflicts, however, can also be the source of innovative ideas and synergy especially when there is much diversity among team members.[11] By having members with a variety of differences, teams can benefit from the wide array of perspectives, styles and skills. Diversity also lessens the occurrence of a dynamic called "group think" in which group members make wrong decisions because they no longer disagree with each other (e.g. The Nixon White House and The Challenger Disaster).[12] For these reasons, some organizations strategically create diversity on their teams by making certain that members come from different work functions, cultural backgrounds, or skill levels. Increased diversity, however, usually requires a longer time for teams to reach the high performance level especially in the earlier stages of the group process.

Facilitative Leadership and School Leadership Teams

In their attempts to reform education, more and more school districts have turned to school-based management teams.[13] Despite its current popularity, however, the literature has shown that it has seldom been fully-implemented and has not generally succeeded in reforming schools.[14] A typical scenario for implementation starts with a superintendent's mandate for schools to change their governance structures with the expectation that greater staff and parent participation would improve results. New structures (e.g. rules, training, procedures) are created but the culture of hierarchical power remains the same. The decision to go to school leadership is mandated from above. The accountability for results is still solely on the principal. The amount of resources given to the ongoing support of such change is not enough to foster sufficient change in the beliefs or the leadership skills of those serving on the team. Teachers and parents on the teams often defer to principals whose belief that they need to be in charge is reinforced. On these teams, a "business as usual" attitude or open hostility infects the group.

Why has this scenario predominated despite the involvement of so many capable, energetic people committed to change? According to Phillip Schlechty, the president of the Center for Leadership in School Reform, it is often because change leaders are not aware of system dynamics and how they affect behavior.[15] These dynamics are rarely perceived because they are embedded in every aspect of our everyday lives. Think, for example, about the relatively simple task of driving home from work. Most of what happens on the road is based on a system of certain procedures, rules, assumptions, technology and past experiences with other drivers that are not consciously considered. We do not question, for example, why we drive on the right side of the road. Yet, if we travel in England, we will soon discover that the right side suddenly becomes the "wrong" side. Cars travel on the left side of the road. If we drove, we would suddenly become very conscious of many of our tacit assumptions about driving a car. Our paradigm, or way of thinking, about driving would have to shift in order to navigate successfully through our changed environment (if we survive the first day that is).

In much the same way we operate our cars in a system of mostly-unobserved dynamics, we also steer ourselves through the complex system known as school. The system impacts on us all the time. When we try to make changes in the system, our efforts are likely to be affected not only by dynamics within the system but also by dynamics in connected systems. Too often, leaders, unaware of systems dynamics, blame the failure of change efforts on people when the real obstacle lies in a systems roadblock. For example, blaming poor student test scores on a teaching staff's ability to use a new reading curriculum may seem justified at first. However, this view may overlook the system's lack of investment in the kind of staff development that would facilitate the adoption of the curriculum. Furthermore, the school system's choices might be related to the political system's willingness to fund testing but not teacher training based on a belief that teachers need to be motivated to work harder and longer in the classroom. This set of dynamics creates a self-perpetuating cycle that impacts negatively on the students who are also part of the system.

In facilitating change to a collaborative school, therefore, change leaders (e.g. informal leaders as well as superintendents and principals) should take a systems perspective. They need to be aware that there is an interplay between a school's structure and culture which maintains the status quo.[16] Structure consists of rules, roles, relationships and procedures. Culture consists of beliefs, assumptions, norms, values and traditions that influence the school's day-to-day operation. Reform efforts generally focus on changing structure without adequately considering how to change the culture of the organization. Thus people in schools receive mixed messages and may eventually adopt a "this too shall pass" attitude towards reform.

In their study of schools that were most effective at using school-based management Odden and Wohletter found that these schools had genuine authority over budget, personnel and curriculum and used that authority to directly affect teaching and learning.[17] They also had principals who were often described as facilitators. In addition, the most effective schools employed the following strategies:

- Essential resources of professional development, important information, and rewards were provided to SBM members.
- Power was dispersed beyond the SBM team to subcommittees and other decision-making groups.

- Building schoolwide capacity for change was an important focus of the team;
- Communication among SBM team, district office and the school community was on-going.
- Feedback was sought and acted upon.
- The SBM team and the school community shared a well-defined vision that they often referred to.

These strategies suggest valuable ways to recognize an effective SBM but they do not give us a sense of how facilitative principals can foster the cultural change that can support such teams. How can leaders foster such a process? First, leaders must use their emotional competencies to make themselves aware of what cultural beliefs and assumptions they hold about schools especially in regards to power. This is not easy to do but, as an example, you can ask yourself:

- What are the meanings that I place on my title, the positions that others hold in the school and district, and the cultural artifacts of power that I value (e.g. my degree, my office, the rituals I and others engage in, etc.)?
- What norms of behavior seem to guide my practice and what do I do when those norms are violated?

You can also seek out and visit schools in places in which the culture of power is much different than your school's and then try to gain insights from that experience (just as you gained insight about America from driving on the left side in England). On your visit (even if it's a virtual tour on the web) be open to information that awakens you to new possibilities. As an added step, you can also use an outside consultant to help you uncover the systemic influences on your perceptions and behaviors. As you become aware, the challenge is to rethink your fundamental assumptions about leadership practices and authority. As this reflective process continues, you may feel some anxiety and defensiveness that you can use as signals that you are uncovering a strong dynamic.

Exploring a school's culture requires more than individual exploration, however.[18] After all, culture is a set of *shared* assumptions and, therefore, the next step is to look outside yourself in order to begin a group inquiry. This process requires the commitment of one or more key groups in the school who want to increase their understanding. It also requires a high level of facilitation skills so you may want to hire an experienced facilitator if no one in the school has these kinds of skills. With good facilitation, the process of uncovering a school's culture can be done in a half or full-day session. Some suggestions for a culture discovery process are described in this chapter's skills section.

Helping your school assess it's own culture and subcultures is not always an easy process. Even more difficult is acting upon what is discovered. According to Edgar Schein, "We must remember that cultural assumptions are the product of past successes."[19] Even if the culture is no longer very conducive to high performance and needs to be changed, for many people in a school the old way "works" and any change produces anxiety. Consider how motivated you are to intervene in the cultural process and if you or others have the needed skills given what you have learned about the system you are in. Remember that to change any elements of an organization's culture is a painful process. Leaders in such change are likely to become targets of anger because, by definition, they must challenge what the group has taken for granted. Be aware that this targeting is part of the natural process of change. It is here where the ability to manage your own emotions and the emotions of others becomes so essential.

If you do decide to act, then your action plan should focus on directly and indirectly developing the self-leadership capabilities of your school based management team and the rest of the school community. If you are lucky, you will be in a school and district in which the structure and culture are already fertile grounds for developing a community of leaders.[20] If you are not so fortunate, you may want to use your negotiation skills with the district superintendent to redesign the school management team initiative to include systems thinking. By reframing the problem from adversarial to collaborative (e.g. "How can we facilitate each other's leadership so that the SBM can have a real impact on teaching and learning in this district?"), a variety of innovative solutions can be generated. By offering to "serve" the superintendent's leadership interests in some way (e.g. offering to lead a team of principals to problem solve SBM issues) you might motivate the superintendent to eliminate some of the systemic constraints on shared leadership.

ACCOUNTABILITY

One of the major challenges for changing the hierarchical culture of leadership to a distributed culture is the question of who is accountable. In the old culture, there is one person at each level who is held accountable. Paul Houston, a superintendent for seventeen years wrote, "I once had a school board president who told me that my job as a superintendent was to be a quick-healing dartboard. And he was a supporter of mine!"[21] He goes on to describe the life cycle of a superintendent:

> They enter a community as a new savior who is thought capable of performing miracles and healings. Sometime later, they are put on trial, marched through the streets in public humiliation, and crucified. Johnathan Kozol once said that he thought that cities needed superintendents because they needed someone to die for their sins. (p. 428)

Though Houston may exaggerate their difficulties, superintendents are being increasingly pressured to produce results more quickly and with less resources. This has a tendency to make them more reactive and less proactive in their approach to their leadership. With their own feet to the fire they are more likely to set the flames higher under their principals especially if test scores are down.

For principals, this higher level of accountability involves more than testing.[22] While every state has created standards, the learning goals are not always clear or strong. Furthermore, assessments are not always aligned with the standards and, therefore, principals are held accountable for what is not being taught. In some schools, parents and teachers are resentful of state mandates and principals are caught in the middle. Moreover, principals are also held accountable for dealing with many of the social problems that have impacted on schools in recent years. In many places such as New York City, school leaders are being threatened with being fired and seeing their schools closed if they do not produce results quickly. In this era of aggressive accountability, it is tempting for principals to meet these challenges with an aggressive, take charge approach even if such an approach becomes counterproductive in the long run.

On the other hand, a facilitative approach to the challenges blurs accountability.[23] Principals may be fearful of entrusting so much power to people who will not share the accountability. In addition, teachers and other members of the school community who take on leadership may fear that the principal will not be a buffer for them if controversy results. All may feel that there is too much ambiguity in their rules.

The fear of being held accountable for a group's decisions often stems from the assumption that the group cannot make as wise a decision as the leader alone. The old joke that a camel is a horse created by a committee illustrates a commonly-held myth about group decisions. The myth presupposes that the group and the leader are in competition to make the best decision. The real question, however, is can a school principal *without* the resources of the members of the group make wiser decisions than the group *including* the principal?[24]

Moreover, faciltative school leaders still have enormous influence on an SBM and its decisions. They bring to the team their diverse experiences in education and they can help the team craft decisions that reflect the needs of not only the school but the district office. Also, if the team uses consensus to make decisions on important matters, the principal will not have to be accountable for any decision that she or he cannot agree to.

A principal might facilitate the empowerment and accountability of the SBM in a variety of ways. Some of these might include:

- Finding resources to provide as much ongoing training and coaching as is necessary to develop the skills that will enable the team to lead effectively.
- Participating in the training on an equal footing with all the other SBM members.
- Facilitating dialogue (or providing a facilitator) early on in the process to help the team come to consensus on many issues but especially on a definition of accountability with realistic expectations that do not focus only on test scores.[25]
- Modeling facilitation, calling attention to it, and encouraging others to take on the role (e.g. rotating chairpersons during meetings).
- Encouraging the use of terms, artifacts, symbols, procedures that suggest that "we are in this together and that we are accountable to each other as well as to others." When names of SBM members are listed, have them written in alphabetical order rather than listing your name first. Acknowledge feelings and manage tensions when the pressures of accountability are being experienced by people who are new to the "hot seat." By reframing the hot seat as a temperature gauge, people can use the information to assess their own performance and develop a plan for action.
- Resist the temptation to immediately take charge even when there is strong sentiment for you to so. Assess the situation to determine if you are the only one who can lead. If not, let there be a temporary vacuum and encourage those who can lead to do so. Resist the added temptation to take charge if that emerging leader does not do the task perfectly. When a member is not carrying out responsibilities, ask the team to act.
- With your team and with other SBM teams in the district, advocate for a new model of shared accountability. According to Doris Alvarez, a former National Principal of the Year, shared accountability would make SBM initiatives more effective and attract more capable candidates for principals' jobs.[26]
- Celebrate successes along the way.

In summary, accountability is just one issue SBM teams must face but it demands an inordinate amount of attention and skilled use of emotional competencies because education is now the veritable gladiators' arena for warring factions in our society.[27] The effectiveness of high EQ leaders to navigate through the process of team building and the development of team leadership will depend largely upon their ability to read the existing system while also leading others to change it.

SCHOOL-WIDE LEADERSHIP

In most schools today, a principal who strives to be a facilitative leader would be considered very successful if the school had a school-based management team that was high performing and collaborative. In some schools, however, there are people and systems in place that have gone beyond SBM to extend leadership throughout the school.[28] As these new models try to redefine what school leadership is or should be within a rapidly-changing information age, questions arise as to who will lead and who will follow.

A useful conceptual model for answering this question was proposed by Gary Crow.[29] Crow views leadership in collaborative settings as both an influence relationship and as systemic. Leadership as a relationship means that principals, teachers, and others in the school community influence each other to do things. This ability to influence, or lead, is not fixed in one person or position. Their leadership is based on their personal attributes, prior experience, their status among their peers, or their vision. A principal and her staff, for example, may be led to adopt a new approach to instruction by a team of teachers who have developed expertise in the method and have used their persuasive skills to advocate for it. In a collaborative school this influence relationship is recognized and is seen as an ongoing attempt to establish parity (i.e. equal status) and reciprocity (i.e. influence works both ways).

Leadership as systemic means that the leadership potential of the larger environment including parents, the community and outside agencies are brought into these notions of who will lead and who will follow. Rather than seeing leadership as a zero sum game in which "if you lead, I lose power," leadership is seen as "the more people take leadership on what we are trying to accomplish, and the more we can help them to do it, the more influence we have." Leadership then can be conceived as not only coming from direct relationships but also from influencing those relationships in indirect systemic ways.

This concept of leadership and organizational structure encourages the development of democratic, collaborative, self-managing teams into what some writers have called "webs of association."[30] These webs are flexible, evolving partnerships of teams guided by shared values and acting synergistically to adapt to a modern, rapidly-changing world. In a school or school district, these webs generate a sense of community, of being connected. This connectedness is maintained through ongoing dialogue that identifies needs, addresses common concerns, resolves conflict, and engages in reflective practice.

In this kind of organizational community, what does leadership look like? Unlike hierarchical leadership, democratic leadership can be found anywhere in the school. As discussed in earlier chapters, leadership is a skill that can be developed in everyone and, if you look hard enough in your current school, you can find it being exhibited by a number of people in informal ways. Moreover, if you could follow all of the people in your school community, you would likely find many exercising leadership in their communities, their places of worship or elsewhere. In the school of the future, these leadership abilities would be identified, developed and tapped into to meet the school's current and future needs.

Depending on those leadership abilities and school needs, the role of the principal is likely to be more fluid and adapted to local situations. In some schools, the principal may function as a "linking leader" who facilitates the smooth interactions between teams and makes sure resources of time, money, and training are allocated where they are needed.[31] In other schools, the principal may function more as a coach who develops instructional leaders who in turn mentor others. In still other schools, there may not even be a position formerly known as Principal and responsibilities for hiring and firing, choosing curriculum and ensuring accountability may be held by teams or by the whole school community.[32] In order to visualize how this model of facilitative leadership differs from leadership in terms of a group's effectiveness, look at Table 8.1 which is taken from Roger Schwarz' *The Skilled Facilitator,* a classic in the field of group facilitation.

IN SUMMARY

In many ways, what we are describing in facilitative leadership is an emotionally intelligent school. It's a school in which everyone, compelled by a common vision, is in the process of becoming emotionally competent. It's what Goleman, Boyatzis and McKee

TABLE 8.1   Moving from Traditional Leadership to Facilitative Leadership [33]

Group Element	Traditional Leader	Facilitative Leader
Group Process		
Communication	Leader controls who communicates with whom.	Leader teaches group members how to communicate effectively, using the ground rules. Group members initiate communication with anyone who has valid information or has an interest in the situation.
Conflict management	Leader manages conflicts among group members.	Leader teaches group members how to manage their own conflicts.
Problem solving	Leader solves problems that group members present.	Leader teaches group members the problem-solving model. Leader ensures that group members have access to relevant information to solve problems. Group members take responsibility for identifying and solving problems they encounter.
Decision making	Leader either makes decisions alone or after consultation with group members.	Group members make many decisions on their own or as a group. Leader and group members jointly make appropriate decisions by consensus.
Boundary management	Leader is largely responsible for communicating, coordinating, and solving problems with people outside the group.	Leader teaches members how to communicate, coordinate, and solve problems with people outside the group. Leader and members jointly determine the boundary-management approach. Leader manages boundaries largely to facilitate group problem solving rather than to solve the problem.
Group Structure		
Group norms	Leader attempts to establish norms implicitly with group.	Leader shares core values, principles, and ground rules with group members as potential bases for group norms. Leader and group members explicitly discuss and agree on group norms.
Group culture	Leader attempts to influence culture implicitly.	Leader shares core values, principles, and ground rules as potential bases for group culture. Leader and group members explicitly discuss the current and desired culture and agree on steps to shape it.

TABLE 8.1   Moving from Traditional Leadership to Facilitative Leadership, Cont'd.

Group Element	Traditional Leader	Facilitative Leader
Sufficient time	Leader decides how much times tasks should take and sets deadlines in consultation with group members.	Leader teaches group members how to plan and manage time. Group members use relevant information and support from leader to set deadlines for their tasks.
Clearly defined roles	Leader defines employees' roles with or without participation from group members.	Group members use relevant information and support from leader to define and agree on their roles.
Appropriate membership	Leader or leader's supervisor decides who will join and leave the group with or without consulting group members.	Leader ensures that group has information and skills necessary to select (and remove) group members. Group members use relevant information and support from leader to discuss and decide what kinds of members they need.
Motivating task	Leader or leader's supervisor designs group members' jobs, sometimes in consultation with group members.	Leader helps members understand what makes a job motivating. Group members use relevant information and support from leader to redesign their jobs.
Clear goals	Leader sets goals based on direction from leader's supervisor and sometimes in consultation with group members.	Leader helps group members learn how to set clear goals. Group members use relevant information and support from leader to discuss and set goals.
Organizational Context Physical environment	Leader takes responsibility for trying to change the physical work environment, sometimes using information from group members.	Group members take responsibility for trying to change the physical work environment with relevant information and support from leader.
Technological and material resources	Leader takes responsibility for obtaining resources.	Group members take responsibility for obtaining resources with relevant information and support from leader.
Training and consultation	Leader takes responsibility for identifying and obtaining training and consultation needed by group.	Leader ensures that group members have knowledge and skills to assess their training and consultation needs. Group members take responsibility for identifying and obtaining training and consultation needed by group.

TABLE 8.1   Moving from Traditional Leadership to Facilitative Leadership, Cont'd.

Group Element	Traditional Leader	Facilitative Leader
Information and feedback	Leader decides what information, including feedback, group members need and provides it, sometimes with participation from group members. Leader provides feedback to group members about their performance.	Group members decide what information they need and obtain it. Leader helps group members learn how to provide and seek feedback effectively. Leader and group members provide feedback to each other and critique their own performances jointly through self-critiques.
Rewards consistent with objectives	Leader (or supervisor above leader's level) designs reward system and decides who receives rewards. Leader focuses primarily on individual extrinsic rewards.	Leader ensures that group members understand the elements of effective reward systems. Group members design reward system and decide who receives rewards. Reward systems include intrinsic and extrinsic rewards and focus on group and individual rewards.
Supportive culture	Leader and group members attempt to influence culture implicitly.	Leader and group members are models of the core values, principles, and ground rules and simultaneously advocate and encourage others to inquire about using them as bases for group culture. Leader and group members explicitly discuss the current and desired culture and agree on steps to shape it.

From *The Skilled Facilitator* by Roger Schwarz, 1994.

call collective emotional competence in which vision is turned into action through processes and not programs.[34] Processes such as action learning, 360° feedback, win-win negotiating and team building. Processes created and maintained by many emotionally resonant leaders. Leaders who care enough to dare, who succeed in the deeds of others, and who embrace change willingly.

Facilitative leadership in some ways represents the ideal goal of the EQ leader because it means that his or her school has the capacity to lead itself. In moving towards this ideal, the challenge for the facilitative leader is to figure out what processes can be put in place to move closer to that ideal at different stages of the school's development. In doing so, EQ leaders will undoubtedly draw upon all the emotional competencies, in themselves and in the people around them. These competencies will be needed to deal with the issues of cultural change, team building, accountability and organizational design. Fortunately, there are models of successful implementation in which communities of learners and leaders significantly improved student performance, staff morale, and a sense of community.[35]

In short, facilitative leadership in schools is promoting revolution in the ways that schools are traditionally managed. Just as cultural revolutions by people of color, women and other disempowered people in the United States improved life in our country, so too will a democratic revolution in education improve life in our schools. In closing, remember the words of Albert Camus:

> *Revolt begins in the human heart. But there comes a time when revolt spreads from heart to spirit, when a feeling becomes an idea, when impulse leads to concerted action. This is the moment of revolution.*[36]

REFLECTIVE QUESTIONS

Focus on times when you are asked either directly or indirectly to assume a leadership role.

1. How do you respond to followers?
2. Do you use power, influence, or both and do your choices reflect a traditional or a facilitative approach to leadership?
3. Is your leadership style consistent with your school system's organizational culture? If not, what emotional reactions do you experience?
4. How hard would it be for you to be more facilitative? Why?
5. During the times that you assume a leadership role are there moments when you naturally fall into a follower's role? What seems to precipitate that switch and what feelings, if any, do you experience at those times?

LESSON FROM THE FIELD

Larry Peterson

I had been retired from education for four years when I received a call from the personnel director at the Salt Lake City Public School District in 1997, asking if I would be willing to come in and interview for a principalship at Glendale Middle School. I was not told everything that was going on at the school when I accepted the position one week before school started.

When I arrived, I found the school in complete disarray. Over fifty percent of the faculty had transferred. There was little communication between faculty members and departments and morale was rock bottom. We had no textbooks and our computer program had been completely dismantled. Everybody was teaching in their own way—making up units as they went along. There was no coherent plan for the school and no core curriculum. Student performance was the lowest in the district. The school had a student mobility rate of about forty-six percent during the school year and some students were in and out of school three times during the year. Over half of the student body came from single parent homes, and about the same percentage was affiliated or had a family member or friend who was gang-related. We were also experiencing major discipline problems because everybody was disciplining in their own way. Glendale had no "glue,"—no guiding philosophy or vision or close-knit school community to hold it together.

Our biggest challenge was reading. Our average student entered seventh grade reading on the fourth grade level. In two years, we needed to get them ready to enter high school reading on the ninth grade level. We were severely challenged on every front. However, I thrive on challenge and it was worth the gamble for those young people. They deserved the best possible education. I walked into the job knowing that it couldn't be any worse after I left—it had only one way to go and that was up. But if I was truly the leader that I thought I was, I believed I could help lead this change. I told myself this staff, this community, and these children can learn to see themselves in a more positive light and achieve dreams that they didn't currently believe were possible.

The first thing I noticed was there was little trust between teachers and administration in the school, so I established an open door policy. My staff did not need an appointment to see me. I set up individual meetings with the teachers so that they could see that I was genuinely interested in them. My main theme was, "Remember we are in this for our students. Nothing comes before serving these students." I also told them, "This is a new administration; this is one that we're going to build on trust. We're going to build our unity and work together toward a common vision for our students." That was where we started. Of course, the teachers tested me and I was always very honest. I listened to each one and took notes. I believe as a school leader that you must be straight with everyone. Educators, parents and students want the truth. If a leader is not telling the truth, it breeds distrust. If you tell the truth and stand by your principles, trust will come.

The school-wide process we used—*In Pursuit of Possibilities*—really helped us. We met regularly. Based on individual conversations with teachers, I presented what the staff perceived was happening, what they did not like, and what they wanted to see happen. We discussed these ideas openly but did not come to any conclusions right away. We just talked and listened to one another. No judgment, no blame, just honest communication about how to serve students better. We discovered common ground that teachers were able to work with. When they left the meetings, they were able to at least speak to one another, to begin planning with one another.

The whole process of building a relationship-centered learning community supported our unity theme. Right from the get-go, we broke up cliques in community building exercises and got them thinking together about the mission statement and our guiding principles. Barriers started to come down. I began to see teachers working to align their subject-area goals and objectives with our common goal.

I made sure that I was in the halls between class changes. I brought teachers together casually in the hall so that there was ongoing conversation. And not just on the professional level, but friendly-type talking so that they began to see each other as both colleagues and people. They talked not just about educational issues, but it was about themselves or their hopes and dreams for young people and our school.

After several months of implementing the process, two staff members stood up and said, "We are one community, we are one unit. We don't want to hear any more negativity or excuses. We can do this. We are a good school, and we can be a really great school. Our students deserve our best effort." I knew at this point that all I had to do was plant some seeds and hang on because they were going to take it from there. They had input into every decision we were making, and because they had become a true community, they were the ones making it happen. I knew they would not—could not—fail.

After one year, our lowest reading group had moved from the pre-primer level to a third grade level. Our average student—including our resource students—gained over a year's growth in 9 months! This was a small miracle for our school. I attribute this directly to the work we did in becoming a unified community, dedicated to students and relentless about the quality of education we were providing to them.

Larry Peterson was principal of Glendale Middle School between 1997–2001. He participated in the "In Pursuit of Possibilities" school transformation process between 1998–2001 and was awarded the Huntsman Award for Excellence in Education in 2001 for his exceptional leadership in turning the school around. He was the only secondary principal in the state of Utah to receive this award in that year.

Chapter 9

Leading the School of the Future

There is nothing more difficult to take in hand, more perilous to conduct, or more uncertain in its success than to take the lead in the introduction of a new order of things.

—Machiavelli in *The Prince*

The world had changed. Not a slight change but a seismic change, a change emanating from the core of human society and rising up, slowly at first but then accelerating. As it spread, the change began to transform the landscape of how people communicate, how they work, and how they learn. The change was first felt by only a small number of people and many of them either dismissed it as a passing thing or tried to adapt it to fit their working models of "how things are." But as the change spread, many people felt its tremors and they responded with fear, anger, confusion or a profound sense of wonder as a child might who first discovers snow. What is this? Can I stop this? Can I use this? What else will I find? The world was changing.

The inventor of the new information technology that precipitated this change could not have predicted how the world would be transformed. He was just trying to solve a classic ongoing human problem: The world is changing rapidly, the population keeps increasing, people want information and knowledge, and existing communication technologies are not meeting this need. He believed that his invention would fill the need and make him a fortune. Like many other trailblazers, however, he lost his business to debtors before his innovation took hold and it was left to others to amass fortunes by developing new products for commerce, government, and education. Education, in particular, was slow to adopt the change and even slower to transform itself to make best use of this modern marvel. Many teachers and school leaders either ignored the change or simply fit the new tools into existing instructional methods that took little advantage of this revolutionary new advance in learning. Some asked, "Why do we need this?"

However, new products soon became less expensive and visionaries pioneered new ways of using these modern wonders in schools and throughout society. The world had changed. The revolution had taken hold.[1]

Today, what was once radical and startling in the 15th Century is so accepted and expected that it's as invisible in our daily lives as our tap water and morning coffee. The invention? It was the printing press and, though Johannes Gutenberg's later life remains relatively obscure today, his printing press and the printed word have transformed our world. If you had thought for a moment that the information technology described above involved computers and digital technology, your assumption would not have been unreasonable. Like the printing press, the computer was invented to meet the information needs of a rapidly changing world. Like the proponents of mass-produced books more than 500 years ago, gurus of "The Digital Age" have "seen" the future and want to lead us, kicking and screaming if need be, into a new and better world. Like education in 15th and 16th Century Europe, it is education today that seems to be the slowest institution to fully integrate the new practices yet it is education that will eventually determine how profound the change will be in society. And like your counterparts in medieval Europe, it is you as an educational leader who is thrust into the middle of the tense interplay between the old and the new.

In this chapter, we will explore how EQ leaders can help their school communities work together to use new technologies in ways that are true to their vision of a caring learning community. Is all this just hype to be taken with a virtual grain of salt or is the new information technology (IT) really a printing-press-like catalyst to a sea of change in how we teach and learn? Will we purchase all the latest gadgets and find that they prove less like the printed book and more like the overhead projector now sitting unused in a classroom or closet? How can we facilitate a process that will increase the probability that investments in technology will produce results without getting rid of all those practices that make us already effective? In terms of human relations, how do we deal with all the feelings that will come with change? What resources are available and what can be done to ensure that there is no digital divide? What might a future school look like? How can we prepare ourselves for the future when we still have a pile of unread books and papers on our desks in the present? All these are important questions for EQ leaders to ask of themselves and others.

In order to help you to answer these questions, this chapter examines IT in schools from an EQ leadership perspective. First, we investigate technology use and its impact on society, schools and students in recent years. Second, we ask you to consider how school design influences school reform efforts and leadership, particularly when technology and collaborative inquiry are being promoted. Finally, we look at the possibilities for future schools along with potential dangers, especially the danger of increasing the digital divide between haves and have-nots.

A NEW WORLD?

In 1976 there were approximately fifty computers in the world.[2] Twenty years later 50,000 computers were being sold every ten hours. In 1985 there were 300,000 registered e-mail users on our planet but only fifteen years later there were 134 million just in the United States. According to the United States Census Bureau, 82 per cent of all classrooms in the United States have a least one computer and the ratio of students to computers is roughly one to four.[3] The percentage of public schools with Internet access has jumped from 50 percent in 1995 to 98 percent in 2001. In that same time span, the percentage of instructional classrooms with Internet access soared from eight percent to 77 percent. Clearly there is a powerful movement to improve schools with technology.

From a leader's perspective, however, these changes can have little meaning unless it significantly improves teaching and learning. Has new technology lived up to its claims of transforming what goes on in schools? In many cases the digital revolution has only succeeded in being a new (and expensive) face on the ubiquitous worksheet. A closer look at Census figures suggests that teachers are primarily using computers and the Internet to engage their students in computer applications (e.g. word processing) and practice drills. What is even more troubling is that the poorer and younger children are, the more likely they will be faced with a computer that drills them.[4] Only about one out of every four teachers who use technology assigns IT tasks that require the application of higher-order thinking skills. That ratio is even higher in schools with large numbers of students in poverty.

In looking back on the printing press' impact on education, however, we see that educational change in response to a new groundbreaking technology is never sudden. The use of printed books in schools in Gutenberg's Europe was minimal at first because these books were still expensive.[5] Moreover, teachers were still trained in methods that emphasized mere recitation. Teachers would read from a book, often Latin from the Bible, and students would repeat what they heard. Teachers would then write a portion of the text and students would copy it. Even when printed books became relatively inexpensive, oral reading remained the standard and teachers often admonished students if they read without speaking. Gradually, however, the educational paradigm shifted as humanists during the Enlightenment promoted learning among the rising middle classes and the printing presses found markets for books printed in German, English and other languages. School leaders and their students were being born into a world that was papered with the printed word.

In much the same way, those of us in schools today may find that the children born in the digital age may be more ready to make good use of technology than we are.[6] Just as medieval schools held onto their Latin texts and outmoded instructional strategies, we may be holding onto our textbooks and teacher-directed instruction. This resistance makes sense since so much of schooling is structured as an adaptation to make best use of the printed word. By their very nature, books are linear and so many aspects of education are designed to create opportunities for students and teachers to easily access or produce information and knowledge in a linear way.[7] The Dewey decimal system, standardized tests, curriculum manuals, graded classes, organizational hierarchy, and school architecture all are shaped by the linear model of print.

The human brain, however, does not just think in a linear way (which makes learning how to read a language more difficult than learning how to speak a language).[8] Reflect on your own thinking, for example, as you search for clues as to why your school's lunchroom has become disruptive. Walk into the lunchroom and your mind automatically makes random connections to dozens of associated thoughts and feelings as you follow your preplanned linear steps of investigation. The conversations you hear, the smells from the kitchen, the movements of the students and the adult aides, the sounds bouncing off the walls stimulate and influence your thinking. If you are an adept problem-solver, your divergent and convergent thinking helps you navigate through these currents of information, venturing up potentially promising streams of information, formulating hypotheses, testing, analyzing, and drawing conclusions. At some point, you might tap into the knowledge of the lunchroom aides but, if you are smart, you will also tap into all the information around you that is pertinent to the problem.

The computer and its offshoot, the Internet, provide tools for expanding upon the linear limits of what Peter Drucker calls our "mental geography" to enhance the learning of higher-order thinking skills.[9] The invention of printing technology eventually enabled students to learn *knowledge* directly without the control of a powerful church monopoly. The invention of information technology enables 21st Century students to acquire *information* and develop knowledge directly without the limits of textbooks or schools. A child who wants to learn about how roller coasters work, for example, can find information in the form of text, graphics, first person accounts, audiovisual simulations and mathematical formulas with a few keystrokes (or voice commands with the latest software) at home. No longer will that student learner be limited to the half-page blurb in the science text or the research that a dedicated but overworked teacher can gather from the public library on a Sunday afternoon. The boundaries for learning have widened to include what is appropriately called the World Wide Web.

For schools to adapt to these new boundaries and to the mental geographies of their incoming students, they must rethink how they use new technologies and how their structures either promote or limit this rethinking. At present, schools that are actively involved in this self-searching process are still the exception but they do seem to share certain characteristics:

1. Technology is viewed as a means to learning rather than a distinct subject area. Technology is primarily integrated into the curriculum.
2. Schools interact with people (e.g. parents, community members, experts) and institutions (e.g. other schools, universities, government agencies) outside the physical boundaries of the school. Technology facilitates these interactions by extending the ability of people to collaborate across distances and time. Face to face interactions (F2F) are still seen as valuable but virtual interactions are also seen as desirable.
3. Teachers, administrators and key members of the learning community are given the time, methods, training and incentives to adapt technology to the specific dynamics of the school. There is the awareness that "plug-in technology" (i.e. technology supposedly able to be used "as is" by any school) is costly and ineffective in the long run. Successful adaptations will all look different.
4. People are aware that the change process takes time and fine-tuning.[10]

TWENTY-FIRST CENTURY TECHNOLOGY AND PREHISTORIC EMOTIONS

The EQ leader is aware that changes that would come with a truly technology-based school or school district are bound to spark emotions and resistance. However, EQ leaders are as accepting of the negative feelings around change as they are of the positive feelings because, as Michael Fullan points out, "with greater emotional intelligence and empathy, initiators of change learn from resistors."[11]

Learn from resistors? What can you learn from someone who's rolling his eyes or trying to find fault in any plan for becoming a technology-based school? Visualize yourself for a moment as a principal standing in front of a staff in which half of its members are the rolling-eyed, fault-finding kind of resistor. How would you feel and what would you do if you wanted to introduce the idea of enhancing the school with technology in front of this group? You planned to show a video of a school similar to yours that had transformed itself with cyber tools but how do you frame the rest of the meeting? You could make a hard sell on the idea, maybe slip in a disguised threat or tell your staff that this is the superintendent's idea and you're just carrying out orders. How do you think you and your staff would respond emotionally to each of these options?

One other option is to suspend your advocacy role for this meeting and use the meeting to promote your staff's learning and your own. After a short light-and-lively gathering experience and the establishment of group guidelines, you might explain the purpose of the meeting in this way:

I know that you have a wide range of feelings and opinions about integrating technology into the curriculum. I feel hopeful that we can use the energy of these feelings and the thought behind these opinions today to talk, in a safe way, about any problems or opportunities we see in using new technology in our school. I think that we can all learn from our different perspectives if we try to suspend our beliefs long enough to fully listen to each other. To help make it easier for you to do this I'd like to lead you in a process that I have written out on this chart. . . .

Ignoring the rolling eyes, you describe the process. First, you randomly divide the staff into two groups. One group will be the Proponents and the other group will be the Critics. Each group will view the video of the Digital School from the perspective of their assigned group and not from their individual viewpoints. For example, a teacher may love the idea of becoming a Digital School but, being in the Critics group, she must try to suspend her true beliefs to find all the problems and flaws in the Digital School's technology-based curriculum. Conversely, a teacher in the Proponents Group must look at the video through a positive lens to find what is working in this model school even if he had walked into this meeting ready to resist to the end.

The video is played. The two groups meet separately, then together, to share their reactions. By going through this process, true dialogue is more likely to be generated, fundamental problems identified and people's fears, both real or imagined, examined carefully. Both proponents and critics have an opportunity to listen to other perspectives and to perhaps experience a shift in their own. No decisions are made at this meeting but information derived from the meeting is used to inform the next steps. Next steps can include going ahead with change in a big way, proceeding cautiously, resolving identified problems before any change is initiated or abandoning the reform for the time being because the time for change is not ripe.

The EQ leader then is someone who is willing to "slow down in order to speed up."[12] By slowing things down enough to learn what people feel and think about change, leaders can discover how to nurture the kind of change no shotgun approach could ever accomplish. EQ leadership in individuals and in organizations means viewing technology through a human lens, embracing it when it preserves our humanness and rejecting it when it infringes upon our humanness. In his book *High Tech High Touch,* John Naisbitt suggests that people need to learn how to live as human beings in this technologically-dominated world much as they learned to do when other technologies that now seem quaint shook the world (e.g. farming, the compass).[13] The school leader that removes blocks from the kindergarten, art instruction from the curriculum, and music from the lives of students in order to pay for more computers needs to press the *Pause* button and engage the minds and hearts of those he serves.

DESIGNED FOR LEARNING AND LEADING IN A DIGITAL AGE

In the process of planning how technology might be used to enhance collaborative, inquiry-based learning, you and your school community need to consider the school's physical environment. Often the school environment is either taken for granted or is seen as a problem without a solution when school reform is considered. Little time or creative thinking is spent exploring how much design affects learning and leading and how to design or redesign schools to foster both. In this section we will undertake such an exploration.

Walk into most schools in the United States and you will be in familiar territory. There will still be the up and down staircases, the general office, the individual classrooms with closed doors facing long corridors, the rather uninviting cafeteria and an assortment of other spaces whose appearance and even smell will likely spark flashbacks of childhood. During your walk you may encounter signs of the 21st century but, for the most part, the space you are in and its design is most deeply rooted in the 19th century. It is not a design conducive to facilitative leadership and a collaborative approach to teaching and learning in a technologically based environment.[14]

Consider the typical middle or high school. It is most likely a very large structure. Upon entering the building, the students move to a room in which a teacher in the front of the room does most of the talking while the students sit in individual workstations (desks). Forty-five minutes later a bell rings and the students move to another room while the teacher in the first room waits for another group of twenty-five or so students. This "assembly line" process continues throughout the day. At some point in the day, a bell will ring and students will hurry to a large cafeteria where they will stand in another assembly line to get standardized food in the most efficient way. Meanwhile, teachers will use the short time periods they have when not teaching to eat, mark papers, prepare for future classes or confer with peers. The year passes and the group of students is passed on to the next group of teachers on another floor and the process continues.

Overseeing all this is the school principal tucked away behind the buffer of the general office where information can be received and channeled over the intercom system. In this context, the physical design of most schools is best suited for individual work, control and conformity. It is not a design that facilitates the ability of teachers, students and other members of the school community to work together in creative and meaningful ways.[15]

In this same school, the informational technology reinforces rather than transforms the rigid linear structures. The most recently renovated space in the school is the computer lab, which has the latest hardware and educational software so that scheduled classes can develop computer skills under the supervision of the computer teacher. There are computers in other classrooms, but most rooms are not wired for the Internet and the computers are few in number and rarely used during class time. This typical arrangement of IT shapes the mental architecture of students and faculty to perceive IT as separate from the normal curriculum rather than an integral part.[16]

Given that most of us never took a course in innovative school design, how can we take a step back from our school's physical "plant" (a word that cries out FACTORY) and consider its design? Franklin Becker and Fritz Steele, authors of *Workplace by Design*, suggest that it is important to look at any workplace in two distinct but connected ways.[17] First, look at the physical setting and determine what message it is giving and what message do you want it to give. Do the size, structure, lighting, furniture and other physical properties of the space convey a message that this a wonderful place to work together? A second way of looking at the workplace is to explore the process by which team members develop and manage the space while connecting it to other spaces in the school. How, for example, will the team make sure the diverse needs of team members are taken into account? How will the work get done and how will people use the space as tasks change? From these two perspectives, a school community might design collaborative settings in many different ways but Becker and Steele suggest five rules of thumb:

1. Create magnet spots with inviting characteristics such as a high-quality food center, comfortable furniture, rich resources and attractive décor.
2. Put collaborative spaces in central, visible locations. Avoid inconvenient leftover sites.
3. Design the areas to foster communication. Round tables and good acoustics make a difference.
4. Don't create so many communal spots that the chances of accidental meetings are greatly decreased.
5. Encourage people to use the spaces. Eliminate norms that convey the message that communicating with one another is "wasting time" or not "real work".

In state-of-the-art schools, the school building is carefully designed to stimulate curiosity and serve as an instructional tool.[18] Designs for learning communities in new

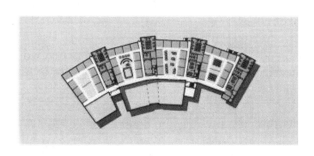

FIGURE 9.1
Courtesy of The School of Environmental Studies
A High School Built for Collaboration. The School of Environmental Studies (SES) in Apple Valley, Minnesota, was designed to foster teamwork and student-centered learning. Photo on left: The school is divided into four "houses" of 100 students. Each house is divided into ten "pods" of ten students with a common meeting area in the middle. For school gatherings a large multipurpose space is centrally located. Photo on right: SES students working in pods they designed themselves.[21]

construction might include a series of small suites of classrooms and support facilities (e.g. computer hubs, teacher office and multi-use meeting spaces, large flexible project areas, etc.) known as "pods".[19] Pods can be connected by a pathway more like a Main Street or museum exhibit space than an all-too-narrow barren hallway. At the center of the school might be the resource center that serves as the accessible support hub of the school replacing the closed-off central office. Cafeteria design might benefit from what works in bookstore cafes and mall food courts by using food stations, natural lighting, comfortable seating and different levels to reduce line time and eliminate the institutional feel of the physical environment. The school could also be built small enough to enable all members of the school community to know each other and be able to work together without massive scheduling problems.[20]

In old schools with design problems, there is much that can be done to achieve many of the same design effects as in the new school design. Large schools can be restructured so that the building houses smaller "families" or academies in which teams of teachers and students work cooperatively with each other over several years. With doses of creativity, classrooms and even hallways can be easily transformed into flexible team project areas that be shared by the team rather than "owned" by one teacher (given that there was consensus for the change). Other rooms can be turned into meeting/work areas. Connected by the Internet, off-site learning environments at museums, universities, zoos or even corporations can be used for exciting learning opportunities but also to develop community-school partnerships. If rewiring the school for the Internet is too difficult or costly in an old school, schools can use the latest wireless technology to connect both desktop and laptop computers to each other in a local area network (LAN), to other schools in the district in a wide area network (WAN) and to the World Wide Web (WWW).[22]

In redesigning schools, facilitative leaders can use a process suggested by the United States Department of Education to build community and leadership capacity.[23] In the first stage, look for people in the school, the district and the community who are interested in and able to lead the master planning process. Support these five or six leaders as they develop an initial action plan for the process. Facilitate communication between this team and the larger community that they represent. In stage two, work together with the leadership group to develop enough funding to insure that the process can include everyone with a stake in the change. During the third stage, help the team select an expert planner from inside or outside the community and work with all involved to develop a cohesive team for the next stage.

In the next two stages, the team can expand its numbers or create a new team that will constitute a core team that guides the project to its completion. This team enlists from the community a large steering committee, which meets the criteria of clout, commitment and diversity. Because the steering committee can have up to 100 members with diverse backgrounds and interests, the facilitative leader provides training and other resources to help members learn the conflict resolution skills and decision-making skills necessary for working together. The leader can also ensure that typically excluded groups such as students and parents are not only represented but that they are heard. This steering committee works together with the school community to create a common understanding of the problem, gather feedback on the process, and build community consensus on a shared vision and possible plans of action. In stage six, the core team develops the master plan based on the information collected by the steering committee. During this stage, the EQ leader can help the team reflect on its process and its plan to make certain that both are in keeping with the shared vision. Finally, the plan is implemented with ongoing assessment and fine-tuning. Here the school leader acts as a coach to help others to assess their progress in terms of the school's action plan and also in terms of their development as leaders.

The School of the Future

No school leader can accurately predict what schools will look like in the future. As leadership guru, Peter Drucker, points out no one's predictions soon after the invention of the printing press or the steam engine foresaw the revolutions that would follow.[24] In its early use, the printing press primarily served to maintain the status quo of the wealthy and powerful and, only later, did Martin Luther and the humanists of the Renaissance discover the true power of the press to spread ideas and transform society. The steam engine and its offspring, the railroad, would lead eventually to factories and big cities and public schools in big cities that were designed in the late 19th century to function like factories. But did James Watt and his contemporaries envision the schools in which you spent your youth? The idea of a public school designed to be as scientifically managed as a factory only came much later, a revolutionary idea at that time but one still shaped by the earlier technology, the printed word.[25]

If leaders cannot predict the future, how can they lead? The answer is that they can raise their awareness of emerging trends, keep themselves updated on new technologies that might serve their school's mission, and act as a catalyst for change. By using their EQ they can facilitate the collaborative processes that learning communities will have to make regarding when to say "Yes" and when to say "Pass" to the latest innovation. Mastering their conflict management skills, they can turn conflicts into opportunities for gathering information, generating new ideas and strengthening working relationships. Finally, they can use technology themselves to foster the EQ development of everyone in their schools.[26]

Emerging Trends

There are a number of educational trends that seem to be emerging from IT best practices:[27]

- Student-centered learning rather than teacher-centered learning.
- Improved instruction that can be tailored to individual learning styles and special needs.

- A changing role for the teacher.
- Communication and collaboration beyond the boundaries of the classroom and the school.
- Flexible restructuring of time to free students and teachers from a fixed nine to three, September to June schedule.
- More focus on life long learning.

The first three trends reflect the power of IT to give immediate and individualized access to both information and knowledge. In the past, the teacher and the textbook primarily determined what the student learned in school but neither the teacher nor the textbook can match the ability of new technologies to provide up-to-date extensive information on any aspect of the curriculum. How many of us have read a textbook that was ten years old and laughed when we noticed its inaccuracies or lack of relevancy to our students' lives? By using IT *and* an inquiry-based instructional approach, the learning process can shift from teacher-directed to more student-directed learning as students engage in both individual and group learning activities that are tailored to the learning styles and needs of each and every student. For example, it is possible that a future student, a kinesthetic learner with a mild visual impairment and a deep interest in history and fantasy, will have a curriculum that adapts easily each day to his needs as well to all other students.[28] In this future, each student may gather information and knowledge on their own inexpensive wireless handheld computer and with that same device make calculations, word process notes, take photos or moving images, store data, and communicate with online mentors or peer collaborators. Some schools already equip students with hand-held computers called personal digital assistants (PDA's) but these devices may someday be replaced by user-friendly electronic "paper" that looks like paper in size, weight and flexibility but is more powerful than any desktop made today.[29]

In this future, the teacher's role changes from being the main source of all information and knowledge to a guide to both knowledge and information. Relieved of being the primary dispenser of information, the teacher is freed to spend more time facilitating group interactions and coaching students one-on-one. Teachers are able then to spend more time developing the EQ of their students, helping them to critically and creatively process their virtual and classroom explorations, and to reflect on their group interactions.

These changes in how students learn and teachers teach has implications for the last three trends as well. If students are not exclusively bound to their teachers and their textbooks and teachers are not bound to the limitations of the textbook manual, both groups can extend their roles beyond the confines of the classroom walls. Students involved in project-based leaning can learn from students, teachers, and experts from around the world or from the school five blocks away. Similarly, teachers can collaborate with others via the Internet or Intranet to share ideas, solve problems and plan. Furthermore, these collaborations do not need to be relegated to a 9 to 3 day, Monday to Friday, September to June in a physical building called a school. Schools can function as hubs for essential face to face (F2F) interactions such as team and community building but many students and teachers can function successfully in their roles while temporarily located elsewhere (e.g. museums, field expeditions, home, internships). Furthermore, if we expand the possibilities we can make room for parents, teachers and administrators to engage in learning themselves in this wider community of learners. Can you picture, for example, communities of learners in schools and in the larger community coming together in virtual and F2F collaboration to learn about the natural, historical and human riches of their state and producing a website based on their research that is actually used by tourists?[30]

In this future school, education looks quite different. Schools might be open all day and all year meeting the needs of students, educators and the larger community. Scheduling, done almost entirely by powerful computers *and not by principals,* flawlessly manage the comings and goings of people who rotate in and out of different sessions and locales. The division of the school day into forty-five-minute periods may be replaced by a more flexible approach that can accommodate the vagaries of a technology-enhanced project-based curriculum. At times, teachers, outside experts, and students of different ages may engage in long term projects that makes use of mentoring, peer tutoring, integrated studies, or service learning. Parents also may be involved in these projects as well as in online courses that enable busy or school-phobic parents to continuously learn in a non-threatening convenient way. Schools may also replace the traditional multiple choice tests with ones that provide ongoing user-friendly information about student learning in academic and social- emotional areas. As part of that ongoing assessment, student portfolios from preK-12 may be digitally stored and instantaneously accessed to provide a developmental portrait of a student's progress (parents might also like a copy!). This information is then programmed so that as soon as an individual (student or adult) accesses technology that technology instantly adapts the learning experience to that person's learning style, interests, language, and prior learning.[31]

In all these scenarios, the mission of the school community must guide the decisions and the implementation of any change effort. The EQ leader must personally become informed about new technologies and how they can or cannot be applied to furthering the school's mission. Working with others, school leaders can make virtual or real visits to see how the technology is being used in similar schools. Based on the results of these visits and ongoing discussions with core constituencies, promising technology could be piloted and assessed. Part of that assessment should include EQ factors including the leader's own reflections after using the technology for an extended amount of time. The investment cost of technology can be great. Therefore, your ability to judge how this innovation "feels" to you and to "read" the emotional reactions in others who use it is crucial. Too many district and school leaders either purchase or accept the latest gadgets without assessing if the emotional field for such seeds of change is ready for sowing. If it is not, the *SMART* School Leader must take the warning and either create a way to prepare the field or look for a different gadget.

For example, Dianne Yee, the principal of a middle school in Saskatchewan, Canada, realized that standard technology workshops were not lessening the fear and frustration levels of her teachers so, with her teachers, she created customized professional development opportunities. These included in-school technology sabbaticals ranging from a half-day to several months during which teachers, working individually or in small teams, engage in their own self-directed, project-based learning. Not only did this approach meet the emotional needs of teachers, it also gave them valuable insights into how powerful technology-based inquiry learning could be for their students. Principal Yee had been wise to "listen" to her teachers' feelings as warnings to put the brakes on technology workshops and ask if there was perhaps another path to travel.[32]

Warnings

There are other important warnings for the EQ leader to consider when the issue of technology becomes the issue. The first is to be aware that the business world, which can be a great source of funding and expertise, can also be a source of a great pressure on schools to adopt the latest "innovation that will transform learning." Businesses can also pressure schools to use technology in ways that are more market-driven than people-driven. "Free" technology given to schools, for example, can carry the hidden costs of lost student and teacher time, commercialization of our schools, and follow-up costs of repair and upgrades. The second warning is that the problem of safety and privacy, despite improving firewalls and other safeguards, still presents a risk to our community of learners and should be considered in planning and implementation. Another warning is to resist, with every emotion-mobilized strategy in your repertoire, any "well, the easiest thing to cut is teacher training" solution to budget problems. The cost of quality professional development is small compared to the cost of unused or misused technology. If the choice is reduced to one or the other (most times there are creative ways to afford both) hold off on the technology and wait for the next price decrease or next bond issue.

An even larger warning for our society as a whole is the threat of creating an even greater "Digital Divide" then what already exists today. Will the financial burdens of integrating technology into the curriculum be so great that only the wealthy school districts are able to take advantage of these modern marvels? Though school superintendents and principals in many historically underfinanced districts have been able to take advantage of government programs (e.g. E-rate) and corporate largesse to integrate technology in meaningful ways, there is a danger that poor children will be left behind or will be faced with computers that merely drill them in the basics. EQ leaders need to mobilize their communities to take advantage of what is currently available to them and to reform school financing so that every child in the future has access to technology and the skills to use it. Electronic equity is possible if we, as a society, will it to be so. For example, our airwaves, which media giants lease for nominal fees, could be leased in the future to finance IT for all schools. We can also move away from using property taxes to finance schools. Just as our society came together to say it is right and just that there should be free public libraries, we can come together to say it is right and just for every school child to have access to IT. Schools leaders in a democracy need to work together and use technology to strive for equity. By connecting people who care about equity issues, the Internet has the potential to power the same democratic yearnings as the printing press did in the 18th and 19th Century.

Thinking about equity issues and democratic yearnings within our school communities, however, is likely to lead to thinking on a global scale because technology has brought us within keystrokes of the rest of humanity. As a school leader you can be certain that some curious eighth grader or impassioned parent will pose a "What about . . ." question. If you have been proactive, however, your school may already be part of a rapidly-growing intercultural global learning network that connects schools around the world and you can probably answer the question. More importantly, you can point to teachers, parents or groups of students who are already taking their recently-gained cultural understanding and applying it to real-world problems. In their book, *Brave New Schools,* Jim Cummins and Dennis Sayers describe how a high school student on Long Island translated an Internet message from a young man describing abuse in a Croatian refugee camp.[33] The message was sent around the world and schools and communities from around the world responded in ways that helped end the horror. In another case, a student-edited magazine used the Internet to find Palestinian and Israeli students to contribute to an issue on the Middle East controversy. The responses led the U.S. students to set up a videoconference with some of those Middle East students who then had an opportunity to communicate with each other for the first time. By supporting such

Web-based interactions with the world, EQ leaders in future schools all around the world will help their students learn, in a very real and active way, from our incredible human diversity.

THE EQ LEADER OF THE FUTURE

In Victor Hugo's novel, *Notre Dame de Paris,* a scholar looks at a printed book, the first he has ever seen, and says "Ceci tuera cela" ("This will kill that") as he shifts his gaze to the massive imposing cathedral before him.[34] While mass production printing did not kill the medieval Church (nor our admiration for the beauty of hand-written script) it did lead to the demise of the Church's monopoly over knowledge. In this chapter we have tried to make the case that information technology may have a similarly revolutionary impact on the educational system's (preschool through university) control on information. Like the medieval cathedral, the Industrial-Age school may remain as part of our connection to the past but not as the primary hope for our future.

As we looked at information technology as a possible bridge to the future, we described some of the dilemmas and opportunities EQ leaders and their learning communities face in crossing that bridge. On one hand, leaders face systemic problems of design, cost, security, staff resistance, and equity when new technologies are considered. On the other hand, leaders have potentially powerful tools to reinvent their places of learning to better foster student-centered learning, higher-order thinking skills, and collaboration both within and outside the confines of time and space. To illustrate how leaders might meet these challenges, we provided some examples of EQ leadership in today's schools and suggestions for leadership in the future.

In reality, however, nothing we do can totally prepare us for the future. There is both wonder and uncertainty in the path ahead. Perhaps, when we find ourselves in a place where the road before us seems strangely unfamiliar, we can humbly remember the words of the poet, Carl Sandburg:

> *I am an idealist. I don't know where I'm going, but I'm on my way.*

REFLECTIVE QUESTIONS

1. What are your thoughts and feelings about information technology?
2. Has there been a pivotal experience that shaped these thoughts and feelings? If so, describe.
3. In your leadership efforts, how have your thoughts, feelings and experiences impacted on your use of technology? On your school's use of technology?
4. What is the prevailing "mental architecture" of the people in your school regarding IT?
5. In overcoming resistance to IT among staff in your school, do you think the process described in this chapter would work? Why or why not?
6. Revisit your school's design (if you are not currently in a school arrange to visit one) and answer the following questions:
   • What aspects of the design impede innovation?
   • What aspects are conducive to innovation?

FIGURE 9.2   Hudson High School
(Courtesy of Sheldon Berman; Rendering by Symmes Maini & McKee Associates, Inc.)

LESSON FROM THE FIELD

Shelley Berman

On the School's Design

We designed the new high school with the concept of democratic community in mind. To create a sense of community you need groupings small enough for teachers and students to get to know each other well and you need a common bond that ties the group together. This meant designing the new high school for clusters much like a middle school. However, rather than assigning students to clusters randomly as we do in our teams at grades 8 and 9, we created thematic clusters in grades 10 through 12 that built on student interest. The four grade 10 through 12 clusters are science, health and the environment; business, engineering and technology; communications, media and the arts; and public policy, education and social service. Students remain in the cluster for three years and build a strong sense of identification with the school, their teachers and their fellow students.

At the same time our desire to create democratic communities in which all students have a voice in decision making meant that we needed public space for democratic deliberation that could be used by each cluster. The end result was a pod-like design with seven to nine rooms surrounding a large group space that could seat the 150 students in the clusters we were creating.

Community also requires time. We built into the weekly schedule one hour a week for clusters to meet to discuss governance issues, plan cluster-based service projects, hear speakers related to the cluster theme or hold advisor-advisee meetings.

We took advantage of this new design to redesign about half of the classrooms in the school into five-sided rooms. These rooms reduce the teaching space at the front of the classroom and lend themselves to horseshoe, circle and group configurations for seating. By its very design we have created spaces that support dialogue and community.

On the Human Side of Schooling

Just as we want to have students participate in school decision-making, we want students to take greater responsibility for their education. This has meant enabling them to pursue their interests within the context of a somewhat standard set of requirements. In addition to the thematic clusters as a way to support student exploration of areas of interest, we implemented a semester-based block schedule. Students take four courses a semester, similar to a college setting. Many of our students have taken advantage of this opportunity and have accelerated their program in particular areas of interest. For example, as a result of block scheduling some of our talented mathematics students have completed AP Calculus by their junior year. This has led to the school offering more advanced courses such as B/C Calculus and Multivariable Calculus.

We have also been able to extend student learning through the many virtual course offerings provided by the Virtual High School Collaborative. This collaborative effort of high schools across the country was developed by the Hudson Public Schools and the Concord Consortium through a grant from the U.S. Department of Education. It now has a membership of over 150 schools and makes available to these schools a wide range of specialized and advanced courses. In addition, through collaborative relationships with area universities, we provide many seniors and some juniors with opportunities to take college courses as part of their high school program.

Lessons Learned

Having a vision has been key to developing alignment between curriculum, instruction, school organization and the very design of the school. The clarity of our vision has also enabled us to hire people who are attracted to this vision of education. In fact, many of our applicants apply because they have heard about what we are doing and want to be part of the innovations we are pursuing.

In spite of the progress we've made, my one caution is that building this kind of consistency in vision and alignment in program takes time. Long term, lasting change never occurs quickly. Leading the change requires patience and persistence. You must educate others to the importance and vitality of the vision and then you have to take advantage of every opportunity to implement the elements that are critical for its success. It is really about knowing in your heart that this is the work that needs to be done and sticking with it in spite of the obstacles. It takes time and commitment.

Sheldon Berman has been the Superintendent of the Hudson Public Schools since 1993. A founder and past President of Educators for Social Responsibility, he is the author of Children's Social Consciousness and Promising Practices in Teaching Social Responsibility *(1997). State University of New York Press. He has also been President of the Massachusetts Association of School Superintendents and selected as 2003 Massachusetts Superintendent of the Year.*

For more information:

- http://www.aasa.org/publications/sa/1999_04/berman.htm. In this online article Shelley, one of the founders of the Virtual High School, describes how virtual learning can prepare students for the future.
- Further information on VHS contact Liz Pape, VHS, Inc., Maynard, MA. She also can be reached at lpape@govhs.org. For a visit to the VHS website go to http://govhs.org.
- For a virtual visit to Hudson High, go to http://www.hudson.k12.ma.us.

Chapter 10

Change and Renewal:
The Leader's Journey

Assistant Principal's Journal, June, 2000

I was several hours away from becoming the Assistant Principal of my school. I had just served five years as Business and Technology Coordinator and personal assistant to the Principal. I was in the office on the last day of school when I heard a commotion in the General Office. An angry neighborhood resident was demanding to see the principal. The principal was inundated with last minute business and asked me to handle it. His parting words to me were,

"Remember make sure he leaves happy."

I work in a school for children with extreme behavioral, emotional and socialization needs that also happens to be located in one of the most exclusive neighborhoods in Manhattan. I walked with the gentleman into the corridor to hear his complaint. The gentleman, of obvious means and education, was very upset and hostile. He reported to me that as he was walking past our school, a child on a parked school bus spit on him from the window. The man continued to say that his wife and children lived in the neighborhood. He didn't want them to get spit on because, "You don't know what is in the spit of kids of their kind."

Alarms went off in my head: Racist, bigot, classist, wimp. I asked him, while my blood continued to heat up, if he could identify the child. He pointed down the hall at a child who was screaming and crying as he was being confronted by our Dean. I responded that the child in question had a history of major emotional problems and that we would make sure that he was dealt with properly. He said he wasn't happy. I assured him that we would take care of it. He repeated that he was unhappy and left.

Two weeks later I was called into the Principal's office. He was holding up a letter addressed to the Mayor, Chancellor, and Superintendent, recounting the episode of that day.

As I replay the events of that day in order to learn from them, I ask myself, "What happened for me in that moment?" Clearly, I felt attacked. When I feel attacked, my survival instinct tells me to defend myself either through withdrawal or counter-attack. I felt that this person had no feelings, empathy or compassion for the children. He also was a man of "means." I grew up without luxury. My students come from the poorest socioeconomic level. I could barely look at this guy, much less console and acknowledge his feelings.

I was on the offense. I did not want to validate this individual whom I had labeled racist. I was angry. But, I know that when I'm angry, there are lessons that I have to look at. So what was I thinking? My thoughts were: he should not be acting like this . . . how irresponsible, insensitive and inconsiderate he is . . . what a cold-hearted person he is. A more productive response to these feelings could have been: I am really upset by this. What specifically am I feeling? Why does it bother me so much? What principles of mine have been violated? What does the school need?

Hindsight and experience has taught me to ask myself, "Did I really want to insult this person and have him leave angry, even after I was given specific instructions from my supervisor?" And, if I'm honest with myself, the answer is clearly, "Yes." I let my anger get the best of me, instead of thinking about what was best for the child and the school. You can't do this as a leader. I know that now, and I work on this every day . . . If I can't control my own emotions, how the heck will I be able to help others with theirs?

As Principal Brandon Davis looks up at his audience, he is filled with emotion. Now, years later, with several years of being a principal under his belt, he shares his story at a principal's professional workshop. He says,

You have to go through these learning moments in order to know that you have a lot of growing to do. At the time I wrote this in my journal, I knew nothing about being a principal. And I was clueless about organizational awareness. Even though I was warned, I still did what I felt like doing. And, my actions came back to bite me. Since that time, I have dealt with hundreds of these kind of moments, and I approach them a heck of a lot differently.

Principal Davis' ability to be so transparent is, indeed, refreshing. He doesn't hide his weaknesses. Instead, he embraces them and talks about how he deals with them now and what he has yet to learn. But, how did this principal learn his leadership lessons? Clearly, as Principal Davis admits, he wasn't born like this. He had to "go within" self assess and choose ways to improve his emotional competencies. He had to find ways to develop those parts of himself that can transform him into the leader he hopes to become.

Where do principals go to develop these critical EQ skills that form the foundation of smart leaders? And, what does that kind of learning require of Brandon and other principals who really want to "be the model" for others?

This chapter asks school leaders to take stock and reflect on where you are now, and where you want to be. It asks you to check in to see if the leader you aspire to be is the one who walks daily through that school door. It reminds you that leadership is a journey of personal and professional development, of inner and outer work; the balance of both, so critical to your success. It validates how much you give as a school leader and offers some ways for you to seek renewal. The more we renew ourselves, the better our work will be in the world. As you read this final chapter, we invite you to find your quiet center, your secret garden and seek comfort and renewal as you continue on your leadership journey.

SETTING THE STAGE FOR RENEWAL

Conversation between Principal and Assistant Principal about a poor teacher lesson:

AP: *I'm going in there and I am going to rip her apart. That lesson was horrid? What's up with her? She knows better than that?*

FIGURE 10.1   Suzhou Garden, China

> **Principal:** *Calm down, for a moment, and think about it. What do you really want her to do?*
>
> **AP:** *I want her to teach the way I know she can. I want her to prepare her lessons and challenge the kids.*
>
> **Principal:** *So, here's an idea. Why don't you go and talk with her and ask her what's going on today? Tell her, "What I saw in here today is nothing like I've seen in the past. Maybe you want to tell me what's going on for you?*
>
> **AP:** *(wide-eyed, trying to save face) Ah, yeah, that's what I can do.*

These three-minute conversations go on all the time between an EQ Principal and those she develops. These brief "on the job," lessons are the kind that help us to reframe and think of another way of doing or saying things. When the lesson to be learned is relevant they can make a real difference. Listen to the following three-minute conversation between a new principal and his seasoned colleague:

> **NP:** *(proudly) I've started writing memos now that lets them know that I'm the boss. I'm just not going to tolerate things like coming late to pick up their kids after lunch, or running in after the bell rings in the morning. From now on, they'll know that if they are late, I am going to write them up.*
>
> **SC:** *So is this happening a lot at the school?*
>
> **NP:** *Well, I have two teachers who do this regularly? I'm sick of it. I've spoken to them and they blatantly do it anyway.*
>
> **SC:** *So, it sounds like these two are really defying you. You may need to come down stronger on them and, I agree, put it in writing.*
>
> **NP:** *Yeah, I plan on it.*
>
> **SC:** *But, the memo to the whole staff. Sounds like that's a bit of overkill when the problem is really with these two teachers, isn't it?*
>
> **NP:** *(holding on to his position) Yeah, but everybody needs to know I mean business.*
>
> **SC:** *(supportive but resolute) Everybody knows you mean business except for these two. Start there and see what happens.*

Learning moments like these can only happen when both teacher and student are willing to learn. These kind of "coaching" experiences require a spirit of trust in the learning environment. They ask the learner to recognize that she's out in the playing field, just waiting to move when the ball comes her way. She would fare much better if she had the skills to anticipate each player's moves. These learning experiences also hold a lot more salt when the person who is giving them models the kinds of behaviors he is asking the learner to acquire. If my actions don't match my words, the lessons I teach will not be heard. Finally, in order to learn better ways of doing things, I may need to repeat the lesson numerous times. Practice makes perfect. The relationship between the teacher and student is a critical ingredient of this learning process. Anthony S. Bryk and Barbara Schneider tell us that if relational trust is present in a school community, one has a good chance of promoting positive, sustained school reform efforts. Relational trust is grounded in the social respect that comes from dialogue with others, personal regard for the members of the learning community, credibility in the role competency of the members and personal integrity of the member.[1]

In an ideal scenario we would each have a personal coach by our side as we assume leadership positions. Short of this, there are a variety of ways that leaders can seek renewal that will lesson the gap between their ideal and real self. The EQ leader finds ways to learn through a balance of personal and professional renewal opportunities.

WHAT IS RENEWAL?

When was the last time you did something special to personally nurture yourself? What was it? What form did it take? Were you home or far away? Were you alone, or with another? How did you feel after you took this time? How did it impact you on the job and in life in general? What about the last time you did something to professionally renew yourself? Where were you? Was it a conference that you attended? Perhaps it was a special institute for education leaders? Maybe it was even a week-long retreat? What did you get out of this experience? How did it impact you on your job and life in general?

Renewal is defined as "to take up something again, or resume where you left off." It is also defined as "to restore, replenish and revive."[2] Both definitions imply that renewal, once taken, equips you to return to the place you were in your life before your renewal with a new frame, a much clearer lens. Every living thing needs to be replenished, refurbished-rejuvenated. Even non-living things need a face lift from time to time. Think of a piano. When the keys don't play, we tune the piano. Soon enough, it plays beautifully again. Renewal allows you to recharge. Once renewed, you can continue on that familiar leadership path with new vitality in body, mind and spirit. Renewal efforts offer you opportunities to reflect upon what you need to be the best that you can be for yourself and others.

Stephen Covey's 7th Habit, "sharpening the saw," addresses the need to renew our physical, social/emotional, mental and spiritual well-being. In *The Seven Habits of Highly Effective People,* Covey illustrates this 7th habit with the following story[3]:

Suppose you were to come upon someone in the woods working feverishly to saw down a tree.

"What are you doing?" you ask.

"Can't you see?" comes the impatient reply. "I'm sawing down this tree."

"You look exhausted!" you exclaim. "How long have you been at it?"

"Over five hours," he returns, "and I'm beat! This is hard work."

"Well, why don't you take a break for a few minutes and sharpen that saw?" you inquire. "I'm sure it would go a lot faster."

"I don't have time to sharpen the saw," the man says emphatically, "I'm too busy sawing!"

Sound like you? Don't worry, you're not alone. Sadly enough, many of us race through life doing our jobs as if this were our last day on earth. Ironically, if this were our final day, I doubt this is what we would be doing. And, what makes us think that working harder is working smarter? Maybe if we took some time to "sharpen that saw," we might gain some fresh insights about more effective ways of getting the job done. Covey says that this seventh habit, which he calls renewal, is key to increasing our ability to optimize the other six habits. According to Covey, this habit promotes vision, sparks continuous improvement, safeguards against burnout and entropy, and puts the organization on a new upward growth path.[4] As we think of sharpening our saws, we realize that personal and professional renewal must go hand in hand. As humans, our minds and hearts are designed to work with our spirits and bodies. When we take the time to improve any aspect of ourselves, all of whom we are reaps the benefits.

Personal renewal means investing in all four human dimensions: physical, emotional, mental and spiritual. Getting that massage, taking that much needed vacation, spending time with loved ones, reading that favorite book and luxuriating at a day at the spa are all desirable forms of personal renewal. Personal renewal takes different forms for each of us. As long as this renewal allows us to "get out of our minds" and into the rest of us, it's doing what it is supposed to do. No matter how much you love your work, you have to love yourself even more.

Professional renewal experiences renew the professional skills that we need to get the job done. The renewal focus for school leaders could be on learning how to use a new instructional strategy or spending a reflective week retreat with trusted colleagues. Both forms of professional renewal ignite passion and encourage you as you gain new perspectives, validate what you do, and plan for trying something new. There are two paradigms that can help us think about the kind of professional development experiences that renew us for our world of work. We call these two paradigms, *outer renewal work* and *inner renewal work*.

Outer professional renewal work is that work that one usually develops and demonstrates outwardly in the world. These opportunities often concentrate on developing skill in the content or pedagogy of a subject area such as literacy or math development, or in technical skills such as management of budgets and human resources. Outer renewal experiences are those that we commonly share with others. You might tell a colleague about your outer renewal experience, "I went to a great workshop on service learning today, or, I can't wait to see Peter Senge next month."

Inner professional renewal work, on the other hand, is not as easily recognized by others. Inner work refers to the more personal skills that the leader develops to strengthen character and leadership behaviors. Characteristically, we don't discuss this work in professional circles unless it is with colleagues with whom we have developed trust. Inner renewal work develops the skills we have been referring to throughout this book. We gain inner work experiences at professional seminars that allow the expression and development of our emotional competencies. Inner renewal work opportunities provide opportunities for relational trust to grow.

Through inner and outer professional renewal experiences, school leaders can nurture themselves and others personally and professionally. Personal and professional, inner and outer renewal experiences go hand in hand to make you better at who you are and who you want to be. Imagine if you spent all your time relaxing or exercising but you never spent time reading professional journals. Your physical health would probably be pretty good, but your professional credibility could be at stake. Conversely, if you spend all your time studying or developing your professional skills, and no time to play, you will lose your stamina, mental acuity and, quite frankly, would not be too much fun to be with!

Every piece of health-related literature you read tells us that smart leaders need balance. And that requires accurately assessing our own needs, not always an easy task. No one can stay at the top of the mountain forever, no matter how good or successful you may be. Achievement-oriented people are drivers. Because performance is so tied into everything they do, it's hard to stop and reflect about renewal. Most of us go until we literally drop. I must admit, that while writing this book, I had to set a timer to stop and take a break. I had to write into my date book things like "take a walk." Today, even as I write this chapter, I cancelled my much-needed acupuncture visit to get in a few more hours of writing.

Balanced, renewed individuals put the saw down from time to time. They seek physical exercise to strengthen the body; study to expand the mind, time with loved ones to feed the heart and religious or spiritual practices to fill the soul. Some people do this well. They are consistent about making sure that all facets of their being are nurtured regularly. Others pretend they are doing this but never follow through. Still others are aware at all times that these four sides of self work best in harmony. They find small ways to nourish themselves daily at home and on the job.

Consider for a moment the tribal wisdom of the Lakota people. In the shape of the medicine wheel four core principles lie at the root of their cultural beliefs[5]:

Belonging: Value is placed on kinship bonds and relationship; we are all part of one another.

Mastery: Success and mastery produce a feeling of both social recognition and inner satisfaction.

Independence: Freedom, autonomy and responsibility are fostered

Generosity: Things are less important than people. Core values of sharing and community responsibility are the norm.

These four principles link directly to the four dimensions of humankind: spiritual, emotional, physical and mental. At all times, it is inherent upon native people to consider all of these dimensions in their daily lives. Doing this assures that life is in harmony and balance. Larry Brendtro and Martin Brokenleg tell us,

Healthy survival or good medicine requires that balance and harmony be always maintained. If spirituality is left out of our lives or teaching, we ignore an essential part of our being and the circle is broken.[6]

We would do well to learn from Native American traditions and strive to balance the four parts of life's wheel. Ask yourself, *In what ways do you assure that you belong? . . . Which relationships in your life give to you? . . . When you are depleted, what nourishes you? . . . When are you most motivated to achieve? . . . What experiences allow you to do your best? . . . Which communities fill you and help you to grow?*

Reflecting on these critical questions helps us balance the cup of giving with that of receiving. Getting the job done goes without saying. But, the quality of how the job is getting done is directly linked to how well we balance our lives.

Some times, we are so caught up in the stress of life, that we easily get locked into our positions, lose our adaptability, get bogged down and don't even know why. As a smart EQ leader, it pays to understand the stress you face, the service you give and seek ways to renew again and again.

STRESS AND THE SCHOOL LEADER

Too often, school leaders are people with saws who won't slow down to take stock and assess their own needs. In fact, one common reason many do not pursue the principal's job is because of the high level stress it causes.[7]

Stress is caused by a variety of these professional and personal circumstances. Extended working hours without any down time can create feelings of being overwhelmed and totally exhausted. At these times we may feel caught in a web of all-too-important commitments. We may find it too difficult to meet these personal and professional commitments. For some of us, too much routine and not enough change cause stress. We all go through different cycles in our lives when we need new challenges, need to climb taller or wider mountains. Another kind of stress can come when we anticipate change to happen but it takes too long. We become impatient and restless. We want to drive it rather than let it take its course. Sometimes, external changes in governance or policy mandates can cause us to have to change our leadership priorities. These can often conflict with our core values and ethics. We may feel we are working for beliefs that are not ours. All of these underlying stressors added to the normal daily demands of the job can cause school leaders to lose their luster and desire professional change. Everyone's cup runs over when stress is relentless.

Today, unlike years ago, we have a lot of information and research available that tells us the ways in which stress not only depletes us but can also impair our healthy body systems. Long-term stress can even lead to chronic diseases. We have known for some time now that "stress and strong emotions, particularly hostility and anger, can contribute to long-term damage to the heart and blood vessels and can precipitate heart attacks.[8]" And, while not conclusive, stress may also be a major factor in depleting our immune system and increasing susceptibility to illness.[9] It's important to remember that stress in and of itself is not a negative thing, but how we react to stress determines how we will be affected by it.

Gary Bloom, a first-year school principal, tells how he finds his job to be stressful and lonely.[10]

> *My first year in the principalship has been a roller coaster ride with ups and downs, successes and failures. It has been isolating, physically and mentally draining, and a huge responsibility. You are a public figure, always in the spotlight, from the moment you leave home in the morning till the time you pull into the garage at night. If I could limit my reflections on the first year principalship it would be one word "isolation."*

School leaders have to balance the physical, emotional and psychological health of their staff, but even more so, their children. Norma Caraballo, a first year elementary school principal tells us of her stress in dealing with a serious disciplinary issue in her school:

> *As a first year principal, I was struggling with all of the normal issues. The climate and behavior issues in the school only added to the stress that I faced each day. One time in particular during a school assembly, I was informed by a small child that some children in the school had homemade sling shots made of paper clips and they were shooting them at him and other children. I immediately collected all the sling shots. Since it was dismissal time, I sent the children home informing them that we would be discussing this more the next day.*

But unbeknownst to her, as the children were leaving school, a student who was angry with the child informer slammed him against a cement wall while another student repeatedly kicked him in the face. Norma arrived at the scene to find the child with eyes closed, blue lips and barely breathing. She continues:

I felt the pain a mother feels at learning that her child has been brutally hurt. I remember screaming out to the child. "Open your eyes, for me. You can't leave me like this. Please, I love you." As I sobbed, leaning over the nurse who was working on him, EMS arrived. They gave him oxygen. Now, somewhat alert, he extended his arms out for me to touch him as a child who reaches out for the one he trusts to keep him safe.

While not all principals have to contend with physically violent incidents, other kinds of violence can be stressors that tear away at the strength of the principal. Joyce, a seasoned K-2 principal arrived late to a scheduled meeting. Apologizing, she explains:

One of my six-year-old girls sexually accosted another six-year-old in the restroom today. Somehow, the children lingered in the rest room five minutes past the others and this happened. Can you believe this? she exclaimed. Six years old! The teacher was standing outside the bathroom waiting for the children when she heard the child scream. She ran into the bathroom and found this happening. These children, these poor children!

Joe, a veteran middle school principal contends with a different kind of stressor. He has been coming to school at 4:30 every morning this month in order to have three hours before school personnel arrived. He is trying to learn the new literacy curriculum his teachers are struggling with in their classrooms. He shares:

When I came into this business, I wasn't the instructional leader. I was supposed to manage the building, keep a safe plant, assure that everyone was doing their job and children were learning. Now, we know that is not enough. I am the instructional leader and I have to get up to snuff. This is the only time I can really spend learning this curriculum so that I can model and supervise those who are using it to teach the children.

Finally, Principal Lois shares the stress she feels from dealing with many new teachers at her school. Every principal knows that if teachers can't teach, children can't learn. This is a common stressor for many school leaders. Lois shares,

I love my job, but I have ten new teachers this year, all of whom need so much work to make them strong instructionally, I'm working more hours than I really have. I can't do anymore. I'm exhausted. But, I can't stop.

While stress management techniques are abundant, they aren't made widely available to school leaders. Still viewed as soft skills, leaders are supposed to find time to acquire them on their own time. Yet, studies tell us the benefits of such stress reducing methods such as support groups, cognitive restructuring strategies (like telling yourself "to relax"), assertive language techniques and crisis intervention strategies.[11] Physiological supports like physical exercise and taking nutrients continue to be very helpful. Increasingly, organizations incorporate strategies such as mindfulness meditation, guided imagery and biofeedback into training modules to help employees manage stress and change the way they think about stressors. Social networking support is critical to leaders who need to bounce off ideas, share stories and ask others in the same line of work how they have handled similar situations.

Renewal efforts allow school leaders to find ways to unleash the stress and gather the fortitude to be the constant support to others. Remember that expression, "You can't get blood out of a stone?" We can't give what we don't have left to give. School leaders need the tools that will comfort and renew them. We would do well to find more opportunities to affirm and nourish leaders, instead of just expecting great results. Ram Dass and Paul Gordon remind us:[12]

We can see now that burnout need not always be an enemy. If not a best friend, it can at least be a catalyst, even a guide, for the inner work, the work on ourselves, which is the foundation of all true service, and the only way, finally to maintain energy and inspira-

tion. If we can view the places where we encounter fatigue and doubt as clues and sign-posts for that inner work, our journey will not only go more lightly but go further, deeper. We will not simply survive. We will grow.

As we recognize the complexities of the school leader's job, we need to take a moment to look at a dynamic that is particular to educators and those in the helping arena. It is the added self-imposed stress that comes from a willful commitment to doing *service* in the world. It comes from the passionate desire to give children all we can; to make the world a better place for children.

The Passion to Serve

When Richard Boyatzis, Anne McKee and Daniel Goleman asked business leaders to explain what drives their performance, responses were summed up in one word—passion.[13] For educational leaders, this passion is embedded in their desire to serve. As we have heard throughout this book, this desire to serve is based on the love of children. Leaders see themselves directly responsible for the educational opportunities their children receive. Many outside of the field of education may lack an understanding of this great compassion and natural empathy that drives educators to give endlessly to their schools. Yet others might say that it is exactly this kind of passion that more leaders need to create a broader ethic of service and compassion in our society and our world.

When we think of those who have lived a life of service to others, the great ones such as Ghandi, Martin Luther King and Mother Theresa come to mind. But every day, in our own backyard, many of the people we know live lives of service. Many of us are inspired by service givers such as members of the police force, fire fighters, clergy members and educators. School leaders probably don't think of themselves as people of service. Yet, this is exactly the role they play in their schools.

Servant leaders, through their actions, create the desire to serve in others. The caring and ethical nature of servant leaders adds richness and meaning to society in general.[14] Thomas Sergiovanni, refers to school leaders as not only servant leaders, but as stewards of the general public who entrust them to care and educate their children.[15] He says,

> *Stewardship involves the leader's personal responsibility to manage her or his life and affairs with prior regard for the rights of other people and for the common welfare. Finally, stewardship involves placing oneself in service to ideas and ideals and to others who are committed to their fulfillment.*

Whether servant or steward, one thing is sure—the school leader's passion is what sustains him and nourishes him when all else fails. If you haven't ever had the opportunity to experience this, ask a SMART school leader a question about his school. You will almost always hear a prideful litany of stories about the many accomplishments of his staff and young people. His response is never about his leadership or accomplishments; it's always about the children. Ever go to a party or dinner engagement with a group of school leaders? They talk nonstop about their schools, the instructional strategies they use, the young people's latest performance and the new equipment or programs their kids are using.

Last week, for example, my partner, an assistant principal, came home from school anxious to share a video tape of his staff and kids taken during their Black History assembly. I stopped working to chat with him, prepare a bite to eat and watch his school video. As we watched he made statements such as,

> *Look, there's Elvin. He's the one I told you about that is really trying to control his anger these days. Hasn't been in trouble all week . . . And, there's Jessica. Look at her get up and read. When she first came to the school she wouldn't dream of reading in public . . .*

FIGURE 10.2 New Orleans, Louisiana

Pointing to an adult who was leading a dance ensemble of adults and young people in vibrant African garb, he added, "That's Adriana, the teacher I told you about. She's such a great teacher. Her kids are really learning." Though I have to admit that I could barely sit through the viewing of this 45-minute poorly taken video, I couldn't help but feel a sense of pride and admiration for this dedicated educator. He, like so many school leaders, demonstrated a passion and commitment to the children and adults of his school.

Educational leaders work not for one child, but for all of the children in their school. Though the opportunities for one-on-one connection with students are lessened, leaders have the potential to multiply their efforts. They do this by empowering this ability in the adults in their school community. Dr. Rene Townsend, my former superintendent and mentor tells me that her greatest motivation to lead her school district of 28,000 young people came from:

> *The desire to serve, to give all kids a chance—I mean all. I have a particular passion for those who start with fewer opportunities and want to give them access to a better life. When things get tough, I think about those kids, and it keeps me going.*

Whether you are leading a school or district, the motivation remains the same. Those who serve know that at the end of the day, when their head hits that pillow, they have done a day's work that matters.

Finding Peace at the Eye of a Storm

Daily renewal is the most assured way of keeping the stress level in check. It isn't enough to wait for that spring or summer vacation. It needs to find its place in your workday. You are probably saying to yourself right now, "What is she nuts? I can't even get time to eat lunch without ten interruptions!" Believe it or not, there are cognitive strategies that can help you create those quiet spaces before, during and after the school day. Remember, personal and professional renewal need to go hand in hand. We don't leave one part of ourselves at the door when we enter our schools. The more we recognize this, the better we will get at the balance we all need. Stephen Covey offers us four ways to nurture ourselves on a regular basis. I know several school principals who follow Covey's work and find these techniques to be helpful.[16]

1. *Keep a Personal Journal:* You have done this throughout the book as an effective tool to increase self-awareness. The more self-aware you are the better chance you have to seek balance.
2. *Listen and Respond to Your Conscience:* By this, Covey means that we need to clear our minds regularly. If your internal compass is plugged in you will be able to see problems coming, avoid possible stressors, gain control and cut potentially difficult moments off at the pass.
3. *Nurture Your Independent Will. Keeping Promises:* Stick to the commitments that you make. Slow them down and follow through. This boosts self-confidence and personal integrity.
4. *Develop Creative Imagination through Visualization:* Play scenes out in your mind. In those scenes practice your best way of dealing with a situation.

You are probably saying, "Okay, this is all well and good, but how do I do this on the job? From the minute I arrive in the morning I am up and running?" Nobody said it's easy. It will probably take a lot of conscious effort to fit a few of these positive practices into your routine. You're not alone. Other EQ leaders who are trying to create that much-needed balance have shared some pointers with us that we think might work for you. In fact, you might even want to post these reminders near your desk:

- Be proactive. Prepare your day as best you can. In your plan allow for two moments in the day when you can take "down time." Tell your assistant principal or administrative assistant that during those twenty minutes or so you need to be undisturbed (short of any crisis that you need to handle!)
- Create a weekly plan of what you will do with your twenty minutes daily. It can't be work. Use those twenty minutes to close your eyes, meditate, pray—whatever nourishes you. I have a friend of mine who literally brought crayons to work and sat and colored for ten minutes when she knew she had to de-stress. Barry, my partner, plays Blockbuster on the computer for about five minutes. If possible, get out of the building. It makes a world of difference.
- Keep toys in your office, teddy bears, and things to look at and feel cuddly inside. Soothing artwork and those meditative water fountains are great!
- Recognize that not everything has to be responded to in the moment. Everyone would love you to take care of everything right away. You have to have your internal compass going to prioritize how your time will be spent.
- Use active listening skills to save a few moments for yourself. When someone demands your attention and you know the situation isn't critical say, "I know that you need my attention to this matter. I can't get to it now, but could we meet at . . . I will be able to give you much more of my quality attention later than I could in this moment."
- Open door policies are great, but not always realistic. Closed doors shut down. Find a balance. Choose a time of the day that is generally the calmest and schedule time for your return phone calls and paper obligations. Be sure it's a time when staff members are less free than other times—not lunchtime, for example!
- Find an out of the way bathroom and sit for a minute where no one can find you.
- Don't respond in anger if you feel it. Put it off. Say nothing rather than exhibit anger. You will only make yourself nuts with negative self-talk later about what you should have done. Use that emotional self-control!
- Keep healthy snacks handy so your blood sugar stays stable and you don't eat out of stress. Also, emotions go haywire when you have eaten too much, or too little.

- Relationships are critical and demand most of your attention. In order to keep people feeling connected, do a classroom round that is not evaluative, just a visit. Those one-minute acknowledgments will buy you much more time later on.
- Be sure that you assign other members of your staff to nurture those relationships. This will take some of the drain off of you. Delegating will help you to renew *you*.
- At the end of the day count the things you did accomplish instead of those you didn't.
- Visit classrooms and talk with the children. There's nothing more renewing than reminding yourself why you are in this business in the first place!

In this section, we spoke about ways that you can individually create spaces for your personal renewal at home and on the job. Ram Dass and Paul Gordon provide us with meaningful words to help us hold on to this critical part of our journey:[17]

> *Nothing may be more important, in all this, than being gentle with ourselves. Whether we're professionals working a sixty- hour week or simply family members called upon to care daily for a sick relative . . . We learn the value of recognizing our limits, forgiving ourselves our bouts of impatience or guilt, acknowledging our own needs. We see that to have compassion for others we must have compassion for ourselves.*

In this next section, we delve more deeply into the kinds of professional renewal experiences that foster professional growth.

CONTINUAL LEARNING: INNER AND OUTER RENEWAL

Most school leaders long to receive opportunities to learn new knowledge and skills that will help them to improve learning in their schools. As we reflect on the kinds of professional development leaders need both the inner and outer paradigms come into play. While outer professional development experiences are more readily available to school leaders, inner renewal work opens the heart and sets the stage for the learning to grow. Remember Principal Davis, whom we met earlier in this chapter? All the outer renewal type workshops he attended could never have taught him what he now knows. It took courage and commitment to stand before his mirror and expose his soul to learn the lessons well.

Rachel Kessler, calls this *soul of leadership*, "a deep connection to the self, the source of what administrators called "personal integrity," "resilience in the face of setbacks, criticism and even misrepresentation" and "the capacity to reflect and create opportunities for silence."[18] Kessler tells us:

> *In schools or districts where the soul of education is welcome and safe, deep connection allows masks to drop away. Colleagues begin to share the joy and success they once feared would spur competition and jealousy. They share the vulnerability and uncertainty they feared would make them look weak in front of peers and superiors. And they rediscover meaning and purpose in their collective responsibility for the children.*

As we think about ways to bring this ability to cultivate "soul" into leadership development, we have to find ways to increase these "deep connections" through mentoring and peer coaching opportunities for both seasoned and fledgling leaders. Non-evaluated peer observation strategies, buddy systems and critical friends groups provide safety in which to learn. Here, leaders reflect, practice, make mistakes and develop new skills. Superintendent Townsend shares:

> *Superintendent meetings, particularly informal meetings are a great source of professional development. The other really outstanding professional development was writing*

the book Eight at the Top with seven other superintendents. It gave us the opportunity to talk about our work, give each other feedback and ideas, and time to reflect on what we do, why we do it and what it all means. The network we created helped each of us enormously, and we all agreed it was the best training/development we ever did.

Recognizing the need to learn together, the last decade has seen Principal Centers and Leadership Academies sprout up across the country. In these places of learning, school leaders share their stories, challenges and strategies for leading schools and districts. The Harvard Principal's Center has served as a model for leadership development across the world.[19] The Center's efforts have been integral in providing leaders with the much needed inner and outer renewal work they desire. Carmen Jimenez, a principal, speaks of her experience at a Harvard Principal Center summer institute:

It freed my soul, my mind and my spirit—it transformed me. So much that I must have impressed someone because I was asked to return the following year as a group leader! Since then I learned about how I liked to learn—and have used this model in my work with principals—I enjoy learning when it involves not only theory but when I can apply theory in practice—I enjoy learning in small intimate groups, I like having discussions where there are many different points of view, with many good readings and especially if the leader is using protocols from critical friends.

In the last decade, organizational development experts have popularized the benefits of executive coaching models. These models provide for skilled coaches to work one-on-one with the leader based on a mutually developed growth plan. Before beginning their coaching experience, leaders participate in personal assessments such as the ECI that help identify areas for development. This training continues over as little time as six months to a period of years. EQ competencies such as self-awareness, self-management and other social skill competencies are often part of this long-term development plan.

In the field of education, this form of coaching, though desirable, often falls outside of the financial capabilities of public schools. Smart organizations and smart leaders however, seek ways to develop and renew themselves whenever possible. Gayle, a colleague of ours, and executive coach to leaders in both the private and public arena presently works with educational leaders in the Atlanta Public Schools. She shares a story about her encounter with one school principal who had been charged with creating a school for middle and high school students identified as having severe behavioral difficulties. Gayle and the principal spoke at length about the politics of her position, the children (whom she wanted to serve with excellence), and all the other stakeholders in her school. Building a team from sometimes disparate interests had been a difficult task. She had become weary from the effort. After listening to the principal describe the actions she had taken, Gayle commented to the principal:

That sounds like a significant achievement, don't you think? Tell me what you thought would happen in the first year of a school with that particular population of students, a brand new faculty and a hesitant community?

Gayle's words gave this novice principal cause to reflect. She had been "beating herself up" for what she had not accomplished, instead of affirming the progress she had made. One month later, she visited Gayle again and said:

You know, I've been thinking about what you said ever since we had that last conversation I never realized how unrealistic some of my expectations were. It was weighing me down and I was disappointed with myself, because I couldn't seem to make things become the way I had envisioned they would be. Somehow a year [though it was really only seven months] seemed like long enough to have accomplished all our year one goals. But so many things got in the way, most of them unexpected. I've begun to realize that getting this school started and keeping the building standing and the students and adults safe was a lot to accomplish. I guess I just thought that so many of the little tasks wouldn't have been as difficult as they turned out to be.

Gayle and the principal talked a little longer about some of her successes, what she had learned and how she might handle upcoming situations. Gayle offered to have the principal call her whenever she felt she needed a perspective shift. Gayle shares:

The pressures of high performance, the weight of student success, the politics of community involvement and the reality of unexpected change take their toll on each of us. As I talk to leaders in school systems across the country, they are all caught in this balancing act. Often times the ability to see your accomplishments through the eyes of someone who understands the enormity of the task you are charged with, but to whom you are not accountable is a helpful gift. I often suggest that leaders work with a coach. A good coach will help to keep you focused on your goal, while charting your progress. Your coach should have no vested interest in the decisions you make, and probably should not be someone from your system. Their role is to support you in maintaining perspective and staying the course.

Finding a personal coach is not always viable, but most of us have a "listening ear" in a friend or trusted colleague nearby. These confidential moments in which you can share your stories are imperative for anyone in the all-too-often isolated leadership position. So, seek a relationship with a trusted buddy (also an EQ leader!). Tell your stories and ask for advice. Be willing to expose yourself and take risks. As you think about ways to renew your inner and outer professional self, the following tips might also be helpful:

- Read books that will allow you to see yourself in them. Join other leaders along their professional journeys. We all have our favorites. One of mine is *Leading with Soul* by Boleman and Deal.[20]
- Attend professional development opportunities that allow you to grapple with yourself as you take in knowledge. Sign up for intensive experiences like those offered by The Harvard Principal Institutes, the Center for Creative Leadership, or the Fetzer Institute's "Courage to Lead" program.[21]
- Push the envelope. Seek out experiences that you think you already have had as well as those you know provide new learning for you. Go with a friend. You'll get much more out of the experience.
- Participate in and facilitate new learning strategies such as microlabs, role plays, paired learning, fishbowls-the kinds we have been using in this book. These experiential strategies allow you and others to feel safe enough to share your deeper feelings.
- Be the change you want to see. Model this kind of renewal with your own staff. Change the *business as usual* meetings into more reflective learning opportunities. Give them a workshop in facilitative leadership or EQ development.
- Relish silence. Find opportunities to allow the silence in when you are receiving or giving new knowledge. Amazingly, many creative moments are sparked by this apparent lull in activity.

As we complete this book, leadership development opportunities that nurture the inner and outer professional development needs are becoming more available. Mae Fong, Middle School Principal of 67 Q in New York City writes in her journal about her recent experience this summer. She attended a week-long training institute offered to her as a member of the Distinguished Faculty of New York City Public Schools. She describes:

Following the personal analysis of our own Emotional Competency data, we attend a day-long seminar to help us understand how to develop our own emotional competencies.

I find this work to be compelling and inspiring. Informed, comparative self-reflection is a powerful motivational tool. Self-reflection of assessments of my performance by respected constituents provides affirmation and motivation for me to set even higher achievement goals . . . We learn methods of conflict resolution, the elements of the negotiation process, negotiation behavior, culture and conflict, anger and emotions and an introduction to the mediation process. We recognize the importance of maintaining a worldview, needs and positions and using bargaining chips and chops to develop reframing questions for resolution of conflict. Collaboration fosters collaboration, and competition begets more competition. In my mission to promote an emotionally intelligent school culture it is wise to improve my negotiation skills. As the principal of a high performing middle school, it is my responsibility to model these self-improvement behaviors that will foster a school culture in which everybody strives to improve their practice.[22]

A Renewal Case Study: The Distinguished Faculty

In the Spring of 2001, Mary Butz, Executive Director of the Office of Leadership Development and founder of the New York City Principal's Institute, took a historic step. She created a system for identifying and renewing fifty star principals of 1150 others in the New York City Public School System. These high performing principals were recognized by their district superintendents because of a number of characteristics. All of them were strong leaders with:

- more than five years experience
- schools that met state standards or that were steadily meeting these standards
- school cultures that were promoting learning
- high level interpersonal skills including the ability to facilitate groups and teach others

Mary's intention was to strengthen the skills of these principals and then have them mentor the newer principals, those with less than three years experience. The principals who signed on as Distinguished Faculty members had to be willing to give of their time, attend renewal sessions for themselves and agree to support up to twelve new principals in a number of ways. Mary explains the thinking behind the Distinguished Faculty model:

When I was a principal, I needed to be in a trusting environment where I could share my concerns. I needed to be among smart people who knew how to do things better than I did. I needed to be with people who could laugh and have a good sense of humor . . . I had a good network in the alternative schools . . .

And despite all the wonderful connections and friends that she had in her own alternative school circles, she still needed a safe place to go to where no one was competing for the same few resources and where trust was explicit. She explains:

*In school communities everyone compares themselves to another. There is always this silent or not so silent competition for the minimal resources in the system. When you are the principal you always have to "rob Peter to pay Paul" . . . there is never enough. There is always someone who is going to be slighted no matter what you do. There is never enough time, never enough resources, and never enough books . . . so even if you have the most dynamic and loving relationship with your staff someone is always angry with you . . . And this struggle for resources and recognition even exists between the best of principals. When one principal would say that they got new materials, another would wonder why they got something, and she didn't. Why was **their** school selected and mine wasn't?*

The difference between those close networks and the Distinguished Faculty group was like being in a family as opposed to going to a summer camp. In the DF group (abbreviation for Distinguished Faculty members) there are common goals, just like at camp. Mama and papa aren't watching. There is no need for sibling rivalry. Instead, there is a clear and noble mission to help others. That's what this camp is all about. This is not the case when you are the principal. Your scores have to go up; your attendance needs to be perfect . . . While these are important to the day-to-day functioning of the school, there is nothing that charges someone more than to be able to just take care of somebody in need. In our case, these DFs, by helping their principal cohorts, were able to effect many more kids and staff than in their own school environments . . . They were ecstatic to be able to do this . . . And, these principals needed to be supported outside of their own environment. Principals need to be with people who respect them for their worth.

Over the two years that I have been privy to work with these principals I have listened to their stories as they worked together, dialogued and broke bread together. I have learned some powerful realities about how they perceive their role as principal. I have observed their dedication, expertise and courage to lead challenging urban schools. These outstanding principals shared many common characteristics. First, these principals love their jobs. They are passionate about education. Second they thrive on dialogue, discussion and the opportunity to share their hopes, their fears and their successes with colleagues who understand and care. Third, their hearts are replete with love and hope for their children and families. Last, they seek opportunities to grow, learn and explore new practices as much as possible. They are continual learners themselves.

I also learned how they need to be affirmed and acknowledged by others. By simply being invited to be a member of the well-respected Distinguished Faculty, these principals were affirmed and renewed. Once they were regarded with respect and dignity, they became totally rejuvenated . . . At the end of the day of a particular training session that I attended with these principals, no fewer than five principals came up to me and told me, *"If it weren't for Mary (who soon became known as Mother Mary), I would have left this job. As much as I love it, I was exhausted, felt unappreciated and was ready to retire."* Mary and her carefully designed renewal program cared about the people side of change. She knew, having lived the reality herself, what it would take to revitalize and sustain these principals.

In their small group cohorts, Distinguished Faculty members worked together to improve their practice and that of others. They attended trainings together, met together in monthly cohorts and took on the responsibility of planning the professional development of new principals. New principals met with them once monthly in study groups, attended summer institutes designed by them and contacted them regularly. They supported their principals regularly by meeting with them at their schools and by answering regular distress phone calls and incessant email needs. One novice principal said to me one day, *"I feel like a babe in the woods. There is so much to learn. These principals make a difference. I have someone to turn to at all times."*

Curriculum for the Distinguished Faculty renewal sessions varied according to the principal's needs. Their training focused on both the outer and the inner renewal work referred to in this chapter. Along with their outer renewal skills such as differentiated instruction techniques and data analysis to drive instruction they also received mentoring and coaching experience based on the work of the National Association of Secondary School Principals and emotional intelligence theory.

Inner and outer renewal experiences came together as they reflected together in their groups. They looked deeply at their leadership style, abilities to analyze and solve problems and make judgments, their sensitivity in interactions with others, their organizational ability. They developed new strategies for addressing resistance to change. They examined their self and social awareness, their abilities to build productive relationships with others. In these sessions, they reflected on their own development and what they needed to do to improve their strength areas. Later, they used this knowledge in their work with their cohort members.

School leaders need ongoing opportunities to collaborate and renew. They need to know that they are valued, cared for and encouraged to grow in an environment of trust and consistent support. Renewal, is an ongoing process. In a time when principals are exiting en masse across the nation, the Distinguished Faculty program serves as a beacon of light and inspiration.

IN SUMMARY

This chapter spoke about the real changes and renewal experiences that help leaders transform themselves into the EQ leaders they hope to be. It explored the kinds of renewal efforts that you as a school leader need to replenish and spark your passion and commitment to your work. We looked at ways you can nurture yourself professionally and personally in body, mind, heart and spirit. We spoke about how to balance your own renewal with the work of service you do in the world. Daily renewal practices were offered as well as short and long-term practices for professional renewal.

As we reach the close of this chapter, the words of Zen Master, Thich Nahat Hanh, ring clear.[23]

From time to time, remind ourselves to relax, to be peaceful, . . . set aside some time for a retreat, a day of mindfulness, when we can walk slowly, smile, drink tea with a friend, enjoy being together as if we are the happiest people on Earth. This is not a retreat, it is a treat.

REFLECTIVE QUESTIONS

1. What are your internal cues that let you know that it is time for renewal? Do you listen to them, or do you just keep on running? Explain.
2. Sit quietly and visualize that special place, that secret garden that fills you with peace and replenishes you. Stay there awhile. Write about the characteristics of that place that renew you.
3. Make a list of at least five ways that you are going to use the contents of this chapter to help you renew on a regular basis.
4. When you reflect on the kinds of learning experiences that help you to grow, what are they like? What do they entail? Where do you go to get these experiences?
5. As you reflect on your Emotional Intelligence competencies, where have you grown? What competencies challenge you? How can you renew yourself in ways that will nourish these competencies?

LESSON FROM THE FIELD

Larry Leverett

It is shortly after the winter holiday season and schools are still on vacation. The usual hubbub of a school district office is replaced by the continual sound of the torrential rain outside. Sitting silently in the outer office of this cozy, New England style school district in the city of Plainfield, New Jersey, Jim and I await our appointment time with Superintendent Larry Leverett. As I take in my surroundings, I immediately notice the Plainfield Public School District's unusual but strong mission statement just above Dr. Leverett's solid wood, chestnut-colored office door. It reads:

> *In partnership with its community we shall do whatever it takes for every student to achieve higher academic standards, no alibis, no excuses, no exceptions.*

The silence is jarred by the sudden opening of the superintendent's office door. With a warm smile and a firm hand shake, he welcomes us. It is good to see him again. The last time I saw him was at a national convening of school superintendents. At that time, he helped CASEL members frame the realities of how to bring social and emotional learning into a school district. Impressed by his passion and strong presence, I made a mental note to learn about his leadership. I wondered if his leadership style reflected the beliefs he espoused. This visit would not only confirm his emotional intelligence, but would also inspire Jim and me to use Larry's story to exemplify so many of the learning points of this book.

Background

Larry came to the Plainfield School District in 1995. He previously held a number of influential positions both in the public and private sector. He wasn't looking for the Plainfield job. But Plainfield was looking for reform and as Larry put it, "I do reform."

> *We've never focused on just creating one good school here . . . The question is, How do we create a system of schools that better serves the children and families? That's where our mission statement comes from, no exceptions, and no excuses. Everybody has a mission statement that hangs on the door but it doesn't mean anything to the organization. Our mission statement is a dynamic statement of our work and commitment.*

Larry's commitment to the children and families of Plainfield is evident and so is his pain. He reveals the depressing statistics that describe the lives of poverty, violence and absentee parenting that so many of his children face. One phenomenon, in particular, gave us pause. A large number of children in Plainfield are being raised not just by single parents, but by grandparents and others. An even greater number are in foster care.

> *At one school, thirty percent of our kids are being raised by grandparents and nonbiologic parents. We had a grandparents' support program where we brought in agencies and legal counsel . . . at least 300 plus children in our system are in foster care . . . So when you start peeling the layers of the onion, you get to see how many challenges we have.*

Given the enormity of the problems the young people of Plainfield are facing, Larry took charge of assuring that the school district would offer all of the educational supports these families need.

Busting the Myths: Changing the Culture

Plainfield had a long standing culture that didn't take kindly to change. When Larry arrived, academic achievement was at an all time low.

> *Eighty-five percent of our children were meeting the minimum state proficiency level of 23 percent in Language Arts and Math . . . this was a disgrace. I hated going into schools in my first year. It pained me to see the children . . . and the putrid quality or lack of quality in the instructional process.*

Larry was determined to dispel the group myths held by school administrators, community members and the teachers union. The first group myths Larry had to "bust open" were those of the school administrators. They were used to doing what they always did. Until Larry arrived, no one had challenged them. Larry recalls one professional development day, shortly after his arrival. The conference had started, and several district leaders were still chatting and drinking coffee in the lobby. Infuriated by their inability to model the kind of leadership he was promoting, he walked over to where they were standing and said, in not such kind words, "Get your selves in here! . . ." He confesses, "And I'm not really proud of that . . . but, I just wanted to bust open the myths."

On his third day of the job, a principal at one of his elementary schools conducted a strip search of a third grade class. She was looking for twelve dollars and change in lunch money, Larry says, "That meant, taking the kid into the cloakroom, pulling down their pants, removing their shoes and socks-for candy money . . . She was up for tenure. I suspended her." Larry wondered how he was going to define himself. This incident clarified his position to everyone in Plainfield.

The culture of Plainfield, at the time, touted the use of shared decision making, but there were no supports for this. There was no training, no structure and no evidence that this was working. Aware that the top down strategies he used had no long-term sustainability, Larry reached out to Jeff Howard and his Efficacy Institute. Within a relatively short time, ninety-five percent of district employees received an efficacy-oriented learning experience with follow-up professional development. This training became part of the district's "reculturation" process. The efficacy belief system became part of Plainfield's cultural norms.

The next myth Larry needed to dispel was the community's belief system that children would always fail in school. There had been two decades of decline in the system. The parents of Plainfield's children and their parents had not been served by the system. Larry knew he had to rebuild their trust. He had to break the myth that this was all their children were capable of doing. This work had to happen before many other change efforts could take place.

> Not only the kids, but the kids' mothers and fathers and aunts and uncles had been miseducated or undereducated. It was a system that had not demonstrated any evidence of willingness to change.

During his first two years in Plainfield the superintendent concentrated on building relationships with community members so that he could put the academic goals in place. These efforts quickly brought successes. In 1996, one year after his appointment, the community supported him by passing a 33.9 million dollar bond referendum to build Washington Community School.

> This just didn't happen here. No one in the state believed we had a chance. This bond was symbolic of the progress that we had made early on in terms of the relationship with schools and the community . . . We built a school in the poorest area of our town, a lovely, wonderful facility that has everything.

Building Relationships: Interest-Based Bargaining

Another part of the reculturation process the superintendent led in Plainfield involved reshaping the relationship between the teacher's union and the administration.

> Before I even set my foot in the district, I was in the offices of the Conflict Management group, founded by Ury and Fisher, in Cambridge, Massachusetts with a board

> *member and the union president. I wanted to change the way we did negotiation . . .*
> *I sold interest-based principal negotiation to them! This changed the tenor of a his-*
> *torically adversarial process that was disruptive to sustaining good communications*
> *and built the relationships necessary for work.*

Larry explained that this first contract set the standard that persisted through all future contracts and established a joint partnership for reform. The former adversarial relationships were replaced by a Leadership Innovation and Change Council that began the talk about shared responsibility for improving the system.

> *I was building the infrastructure to help us change. I couldn't allow the myths to stand. I*
> *just couldn't. So I just had to be real hard on the myths and hard on the people at that*
> *time. Now I'm hard on issues and softer on people.*

But what steps did the superintendent take to convince union leaders to change the formerly adversarial relationship? Four strategies became clear. He confronted the truth, built relationships based on people's strengths, educated others, and modeled his beliefs. Larry appealed to union leaders sense of ethics by using the data about the history of failure that existed.

> *I put the mirror up about the history of relationship and communications. If we were to*
> *do real work in this district we couldn't do that work with this type of communication*
> *and these types of relationships. And the place where the fight always damages the abil-*
> *ity to communicate in the relationship is at the bargaining table.*

Larry built relationships based on trust. He noticed immediately that the union president was a strong leader who got things done in the organization and was able to influence the school board. Rather than alienate this leader, he used his strengths, one of which was building relationships. Involving him from the beginning in the education process won his favor and, ultimately, that of the union members.

> *You have to educate. Not just, "here is an article, here are places". You say, "let's talk. Let's*
> *learn about this together."*

Larry realized the success or failure of the interest-based process would fall in his lap. He was personally responsible for making it all work. He had to be the living example of the norms he was asking others to embrace. He struggled internally in those early days to contain his anger and be supportive of others in this process.

> *I had to work responsibly and model interest-based approaches to develop the commit-*
> *ment. I had to be principled about how I went about helping people to accept this major*
> *departure from the way we've been doing things for decades . . . my walk, my talk, these*
> *kinds of things had to be well-aligned . . . I had to work with that myself because I wanted*
> *to do this change in the way that the relationship was saved. I couldn't be irresponsible.*

Emotionally Intelligent Leadership

How far Larry's EQ leadership has grown since his first days as superintendent is evident in his self-reflection on his own self-directed learning. Recall his earlier story about his angry outburst with his principals on that first professional day.

> *That is where I was when I started. That's where my head was for the first year and a half*
> *or so. I was a very weak-sided leader . . . I did break the back of that organization but I*

didn't like being that kind of a leader, very direct, very controlling, very confrontational . . . But I really hated what was going on here in terms of what the kids were given . . . I was angry about it, and it was personal. I wasn't very strong-sided.

Larry knew that he had to confront the compelling needs of his district in ways other than by commanding. So, he brought in an organizational development consultant through a negotiated partnership with AT&T. Denise Larratta became his full time coach.

. . . She knew complexity, she knew about total quality management, she knew organizational theory, change theory, she had a lot of skills . . . Having her as a coach really helped me to find a way to channel the hostility that I had about the organization into more strong-side, productive vehicles. She provided me with some bridges to move me from negative emotionality to one that was more emotionally intelligent. She took the change process that was more theory-based and started to work with me on some of the major organizational development challenges.

Larry worked with Denise over three years, during which time he implemented some of the major changes in his district. Larry's work with his coach is unprecedented in the education arena. Few leaders would both recognize their need and then seek out ways to secure this kind of guidance. We asked him how he managed to obtain the funding to bring in Denise. He had secured a grant from AT&T. They offered executive coaching and, recognizing his need, he embraced it.

Raising the Standards

We were anxious to hear about whether or not all of these efforts were impacting the academic success or failure of his students. Larry explained that by 1997, two years after his appointment, he began working on his strategic plan to improve instruction.

Everything was in bad shape and we wanted to fix it all. We eventually got the focus message, and began in earnest in 97–98 to make Language Arts Literacy our focus.

Last year, Larry started laying the ground work for a more systemized math change effort based on what he had learned from his literacy efforts.

Go to Clepton School, the Jefferson School, the Evergreen School . . . and you will see classrooms that look very similar. You will see standards-based bulletin boards. You will be able to speak with children about the rituals and routines of reading workshop and writing workshop. You should be able to have a conversation with them about how to use rubrics. You should be able to examine student work and see peer-to-peer review.

But what about the tests, we hesitantly asked? Were the children passing the tests?

Test taking skills, test prep booklets, dittos that focus on discrete skills, we just did not and have not approached it that way. For example, our math program is called, "Elementary Math Investigations." It is very concept-driven, inquiry-based, suburban if you will. It's not the drill and kill you use to get more kids passing tests.

Larry explains that while all these wonderful changes were happening in the district the pressure was on him to improve the test scores. He shares, "Bottom line, that's what people want to see." Finally, in 2000–2001, two of his seven elementary schools met or exceeded the state standards in grade four language, and in 2001–02, seven out of ten schools met it. . . . Smiling he says, "No test preps, no little booklets, no drill to kill."

Larry is still concerned about math instruction because the scores are not yet where he wants them to be. But, what he does see is good learning going on and that gives him hope.

> *I visited five math classes at the middle school the other day. I was pleased with four out of five middle school math classes. While in one classroom I was emotionally touched, almost to tears because I saw the kids getting such good instruction . . . It really gets to me when it's bad, and it gets to me when it's good. I walked into one middle school math class and the kids were involved in a heated argument. The argument was over the rate at which a person walked from one location to another. It went on for about seven minutes. The teacher was facilitating, managing the conversation and the kids, owned it entirely. . . . It's that whole idea about accountable talk, which we are learning how to do in our classrooms.*

Teacher professional development is the key to instructional improvement in Plainfield. And Larry believes leaders need to use both pressure and support in this process.

> *Pressure sends the message that things have to be different. And if we expect things to be different we are going to provide you with support. Low pressure, no support, no change. All support, no pressure, no change. Balance pressure and support and that's the way we work.*

Larry tells us he educated the school board about the critical nature of professional development. Plainfield spends 2.5 to 3 percent of the gross salary budget on professional development.

SEL at the Core of Learning

According to Larry Leverett, you can't have standards-based instruction without social and emotional learning. In Plainfield, SEL aligns perfectly with the district's instructional goals.

> *Standard-based instruction requires lots of dialogue, more acceptance and responsibility by kids for their learning. It requires giving and receiving feedback; it requires a classroom that moves a lot of the power and control from the teacher to the kids. It requires students to work in peer-to-peer relationships . . . in order to really create a standard-based instructional environment, you have to have social-emotional learning.*

Because his children often arrive at the school door rightfully angry, hurt, despondent, hostile and not feeling good about themselves he believes you have to help them find ways to deal with their emotions. Kids have to have social skills to negotiate and take on responsibilities in a standard-structured environment. They need these same skills for survival in families, on the play ground and in their community. If we don't provide these vehicles for children then teaching becomes all about managing. He says, "It gives the adults the excuse to manage the kids."

Larry makes the point that SEL is not only targeted for kids, but also for adults.

> *Many educators show up at the schoolhouse door exposed to the same levels of issues as the children and families who they serve . . . Teachers have divorces, they are in abusive relationships . . . drugs, alcohol, mental illness.*

There are a variety of SEL programs and projects in Plainfield. Larry mentions two that have been instrumental both the Laws of Life essay program, and The Social Decision Making Program. He makes it clear that while he is the "keeper of the vision" within the organizational context he cannot do it alone. He worked hard to create ownership. In Plainfield the SEL work is done by people who are not in positions of formal authority such as social workers, school psychologists and guidance counselors. Larry believes that the SEL work goes deeper into the organization when various people carry the SEL mission with them. Their influence will continue to impact the formal organizational structure.

Renewal

As the interview draws to a close, Jim asks Larry how he maintains his integrity and balances his heavy load. He admits that he is not a real exercise buff, although he did buy the treadmill when he got the job. He said, "I knew that I had to be physically in a different place in order to do this hard work." He also loves gospel music:

> *While I'm on a treadmill that's in the basement of my house with my surround sound and five disc CD player, Gospel is basically the only thing that's on there. I walk the treadmill, do sit ups, lift little lightweights and get pumped up.*

On his morning ride to Plainfield he listens to his Gospel music.

> *I try to frame my mind on the positive, the spiritual, the uplifting; get support to strengthen me. I have a responsibility to stay strong-sided even in the midst of all of this adversity, stress and challenge.*

To Larry, the leader needs to be a person who values people and builds them up. Larry confirms that to be able to do this you have to keep yourself supported. He says, "My spirituality helps. Being physically healthy makes my disposition a bit better. I have energy because it takes psychic and physical energy to do this work." Larry says that being a continual learner helps him too. "You have to understand what motivates people within the organization, you've got to understand the place of the individual in the organizational goals." Finally, Larry tells us that we need to have people to talk to when we are feeling stressed. He misses his Denise, but he does go to others in his organization.

> *I mean from time to time I need to cry, you know get it out or I need someone to argue hard with me. So you build up a support network in the district or outside . . . And you don't take it home. You just keep doing maintenance on yourself.*

Larry Leverett is indeed, Superintendent Emotionally Smart, whom you met in the Project Based Learning activity in the skills section of Chapter One. In so many ways, his leadership behaviors are replete with EQ and IQ. As we stand to leave Larry's office, Jim catches my eye and directs my attention to a sign behind us. In large print letters are the words, STAY ON YOUR STRONG SIDE. Noting our observation, Larry nods, "Yeah, I remind myself about this every day. The tendency to be weak is always there. A little reminder helps."

Epilogue

"I long to accomplish a great and noble task, but it is my chief duty to accomplish small tasks as if they were great and noble."

—Helen Keller

In our own small way, we hope that by writing this book we have increased your ability to accomplish a truly great and noble task—to lead a school community that cares about the people side of change. In the many hundreds of small tasks that we accomplished to bring this book to life, we hope that we produced at least one thing—a phrase, an image, an activity—which moved you to look inside yourself and learn. It is hope, after all, which keeps so many of us in education beyond the bell and beyond the limits of the possible.

From that hope also grows expectations. We expect that you will see this book as only one part of your learning journey. The leaders we highlight in this book are all excellent leaders, but they consider themselves learners still. Engage in self-directed learning. Continue your journal. Join or start a support group. Get feedback. "Hire" a coach. Be a coach to someone else. Read more. Reflect. Practice, practice, practice.

We also expect you to apply what you have learned to a school setting as soon as possible even if you have to volunteer in your local school and even if the biggest group you will lead is a reading group or a parents' school committee. Lead or facilitate leadership. If you are already leading a school or a school district, apply one new approach or skill this week and be sure to keep your sense of humor when the "textbook answer" doesn't work. Remember the "textbook" advice we gave you to be flexible in approaching any situation. Like good teaching or good dancing, leading is an art and you need a flexible brushstroke.

We also expect you to consider EQ leadership as a science, complete with hypothesis testing and problem solving. Become adept at observing others and checking out your assumptions. Try to disprove your most strongly-held beliefs by searching for disconfirming evidence. Collect data on yourself as well as on your school and evaluate the data with clear and objective criteria. "Publish" your findings as widely as possible so that others in your school will learn the value of transparency as well as the findings. Encourage others to take on their own action research projects centered on the school's mission.

In Chapter One, we presented the road map for the inner and outer journey you would take with *SMART* SCHOOL LEADERS and now you can stop and reflect on just how much of the social-emotional landscape you took in. Reflect on which chapter,

Lesson in the Field, reading or skill activity had the most impact on your learning. Which did you have the strongest emotional reaction to and which emotional reaction led to the most learning or the least? Did you take full advantage of the exercises that you were asked to do alone and what did you learn about yourself from the exercises you did with others? What gaps in learning did you discover from these exercises and which do you plan to narrow in the future? Have you formulated a plan, or a learning agenda as Boyatzis calls it, which would build upon your strengths while reducing the gaps? Be mindful that you are in the driver's seat on this leadership journey.

Moving through Chapters Two through Four, you shifted from self-awareness and regulation into social awareness. From there you traveled into the part of the book which asked you to examine some of your concepts and practices in regards to schools and the groups that make up the school community. Chapters Five through Eight presented a vision of education that may be more inclusive, more progressive and more democratic than the schools we ourselves went to or the ones we now work in. Does this vision resonate with yours and how does your model of leadership "fit" with the models that were portrayed in both theory and in real-life stories in these chapters?

In Chapter Nine, we accelerated into the future and asked you to look forward at what may be possible in the Twenty-first Century. Will technology and new school structures improve schools, make them obsolete, or have little real impact? The authors think that education will be transformed if we do not forget to make sure that our designs and our hearts are open to emotional learning. Our ability to plan for the future is critical—SMART goals (simple, measurable, actionable, reasonable, timely) help SMART leaders create SMART schools.

Finally, we concluded this book with a return trip to the inner self. In Chapter Ten, we explored the process of renewal that EQ leaders use to replenish themselves for the next part of the journey. It is fitting that we end where we began—with you. In the end, it is up to you what kind of leader you will be. If there was a theme that ran through this book, it is the simple notion that EQ leadership can be learned. It is not easy but it can be done. The road lies just ahead.

SKILLS SECTION

FOR INDIVIDUAL READERS

The activities in this section are designed to provide individual and group learning experience in skills related to many of the emotional competencies covered in this book. If you are teaching an educational leadership course or leading a professional development workshop for practicing school leaders, please read the note below. If you are reading this book for your own individual use or are considering using these skill activities with a different audience than aspiring or practicing school leaders, many of these activities can be used as is or with slight modifications.

NOTE TO COURSE INSTRUCTOR OR PROFESSIONAL DEVELOPMENT FACILITATORS

The activities in this section are intended to give participants opportunities to learn and practice skills. It is likely that students or even practicing school leaders will lack mastery in many of these skills which, by their very nature, evoke emotion. It is important, therefore, that you follow certain guidelines before assigning these activities:

1. If possible, experience the activities yourself.
2. Develop some trust among students or participants. This book's aim is to develop leadership, and trust building is part of that process. By modeling trust building in your class or group, you will not only be teaching the skill but you will also set the climate for learning the various skills in this section.
3. Before introducing the activities in class, you should lead participants in a brief warm-up to get them interacting. Make it fast. Make it fun.
4. Encourage all students to participate but allow students to pass on the activity if any feel too uncomfortable. If any students do pass, have them observe and take notes. Later, meet with them to help process observations and find out how you might create more safety for them.
5. If you feel too uncomfortable to follow the guidelines above, reflect on your emotions. What are the underlying feelings? Assess what is there about these guidelines or the following activities that are triggering these feelings. The causes may vary. There may be a clash between your instructional beliefs and this hands-on approach. Or it may be that you do not believe that you have the necessary facilitation skills for this kind of learning. If either is the case you may want to read Roger Schwartz's book (see references) which can provide you with the rationale for this learning and a deeper understanding of facilitation. In the end, however, you must find the approach that fits your own teaching and learning style so feel free to adapt, eliminate, or add to any activity.

Chapter One Skills Section

In this section, activities are presented that introduce EQ knowledge and competencies.

ACTIVITY 1.1   EQ REFLECTION

This handout serves as a reflection tool. Each question addresses one of the key components of the Emotional Competence Framework and is directly related to the competencies in the Emotional Competency Inventory. These questions can be used to spark a daily journal entry or as a "gathering" at the beginning of a class or staff meeting.

ACTIVITY 1.2   EQ COMPETENCIES FOR SCHOOL LEADERS

The purpose of this activity is to help learners increase their awareness of what the competencies might look like in the actions and words of an EQ leader. Learners will write one observable behavior and one statement of a leader who demonstrates strength in each of the competencies. To help learners focus on the competencies, they may refer to Appendix B from *Primal Leadership* (in the Readings Section of this book) or their ECIU competency assessment results. If done in groups, divide up the competencies and have individuals share their responses with the entire group when finished. Note the example provided in the emotional self-awareness competency.

ACTIVITY 1.3   THE EQ ROLE-PLAY: SELF-AWARENESS

This activity introduces the role play strategy as a tool for developing emotional competencies. This first role play is used to increase self-awareness. Read the rules for conducting the role-play before facilitating the role-play.

ACTIVITY 1.4   PROBLEM-BASED LEARNING ACTIVITY

Problem-based learning (PBL) has increasingly become a desired mode of professional development for aspiring school leaders. It can also assist current school leaders as they grapple with the reality of their own problems and dilemmas in their schools. PBL allows learners to bring prior knowledge together with new knowledge as they analyze and take steps to solve problems. Participants develop problem solving ability while implementing the strategies they propose. They learn and reflect upon their leadership skills and emotional competencies as they work in teams. To learn more about PBL we recommend that you read *Implementing Problem-Based Learning in Leadership Development.*[1]

---

[1]Edwin M.Bridges and Philip Hallinger. *Implementing Problem-Based Learning in Leadership Development.* (Oregon: ERIC Clearinghouse on Educational Management, 1995)

Overview

- *Guide the Process:* The instructor's task is to step back and guide the process, not direct it. In our experience, many students do not want the responsibility of active learning. They want the instructor to do all the work and they want to be the recipients of this work. You will probably have to do some paradigm shifting and create some emotional support before students fully embrace this methodology.
- *Produce Products:* Participants report what they do to resolve the problem. They also take action to implement the solution. For example, if the problem solution is to seek community support for violence prevention, they might make phone calls, write letters, hold meetings and conduct interviews. They document their efforts.
- *Team Collaboration:* Group participation gives participants experience in working together. Questions on the handout guide their collaborative thinking.

Recommended Procedures for the PBL Instructor:

- *Time Frames:* Decide on how much of class time you will use for PBL development. Some Instructors or Group Leaders might want PBL to extend over the duration of a course. Others might allocate five or six sessions to its development. Clarify time frames in the first class. If you use PBL during class allow a minimum of forty-five minutes.
- *Your Role:* Introduce PBL approach. Distribute the handout provided. Assign learners to teams of no more than seven people. Assign roles of Team leader, Facilitator and Recorder. Be sure group members understand their responsibilities.
- *EQ Focus:* We suggest that your students complete the ECIU inventory and receive an orientation to the course content and methodology before you begin PBL. Since the major focus of this book is to develop the emotional competencies of school leaders, we want participants to be grounded in theory. It also helps for them to know their strengths and limitations before they work with others. We recommend that each participant keep a reflective log handy to record their feelings as they work in teams.
- *Select a Problem:* Each team will assume the role of *Principal on the Rise* as they resolve their problem. Each selects a problem that they would like to develop during the course. Note: There are many problems in *District Anywhere*. As principal of school, *On the Rise,* teams might select any problem. These might include: a) strategies to increase community-school based programs; b) violence and other prevention strategies; c) academic instruction issues; d) new teacher development, and parental involvement. Feel free to brainstorm additional problems with your class or group. Ask each team to select, define and submit their plan to you.
- In addition to this textbook, teams might also use other resources that you or they obtain. These might include additional readings, school based comprehensive education plans, interviews with practitioners, school documents and websites.

How To Evaluate

- At each meeting, have the Recorder submit an account to you of the team's progress. You should establish benchmarks for the students so they know that they are within the timeframe and product expectations for completion.
- The assessment of the project is primarily based on the final product. This includes a written report as well as an oral presentation to *Superintendent Emotionally Smart*. We suggest that each group submit a two-page summary of their group's findings and process. They should attach any relevant documents that they produced as exhibits of their work during the sessions provided. Allow fifteen to twenty minutes per group for final presentations of their work. Be sure to have learners submit an individual reflection of their learning during the process. Reflective logs can be used for this purpose.

How well am I aware of my own feelings?
Do I recognize my own cues and triggers?
Do I see how my emotions affect my performance?
Can I laugh at my mistakes and learn from them?
Do I have presence?
Do I believe that I am good at what I do?
Can I hear you when you give me positive feedback?
Can I remain calm under stress?

Can I control my impulses?
Do my actions reflect my beliefs?
Am I an ethical leader?
Do I follow through on commitments?
Can I smoothly handle all the demands on me?
Can I change my plan midstream even if I believe I'm right?
Can I make a difficult situation positive?
Do I take calculated risks?
Do I set measurable goals for myself and others?
Can I get out of the box and embrace new challenges regularly?

Can I see, and hear and observe the perspective of others?
Am I sensitive to the multitude of differences in others?
Do I embrace these differences?
Can I really listen without judgment?
How well do I know the political current of my school/district?
Can I see and understand power relationships and utilize them positively?
Do I really understand and influence the culture in which I work?
Do I know what my people need to thrive? Am I available to them when needed?

Do I mentor and coach others effectively?
Do I give constructive feedback to others?
Do I see the strengths of others?
Is my vision viewed as valuable by others?
Can I motivate others?
Am I talented at persuading, convincing and getting others to
    value what I value?
Do I engage others verbally and nonverbally?
Can I energize and guide others to make a needed change?
Do I really know how to manage conflict positively?
Am I gifted at nurturing relationships and building community?
Can I work well in a team and encourage others to do the same?

ACTIVITY 1.2   EQ COMPETENCIES FOR SCHOOL LEADERS

Self Awareness
Emotional Self Awareness
Behavior: The school leader keeps a reflective journal on his desk. The school leader asks a teacher to comment on the quality of his feedback in a post observation conference.
Audible Statement: The school leader says, "I know that I have been edgy lately. Let me tell you why."
Accurate Self Assessment
Behavior:
Audible Statement:
Self Confidence
Behavior:
Audible Statement:

Self Management
Emotional Self Control
Behavior:
Audible Statement:
Transparency
Behavior:
Audible Statement:
Optimism
Behavior:
Audible Statement:
Adaptability
Behavior:
Audible Statement:
Achievement Orientation
Behavior:
Audible Statement:
Initiative
Behavior:
Audible Statement:

ACTIVITY 1.2   EQ COMPETENCIES FOR SCHOOL LEADERS, Continued

Social Awareness
Empathy *Behavior:* *Audible Statement:*
Organizational Awareness *Behavior:* *Audible Statement:*
Service Orientation *Behavior:*   *Audible Statement:*

Relationship Management
Developing Others *Behavior:* *Audible Statement*
Inspirational Leadership *Behavior:* *Audible Statement:*
Influence *Behavior:* *Audible Statement:*
Change Catalyst *Behavior:* *Audible Statement:*
Conflict Management *Behavior:* *Audible Statement:*
Teamwork and Collaboration *Behavior:*   *Audible Statement:*

(Based on the work of Goleman, D., Boyatzis, R.& McKee, A. *Primal Leadership*, 2002)

Basic Procedures for Conducting the Role-play

In order to maximize the learning from the role-play, set up your learning environment so that it is conducive for the characters who are playing the given parts as well as for the audience. Place three chairs in the center of the room for the two characters and the facilitator. Place the remaining chairs in a circle surrounding these three chairs. This technique is often called a "fishbowl" because it is as if the central characters are engaged in a private conversation with the onlookers. The class participants silently observe the action. Best practice is for the facilitator to act as the bridge between the audience and the actors. Use the Freeze Action and Resume Action cues for points of processing and discussion during the role play. You may choose to give the school leader some "tools" to utilize as the role play continues. In advanced facilitation role-plays, the facilitator may invite the audience to freeze the role-play and intervene in the competency development of the main character, the school leader.

The following guidelines are provided to assist participants in developing their role plays.

1. Use positive, open body language and communication.
2. Use active listening skills to hear the messages that the characters are saying, or not saying. Active listening skills, remember, include: paraphrasing, reflecting, clarifying, encouraging, summarizing and affirming. Choose fictitious names to avoid over personalizing of the role play.
3. Respond to the facilitator's questions as best you can, letting the audience hear your "self-talk" rather than engage in a conversation. Self-talk, the private conversation we have with ourselves in our mind can be a wonderful tool to help us reflect on our own actions and decisions. Self-talk can also be destructive and stress producing. Being aware of our own self-talk is part of the reflective process.
4. Have fun with this. Be creative and follow your instincts.

When the role-play has ended, the facilitator will ask questions of the audience to determine what were the most and least helpful strategies used in the development of the school leader's emotional competencies. The facilitator/ instructor should be sure to allow the participants who played the characters in the role-play to explore their feelings and awareness as you and the audience explore the answers to the suggested questions.

SELF-AWARENESS ROLE-PLAY

The foundation of emotional intelligence is *self-awareness*. This is the threshold competency for so many of the other emotional competencies. This role-play is designed to help the leader enhance self-awareness, and the impact it has on one's relationships. Self-awareness is knowing what we are feeling in the moment and using those preferences to guide our decision making; having a realistic assessment of our own abilities and a well-grounded sense of self-confidence (Goleman, 1995, p. 318). There are three leadership competencies we will be addressing in this role-play. They are:

- emotional self-awareness: recognizing our emotions and their effects.
- accurate self-assessment: knowing our strengths and limits.
- self-confidence: a strong sense of our self-worth and capabilities.

As this is the first role play in the book, the entire dialogue is scripted. More advanced facilitators are welcome to develop the role play independent of the given script. Special thanks to Dr. Robin Stern for developing this role play with us.

Scenario: *Principal Sharp has been at the helm of EQ Middle school for two years. She was placed at this school because she has an excellent knowledge of instruction. At her former school, while she was an assistant principal, students' achievement scores in literacy increased by 20% over three years. Now, as head of EQ Middle school, Principal Sharp hopes to be able to do the same, but the culture of this school is a bit more difficult. There are a handful of veteran teachers who are accustomed to doing things their own way. Additionally, the assistant principal who is working with Principal Sharp is somewhat resistant to change. In this scenario, Principal Sharp and Assistant Principal APX are seated in the office on Monday afternoon at 4:00 p.m. They begin to discuss the upcoming meeting that they will be having with their staff on Thursday afternoon. Principal Sharp has a well-thought out plan as to how she wants to go about improving instruction in this school.*

Character Notes: Principal Sharp can be defined as an autocratic leader. She believes, however, that she is collaborative. Given the focus on accountability, Principal Sharp knows the only way that she can assure to input the changes she needs is to lead with her very clear vision. Assistant Principal APX has been at EQ Middle school for ten years. She knows the staff and is well-respected and trusted. She is a reflective leader and quite self-aware.

BEGIN ROLE PLAY

PS: *So, here's how I plan to implement the new literacy program. I hope you agree.*

APX: *I think we should ask the team what direction they want to take. That's how we are accustomed to making large-scale instructional decisions.*

PS: *I know, but that's not how I work. I'm convinced that this plan I have will work. It's what I used at my other school and you know how well we did in our test results, and in such a short time!*

APX: *Well, Frieda and Martha have been leading the literacy and math development now for about ten years. I am sure that they will have lots to say about the direction that you are hoping to take us. They are very committed to literacy development. They seem to think that the program we have is a good one. They see the problem not as the program, but more the schedule and time we've been devoting to literacy.*

PS: *Well, Frieda and Martha will have to learn how to collaborate with me. New leadership brings new changes and you'll find that I am very effective at what I do. They'll adapt.*

APX: *(looking annoyed) That's not the point.*

FREEZE ACTION

Facilitator: *Principal Sharp, What are you feeling right now?*

PS: *I don't know what I'm feeling. It seems that APX doesn't want to agree with my approach to this change.*

Facilitator: *And how does that make you feel? Can you put an emotion to that? Are you angry, frustrated, tense?*

PS: (*Squirming a bit*)   *I guess I'm annoyed, and a little tense. I'd like her to cooperate with me more. We have a lot to do and so little time to do it in. I don't know why she's worrying so much about Frieda and Martha.*

Facilitator: *Well, how do you usually react to people when you are annoyed and tense?*

PS: *Well, I don't know . . . I guess, I usually get more insistent. After all, I'm the person who is accountable for getting things done.*

Facilitator: *How do you imagine APX is feeling right now?*

PS: *Well, she is probably annoyed with me. She must think I'm stubborn, wanting things my way. But, it isn't that. I really like to collaborate.*

Facilitator: *Well, why don't we find out how APX sees you? Let's go back and talk with APX and try to clarify what her feelings are before we make an assumption.*

PS: *Okay, I'll give it a try.*

RESUME ACTION

PS: *Well wait a minute, Are you saying that Frieda and Martha would want to be part of shaping the direction more?*

APX: *Well, I am not sure, but I know that they would love it if you were to involve them more.*

PS: *What do you mean? I always involve them in decisions in these areas.*

APX: *Look, I know you want to collaborate, but that's not what you really do.*

PS: (*defensive, pauses and then asks*)

What do you mean?

APX: *Do you remember last years math book adoption process? You had the whole system set up and done. You didn't consult with either of them, or me.*

PS: (*defensive*) *Well, we were forced to make a decision in two days. I had no choice. It turned out great. Everyone is happy with the new series.*

APX: (*frustrated*)*Tell Martha and Frieda that.*

FREEZE ACTION

Facilitator: *How are things going now?*

PS: *Okay, but she still doesn't get what I'm trying to do.*

Facilitator: *How do you know this? What are you hearing APX tell you?*

PS: *Well look at her. And listen to her. She keeps bringing Martha and Frieda into it.*

Facilitator: *What are you feeling right now?*

P.S.: *Tense, annoyed.*

Facilitator: *Is that a familiar feeling?*

PS: *Well, I guess. It's the same thing I was feeling a little while ago when APX disagreed with my approach.*

Facilitator: *And, how do you react in the conversation when you feel annoyed or tense?*

PS: *Well, I guess I . . . Well, I dig in my heels and take action.*

Facilitator: *I bet inside you are saying something like, "Just let me do what I want to do. I know what I'm doing."*

PS: *Exactly! That's what works best for me.*

Facilitator: *Apparently, it works for you, but not for APX, or Martha or Frieda.*

PS: *(defensive and then) I guess . . .*

Facilitator: *Why not go back to APX and let her know that you hear her and you are open to listening to what she has to say.*

PS: *(sighs)   I'll give it a try . . .*

RESUME ACTION

PS: *Look, APX, I think we are both getting a little tense here. We both want to do the right thing. I know I have some very definite ideas, but I think you are right; I have to listen more to what others have to say.*

APX: *(with a smile) Thank you for hearing me. And I'm sure that spirit would be well appreciated by the staff, especially Martha and Frieda.*

Role Play Deconstruction:

Ask the audience (participants) to respond to the following questions. Have the characters remain in the fishbowl, but come out of character. Be sure to allow each character to debrief their feelings and awareness as the audience responds to the questions.

1. What were the underlying motivations and basic assumptions that were driving Principal Sharp? How aware do you think she was of that motivation? What feelings are connected to these? Is Principal Sharp aware of these?
2. What do you think Principal Sharp feels about Assistant Principal APX's comments? Is she aware of her feelings? How can you tell?
3. Developing the competency of self-awareness is an ongoing process. What might be three techniques or strategies that you could suggest to Principal Sharp to further develop this competency?
4. Given the reality of the job of the school principal, how realistic is it for Principal Sharp to improve this competency? How will it impact her role as principal?

LEARNING OBJECTIVES: THROUGH ACTUAL LEADERSHIP EXPERIENCES:

1. Analyze, plan and implement a possible resolution to a critical leadership problem.
2. Identify and reflect on the leadership behaviors an EQ leader uses to promote change.
3. Increase skills in using EQ competencies to design and implement an action plan that will improve a critical problem.

The Problem: Please read the problem indicated below and the task that you are assigned to complete as *Principal On the Rise* in *District Anywhere*. Ask your instructor for help if you do not fully understand the problem or the PBL process.

Description of School District Anywhere

School District Anywhere is situated in an urban city with a population of 48,000. Sixty two percent of the residents are African Americans, 21 percent are White-Ethnics, 1 percent Asian Americans and 16 percent represent other groups. The outwardly modest, well-kept mostly two story houses that line the streets of School District Anywhere mask the inner conflict that exists in many of this city's families. The outer trappings resemble a middle-class environment with few problems. In reality, this community has a disproportionate share of violence and criminality. The school district serves 7,526 students, 99 percent of whom are children of color. African Americans comprise 71 percent of students and 28 percent are Latinos. All ten elementary schools are Title I schools. There are two middle schools, and one high school. Close to 1000 students are designated as English language learners. Student mobility rate is 22 percent.

In many of the households in District Anywhere, families struggle with economic, emotional and social instability resulting from drug and alcohol use, AIDS and absent parents, often in jail. Many children (approximately 300) are in foster care. Many single parents are living in poverty. On a daily basis, *Anywhere's* schools receive children impacted by issues of emotional and physical abuse and neglect. The number of domestic violence incidents in this city is higher than all of the surrounding major cities in the state.

Superintendent Emotionally Smart has been in the district since April 1995. He was voted in by a three–two vote of the five member Board of Trustees. Born and raised in the northern region of the state, in a small, former industrial town, Superintendent ES has had a wide range of experiences that have prepared him for this job in both the private and public sectors. He came to *District Anywhere* because the job called for a "reform oriented," leader. He was ready for the challenge and wanted to *give back* to a K-12 community.

Academically, 80 percent of the children met the *minimum* level of proficiency established by the state, which is the 23rd percentile in Language Arts and Math for elementary. There is a 20 percent drop out rate for high school students between freshman and senior years. Of those who do graduate, 40 percent plan on attending a four-year college and 25 percent plan on attending a two-year college.

The culture of *District Anywhere* is extremely challenging. Folks in leadership positions have been there over time. They are resistant to change and unreceptive to new blood in the district. There are structures for shared decision-making in place, but decisions made top-down, or bottom-up are not helping the children. Union membership is very strong in this district. Historically, negotiations have been an adversarial process that is disruptive to sustaining good communications and building relationships. The Chairperson of the local chapter has been known to be divisive and foster adversarial relations with the former superintendent. Shortly after Superintendent ES took the job, the Chairperson informed him that he would not be easy to work with. There are a large number of uncertified teachers in District Anywhere. Many of these teachers are fresh out of college. There has not been a culture of educational improvement in the district. Seasoned teachers use longstanding traditional methods of teaching. Many teachers have not yet obtained their Masters degrees. Teachers report children as undisciplined and suspensions are on the rise, especially at the middle school.

Superintendent Emotionally Smart recognizes that he needs someone to dialogue with whom he can think *out of the box* regarding initiatives that need to take place. He reaches out to equally smart leaders in the district, like you, *Principal on the Rise*.

Your Role

You are a well-respected principal of a moderately successful school (elementary, middle, high school of your choice) in the district. Academically, children are approaching state standards, but still have a way to go, especially in mathematics. You have a fairly strong teaching staff. Many teachers, however, are new to your school. There are, as always, a few old guard resistors that just want to keep things the way they are. Community members and parents are generally supportive of your efforts. As leader, you struggle with the issues that were described above in *District Anywhere,* especially those regarding the young people. You have several leadership positions in your school including one assistant principal, a school counselor and a nurse.

Superintendent Emotionally Smart regards you highly. He counts on you to implement many of the initiatives that he is promoting. In fact, he would like your school to be a model school for the district. You recognize that change is terribly needed in *District Anywhere,* and that Superintendent ES will need your help. This is a chance to make substantive changes with real support. You have also read Dan Goleman's books on emotional intelligence and have taken the Emotional Competency Inventory. Your personal competencies and social competencies are in the moderate to high range, and you know your strengths and limitations.

Your Task

As you read and dialogue about the issues in the book, you will also work as a team on your Problem Based Learning. Here are your responsibilities as a PBL team member:

1. Delineate the problems that exist in *District Anywhere* and specifically in *Principal On the Rise's* school. Select the level that you will address (elementary, middle, high.) Select the one problem that your team will be developing over this course or series of workshops.
2. Use the book chapter content and any other resources you may need to inform the steps that you will take as you develop your solutions to the problem. Answer the general questions below after each chapter reading to determine if the chapter has provided you with any insights that can help you with your problem.
3. By the second meeting of your team, submit a problem analysis plan to your Instructor. This will delineate the general direction and steps that your team plans to pursue as you develop your problem's solution.
4. Set a timeline for the sessions that you will be working together. Assign roles other than those that your Instructor has appointed (Team Leader, Facilitator and

Recorder.) Distribute work roles for members of the group as they are needed to resolve your problem.

5. After each work session, complete a log reflection in you EQ reflective log as to the leadership roles you took during the session. Comment on the emotional intelligence competencies you utilized or could have utilized.

Chapter and Reading Guiding Questions

Answer the following questions in your team as you complete the chapters and readings in *SMART* School Leaders.

1. How are the steps I am taking in my PBL part of my larger school vision?
2. What theory, conceptual framework or essential questions should I consider to assist me in implementing my PBL product?
3. As an EQ leader, which competencies are critical to me? Are these my strengths or limitations? How can they assist me?
4. What new strategies might I use to assist me in resolving my PBL?
5. What challenges might I face as I implement my PBL? How can I best prepare for these?

The Product: Each team is required to prepare and submit a final product that includes:

1. A two-page report to the Superintendent outlining the steps that you have taken to resolve your problem. You could even have suggestions for the Superintendent, if applicable. Provide supporting evidence in the forms of memos, phone logs, emails, interview transcripts, etc.
2. A 15–20 minute presentation for your colleagues during which time you will present the problem you addressed and the steps you took to address it. Provide evidence of your efforts.
3. Evidence of the team's learning, including your EQ learning in a one to two page reflection paper.

Chapter Two Skills Section

The activities in this section are designed to help increase self-awareness.

ACTIVITY 2.1   THE REFLECTIVE LOG

One of the best ways to develop an ability to reflect is to keep a reflective log. This log is similar to a diary, except there is a more conscious effort to include the underlying emotional and metacognitive processes often overlooked when we write. If you use this book for a course or a professional group, ask learners to join you in keeping a log. Give them these instructions:

> *The focus of this ongoing activity is fine tuning our emotional awareness. You will be required to write each day in a reflective log, a special kind of journal that significantly improves one's ability to reflect on their experiences. As you write in your log each day, divide each page into two sections with a vertical line (see sample below) or you can buy a steno pad, which is already divided. On each page's right side, write down any events that evoke either positive or negative emotions during the day. Do not write about any events that you would not want me to know about as I need to review your logs as part of the feedback process. I may ask for volunteers to share insightful passages with the group.*
>
> *On the left-hand side, write down or draw your reflections about the event. On the left side you will also note any emotional awareness or regulation strategies that you tried and what results you obtained. Look now at the sample page in your book (review). Now look at the Prompt Cards. These cards are specifically designed to foster reflection on each chapter's topic and can be cut out and used as a bookmark for your journal. Carry your log with you each day and write during the experience rather than afterwards. Any questions?*

Because a journal is used in this activity it might be helpful to have access to an inexpensive stock of journals that students can purchase from you at the beginning of the course.

ACTIVITY 2.2   PERSONAL VALUE AWARENESS

This activity asks individuals to tap into their value system to identify core values that guide them. An activity sheet with directions is provided.

ACTIVITY 2.3   AWARENESS FROM INTERACTION WITH OTHERS

This activity uses the strategies, THINK-PAIR-SHARE and MICROLAB. The authors often use these to facilitate reflection in group settings (e.g. courses, faculty meetings, parent workshops, strategic planning, classroom activities). They both involve wait time, active listening, and a structured approach to establishing trust. They are also excellent strategies for school and district leaders to use when open communication on sensitive topics is desired. Additionally, school leaders can encourage teachers to use these tools for facilitating discussion on topics in the curriculum (e.g. "What conditions in both North and South led to the Civil War?"

Think-Pair-Share Directions

1. Before meeting with the group, formulate a question or statement you would like them to comment on in the safety of a small group. For example, you might ask, "What strong feeling have you had most recently and how has it affected you?"
2. Tell the group:

   Think-Pair-Share is an activity that will give you an opportunity to reflect on a thought-provoking question that taps into your emotional experiences. The activity consists of three stages: Silent thinking stage after I read a question; pair stage in which you will share your thoughts with a partner, and finally, a large group stage in which volunteers will be asked to share their own thoughts; not those of their partners. Are there any questions?

3. Say,

   After I read this question, I'd like you to sit in silence for 30 seconds and think about your response. By thinking silently at first you give yourself what is called "wait time" which has been shown to improve the quality of the thinking process.

4. Ask the question and use a timer to alert the group at the end of thirty seconds.
5. Have groups pair up. People choose partners or are randomly assigned (e.g. each person receives a playing card and finds a person who can make a matching pair [two Jacks]). Partners face each other and take turns (1-2 minutes each) sharing their responses.
6. Lead a large group discussion (10-15 minutes) on their responses. At the end, ask the group to reflect on the activity. Ask, "What insights or awareness did you gain from this activity?"
7. If there is time, you might want to divide the group into teams of five to discuss ways that they might apply Think-Pair-Share in their own work with groups.

Microlab Activity Directions

1. First formulate three or four statements or questions that you would like your group members to share in a small group experience. For example:

   - When I feel _____ I can tell because I can sense it in the following parts of my body _____
   - How has your cultural beliefs affected your ability to access your emotions?
   - The self-regulation strategies that work best for me seem to be _____

2. Give information. Tell the group (you may want some information listed on chart paper):

   A microlab is a small group experience which helps you learn something about yourself through speaking and listening with others. In a few minutes I will ask you to form groups of four (groups of three are also fine) and sit in a circle. I will then read a series of questions one by one and ask you to respond to each. In order to ensure a climate of open communication, I need you to agree to four guidelines. The first is that you take turns answering the question and, if it is not your turn to speak, you listen and do not interrupt. The second guideline is that this a timed activity and each small group has to monitor its allotted time to make sure that each member has roughly the same amount of time to speak. If each person has finished and there is time still remaining, you may then engage in discussion if you wish. The third guideline is that you should share to the level that you feel comfortable and anyone can pass if he or she chooses. The final guideline is that whatever you say in the small group must remain confidential when we return to the large group. If you want to share what you said in the small group, please do, but do not share what anyone else said. By a show of hands, how many of you agree to these guidelines?

3. Divide the group into fours (playing cards or puzzle pieces can be used).

4. Ask the first question and give the whole group enough time (4–6 minutes) to have a go around. With four minutes, for example, each person would have one minute. Help them keep track of time by letting them know when half the time is up. Observe the groups to make sure that people are following the guidelines. Ask the rest of the questions following the same format. Circulate around the room to observe the process.

5. When all the questions have been responded to, ask everyone to return to their original places. Process the experience by asking a few volunteers to share their answers to a question. Ask the whole group what they liked and did not like about the microlab experience. Elicit any insights, feelings, or training points. Brainstorm ways that they might use the microlab technique in their workplace. Thank the group for their involvement.

ACTIVITY 2.4.   ACKNOWLEDGING FEELINGS

School leaders can help students develop their self-awareness. In this exercise, learners guess the underlying feelings reflected in typical statements that students utter to administrators. The statements are listed on the activity sheet with room for written responses. After completing the sheet, learners should discuss their answers in small groups. Practicing leaders can use this exercise with their staff. Good follow up activities:

1. Ask volunteers to role-play interactions between school leaders and students using the statements on the activity sheet.

2. Have small groups develop other Acknowledging Feelings scenarios between principal and teacher or between principal and parent.

3. Have a group use this skill in their workplace and report back to the large group.

A Sample Entry for A Reflective Log

Reflections	Events
Feeling excited and proud. Cues: big smile on my face, pleasant sensation flowing throughout my body but especially in my head. Have a hard time sitting still. Triggers: the promotion, mental pictures of myself in new office, sun outside. Intensity: Very strong. 5 on a scale of 1-5. Other feelings: Annoyed. Cues: Sighing. Gritted teeth. Trigger: Joan's not here and I wanted to share this moment with her. Intensity: Low. 1 on scale. I'm thinking that she could not have known and I do not want to spoil this moment. Used self-talk. I feel the tension decrease.	I just received a call from Mrs. Burke that the school board selected me for the principal's position at the new school. When I hung up the phone I called out Joan's name because I wanted to tell her but she did not answer. She might have gone next door to visit her friend.
	Joan walks in and sees two glasses of champagne. She yells out "Yes?" I guess I shook my head because she threw her arms around me and we almost fell to the floor.

Journal Questions Prompt Cards

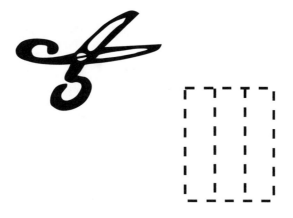

Directions:

On the next three pages are questions that can help you to maximize your social and emotional learning as you use your journal. These questions, called Prompt Questions, were written to facilitate your reflection on topics covered in Chapters 2 through 10. Cut out each Prompt Card and use it as a bookmark for your journal while you are learning and applying the concepts of that chapter in your everyday experience. For example, a question on the Emotional Awareness Prompt Card asks you to notice the physical sensations, or "cues", that you are feeling when you are involved in an emotional experience. By trying to answer this question in a reflective way in your journal, you not only fine-tune your emotional awareness but also record the reflection for future reflection and learning.

The Art of Reflection
Prompt Card

1. Close your eyes and ask yourself, "What am I feeling?"
2. What are the physical cues that let me know that I am experiencing emotions?
3. What event or thought triggered this emotion?
4. Am I feeling any other emotions other than the one I first named? What are they and what are the cues, triggers and intensity level of these emotions?
5. How does this awareness make me feel and why?
6. Once aware of my emotions, what works or doesn't work in terms of managing (enhancing as well as defusing) emotions?
7. What have I learned from my emotional experiences and how can I apply this learning tomorrow?

Am I the Model?
Prompt Card

1. What emotions am I expressing to this person(s)?
2. How am I expressing the emotions and what are my thought processes before, during and after that expression?
3. What nonverbal messages do I send and are they consistent with my verbal statements? What assumptions am I making?
4. In communications with others, how able am I to "read" the other person's meaning and how do I test that assumption?
5. What have I done today to influence others to create a caring learning environment?
6. As an EQ model, what could I do differently in similar situations?

Embracing Conflict in Ourselves and Others Prompt Card

1. In this conflict, what are the underlying interests? Mine? The other person's? Shared by both?
2. What strategies are the other party and I using to increase the probability that this conflict will be constructive rather than destructive?
3. Am I rushing to a solution and, if so, why?
4. What did I do to promote constructive conflict or to buffer others to prevent conflict?
5. If others come to me to intervene in a conflict, how do I decide if I should?
6. In reflecting upon how I dealt with conflict today, what did I do well and what could I do differently?

Leading SEL Communities Prompt Card	The People Side of Change Prompt Card	The Purpose of School Prompt Card
ò	ò	ò
1. What have I done today to promote SEL in my school? 2. When and where did I model the behavior that I want others to follow? 3. What evidence do I have that teachers use modeling? 4. What evidence do I have that teachers are teaching the SEL competencies? 5. What did I do today to assess my school's climate and how do I know its accurate? 6. Thinking about my day, what is one thing that I would like to do tomorrow to create a better school climate?	1. Have I done anything today to create a *shared* vision? 2. What have I done to increase my self-motivation? 3. What have I done to increase the intrinsic motivation of someone else? 4. Which leadership styles did I employ today? 5. Were my choices of style congruent to each teacher's abilities and readiness? 6. What have I done to sustain desired change in self and others?	1. What if anything did I do today to empower someone else? 2. How did I create safety for experimentation today? 3. How will I or did I value the diversity around me? 4. Was there an opportunity for me to play the Believing Game? Did I play? Why? 5. What did I learn about myself from my interactions with people who are different from me? 6. What do I think they learned from me?
ñ	ñ	ñ

ð

Facilitative Leadership Prompt Card

1. When someone comes to me to solve his or her problem, what am I thinking and feeling? Why?

2. When I follow another person's lead, how do I interact with the leader and with others? What influences me?

3. As I interact in this team situation, what role(s) am I playing?

4. Do my actions in this collaborative effort, reflect my core values? If not, what other values may actually be guiding me?

5. What organizational constraints affect this situation now? What do I do to perpetuate or eliminate constraints?

6. Who is accountable in this situation and for what?

7. If I were not here, how would this group's behavior be different? Why?

ñ

Leading the School of the Future Prompt Card

ð

1. Have I thought about my long-term vision and, if so, what did I think and feel?

2. How was technology used in my work? In other's work?

3. Is or was the technology use in keeping with my vision?

4. What do I notice about the physical environment that either hinders or enhances my work? The work of others?

5. What have I done today or what shall I do to keep informed about new developments that might affect my work in the future?

6. How do I feel about the distant future? The near future?

ñ

Change and Renewal Prompt Card

ð

1. How do I know when I have had enough? Am I able to pull back and take care of me?

2. Is it time to replenish? Make arrangements immediately to nourish your heart and soul.

3. What professional skills do I need to renew? How will I make that happen?

4. Who is my trusted "buddy?" When did I last arrange phone time, or a visit to bounce off my ideas and challenges?

5. Who knows better than I the many ways that I need to renew?

6. How do I allow others to renew in my school?

ñ

ACTIVITY 2.2 PERSONAL VALUE AWARENESS

Directions:

1. Read the list of values below. If there are additional values that are important to you, write them in the spaces provided.
2. Write a check next to the 10 values that are the most important to you.
3. From those selected ten, circle the five that have the most meaning to you in this part of your life.
4. Reflect on how these core values interact with how you think, feel and act in the role of school leader.

_____ Achievement

_____ Adventure

_____ Affection

_____ Beauty (Aesthetic)

_____ Beauty (Physical)

_____ Change and variety

_____ Challenge (Physical)

_____ Community

_____ Competence

_____ Competition

_____ Cooperation

_____ Creativity

_____ Democracy

_____ Effectiveness

_____ Efficiency

_____ Excellence

_____ Fame

_____ Family

_____ Good health

_____ Honesty

_____ Independence

_____ Integrity

_____ Money

_____ Nature

_____ Novelty

_____ Pleasure

_____ Power

_____ Privacy

_____ Public service

_____ Recognition

_____ Religion

_____ Reputation

_____ Responsibility

_____ Security (job)

_____ Self-respect

_____ Serenity

_____ Social Justice

_____ Status

_____ Time

_____ Truth

_____ Wisdom

_____ Working hard

Additional values:

_____

_____

ACTIVITY 2.4 ACKNOWLEDGING FEELINGS

Below are some statements young people might make in schools that reflect underlying feelings. Think of responses that involve accepting the student's feelings. Write your answers below the statement. Example: I didn't ever think that I'd get a 95 on the chemistry test. It was so hard. Possible responses: It sounds like you're surprised that you did so well . . . or . . . Are you feeling proud of what you did? Remember, acknowledging does not mean agreement.

1. I hate doing all this homework every single day.

2. I'm really dumb in Spanish.

3. I'm going to fail the test anyway no matter what you say!

4. My father is going to kill me when he finds out I lost my jacket.

5. I'm fine. Who cares anyway?

6. I hate her. She never answers anybody's questions.

7. It was my brother who scored the final basket. How cool!

8. You can't make me leave him alone. My mother said that if someone bothers me I should hit him.

9. I don't know why I was given a failing grade. Every test but one was over an 80.

Chapter Three Skills Section

In this section are activities that will help develop social awareness skills.

ACTIVITY 3.1   ACTIVE LISTENING TRIADS

In this activity, groups of three will help each other practice active listening skills. Three partners will take turns playing the role of speaker, listener and observer. The speaker selects a topic from the list below. The listener uses active listening techniques to affirm the speaker and to find out more information. Meanwhile, the observer will use the handout for activity 3.1 to record observations of the listener's behaviors. At the end of each 2–3 minute round, the observer and the speaker give brief feedback to the listener.

- Topics (Announce or chart these):
  - A strong feeling that you have experienced recently.
  - Someone who has been a mentor in my life.
  - A time in my life when. . . .

ACTIVITY 3.2   OBSERVING NONVERBAL COMMUNICATION

Awareness of nonverbal communication channels and social awareness are developed in this exercise. It can be done as an individual or a group exercise. Individual readers can go right to Activity Sheet 3.2 and follow directions. If used as a group activity, first have participants brainstorm and chart a list of feeling words. As a warm-up to the activity, select one of the words and walk by the group saying "My name is ____ (fill in your name) but act out the feeling word you selected. For example, you select the word "anxious" so your body language would reflect that feeling as you told the group your name. Have the group guess the emotion using clues from your body language. Invite a few volunteers to continue the feeling charades with different emotions.

After the warm-up, have participants turn to Activity Sheet 3.2. Read the directions together and then show a soundless four-minute clip from a dramatic movie that you previewed before this meeting or class. After viewing the clip have learners pair up and compare notes. Process in large group with the following questions:

1. How many people felt that this activity was difficult and can you explain why?
2. What strategies did you use to determine the meaning of the nonverbal communication?
3. Were there any additional insights or awareness?
4. How else can you practice this skill?

ACTIVITY 3.3   UNDERSTANDING ANOTHER POINT OF VIEW

This activity is designed to be done as an individual learning exercise that develops the ability to entertain the perspectives of another. Learners can write on the sheets provided. If desired the activity can be done by a small group.

ACTIVITY 3.4   I MESSAGES FOR ADMINISTRATORS

Assertiveness skills are focused on in this exercise. Learners should review the formula for an I Message and craft such assertions for each one of the situations on the handout provided. Partners can give each other feedback. If this is done in a class or other group experience, learners should then be given opportunities to pair up and to deliver each I Message. After participants rehearse situations in pairs ask for volunteer pairs to role-play the situations in a fishbowl. Group and facilitator should give feedback. If the group's skills are advanced, set up the role play so that the receiver of the I Message is defensive and the sender must use communication skills to decrease defensiveness. Follow up assignments:

- Learners craft I Messages, with both positive and negative feelings, to people they know. They rehearse delivery with a partner and use feedback to improve the message or delivery. Whether learners actually use their I Messages with others is their choice but encourage them to do so (suggest that they start with someone they trust who might be receptive).
- Learners create and write down scenarios when I Messages might be used. The handout can be used as a model. Learners trade worksheets with each other and fashion I Messages. Sheets are then returned and messages analyzed by the writer.
- Movies on video can be used as learning tools. Learners observe interactions between characters and classify them as avoiding, assertive, or aggressive. Have them note when verbal and nonverbal communication is inconsistent (e.g. a hero's words are assertive but gestures are avoiding). Stop the video at key points and ask learners to craft and deliver an I Message.

ACTIVITY 3.5   SELF-DIRECTED LEARNING PATH

This exercise asks learners to use Boyatzis' Five Discoveries to chart out what they would like to learn while reading this book. See activity sheet.

Silently observe the listener. Note examples of effective and ineffective listening behaviors on this grid. These notes will help you provide feedback to the listener at end of his or her turn.

Active Listening Behaviors	Examples of listener's listening behaviors	Examples of listener's obstacles to communication
1. Nonverbal listening responses: • Eye contact • Position of body • Gestures • Nods • Other		
2. Reflecting feelings		
3. Paraphrasing		
4. Clarifying questions		
5. Encouraging or summarizing statements		

ACTIVITY 3.2   VIDEO OBSERVATION FORM

1. Directions:Watch a four minute video clip of a dramatic movie that you have never seen. Either start at the beginning or at a spot when two or more characters are interacting. Press the mute button on your remote control or turn down the TV so you cannot hear the characters. Observe all the characters but record your guesses on the nonverbal communication of only one character.

Name of Movie _____ Character I observed _____

Body Language Noted Facial expressions, gestures, proximal distance, other body language	My guesses to the character's emotions based on my reading of nonverbal communication

2. After watching the video clip, play the segment again with sound. Compare the words to the emotions you "heard" from the body language. Also, listen for the tone of voice. Are there any differences and, if so, how do you explain those differences? Try observing people in real situations and make guesses about any emotions expressed nonverbally.

ACTIVITY 3.3   UNDERSTANDING ANOTHER POINT OF VIEW

Understanding someone else's Point of View (POV) requires that we examine our own belief systems as well as those of others. In order to do that it is useful to dialogue with others, to look at beliefs from their perspective and to evaluate the accuracy and justification of our beliefs. Useful questions to ask are:

1. How well do our beliefs explain the world around us?
2. How well do these beliefs predict the future?
3. How well does evidence support our beliefs?
4. How reliable is the information that we use to support these beliefs?

POV ACTIVITY 1:

Consider the following contrasting viewpoints. In each of these cases, both people are being exposed to the same phenomenon, yet each has a totally different perception of it. Try putting yourself in both perspectives. Under each perspective write possible reasons why you, as that person, might have this opinion.

1a. I think parents have too much influence on school decision-making because they cannot be as objective or as well-informed on educational issues as educators.

b. I think parents need to have more of a role in school decision-making because educators would benefit from their involvement and different perspectives.

2a. I think (insert the name of a recent action movie) was a wonderful movie because the special effects were so visually exciting.

b. I think (same movie) was a terrible movie because it relied too much on special effects and not enough on character development.

3a. I like the workshop approach to learning because it gives me the opportunity to learn from experience.

b. I dislike workshops because I don't feel that I get all the information I need to help me toward my goal.

221

POV ACTIVITY 2:

Think about the following situation:

> *Julie, an experienced teacher, has a problem. She feels that the principal should help her and several colleagues to set up, in the school building, a mini-school that would re-structure and integrate the curriculum.* **The principal,** *proud of the school's reputation for good morale among teachers and students, thinks the idea has some merit, but refuses to implement it because she feels that the shifting of classrooms, schedules and students would anger too many people and disrupt harmony.* **Ron** *is one teacher who does not want to switch rooms, since he endured teaching in the basement before getting this room five years ago. He also believes that teachers who run to try out the latest craze get all the perks while excellent teachers who quietly do their own thing get little support. One of Ron's students,* **Lynn,** *wants the mini-school to happen because "it would be awesome to be with all my friends working together on projects." However, she also wants permis-sion to attend Ron's math class since his students always do best in math (the mini-school teachers would teach math to their students). Lynn's mother,* **Joyce,** *the PTA president, is pushing for the mini-school because many parents want the choice even though she is per-sonally against the mini-school for her daughter. "I know her grades would go down if she was socializing with her friends all day," Joyce says, "and that's my final word on that subject!" Who is right?*

Analyze the problem by using the following method:

- What is the problem from your perspective?
- Describe the problem from the POV of each person below (include possible feelings):

Julie:

The principal:

Ron:

Lynn:

Joyce:

> Structure:
> - I feel . . . *(state the emotion)*
> - when you . . . *(state the specific behavior)*
> - because . . . *(state the effect the behavior has on you)*

Complete the following examples:

1. A teacher arrived 5–10 minutes late several times this year. You have spoken to him but today it happened again. You've asked to speak to him during his prep.

I feel _____

when you _____

because _____

2. A staff developer borrowed your copy of the Standards recently. Each time she forgot to give it back when promised. Now, she has done it again.

When you _____

I feel _____

because _____

3. Your district superintendent has recently given you several new projects over and above your regular responsibilities. She has just asked you to take on another.

I feel _____

when you _____

because _____

Write an I Message below that you would like to give a real person in your life (a colleague, a friend, a co-worker, a student, a relative, your spouse or partner).

What is the situation?

What is your immediate goal?

What is your long-term goal?

I Message _____

ACTIVITY 3.5   SELF-DIRECTED LEARNING PATH EXERCISE

1. **The First Discovery:** *My ideal self—Who do I want to be as a leader?*
   - First write below what you think you **ought to say** if someone asked you this question:

   - Now put a line through any part of the answer above that does not accurately reflect what you truly believe you should be as a leader. Once done rewrite your answer in the space below joining anything not crossed out above with anything that *feels* right as an answer but which you did not initially include.

2. **The Second Discovery:** *My real self—Who am I? What are my strengths and gaps?*
   - Before you answer this question, refer to your ECIU results (see Chapter 1). If you did not take the ECUI, ask three people you know to be as honest as they can and tell you what they think your strengths and gaps are as a leader. Tell them that you will listen to them and at the end will only ask questions to clarify, not to refute or defend. Write a brief summary of their appraisals below:

   Strengths

   Gaps

   - When done getting feedback, use that information and ask yourself "where are their appraisals similar to my own and where are they different?" Ask yourself are the inconsistencies because of their misperceptions or yours or both. Now, based on what you discover, write your strengths and gaps:

   Strengths

   Gaps

3. **The Third Discovery:** *My learning agenda—Building on my strengths while reducing the gaps.*
   - Write a learning agenda (a short action plan) for your self-directed learning of leadership concepts and skills. The agenda's time frame will be the amount of time allotted for reading this book. First think of what you can do to build upon your strengths and then ask how you can narrow the gaps. Write your plan below and make sure that you have both short and long term goals.

4. **The Fourth Discovery:** *Experimenting with and practicing new behaviors, thoughts, and feelings to the point of mastery.*
   - List below the behaviors, thoughts and feelings that you would like to experiment with or practice during the time you will be involved with this book. Write at least two of each.

5. **The Fifth Discovery:** *Developing supportive and trusting relationships that make change possible. Write down the names of people whom you might:*
   - Relate to as your mentor or coach.
   - Relate to as your peer learners.
   - Relate to as _____ (you fill in) in your learning process.

Chapter Four Skills Section

Learning how to deal better with conflict is a difficult skill to learn because this kind of learning is not so cut and dry as learning how to solve a mathematical equation or to edit an essay. In order to learn how to embrace conflict, in ourselves and others, we need to unlearn methods that are hard-wired into our brains, work with the emotions that are evoked, apply new strategies and assess our progress. The activities in this section will help in that process, but are also designed to help readers to identify gaps in their learning so that they can best make use of self-directed learning elsewhere.

4.1 THE CONFLICT SPIRAL

Introduce activity by showing chart of spiral and saying the following:
This Conflict Spiral depicts the dynamic process of interpersonal conflict. This process consists of different stages, each of which can influence the other. For example, a student believes that her world is an unsafe place and she must be ready to fight if someone attacks her. When someone steps on her foot at lunch her belief prompts her to perceive the situation as a battlefield and the other person as the enemy. And there may be aspects of the other person or the time and place that do trigger that reaction. Her behavioral response is to lash out because she does not have the self-awareness and management skills to slow down the action and analyze the situation. The outcomes are destructive. The conflict spirals out of control and further solidifies her POV that the world is dangerous. This spiral can lead to a destructive pattern. The spiral is not preordained, however, and new learning can change the pattern at any or all stages of the process. Learning can lead to a constructive spiral of improved relationships and success in life.

Learners use Activity Sheet 4.1 to analyze one conflict. The exercise can be done individually or, if a video is used to show a conflict, as a group. Directions are written on the sheet but you may want to tap into learners' prior knowledge by asking them to share examples of how conflicts in their lives spiraled constructively or destructively.

4.2 DE-ESCALATING A CONFLICT

This activity is useful for developing the ability of people to stay centered and step to the side when confronted by an angry individual—something that every school leader has experienced. Learners can do this activity in pairs but it is suggested that triads be used instead enabling the third person to observe and give feedback to the person trying to defuse the situation. A handout is provided which explains the activity to learners. It is wise, however, to review communication and empathy skills beforehand and to model the effective use of both to de-escalate a conflict situation.

4.3   SCHOOL COMMUNITY PROBLEM SOLVING ROLE-PLAY

As a group activity, this exercise gives participants a chance to take on the role of school based management team members working collaboratively to solve a school problem. Hand each learner the introduction sheet entitled, *School Community Problem Solving Role-Play*. Read it aloud while they read it silently and answer any questions. Break your group into smaller groups of five to seven members and hand out role cards (copy form sheets below on card stock and cut beforehand) so that each person in the group gets a different role. Allow learners to read their role instructions but make sure that they do not share the instructions with each other. Give groups at least 30 minutes to problem-solve, five to ten minutes to prepare a presentation and no more than three minutes for each group to present their solutions. If desired, groups can meet outside of class time.

ACTIVITY 4.4   MEDIATION SKILLS BUILDING

In this activity, learners will practice their active listening and interviewing skills to conduct one part of an adult mediation—the Caucus Interview. See activity sheet for instructions and form. To facilitate this activity it is suggested that you form triads (groups of three). Circulate around to each triad to help them follow the process. If you are able to do so, it is helpful to model a complete mediation beforehand. An alternative is to show a video of a mediation with adults or students.

ACTIVITY 4.5   REFLECTING ON THE FOUR STAGES OF NEGOTIATIONS

This activity is intended to help the learner learn by doing. The activity sheet provided will guide them through the negotiation process in an actual conflict that the learner is experiencing. If the learner is a student in a course, the student should first consult with the course instructor to determine with the student if the student is ready to undertake this task. Consideration should be given to the skills and attitude of the student, the difficulty of the conflict situation that the student will attempt to negotiate, and the availability of the course instructor to act as a mentor through the process. If a student is able and willing to negotiate a real problem but reports that he or she is not currently involved in an interpersonal conflict, then the instructor may create a mock negotiation. Some students may narrowly define conflict as an escalated destructive conflict and will easily find a conflict to negotiate if the actual definition is made clearer.

ACTIVITY 4.6   EVALUATING A SOLUTION USING CRITERIA FOR A WIN-WIN SOLUTION

This activity can be used in a variety of ways. It may be used by individual learners or by a whole group to evaluate solutions in activities 4.3 or 4.5. It may also be used to evaluate fictional solutions to conflicts in movies or books, and in historical and current societal conflicts. In introducing the exercise, emphasize that these criteria represent an ideal to work towards and, depending on the circumstances, the most effective solution to a conflict may be a compromise or a legal agreement after a court case.

Directions: Reflect on a conflict that you have been involved in as a participant or as an observer. Analyze the conflict and answer these questions:

1. What do you think were the disputants' points-of-view that they brought into the conflict that might have influenced how they perceived the conflict situation?

2. What about the conflict situation (include the other party) triggered a reaction?

3. What were the behavioral responses to the conflict and were they measured and skilled?

4. What were the outcomes and did they serve anyone's interests?

5. How do you think the outcomes changed or reinforced each party's POV?

6. If the conflict progressed into a destructive spiral, what actions could either or both of the parties have taken at each stage of the spiral to change the course of the conflict?

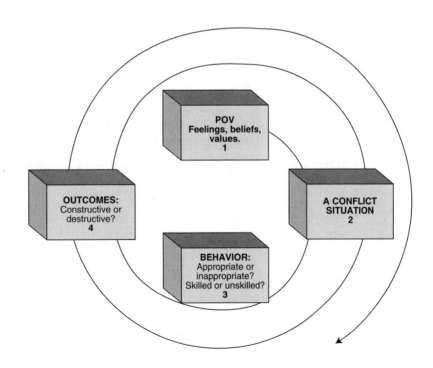

ACTIVITY 4.2   DE-ESCALATING A CONFLICT

Often school leaders are confronted with angry adults or students and find it necessary to de-escalate the situation before working towards a solution of whatever problem is triggering the anger. In this activity, you will work with two partners and take turns using the techniques described in Chapter Four for opening up communication and avoiding OFF switches to open communication in an emotionally escalating situation.

Steps:

1. Brainstorm with your partners several typical conflicts that may result in escalating conflicts in schools that involve only two parties. Make sure that some of the conflicts involve the school or district leader.

2. Select one conflict to role play and give each other roles:

   • One person plays an angry person whose emotions are escalating. This person will make it challenging but not impossible for the other party to de-escalate.

   • One person plays the person trying to de-escalate the conflict using good communication and empathy skills.

   • One person will act as an observer who will give feedback at the end of the role-play to the person defusing the situation. The observer will remain silent during the role-play unless it becomes clear that the angry person is making it too difficult for the defuser. If that happens, the observer can interrupt the role-play and remind the actor to make the task possible for the defuser.

3. Role-Play—Two minutes maximum followed by one minute of feedback.

4. Switch roles for two more role-plays so that each member of the triad gets an opportunity to play all three roles.

5. If this activity is done in a class, then the large group should be reassembled and the activity processed. Possible questions:

   • What was easy and hard about de-escalating a conflict?

   • What strategies seemed to work best for you?

   • When would you use these strategies in your work? What other strategies would you use?

For the past two years students, parents, teachers, administrators and local community members have worked together to create a true learning community in your school, The World Academy. It has not been easy but the spirit of community can be seen in the student-centered cooperative learning approach, in the opportunities for shared-decision making and in better communication among all constituencies.

Not everything has changed, however. One glaring holdover has been the lunch-room. During lunch, many students have been disruptive and leave the space a mess. Students and parents complain that students have been verbally harassed. Teachers complain that their students come back from lunch in an emotional state that impairs learning. The principal is concerned that the issue will undermine the community "spirit" that has just begun to flourish. Recently, a committee of teachers suggested that handing out stickers and stars for good behavior might work. Rather than criticize or accept the decision, the principal reminded the committee that their shared vision requires that every activity be a *meaningful* learning experience and that important community problems need community solutions. The teachers reflected on this and decided to form a new committee with representatives from all members.

Your task is to pretend that you are person on that committee. You will represent your constituency (students, parents, teachers, administrators, etc.) in developing a plan that might solve The Lunchroom Problem in a way that reflects the values of your shared vision. Please read the Role-Play Card that is given to you. The card will describe *your* role and the point of view you will take in the committee meeting. There is a different card for each role on the committee but these role instructions should not be shared. Instead you and the other members will have to *act out* your roles and try to figure out, using your verbal and nonverbal skills what the other people in the committee bring to the table. Remember, however, that you want to solve this problem and that the activity is limited by time so do not get stuck into an "I will not be moved" attitude (which happens sometimes in groups).

Begin your group meeting with a Go-Around to share just your names (make up a name) and your school role (e.g. "Hi, my name is Lonnie Moore and I am a lunchroom aide"). If possible, wear name tags with your made-up name (the name cannot be the name of anyone in either the small or large group).

Parent's Role for School Community
Problem Solving Role-Play

You are a **PARENT** and you have discovered that most parents generally agree that the lunchroom is not a great place to be. They seem to agree that there is too much noise, that the food does not appeal to many of the kids (your own, for example), that the space itself is not inviting, that there are two few adults supervising, and that some kids are more disruptive than others. Parents have different ideas on solving this problem. Their ideas range from using in-school suspensions to serving meals family-style. You have sought out these ideas and you know that the bottom line for these parents is the students' safety and emotional health. Your own point of view is that there has to be something for the kids to do after they finish eating. Students have nothing to do and lunch room aides sometimes yell when the kids move around too much. Both your daughter and son, for example, inherited your "activity" gene and they don't have enough ways to "let off steam" in school. You think that some parents like yourself would be willing to donate time to lead activities but there may be regulations against that. You are a little nervous about suggesting anything because you are not sure the educators are willing to listen to ideas on this particular issue (other issues they have listened).

Teacher's Role for School Community
Problem Solving Role-Play

You have been a **TEACHER** in this school for a number of years and you have seen some positive changes in the school climate in the last two years. You like the spirit of collaboration but you are not sure that this is an issue in which students and parents should have a say. You were the teacher who came up with the idea of a reward system for well-behaved students at lunch and most of the other teachers went along with it though you must admit that they didn't love it. They quickly abandoned the idea when the principal asked them to reflect on whether my idea fits our vision. It doesn't, but what else is going to work? The only two things that might work would be to have a lot of teachers on lunch duty or teaching the kids to police themselves. If the kids could learn how to regulate themselves that could work, but why should the most disruptive kids do that? They are having a jolly good time causing chaos. There's that one class in particular. Maybe that class should have lunch up in their room. No, that wouldn't fit our vision either. You will make a sincere attempt to listen to others' ideas at the meeting. And you will pass on the wishes of the teachers you surveyed.

Principal's Role for School Community Problem Solving Role-Play

You are the **PRINCIPAL** and your concern is maintaining a safe lunchroom and the school's spirit of community. Unlike the other people on this committee, the buck stops with you and, whatever the group decides together, you know that you are ultimately accountable to the Superintendent. Therefore, you want to encourage people to communicate, share ideas and make decisions collaboratively, but you have to be the guardian of the law here. It's a tough role for you to play because most people in the school still look to you to take charge and you get flack if you do and flack if you don't. You will keep reminding yourself to keep sight of the school's vision. In that spirit, you'll try to get others to share their ideas first and then you will give your perspective. You're not sure what ideas would work but you do not want any tough love approaches. You're hoping that someone will come up with a creative idea on how we can make the lunchroom such a positive experience that it sets the tone for the rest of the day. Maybe you'll try coming up with a wild idea and see how they will react. You're especially interested to see what ideas the students came up with.

Student's Role for School Community Problem Solving Role-Play

You are a **STUDENT** and you and your class first talked about the problems during lunch at a classroom meeting. Your teacher brought up the problem and said some teachers thought giving stickers to kids who behaved was a good solution. You didn't think that would work with your class because it is your class that usually gets in trouble at lunch and the most disruptive kids don't even like stickers. You do not think the aides would give out rewards to your class anyway. The aides yell a lot, but they're not really mean. Everybody yells a lot because it's so noisy and kids want to talk and have some fun. Sometimes it's not so much fun, though, because so many kids are calling each other names and pushing each other on the food lines. There's a lot of cutting and that's how a lot of arguments start. And then when you get your food, it does not taste good and a lot of it gets thrown around. You are pretty popular and you are the president of the student council so neither the kids nor the aides pick on you but you think the lunchroom could be a lot better. The student council surveyed the students to come up with ways to make the lunchroom better for kids and you'll bring the list. You're a little scared to be with all these adults. You know that sometimes adults ask for your opinion but don't really want it. You're also missing your gym period.

Volunteer's Role for School Community
Problem Solving Role-Play

You are a **VOLUNTEER FROM THE COMMUNITY** who has been instrumental in getting business support for the school. You are a reading tutor with some of the students who most often get in trouble in the lunchroom. When you heard about this committee, you asked if you could join because you wanted to help find a solution that does not come down hard on "your" kids and you want to offer a different perspective. You are a retired small business owner (construction company) who still maintains ties to many small businesses (restaurants, newsstands, retail, etc.) in the diverse, working-class neighborhood. From your experience, you have learned how to solve tough problems and you bring a sense of optimism. You are not afraid to speak up but you also know that most of the people in this meeting, other than a student you tutor, know each other a lot better than they know you. You will try to sit next to your "reading buddy" and say something funny to break the ice. You have not spent any significant time in the cafeteria so you will try to learn more about the problem in the meeting. In your culture, sitting down to eat is a way to create community so you are interested in finding ways to help your school community recreate that same process.

School Aide's Role for School Community
Problem Solving Role-Play

You are a **SCHOOL AIDE** who helps supervise students in the lunchroom. You love the students but they can drive you up a wall. The noise level, the long lines, the mess and the conflicts that they bring to you! And you have too many kids for the number of adults. Now, most of the time you keep order but if it's a rainy day or too many kids rose on the wrong side of the bed that morning, you not only get a headache but some of the teachers complain that you must not be doing a good job! You are feeling angry because this has gone on too long but you will try to give your views without blaming anyone. You expect that others at the meeting will try to blame you, but you will stay cool (unless they continue). From your perspective, you and the other aides need help and the students need to have a little fun but not at each other's expense. Some of these children really need a good hug a day and to have somebody look out for them, but, as it stands now, you feel more like a prison guard (especially, on rainy days).

Custodian's Role for School Community
Problem Solving Role-Play

You are the **CUSTODIAN** and you want this school to have a real community "feel" to it. Except for a few teachers, you have been here longer than anyone else. You take pride in the fact that most people feel good about the job that you and your staff do. You have your limits, however, and the limits usually relate to three things: the regulations, the regulations and the regulations. You can bend them, but you will not break them. As far as the lunchroom goes, your staff does its best keeping it clean and safe but sometimes the kids make too much mess. But you were a kid once and all you wanted to do for lunch was run outside. Whatever this new plan is you want to make sure it follows the fire codes and does not put extra burdens on your staff (you get budget cuts too). You might throw out an idea if something pops into your mind. You are always willing to horse trade if the other party throws something on the table. You're curious about how this meeting is going to go.

As a third party in a conflict, the school leader may choose to act as a mediator if he or she thinks it appropriate. In this activity, you will be teamed with two partners to practice one stage of a mediation between two adults. This is the beginning stage in which you are attempting to gain information that will help you and the two parties better understand the problem at the heart of the conflict. You and your partners will take turns playing a mediator and two adults in a conflict at school. The adults should be of equal power. For example two teachers are in a conflict over how they treat one another in meetings or two parents are in conflict about one seeming to shirk responsibility for an upcoming fundraiser. The steps for this activity are:

1. Decide on who will play the principal first, second and third.

2. In the first role-play the two adults in conflict should confer and decide out of earshot of the "principal" who they are, what their relationship is and what the conflict is about. First, they should agree on their positions, or wants, that have triggered this conflict. Next, they should decide what their interests are (e.g. I may be arguing about using the copying machine, but my interests may consist of my need to do a good job and my value that people should be treated with respect). Remember that in real life these interests are often hidden in the disputant. This should take no more than five minutes.

3. After five minutes, the "principal" returns to meet with both adults who have asked the principal to mediate their dispute. The adults know about mediation and have signed an agreement to abide by the guidelines. The principal will now meet with them briefly to listen while each person answers, "Can you tell me again what happened?" After listening to both parties, the principal will meet (caucus) individually with each party to find out more. The principal will use a copy of the following sheet, *Mediation Caucus Interview,* to help him or her explore the problem with each party in order to uncover information and feelings that will help guide the following stages of the mediation. During an actual caucus, the mediator meets alone with each party but in this activity, the disputant who is not being interviewed at the time can step out of role and observe the principal's actions for good active listening skills. The observer can also stop the action if it seems that the other disputant is making it too difficult for the principal (aim to make it challenging but not impossible in the amount of time you have). Give ten minutes for each interview. At the end of the interviews the person playing the principal should have one minute for self-feedback followed by one-minute feedback each from partners.

4. Each person in turn should have an opportunity to play the principal and go through the above process.

For further information on the mediation process, read Karl Slaikeu's book (see references).

Mediation Caucus Interview

Name of Party _____

Position	
Needs, Concerns & Interests	
BATNA	
Possible Solutions	
Other info	

It is useful to reflect on times when you were involved in trying to negotiate with some one else. Take notice of times when you were involved in a situation in which you sought a win-win solution. Select at least one of those negotiations (successful or unsuccessful) to reflect on. Use the questions below to help you. Write a one-to-two-page retrospective report that describes the conflict situation and includes your reflections on the four stages. Disguise the identity of the other party. At the end, summarize the report and include anything that you learned about yourself as a negotiator. The criteria for an effective report are the depth of the reflection, the thoroughness of the effort in the negotiation and the mechanics of writing, and *not* whether or not the outcome of the negotiation was successful.

PREPARATION FOR NEGOTIATION

Were you able to prepare beforehand? Why or why not? If you did prepare, what specifically did you do and what was helpful? For example, did you consider the specific situation you face, including the kind of relationship you have with the other party and whether this conflict represents a high or low stakes situation? Did you consider the other party's negotiation style and your own? Were you able to identify your interests (your needs, values, feelings)? Did you try to stand in the other person's shoes so that you could guess what his or her interests might be? Did you assess your alternatives to negotiation? Was the most conducive time and place for negotiation considered? Reflect on what was easy or hard for you in this stage of negotiation.

COMMUNICATION STAGE

Did you use active listening? What specific techniques did you use? How did that feel? What was the other person's response? Did you learn anything new about the problem or the other person by listening to them? Were you able to express your feelings and point of view effectively? What was the other person's response? How did you respond to his or her reaction? Were you and the other person able to stay focused on interests rather than positions? If you were, how did you do it and how did it feel?

PROBLEM FINDING AND SOLVING STAGE

Were both of you able to reach an agreement as to the nature of the problem? Did you generate a number of possible solutions? What criteria did you both use to evaluate and choose a solution? Did you agree on one solution? Why or why not?

COMMITMENT STAGE

If an agreement was reached, was it specific and were all parties responsible for carrying out the agreement? Was the agreement written up and were any provisions made for evaluating the agreement in the future? Do you think the solution will last? Why or why not? What did you learn from your experience? What did you do well? What could you have done differently?

ACTIVITY 4.6   WIN-WIN EVALUATING A SOLUTION USING CRITERIA FOR A SOLUTION

Directions:

Use the questions below to evaluate a negotiated or mediated solution to a problem based on criteria for a win-win solution. Write your answers as fully as you can in the spaces provided. If you are not able to answer a question write the reasons for this decision.

What is the solution?

Criteria

1. Have both disputants agreed on a solution?

2. Do both disputants believe that this solution is a win-win? How do you know?

3. Is the resolution specific? Does it answer who, what, where, when and how?

4. Do both disputants share responsibility for making the solution work? Is that responsibility balanced? How so?

5. Is the solution realistic? Can both disputants really do what they have agreed to do? Explain.

6. Does the solution solve the problem for good? Saying "I'm sorry" may seem like a solution but it may not deal with the underlying need or concern.

Chapter Five Skills Section

The activities below reinforce EQ competencies described in Chapter Five and can be used to help school leaders build a socially and emotionally based climate and culture in their school.

ACTIVITY 5.1: PEACEABLE SCHOOL CLIMATE REFLECTION: (APPROXIMATE TIME: 30 MINUTES)

Using Taguiri's four dimensional areas of organizational climate, learners will reflect on a school's climate. A Peaceable School Climate worksheet is provided.

ACTIVITY 5.2 PEACEABLE SCHOOL CULTURAL NORMS
(APPROXIMATE TIME: 30 MINUTES)

Norms of behavior, the way people act and treat one another, demonstrate the values and beliefs of the people in the organization. In a school, they are the physical manifestation of the school's culture. They represent people's deeper values, and stem from cultural, religious, moral and personal behavioral expectations. In schools, discussing norms of behaviors allows everyone to become clear about expected behaviors, and the nature of relationships.

In small groups of five, draw a large picture of a schoolhouse on a piece of chart paper. Each member of the group should assume the role of a key stakeholder of their school: Principal, Teacher, Parent, Student, Teacher's Assistant, etc. Participants should select a facilitator to guide their group. Write the words, "The Way We Are," inside the house. On the outside of the house, write the words, "The Way We Aren't."

- Distribute markers to everyone in the group. For about five minutes, in silence, members of each group write their desired positive behaviors *inside* the house. A group member who has assumed the role of teacher, for example, might write, "All teachers speak kindly about children," or "Share power with young people." The group member who has assumed the role of the principal might write, "Communicates clearly," or "shares decisions." The parent might say, "Assists others," or "attends meetings." The student might write, "Completes assignments." The facilitator should be sure that everyone contributes a number of ideas to the schoolhouse.
- Repeat the same exercise, only this time, have each group member reflect on the behaviors they believe should *not* be expressed in their school. Members might write, "Criticize others," or "Use vulgar language," or "Backstab someone." Dialogue within small groups.
- Now ask the small group facilitators to help members of the group find common themes in the behaviors they see inside the house. Responses might include, "treat people kindly," or, "confront conflict peacefully." As a group, compose a list of five to ten norms that seem to be important to all members.

- Debrief this exercise with participants. Ask them to share their agreed upon list of norms. Were there any commonalities across groups? What awareness did they have while doing this activity? How might this activity help establish cultural norms for a school staff? How might they extend this activity?

Source: *The concept for this activity was adapted with permission from The Caring Being activity in the Adventures in Peacemaking Guide from Educator's for Social Responsibility, www.esrnational.org.*

ACTIVITY 5.3: PREVENTATIVE SAFETY IN THE SCHOOLHOUSE (APPROXIMATE TIME: 60 MINUTES)

In small groups, participants identify the major issues of safety (physical, social and emotional) that concern school leaders. Leaders should use the questions provided to help them devise a plan for involving their staff in addressing the safety concerns that are raised.

ACTIVITY 5.4: BUILDING THE SEL SCHOOLHOUSE
(APPROXIMATE TIME: 45 MINUTES)

Individually or in small groups, participants will create their SEL schoolhouse based on the concepts discussed in the chapter and their own school's or organization's data. The schoolhouse windows should represent integrated SEL activities. We suggest that before participants complete this activity, they visit the CASEL website at www.casel.org. The website provides research-based information about such SEL programs as The Resolving Conflict Creatively, The Responsive Classroom, PATHS, Social Decision-Making and Problem Solving. Participants should also evaluate and include the SEL efforts they may already have at their schools. This activity can be helpful for school leaders as they develop an SEL implementation plan with their staffs. Participants should reflect on the needs of the community of learners in their school before they design and complete their schoolhouses.

ACTIVITY 5.5   SEL IMPLEMENTATION PROBLEM
(APPROXIMATE TIME: 60 MINUTES)

This problem, contributed by Dr. Jacqui Norris, is based on a true account of challenges she encountered while a new principal at her former school. In 1992, Dr. Norris became an intermediate school principal who was responsible for opening a newly reorganized fourth and fifth grade building under a state desegregation mandate. Through her efforts and with a federally funded Goals 2000 grant, all fourth and fifth grade teachers in the district were trained in "Social Decision-Making and Problem Solving (SDM/PS)," a nationally recognized and award winning program. After assuming the central administration position of Director of Teaching and Learning, Dr. Norris facilitated the training in SDM/PS for all K-8 teachers, counselors, paraprofessionals and child study team members in Piscataway Township School District. Presently, Dr. Norris is an Assistant Professor of Education at The College of New Jersey.

In this activity, you will explore your organizational climate in light of Renato Taguiri's four dimensions. Thinking about climate from the four dimensions will help you expand your organizational awareness competency. It will also help to create or further develop your ideas about peaceable schools. As you reflect on the questions for each dimension below, create symbols or pictures to illustrate the dimension's characteristics in your school and draw them on the following *My Peaceable School Climate* worksheet. For example, if you are working in the Ecology box, you might use dull colors or vibrant colors to depict your school's physical environment. You might draw stairs if there are lots of them, or pods if your classrooms are arranged in this way. In *Milieu*, you might show your school's diversity or represent, in some way, the relationships that exist in your school and community. Do the same for the last two dimensions. As you do this activity, think of the strengths you have in each dimension, as well as the challenges. If feelings come up, depict them as well. Be creative. When finished share your illustrations with a partner. Be sure to highlight a strength and a challenge in each area and state why it is that way. Hopefully, this activity will help you to focus on areas of your school climate that you might not have had a chance to think about for a while. Before you finish, make a plan to tackle one of your challenges in the upcoming month.

ECOLOGY:

Ecology refers to the physical and material environment of the school. The ecology of a peaceable school is clean, safe, warm and nurturing. Paint is fresh. Walls are graffiti-free. Children and adults are proud of their school and work to preserve its beauty and warmth. In North American classrooms, teachers involve young people in a variety of small group and whole group activities. Subsequently, desks and tables do not remain static, but are arranged so that young people can interact with one another throughout the school day. The teacher's desk is situated wherever it best serves the students. The classroom and school walls, gardens or urban city lots reflect the beliefs, values and norms of the peaceable culture through art displays and a variety of children's work and dedication. As you reflect think about the following:

When you walk around this school can you see the hard work of everyone in the school? Do people feel physically safe in this school? Is the ecology of this school what you aspire to, or is there work to be done?

MILIEU:

Milieu encompasses all of the social dimensions of the school. In a peaceable school, the morale of all adults and children, is high. Relationships matter. The social relations that are honored and supported by the school leader contribute immensely to the school's climate. The culture of a school manifests itself in the social relationships that form in the school. As you reflect think about the following:

What are the social dimensions of my school? Is it reflective of the diversity of the school's community? Are adults and young people actively involved? Are certain groups favored over others? What relationships are fostered and valued? Is the outside community visible in the interior of the school and visa versa? Do children and adults feel emotionally and socially safe in this school?

SOCIAL SYSTEM:

As school leader, you set the tone for the social system, the administrative structure that exists in your school. The administrative structure will reflect the leadership styles that you choose to model and support. If governance teams exist, teams will have established their organizational norms. Facilitative leadership and consensus-building strategies are used as a common form of decision making. As you reflect, ask yourself:

Do I strive to model democratic principles and to share leadership wherever possible? Are governance teams common? Do I allow decisions to be made top down and bottom up based on a variety of factors such as time, resources and commitment level? Do I have the respect and support of all constituencies? Are students involved in school wide decision making, as appropriate? As I visit classrooms, do teachers lead "negotiated" classrooms in which young people have a voice in decision making?

CULTURE

The peaceable school is grounded in core values, beliefs and norms of the school community that promote peaceful means to resolve conflict and make decisions. Collaboration and cooperation are regarded as essential tools in learning and decision making. Nonviolence is esteemed and rewarded. Diversity is honored. Discrimination of any form is abhorred. As you reflect on your school's culture, ask yourself:

Is this my school? Is the development of the social and emotional aspects of young people equal to the efforts we place on cognitive development? Are there structures established to support SEL in the school ? How is conflict handled? Are adults and young people valued members of the school community and the community at large? Are social responsibility and service promoted and encouraged?

The ecology, milieu, social systems and culture of a school that embraces SEL are very specific. As the educational leader of the school or educational system, your vision needs to be clear and it needs to be shared by everyone—teachers, parents, students and community members. Bringing others along to embrace the vision you have requires your commitment to learning about who your constituents are. What do they value? What do they need to grow and move forward towards this commitment?

(Courtesy of Resolving Conflict Creatively Program of Educators for Social Responsibility)

ECOLOGY/PHYSICAL ENVIRONMENT

MILIEU/RELATIONSHIPS

SOCIAL SYSTEM/ADMINISTRATIVE STRUCTURE

CULTURE-VALUES, NORMS, BELIEFS

ACTIVITY 5.3:   PREVENTATIVE SAFETY IN YOUR SCHOOL

Entrance	Nurse's Offices	H A L L	Classroom	Assistant Principal's Office	Gymnasium/Multipurpose Room		
Security					Classroom	Bathrooms	Classroom
Student Welcome Office	Custodial Offices			Mediation Room		Locker Rooms	
			Classroom				
HALL					Computer Room		
Administrative Offices				Bathrooms			
			HALL				
		H A L L	Classroom	Cafeteria	Bathrooms	Counselor's Office	Closet
Reception Area					Parent Office		Exit
Principal's Office							

Instructions:

The goal of this activity is to provide you with opportunities to think about physical space in terms of how you would support a SEL culture at your school. Please feel free to use the diagram above, or bring in a diagram of your own school to do this activity. Use the data from the minicase below as you respond to the questions. If you choose to use an actual school's data, have one member of the group supply the data from their school's profile to respond to the questions. Facilitators should plan in advance so that groups are ready to participate in this activity.

- As you look at your school's diagram, think about the physical, social and emotional safety issues that might challenge you. What areas might be unsafe? What kinds of safety issues might arise in this school space? Where are the places for adults and young people to express their voices as part of the school community? How can space be redesigned to promote the culture of caring that you envision? How will you plan for assuring the safety of everyone in this school? As school administrator, what challenges might you face as you plan to address these safety issues? How might you be proactive in dealing with them?
- Based on the questions you discussed above, plan a brief presentation that identifies the safety concerns of your group's school. Explain how you might address them.

Minicase:

In K-8 *School Unknown* the milieu is such that adults and young people work together to create a caring community of learners. The principal and faculty are experts on education, curriculum and implementing pedagogical practice. Parents are involved in this community. Parent teacher conferences usually have a 75 to 85 percent attendance rate. Parents work in various offices, assisting the school administration with many areas such as attendance, lunchtime activities and supervision of free areas. Recently, they organized the peer mediation program. The community uses the building after four o'clock in the afternoon and on weekends for a number of activities including but not limited to sports and recreational activities. Students are generally motivated to learn in this diverse school. Academic achievement is a real focus. Classes are rigorous and 30 to 40 percent of this school's graduates go on to other competitive institutions. Classes are tracked by ability. It is not uncommon to see congregations of young people in hallways. Teachers complain about kids arriving late to class, after the school bell. There is a bilingual track of children in this school who are learning English as a second language. The school has recently adopted an inclusion model for addressing the needs of special education youth.

ACTIVITY 5.5   SEL IMPLEMENTATION PROBLEM

THE PROBLEM

Principal J is a first year African American principal, in an elementary school newly-configured to meet a desegregation mandate from the New Jersey State Department of Education. Before the changes took place, the school's population was predominately white with a 45 percent minority population. It sat in the most affluent section of the township, near Rutgers University. The common factor that joined the diverse populations of this community together was its educational focus. All families in this community are well-educated, and expect the same for their children. The desegregation efforts have brought in children from schools in the southern half of the township. Of these students, approximately 40 percent are minority and middle class, while 60 percent of the students are minority and poor. Residents in the immediate neighborhood do not embrace the school's reorganization. These community members pride themselves in the high academic achievement of their children. They, under no circumstances, embrace this influx of new students who they fear will lower the educational standards.

Issues of class and socioeconomic status are equally as challenging as racial and ethnicity changes. The culture of the school has changed. The new arrivals come from schools where there had been different behavioral norms. Many students are referred to the principal's office for using intimidation, teasing and name-calling. Student's first response to frustration and any kind of conflict is to push and punch. Principal J knows she has to take some action to change the norms of behavior and establish a united school culture. She and her staff explore a conflict resolution and anti-bullying program as a means to de-escalate the ensuing violence. The staff decided on a nationally-recognized program that has been applauded for its effectiveness in helping children develop greater prosocial interactions. Principal J hopes that students will learn to recognize their own emotions, develop self-regulation skills, empathy and a host of other social skills.

Teachers attend a presentation that provides an overview of the program. They verbalize their support for "someone" to teach these skills to the students. Principal J moves ahead with the program. All teachers go through the training sessions in the spring. Some quickly grasp the philosophy of the approach and immediately begin teaching lessons to their children. Others proceed with cautious optimism. Of this group, many expressed discomfort in working with emotions. They are uncomfortable asking students to express their feelings about real-life or contrived situations, such as role-plays. To them, SEL skills are soft and not cognitively based. Others feel that these skills should not be taught at school. The parents should teach these skills at home. The schools' job is to teach academics. Still other teachers say and do nothing. Principal J encourages them to try just one of the strategies in the classroom. She offers to teach demonstration lessons and even invites graduate students trained in the program to assist them. Principal J says, "We know not to mandate the change. We want to build the capacity of the teacher to see these strategies not as add-ons, but as new teaching methods."

Funding is another major concern. The training initially began with a small grant from a local nonprofit organization. With this money, Principal J bought teacher manuals and paid for substitute teachers. By the second year of implementation, the school receives a Goals 2000 federal grant. Now, all the fourth and fifth grade teachers in the school receive additional training and support. Principal J and her staff are beginning to see wonderful changes in her school. Teachers and parents share stories that these skills are making a difference in their children's behavior and attitude toward school. Some teachers report having more time for instruction because disruptive behaviors have decreased. Children are learning how to work together cooperatively in support of each other. The number of children being sent to the principal's office has started to decrease.

By year three, however, efforts at full implementation are unsuccessful. The teachers who embraced the philosophy recognized the connection between learning and emotions. They incorporated the new strategies into their teaching style and classroom management approach. The most challenging group of teachers verbalized support for teaching the skills but then in their classrooms did not follow through with the lessons. They understood why the skills were important but felt that teaching them reduced time needed to teach academic content. Others never "bought in" and even spoke negatively about the efforts. Shortly after this, Principal J retired from the district. When she left, so did the program efforts. Children still do not receive the consistent social and emotional development that Principal J worked so hard to implement.

Instructions:

In your small groups answer the following questions:

1. Identify the major issues that Principal J confronted as leader of this school.
2. Dialogue about the steps that Principal J took to resolve her school's issues. Are you in agreement with the steps she took? Do you agree that an SEL program was needed? What were the organizational issues that she confronted? Were there any other steps that you might have considered to address the issues that resulted from the desegregation action?
3. Analyze the issues of SEL implementation that Principal J faced. Talk about the steps she took to create ownership at her school? Why do you think they may have failed? What might you have recommended to her if you were her EQ coach at the time?
4. Devise a plan for next steps at Principal J's school. Write a letter to her outlining your recommendations. She is anticipating your mail.

Chapter Six Skills Section

In this section, activities draw upon EQ competencies described in Chapter Six.

ACTIVITY 6.1   DREAMING A VISION

This is a reflective tool to help leaders develop their personal vision. Peter Senge and others change leaders remind us that our personal vision cannot be far removed from our school vision. If possible, read the chapter on Personal Mastery in Senge's *The Fifth Discipline* before you do this activity. After everyone has completed this activity, it would be helpful to debrief the exercise. *What did people find easy to do? What was difficult about this exercise? How many recognized that they were not sure about the answers to the questions? How many envision clear goals? In what ways do these personal visions impact upon our collective school shared visions?*

ACTIVITY 6.2   A TRUSTING REFLECTION

Trust is a critical element for any change to happen. Before you continue, spend a moment, either alone or in a microlab, answering these questions about what trust means to you. Remember, everyone has different perspectives and expectations. It would be great to dialogue with your own staff about the ingredients that need to be present to build trust in your school organizations.

1. Think about one person whom you trust *implicitly*. List the qualities of this person.
2. Now focus on one professional colleague whom you trust. How did this person gain your trust?
3. Thinking about your organization, where do you see "pockets of trust"? Which relationships appear to exhibit trust within them? Which do not? Why?
4. Consider one relationship of individuals or groups in your school: teacher-teacher, PTA/principal, new teachers/seasoned teachers, classified personnel/teacher. Describe two or three behaviors that lead you to believe that trust exists in this relationship. What are the benefits gained from this trusting relationship?
5. Consider one relationship that is not trusting, one that may be divisive. What behaviors do you see that reveal a lack of trust? State specific action/behaviors that might foster trust building. What EQ competencies does the leader need to be a facilitator and model of trust building in the organization? What obstacles might leaders encounter along the way? How might they prepare for these?

ACTIVITY 6.3   INTRINSIC MOTIVATORS

In this activity, learners will be guided in an exploration of what motivates themselves and others and how to increase inner motivation. *Materials Needed:* Chart paper, masking tape, rulers, crayons or markers, *What Motivates Me?* circles.
Steps to Follow:

1. Briefly review the section in Chapter Six on intrinsic motivation, especially the four intrinsic motivators proposed by Thomas (2002).
2. <u>Slicing the Motivation Pie</u>—Ask learners to look at the activity sheet entitled *What Motivates Me?*. Display the circle below on chart paper as an example. Point out, that for the person represented by this circle, a sense of progress is more important than all other intrinsic motivators, and competence appears to be more important than the remaining two motivators. Direct learners to use a marker or crayon to divide the circle into four slices that represent to what degree Thomas' four motivators are generally important to them. When done ask them to reflect silently for one minute to two questions: "Based on how you divided up the pie, what are the intrinsic motivators that are most important to you and why? Has this changed over the years?"

3. <u>Shading the Motivation Pie</u>—Ask participants to think about their current work (either employed or as a student). Ask them to use a pencil to shade in each slice in their circles to the degree that their current work is providing fulfillment in each motivator. Use the circle on your chart paper to give an example. Say, "For example, progress is very important to me but my work is presently affording me little progress so I shade in only 10 percent of the slice." Shade in 10 percent of the progress slice. Say, "Are there any questions?"
4. <u>Reflect on your Pie.</u> After participants shade in their four slices, pair them with a partner. Have learners show their pies to each other and answer the following questions that you are now displaying: *What motivates you and how does your work currently provide you with the factors you need? What do you do that prevents you from enlarging the pie? What can you do differently to change either the context or your attitudes so that your work will be more motivating?*
5. Have partners develop goals and an action plan for increasing their motivation.
6. Bring people back to the large group and process the activity:
   • What insights did you discover while doing this activity?

- As school leader, how could you find out what motivators your staff members value most and how they assess their current work? (Chart their ideas and elicit structures and policies that could be put into place to increase intrinsic motivation at work.)

ACTIVITY 6.4   BUILDING A RELATIONSHIP-CENTERED LEARNING COMMUNITY EXERCISE

This activity is based on the work done by Sue Keister in Salt Lake City public schools. In this activity, participants reflect on a learning community as a school of possibilities. This is a great activity for envisioning the purpose of your school and beginning to think about the change process needed to arrive at this vision.

ACTIVITY 6.5   TRANSPARENCY ROLE-PLAY

This role-play is designed to provide learners with practice in recognizing the importance of the leader's "trustworthiness." Richard Boyatzis, Anne McKee and Daniel Goleman call this competency "transparency" in *Primal Leadership*. You may notice that leaders who have a strength in this competency are often more approachable and more trusted by staff. Before you lead the role-play, talk about what behaviors depict a strength in transparency.

ACTIVITY 6.6   PLANNING FOR CHANGE WITH AN IC MAP

In Chapter Six we spoke about the use of an Innovation Configuration Map to assist with long term planning of an innovation. In this activity, participants are asked to use the IC map as a planning device for a school change effort. The innovation configuration map is part of the Concerns Based Adoption Model (CBAM), a model used to design and monitor change. The IC helps one think about the best-case scenario for implementing a change effort as well as the least-acceptable forms of the innovation's implementation. In the following activity, learners will develop an IC map either individually or in a group. In order to construct the map with a group, participants will have to come to consensus about the outcomes they expect for the change process and the individual components of the change process they develop. Introduce the activity and then ask participants to use the *Planning for Change with an IC Map* worksheet as a guide.

ACTIVITY 6.1   LIVING MY DREAM: DEVELOPING MY PERSONAL VISION

Describe what you hope for in each of these areas as you progress through the next five years. Speak from your voice, five years from now. Write in the present tense. Write as if you already have achieved these dreams. (approximate time: 15 minutes)

Self image   I am . . .

Material   I own . . .
Possessions

Home   My home is . . .

Relationship   My relationship is . . .
(partner)

Adapted from *The Fifth Discipline Fieldbook,* (Senge, 1994)

Personal Vision Continued . . .

Relationships with Others

Health   I am . . .

Professional Goal   I am . . .

Personal Growth   I am . . .

Life Purpose   I am . . .

Adapted from *The Fifth Discipline Fieldbook,* (Senge, 1994)

Directions:

To what degree does a sense of meaningfulness, choice, competence, or progress generally motivate you? Divide the "pie" below into four pieces based on the degree to which each of the intrinsic rewards move you to action. For example, you may believe that you are moved twice as much by the feeling that your work is progressing well than by the feeling that you had a choice in selecting or modifying the task. In that case, make the "Sense of Progress" piece twice as big as the "Sense of Choice" piece.

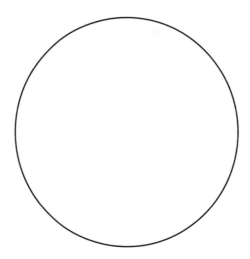

Follow up:

After you have divided your circle into four pieces, shade in each piece to the degree that your current work is satisfying your intrinsic needs for these rewards. For example, if I feel little passion for my work now because what I am doing does not "make a difference", I might shade in only a small section of that piece. Reflect on your pie graph after you finish.

ACTIVITY 6.4   BUILDING A RELATIONSHIP-CENTERED LEARNING COMMUNITY EXERCISE

Before participating in the following three activities, please read the article, *Schools of Possibilities: Becoming a Relationship-Centered Learning Community* by Sue Keister located in the Readings section of this book.

Part I:

Individually, or in groups of three or four, respond to the questions below. Be prepared to debrief your responses with the whole class. (Approximate time: 30 minutes)

1. According to the author, when is a school a learning community of reciprocal relationships in pursuit of every participant's potential?
2. Describe the qualities and characteristics of the relationship-centered leader.
3. Given your school community, can you see developing a relationship-centered school that hopes to "liberate the collective intelligence and imagination of the whole learning community?" Explain.
4. As you self-reflect on your leadership competencies in terms of emotional intelligence, what strengths do you bring to this process? Where might you need assistance from others?

Part II:

Based on your reading, reflect and dialogue on the following questions. In answering the questions, think about you and your own school, but do not get stuck thinking about where it is now. Allow yourself to envision the possibilities. Assign a recorder to jot down your ideas. Try not to get bogged down. Debrief the activity when done. (Approximate time: 30 minutes)

Inner Journey	Outer Journey
How do I live my core beliefs and values?	*What has meaning for us here?*
What kind of relationships do I foster and nurture?	*What makes our community viable?*
How do I contribute? How do I support others?	*How do we approach change?*
What surprises me? What challenges me? Opens me?	*How can we better serve our community*
What am I willing to do differently?	*of learners?*

Part III:

Now it's time to take your reflections about your relationship-centered school into action. Ask yourselves: *What kind of school do we want to be? What is our image of young people? What is the role of adults here? What do we believe about teaching and learning? How can we support everyone's potential?* With your colleagues, create about four or five guiding principles about teaching and learning and the relationships between young people and adults in your school setting. You may choose to do this individually and then come back and debrief these together in groups. Once this is done, have a conversation about ways to move your school to be reflective of these principles. Here are two examples of guiding principles from Sue Keister's work with Salt Lake City middle schools: (Approximate time: 30 minutes)

- Every student has at least one advocate who is sensitive and responsive to the needs of the whole child—academic/intellectual, social, emotional, physical and ethical.
- Teachers and students become partners in learning when they are characterized by friendliness, fairness, flexibility, and forgiveness; they engage teachers and learners through inquiry-based, hands-on, relevant and reflective education.

Leaders who are transparent live their values. Transparency—an authentic openness to others about one's feelings, beliefs, and actions—allows integrity. Such leaders openly admit mistakes or faults, and confront unethical behavior in others rather than turn a blind eye (Goleman, Boyatzis, McKee, 2002).

Please refer to role-play guidelines in the skills section of Chapter One before engaging in this role-play. Remember, the purpose of the EQ role-plays is to work on developing the EQ competency in the educational leader. As you begin this scenario, focus on the transparency of the leader, Principal Ingrid.

Scenario

Principal Ingrid has been at Little One Elementary school for five years. When Ingrid first came to this small, suburban school it had about 500 children. The mostly white, middle-class students come from a combination of blue-collar and professional backgrounds ranging from middle to upper socioeconomic levels. The Parents Association, in response to their good feeling about the administration, has raised a lot of money and been very active in keeping the school a district leader in the forefront of the local news.

In the past two years, however, the population of Little One Elementary school has shifted. The total population has increased to nearly 1,000 children and 40 percent of these students from African American and Latino backgrounds. Recently, an increasing number of Russian immigrant children have moved to the community. At Little One, parents and teachers alike were used to the tracking system that had always been in place. Traditionally, community members knew who were the high-performing children and who were in the lower-tracked classes. Up until now, Principal Ingrid had concentrated her time on bringing in the latest methods in math and literacy instruction. She hadn't given any thought to working on integrating the classes and making them more homogeneous. Now, however, a powerful group of parents representing the minority populations are pushing for de-tracked classes. Ingrid has been supported by the longstanding largely-white community. Now, these same parents are threatening to withdraw their children from the school if the classes are de-tracked. They feel their children will be mixed with other lower-performing children and will lose out in school. Ingrid feels helpless and unsure as to what she should do with the classes. She recognizes that the top classes are still predominantly composed of white children who have excelled on the state-mandated standardized tests.

In this scenario, Parent Association President Talia meets with Principal Ingrid to discuss this dilemma. Parent Talia has a child in the high class and is certain that Principal Ingrid will make the right decision to keep the classes tracked and maintain the "integrity" of the school.

Tuesday morning at Little One Elementary School

T: *Good morning—how's the family?*

P: *Fine, thank you—glad we finally are sitting down—I am sorry that my calendar has been so full! Busy working for our kids! I was at an ASCD conference—great speakers, great town.*

T: *Yes—I am glad I am here too.*

P: *You had a specific issue?*

T: *Yes—well, I know it worries all of us that our school is in jeopardy of going downhill because of some of the new elements in town.*

P: *I am not sure what you are referring to.*

STOP ACTION—point out her tension starting—ask audience if they feel tense too

T: *Well, we have always had the best classes here and as you know my daughter is in Honors—you must realize that we can't get rid of the Honors Program. It's not that I have anything against the newcomers, you know, it's just that I want my daughter to get the best education. We all know that is not possible if you put all the kids together.*

P: *You are talking about the decision to do away with tracking—in favor of a more unified and integrated education here at Excellent High? We have a deep commitment to diversity here, Talia. And, this is the direction the whole country is going in.*

T: *Fine, fine but the school's reputation and the standing of the community is based on the integrity of this school—the commitment to excellence—the pride in the crème of the crop—our PA is dedicated to those ideals.*

P: *The PA, I hope is dedicated to good education, the best for your kids—we have that.*

T: *You know what we are really talking about here. I want my kids to be in class with the best kids.*

STOP ACTION—What is the internal conversation of Principal Ingrid? What is she battling with emotionally? What are the political forces that she needs to contend with? What is Parent Talia's major concern here? RESUME ACTION

P: *I believe that your kids' educational needs will be served in this way. I am sure we can win all the regional kudos for integration and diversity as well as the areas we traditionally have been succeeding at.*

T: *Maybe so—but you won't have the support of the PA in this new direction—I am telling you that now.*

P: *Are you speaking for everyone or just yourself?*

T: *I am speaking for all of us—we are very unhappy with this decision. But, I am sure that knowing our feelings about it, you will consider going back to the old way—we are your best advocates. We believe in you, we support your programs. My goodness, we have three events a year to raise money for this school—PLUS a raffle—we love it the way it has been. We are looking out for the best for our kids—the best means the top. Integration is great as a concept—let someone else sacrifice their kids to it. Not us.*

P: *I hear what you are saying—I hear your concerns—I am not comfortable with what you are asking. I need some time to think this through.*

STOP ACTION. Debrief:

1. What conversation is the Principal having with herself? What is her anticipated loss? Gain? Has this principal been trusted to this point? By whom? What are her apparent values here? What steps must she take before her next meeting with Parent Talia?
2. What is the conversation that the PTA president is having with herself? What are her hopes and fears? What, if anything, will change for Parent Talia when she meets with Principal Ingrid next week?

Problem Solving:

Divide the class into several small groups. Dialogue about the possible directions this conflict can go. Then, in triads, continue the role-play. Each group member should role play the parts of Principal Ingrid, Parent Talia and an Observer. Assume that it is now one week later and Principal Ingrid is meeting again with Parent Talia. Decide the course of action that Principal Ingrid will take. Plot the strategies that she will use. As best as possible, resolve the moral dilemma presented by using the leader's EQ skills, particularly, the EQ competency of transparency. As you move forward in your groups, think about the road ahead for Principal Ingrid. What are the short-term and long-term consequences of the actions she will take? Be prepared to explain your actions.

Role-Play Debrief:

1. Ask several groups to share back the outcome of their role play. What actions transpired? What will be the results of these words and actions?
2. Reflect on your own competencies in the area of transparency. Are you trusted by others? How do you demonstrate this in your work life? Be specific about your behaviors that demonstrate this competency, or lack thereof.
3. Think back to the values you ascribed to in Chapter Two. What would you do if you had to compromise one of these values? Pair share this with a colleague in your class.
4. In triads, tell of a time professionally, when either a) your sincerity and trustworthiness were challenged by a colleague, supervisor, community member? Describe your words actions and feelings at the time.
5. Name three actions you can take to increase your transparency competency.

Decide on the innovation you will be mapping. This could be any change that you plan to implement over a period of time. Most change efforts take years to develop. It might be implementation of an SEL program, a new school discipline program, a new literacy program, a block schedule or any substantial change innovation.

1. Now you will have to operationalize the innovation. In order to do this, decide on what the components of this innovation would look like. One way to think about this is by answering these three questions proposed by Hall and Hord:
   a. What does the innovation look like when it is in use?
   b. What would I see in classrooms where it is used well and not used well?
   c. What will teachers and students be doing when the innovation is in use?

It helps to think backwards from what you hope to see and then begin the steps to get there. Let's say, for example that you want to implement an SEL program. Answer the above questions and then decide on the number of components you need to put in place as you implement this innovation. These components might include: Teacher training, Staff development follow up, Curriculum Infusion, Student Involvement and School-wide Activities.

2. Once you are clear on the components that you will operationalize, you are ready to flush them out. Think about how they would look on a continuum from *Best Case* scenario of implementation to *Least Acceptable*. You can use your own language for your innovation configuration map, if you choose. You will find that other components might come up as you work. Be flexible. The purpose of this tool is to help you gain a systemic view of the change process.

3. Now you are ready to draw your map. An example of three possible components of a sample innovative configuration map for SEL implementation is provided in this section. Use the sample map provided, or draw your own map on a piece of paper. Design away!

Sample IC MAP for SEL Implementation Components

Components	Best Case	Good Case	Acceptable Case
Teacher training	All teachers are trained in program methodology and willing to implement in classroom.	All teachers are trained and a cadre of teachers agree to teach lessons in classroom each year.	Certain grade levels are trained and of these most agree to teach in the classroom.
Staff development follow up	All teachers receive follow up support in the classroom.	Those who will teach receive follow up support in the classroom.	Three teachers from each grade level receive follow up support.
Curriculum Infusion	All teachers agree to infuse required lessons into their regular instruction.	Trained teachers infuse lessons into their classes. These teachers also rotate teaching assignments to assure that all young people get lessons.	Trained teachers only teach lessons in their classrooms. However, opportunities are provided for lessons to be taught as an elective class by trained teachers.

Chapter Seven Skills Section

In this section, activities are presented that help to develop the EQ competency, empathy.

ACTIVITY 7.1   DIVERSITY GATHERING

The Diversity Gathering allows a group to learn about each other's ethnic and cultural background as they share information about their names. This non-threatening activity can be used early on in a group's formation. We have had very positive results using this activity with both children and adults. This activity could take about 40 minutes in a group of thirty-five participants.

- Ask the participants to write their first and last name on a large index card.
- Invite the participants to sit in a large circle with their name cards.
- Ask them to share briefly any information they may know about their name/heritage. As they share they might include: a) significance of first or last name; b) who named them? c) who they might have been named after? d) what part of the world they feel connected to? e) any thing special about their names. Example: "My name is Janet Patti. My mother called me Janet because she liked the name. Patti is my father's name. I'm third generation Italian American. My grandfather emigrated from Sicily. Patti has never been shortened. I always liked my name because I didn't have a lot of letters to write in grade school!

Note: Be sensitive to the fact that some participants may have been adopted and do not have any connection to their heritage. You should always allow any participant to "Pass" if they wish.

ACTIVITY 7.2   DIVERSITY MICROLAB

This activity is designed to open up the dialogue about differences. Hearing one another's stories helps to increase empathy, create trust and builds bonds. Before you use the diversity microlab, be sure that you have established group ground rules. It is imperative that participants feel they can share in an environment of safety and support. Please refer to the guidelines for using a Microlab in the skills section of Chapter Three. Use the following questions for this microlab:

- Share where your family members are from? Where were you born? What is your ethnic and racial background?
- How connected do you feel to your ethnic and racial background? What was it like for you being a member of this group when you were growing up? Were there others like you in you home and school environment?
- When is the first time you experienced prejudice and discrimination? What happened, and to whom? What did you do?

- What do you love about being from your background? What, if anything, has been difficult or hard?

When the microlab is finished, debrief with the whole group. Choose two or three questions and encourage participants to share their feelings. Facilitate a dialogue about these often difficult diversity issues. Be aware that this microlab can bring out strong emotions for some people. *Note: This activity is used with permission from the development work of Educator's for Social Responsibility.*

ACTIVITY 7.3   USE OF MEDIA TO CREATE A SAFE PLACE AND OPEN DIALOGUE

There are four different videos that we have used regularly to dialogue about varying issues of diversity. The three videos are listed below with a brief description of each topic and information as to how to obtain them.

Names Can Really Hurt You:

This powerful documentary focuses on the work of nationally-known violence prevention expert, Linda Lantieri, in the area of prejudice reduction with New York City seventh through ninth graders. As Director of the Resolving Conflict Creatively Program, Linda facilitated a two-week seminar with these students in which she helped them move from an intellectual understanding of prejudice and discrimination to a true experience of how it impacts their lives. As a school leader, this video could be used to promote dialogue with your staff around these issues. It can also be used as part of young people's curriculum. It can be obtained by contacting the Anti Defamation League at 1-800-343-5540 or via the website at www.adl.org.

Eye of the Storm

This classic documentary tells the story of Jane Elliot who in the 1960's conducted an experiment with third graders to teach them the impact of prejudice and discrimination. This video opens up the conversation around the impact that names and labels can give to people who are different. It provides a clear and accurate example of the concept of internalized oppression. You can also obtain the video called *A Class Divided* in which these children were interviewed fifteen years after this classroom experiment. These videos can be obtained from The Anti Defamation League at 1-800-343-5540 or via the website at www.adl.org.

It's Elementary: Talking About Gay issues in School

This video created by Academy Award winning Debra Chasnoff and producer Helen S. Cohen documents school teachers in grades one through eight as they talk about gay issues in age-appropriate ways with their students. This film has won numerous awards for excellence and is being used in thousands of educational institutions. It is intended to open the public dialogue about gay and lesbian issues in schools. For information about the film or to order this film for educational purposes please visit the Women's Educational Media website at www.womedia.org.

ACTIVITY 7.4   THE BELIEVING GAME

This activity is an exercise that helps us "try on" other perspectives in order to more deeply understand the values and assumptions behind opinions different from our own. Procedures as to how to conduct this game can be found on the next few pages.

ACTIVITY 7.5   THE GALLERY WALK

The Gallery Walk format is a helpful tool for school leaders. It can be used to involve all members of the school community in thinking about major issues that link to the mission and vision of the school. The Gallery Walk is used in Activity 7.6. The format of the Gallery Walk used here has been contributed by Dr. Marcia Kalb Knoll and can be found in the *Administrator's Guide to Student Achievement & Higher Test Scores* published by Prentice Hall, 2002.

ACTIVITY 7.6   THINKING ABOUT HOW TO CREATE A DEMOCRATIC SCHOOL CULTURE AND CLIMATE

This activity is designed to help participants think about the school structures that can support democratic practices. It utilizes the Gallery Walk strategy as you work in groups to create a democratic school culture.

ACTIVITY 7.7   THE ANGRY PARENT DILEMMA

This activity provides participants an opportunity to work on both de-escalating skills and problem solving skills in the context of school administration. In this activity, the assistant principal, acting on behalf of the school principal, encounters a situation with a very angry parent and must seek ways to resolve it.

About the Game

As stated in Chapter Seven, The Believing Game is based on the concept of "method-ological belief" developed by educator Peter Elbow. Methodological belief, is meant to encourage us to suspend judgment and criticism when we first listen to or read about a new perspective or a contradictory point of view. After hearing or reading a particular position, participants are invited to ask questions that might help them to further understand a position in order to believe it more fully. The Believing Game works best with a controversial issue on which there is deeply divided opinion about who is right and who is wrong and what is the right or wrong thing to do. Issues can be current or historical, real or fictional. "Believing" invites us to be more flexible, to recognize that everyone has a "piece of the truth." Believing helps us move beyond absolutes to more tentative opinions, more original interpretations, and solutions that truly consider all points of view.

The Activity

This activity is designed for use with a class size audience. If you are working alone, you can use the questions for reflection. Facilitators should work with issues that are critical for school leaders. Possible Hot Issues for School Leaders could be: (a) Inclusion or non-inclusion of special education students into regular education; (b) Use of tracking or homogeneously structured groups; (c) Use of traditional mathematics teaching strategies versus a "hands-on" math approach or a strict phonics-based reading method versus a blended literacy approach; (d) Teacher union rights and leaders' ability to evaluate teachers; (e) Gifted education versus heterogeneous classes in regular education.

Setting up the Game

- Ask two or more people to assist you in role playing a particular perspective in the Hot Issues listed. You may use one of the situations presented, or you can select your own hot issue. If you decide not to do this with a panel of presenters, you could use an editorial, a magazine article or a video clip to stimulate the different perspectives.
- Ask students to prepare their presentation on their "hot issue" prior to the class or seminar. Participants should become familiar with the supporting evidence for the perspective they will take.
- Remind the participants who are listening that they are to approach the presentation by suspending doubt and believing as truth what they are hearing, watching, or reading.
- Set up the time frames you hope to allow for each of the steps of the game. Be aware that this activity could easily take up two or more hours, depending on the number of perspectives you present.

Playing the Game

- Perspective one is presented by a participant.(approximately 3 minutes)
- Participants ask clarifying questions that will help them have a deeper understanding of the perspective being presented.
- Participants jot down the essentials of the perspective presented.

- Participants re-read what they have written, and check or underline what they can affirm, believe, or agree with.
- Participants pair share with a partner to find their points of *agreement*.
- Debrief the "Believing" of Perspective #1: as a whole group (or alone). Was it difficult to believe? What got in the way? Did you come to understanding this viewpoint differently than before? Is "believing" different than careful listening?
- Participants pair share again with their partners to analyze Perspective #1's position. Examine the facts presented (find examples of omissions, distortions, loaded language, etc.), raise concerns and objections, and examine underlying positions and values. How do the values, assumptions, and opinions of this position match or conflict with you own? Share whole group.
- Participants work in groups of four to try and find places of common ground with Perspective #1. Try to agree with values, assumptions, concerns and recommendations that are part of this position. Is there anything about this position that you could possible agree with and use as a place to negotiate if you were to have to do this with this person?
- Repeat the same procedures for Perspective #2 and any other perspectives you might bring into this activity.

Reflecting on the Game

Once all perspectives are presented, debrief and review the entire process. Possible questions to ask:

- What emotions came up for you as you were listening to the different perspectives?
- Were you able to let go of your position and really hear the other person's point of view? If so, what techniques did you use to be able to do this? If not, why?
- Was there any new information that you considered when listening to a perspective that you normally would not have listened to at all? Explain.
- Were there any values or concerns that were common to all perspectives?
- What, if anything, about the person's words, body language and demeanor helped or hindered you to believe their perspective?

Note: You can extend this activity by using new information and understandings to explore possible alternative solutions that incorporate the underlying values and concerns of all positions presented.

Excerpted and adapted from Conflict in Context: Understanding Local to Global Security *by Gayle Mertz and Carol Miller Lieber (Educators for Social Responsibility, 2001) pp. 216–219, or @www.esrnational.org*

The purpose of a Gallery Walk is to provide groups with the opportunity to think together, process and organize information. A Gallery Walk works best with small groups of three, four or five people so that everyone has both the opportunity and the obligation to contribute.

Steps to Follow:

1. Hang pages of newsprint on flat surfaces around the walls of the room. Spread the newsprint as far as possible. Write one topic on each page and number the topics in order. The number of pages matches the number of concepts to be addressed.

2. Ask the participants to count off to three, four, five or six. The count off number you use depends on how many topics are posted for reflection. Each posted topic needs a group. If there were five posted topics and 30 participants, each group would have 6 members. Try to keep the groups as equal as possible. After the count off, tell the participants that each person with the same count off number (1, 2 etc.) will be in the same group. Since people who know each other tend to sit together, this strategy will encourage the participants to speak with new people.

3. Tell the participants that each group is to read and then discuss the topic, form a response and record the response on the newsprint. Each group will rotate to each posted topic. As the groups come to topics that have responses from other groups, they are to read and discuss the responses. Those responses with which they agree should be checked. Those with which they do not agree should be marked with a minus and a comment should be made. Additional responses should be recorded.

4. Give each group a topic with which to start. Group I goes to topic #1, etc. Each group will have about three minutes to talk about and write a response to the posted topic. (Note: Allow more time for the initial topic.) When the three minutes are up, a signal is given and each group moves in order, to the next topic. Group 1 goes next to topic 2, etc. until each group has had an opportunity to respond to each posted topic.

5. Ask each group to select a recorder. Give them a different color marker for writing their response. The colors will be helpful later in identifying which group made a particular statement for clarification. Each group is also asked to select a spokesperson who will summarize the work of all the groups written on the newsprint for the topic where the group started.

6. Ask the spokesperson for each group summarizes the information of the first topic his/her group addressed. All participants are encouraged to add information and opinions. The summarized information may be processed in additional ways. For example, the participants may be asked to prioritize the points made for a master summary.

Contributed by Dr. Marcia Knoll, Hunter College and published in the Administrator's Guide to Student Achievement & Higher Test Scores. *(Prentice Hall, 2002).*

A democratic school's culture and climate reflects many of the norms of behavior and ways of doing things we have been addressing throughout this book. This awareness should permeate the daily management of the school. Democratic practices should filter throughout all of the school's organizational structures. In this activity, participants will define what these constructs would look like in such a school. Use the Gallery Walk format described in Activity 7.5 and the topics and questions provided below for this activity. (Approximate time: One hour and 15 minutes)

Organizational Structures

A. *Personnel:* Who works in this school? What do they look like, sound like? What positions are valued in this school? How do these people relate to one another?

B. *Curriculum:* This includes the regular curricula and the hidden curricula. What kinds of curricula are used? What subjects are taught and emphasized? What regular activities flow from the curriculum into the school?

C. *Instruction:* What instructional methodologies are promoted in this school? How do adults and children learn about learning? How do adults teach?

D. *Evaluation and Assessment:* What learning is assessed? What methods are used to assess that learning? How is learning monitored? How is teaching monitored? How do adults monitor their learning? How do young people monitor their learning? What vehicles exist for reflection about teaching and learning?

E. *Building and Facilities Usage:* What does this building look like? Who maintains it? What is the layout of this school? Where do people come together in this building? What is on the walls? What makes people feel safe in this building?

F. *Governance:* Who is in charge in this building? How do you know that? What are the power structures in this school? Who makes decisions and about what? How is this governance structure conveyed to everyone in the school?

G. *Finances: and Resources:* Where do the finances come from to run this school? Who is in charge of them? Who decides how they are allocated? What other resources are available? How are they recruited and who manages them?

H. *Parents and Community Relations:* What is the role of parents in this school? Where do you see them connected to the school both in and out of the building? With whom does the school have relationships with from the broader community? How do you see this in the school?

Before You Begin:

Think about the realities of the community this school serves. As a whole group, (or individually if working alone), decide what the demographics and realities are of this particular population. Think about the needs of this population considering ethnicity, socioeconomic factors, accessibility to services and any cultural values or beliefs that stem from this community. Consider these as you go about designing your democratic school.

Whole Group Debrief

- Ask the larger group to dialogue about the reality of promoting this kind of culture in your school.
- Allow five minutes for participants to reflect on their learning silently in their reflective logs.

The following role-play and activities are designed to increase your awareness and skill level in the use of effective conflict resolution and problem solving strategies school leaders need to address controversial issues in schools. As you progress through the steps indicated below you will: First, use your communication and conflict resolution skills to defuse the situation. Second, use your problem solving skills to delineate steps that you would take, as an administrator, to resolve the problem. Third, reflect on the leadership behaviors and strategies needed by a school administrator. Finally, you will reflect on your own skill in these areas (Approximate time: One hour and 30 minutes)

> *Scenario:* You are the assistant principal of *Happy School Elementary.* Your school of 600 children in grades K-5 is an urban oasis. Children here get along well. Teachers are collegial and collaborative. They teach conflict resolution to children as part of their regular curriculum. Parents are involved in the school. They attend workshops provided by staff members. But, there is a problem that has come up this week. *Parent I Won't Have It!* has left two messages in the past two days for the principal regarding an issue that appears to be happening in her son's third-grade classroom. Evidently, *Teacher Special,* a two-year teacher, who is loved by her students and well-liked by staff, has been sharing a proverb or two from the Bible in her class. *Parent, I Won't Have It!* is a practicing Buddhist. She is irate. She does not want her child exposed to this. If anything spiritual were to be done at all, she would love to have all children meditate.
>
> Principal *Take Care of Everything* is at a two-day conference and you are in charge of the building. Today, your secretary warns you that *Parent, I Won't Have It!* is on her way over to the school and ready to go to the school board if she doesn't get satisfaction.

Please use the following steps as you work through this problem. This is a more advanced role play activity. It combines several strategies including de-escalating anger, problem solving and negotiation. It also involves the leader's use of a number of EI competencies such as emotional self-control, conflict management and empathy. Approximate times are provided.

a) On a piece of paper, list the steps that you (individually) would take, as the Assistant Principal, knowing that this parent is on her way to speak with you. What must you consider? Who, if anyone will you consult? (Three minutes)
b) Set up the role play in a triad, Parent, Assistant Principal, and Observer. The Assistant Principal's first job is to de-escalate this parent using effective conflict resolution strategies. Remember, you are the listener here. Observer, pay particular attention to AP's use of active listening strategies. (Four minutes)
c) (Freeze Action) Debrief in your triad. Is the AP effectively de-escalating the parent? Allow each member to provide feedback regarding their actions and feelings. (Three minutes)
d) Once you have de-escalated this parent you will have to begin to resolve this problem. In your group, define the problem. Dialogue about possible strategies that you will take to resolve this issue. (Four minutes)
e) Resume the role-play. Armed with your strategies, meet with this parent again and let her know your course of action. At this point, you should draw upon your negotiation skills discussed earlier in Chapter Four. (Five minutes)
f) Whole class Debrief/Individual Reflective Response. (Three minutes)
g) Take a moment alone with your reflective log to note the EQ competencies that you had to draw upon as you worked through these issues.

Chapter Eight Skills Section

In this section, activities are presented which draw upon EQ competencies relating to team work and empowering others.

ACTIVITY 8.1   TEAM INVENTORY

This activity is designed to help develop team-assessment skills that are very important in facilitative leadership. It can be used to assess a team in which each learner is or was a member. A scoring key is provided. Follow up discussion either in small groups or one large group should focus on the following questions: What did we find out about our teams that was most surprising? What team characteristics are generally most lacking in our group's teams? What could you do to create better teams?

ACTIVITY 8.2   TEAM CASE STUDY

Divide group into five teams. Say, *Facilitative leaders believe in the value of team decision-making. In this activity you will role-play as members of a SBM to decide on the ideal makeup of a new working team in your school. In your decision-making, please try to reach consensus on the ideal characteristics of the kind of people you want on the new team.*

Give Instructions:

1.) First, ask each team to use a go-around to briefly answer (about one minute response per person to each question) the following questions:
   * Based on your own experience, what is the most rewarding aspect of working on a school team? What is the most challenging aspect? (If participants have never worked on a school team, they can substitute any team experience).
   * What do you believe you bring to this current team that might help it successfully complete a task (give them information if necessary)?
2) Review Activity Sheet 8.2 and assign each SBM to a particular case (staff development, curriculum, new school design, service learning, budget, parent involvement). Their task is to design the ideal team. In their thinking about the new team's makeup, members need to look at their purpose and the particular situation. They must try to reach consensus on team composition, size and any other factor (diversity, expert knowledge or skills, team skills) that might affect team performance. Give each team a sheet of chart paper and a few magic markers to use for a "presentation" of their ideal team to the rest of the class. In their presentation they can use words, pictures and symbols. The only conditions are that the presentation be no longer than three minutes and that all members must have some role in its creation and implementation.
3) Facilitate team presentations.

4) Give teams time to evaluate the team's performance. In their own groups, they should answer the question: "As a team, what did we do well and what could we have done differently in our decision making and our presentation?"

Process the activity:

A. What factors did you agree on? What factors did you disagree on? Why?
B. What was there about your teams that made it easy or hard to do this activity? Examples of responses:
  • Five to seven is a size that can make decisions easily yet is large enough to generate ideas.
  • There were no clear roles. The group had to develop them.
  • The individual skills of group members affected the presentation (e.g., artistic types might have done drawings).
C. What feelings were triggered by this activity? Why? What did you do with these feelings?
D. How might you apply what you learned here in a school setting?

ACTIVITY 8.3   UNCOVERING YOUR ORGANIZATION'S CULTURE

This is a cultural analysis that one can use in a school setting. This activity requires a considerable amount of effort and the participation of a school or school district. Therefore, if this activity is considered for a course, it might be undertaken in place of a paper. It might also be considered as a group project. The outcome of the project could be a process report or an introspective account of the process in a journal. On the other hand, if the reader of this book is currently a practicing school leader then this activity might be part of a strategic planning initiative. An activity sheet is provided.

ACTIVITY 8.4   CONCENTRIC CIRCLES ON LEADERSHIP

This activity is used with large groups but individual learners can profit from reflecting on the questions below. Concentric Circles is a strategy similar to microlabs (see Chapter Two Skills Section) in that participants learn from interaction with others. What is different is the fact that the group is divided into two subgroups facing each other in two concentric circles. A large open space is needed (if no large space is available use the microlab approach).

Directions:

1. Separate the large group by asking them to count off by 1's and 2's. Ask the 1's to form a circle in the middle of the room. Ask the 2's to find a person in the first group to stand behind. Ask the 1's to turn around and say hello to their partners.
2. Tell the group that it will be asked a series of questions and they will have one minute each to share their answers with the person standing in front of them. They will take turns speaking and listening. Say, "Whatever is said is strictly confidential unless you want to later reveal to the large group what you, and not your partner, said. Share to your own comfort level and, if you feel you must, you can pass on a question."

3. Ask the first question: *"From your point of view what is the role of a school leader?"* Give two minutes for the partners to finish. Let the group know when half the time is up.

4. Say, *"Now say goodbye to your partner and I want the inner circle to move two people to their right. Say hello to your new partner."* This movement continues after each question so that learners have the opportunity to engage with a different partner each time. You may want to have the outer circle move or change the direction to make the transition more novel.

5. Continue the process with two or three more questions. Sample questions:
   - *Who has been a mentor (living or dead) to you and what were the leadership qualities that you most admire in that person?*
   - *If you wanted to be a more facilitative leader than you are now, what changes would need to occur in you, in the people you work with, and in the larger system? If the group members are not practicing leaders ask them to imagine working in a school system that they know.*
   - *What is the hardest thing emotionally for you to deal with in trying to get others to take on more leadership?*
   - *What is the most rewarding aspect emotionally of seeing someone you lead become more of a leader?*

6. Have the group affirm their good work (a group cheer?), bring them back to the large group and help them process their experiences. Possible process questions:
   - *Who were some of your mentors and in what way did they influence you?*
   - *Are there some common qualities in the people who become our heroes?*
   - *For you, what represents your major challenge in terms of becoming a more facilitative leader: the intrapersonal, the interpersonal, or the systemic?*
   - *What other insights did you gain from this activity?*
   - *Would you use the concentric circle strategy in a school setting? How?*

A good follow-up to this activity would be to lead a brainstorm of ways that school leaders could mentor others in the process of taking on leadership roles in a school.

ACTIVITY 8.5   CONFLICT ROLE-PLAY BETWEEN A PRINCIPAL AND A SUPERINTENDENT

In Chapter Four we described a real conflict between Hilda and her school superintendent about a plan to break up her large school into smaller academies. Hilda decided the risk was too great to try to negotiate with her supervisor. In this activity, learners role-play a principal and a superintendent who do get together to negotiate a win-win solution to the problem. The activity can be done in a fishbowl setting. Two volunteers will begin while the rest of the group sits in a circle around the pair. An empty chair sits next to the pair and, during the role-play, learners from the large circle can sit in the chair to ask the pair a question to help the process. Following the negotiation, group discussion should focus on not only the negotiation but also on systemic issues that were not discussed.

Please think of a team or working group that you are a member of and use this inventory to assess your perceptions of its effectiveness in creating teamwork. Circle the number that reflects your response to the following questions:

1) To what level does your group work as a team?

1	2	3	4	5
Always	Mostly	Sometimes	Seldomly	Never

2) To what level do *you* personally contribute to helping the group work as a team?

1	2	3	4	5
Never	Seldomly	Sometimes	Mostly	Always

3) To what extent do team members take personal responsibility for the work of the team?

1	2	3	4	5
Each person does	Most of us do	About half does	Only a few do	One does

4) To what extent do *you* take responsibility for the work of the team?

1	2	3	4	5
A great deal	A lot	Average	Not much	None

5) How well do you understand the goals of your team?

1	2	3	4	5
Fully	Mostly	Somewhat	Not sure	Not at all

6) To what extent do you agree with the team's goals?

1	2	3	4	5
Not at all	A little	50\50	Mostly	Completely

7) How much do you feel part of the team?

1	2	3	4	5
Not at all	A little	50\50	Mostly	Completely

8) How much do you think that other members feel part of the team?

1	2	3	4	5
Not at all	A little	50\50	Mostly	Completely

9) How are important decisions made?

1	2	3	4	5
The leader has all the power	The leader & few allies share	Majority vote	Majority decides but effort is made for consensus	Consensus mostly

10) How are differences or conflicts handled by your team?

1	2	3	4	5
Effectively Members use excellent skills	Mostly Effective	Some problems are not discussed	Most conflicts are not discussed	Poorly There are open battles

11) How safe do you feel to publicly voice your thoughts, feelings and differences of opinion within the group?

1	2	3	4	5
Completely	Safe most times	Sometimes safe	Rarely safe	Never

Scoring Key
1.   Reverse scoring on items 1, 3, 4, 5, 10 and 11. If you circled the number 1 on question three, change score to 5; if you circled 2 score it 4; score 3 remains the same, score 4 becomes 2, and score 5 changes to 1.
2.   Add up all scores. The total scores will range from 11 to 55. Team Assessment Scores on the low end reflect your belief that your team is not functioning as a true team. Scores in the upper range reflect your belief that your team is higher functioning.
3.   Items 2, 4, 5, 7, and 11 reflect your perceptions of your own personal interactions in the team. Add up your scores on these items. The scores will range from 5 to 25. If your scoring on these items is consistent with the scoring on the rest of the items than low scores are very much a group dynamic. However, if the scores on these items are low and other scores are high then you might ask yourself if you are experiencing personal difficulties that keep you from full involvement with the team or group (if not then you may be scapegoated).

Note: This assessment represents *your* perceptions. To assess the team more accurately, ask other team members to share results of their assessments.

1. Your team is an SBM team in a large regional high school in a rural farming community. The team has decided to form a new team that will be responsible for all aspects of professional development for all members of the school staff. In the past, the school district mandated most of the professional development, but the district has now shifted that responsibility to each school.

2. Your team is an SBM team in a small alternative elementary school of 200 students that wants to form a curriculum planning team. The curriculum must meet your state standards but it does not have to be taken from any district-mandated list. Your school's mission is to provide the best education for every child while honoring the great diversity that exists in your large urban community.

3. Your team is an SBM team in a magnet high school located in a large urban setting and dedicated to the performing arts. Your school has a renowned staff many of whom are professional artists. It also has an ancient run-down building that is scheduled to be torn down in five years. A new building is going to be erected on a different site nearby. Your SBM team has been given the task of forming a planning team that will help design the new building to meet the needs of the school community and hire contractors.

4. Your team is an SBM team in a suburban middle school. The town residents voted down the last two school budgets. Funding, therefore, is a major issue for your school, especially because the school has been trying to become a technology enhanced learning community. The school has a great deal of discretion as to how it spends the money it receives from the school district. Your SBM team has decided to form a working team to develop a strategy for dealing with the budget crisis while still meeting present and future needs.

5. Your team is an SBM team in an elementary school in an economically depressed community. Most of your parents are from the same ethnic background evenly mixed between recent immigrants (some illegal) and first or second-generation citizens who work long and hard in poorly paying jobs. There is also a small, but growing, population of transient families from a different ethnic background who are temporarily housed in neighborhood shelters. Previously, the school's efforts to involve parents has been hindered by tensions among the different groups of parents, language and cultural differences, lack of funds and a lack of willingness by the last administration to make parent involvement a priority (an attitude shared by some of the staff). Your SBM and a majority of the staff, however, want to make the school inviting for parents and foster a collaborative spirit. To do so, the SBM has decided to form a parent involvement team.

INTRODUCTION

Cultural assumptions are so much a part of our everyday work lives that we are often unaware of them. They can be uncovered, however, with effective facilitation either by you or by a facilitator from outside your school or school district. The suggested activity below is a group exercise designed for any group consisting of three to fifty persons. Participation should be voluntary and include a diverse cross-section of the school community. Some newcomers to the organization are especially useful.

The room that you use can be on or off site but should be large and comfortable as this process will take several hours. The room should have an abundance of wall space for hanging chart paper. In addition to flip charts, the facilitator should have markers and masking tape and have enlisted others who will write on charts as needed. The agenda should include adequate time for breaks (approximately every one and a half-hours) and a lunch or refreshments.

Step One: Define the Problem

Participants will be more motivated to explore the school's culture if it is related to a problem that is significant to them as members of the school community. The problem can be something they want to fix or one they anticipate having to solve in the near future. It is useful to identify and write down the problem in the form of a question. Examples of problems might be:

- How can we work together more collaboratively?
- How can we help everyone, both adults and students, become a learner?
- In what ways can we make better use of our diversity to teach the children?
- What are the most creative ways that we can make use of available technology?

Step Two: Review the Concept of Culture

Participants should have been given the opportunity to be informed about this concept prior to the meeting. Readings, videos, discussion groups or any other educational tool could be used to develop the group's prior knowledge. During Step Two, make sure that the group shares a common definition of organizational culture and that all understand the meanings of artifacts, espoused values and shared tacit assumptions.

Step Three: Identify Cultural Artifacts

Help group members list artifacts that characterize their school community. Artifacts represent the first level of culture and are the easiest to observe. Artifacts are the phenomena that one sees, hears and feels when one encounters a culture. Think of what you first noticed when you have traveled to other cultures and then ask your group to try to use a *visitor's* senses to list as many artifacts of your school as possible. Some artifacts might include jargon, physical structures, organizational charts, how meetings are conducted, dress codes, methods of communicating, initiation rites and decision-making rules or ceremonies. Some artifacts might be similar to those of other schools or school districts and some might be unique to your school or district. For example, one charter school in New York City was built in a renovated commercial building and its physical design was purposely created to augment its specialized curriculum studying the city's physical environment.

This step can be accomplished by eliciting ideas from the whole group or breaking the large groups into smaller groups. The results might fill ten or more pages of chart paper that can be taped onto walls.

Step Four: Identify Your School or District's Values

If you have done strategic planning with this group, your group may have already explicitly stated their espoused values. If so, post them and find out if there is still agreement. If not, spend some time with the group identifying these values and posting them separately from the list of artifacts.

Step Five: Compare Values with Artifacts

Ask group members to silently look over the list of artifacts and espoused values. Where do the artifacts and values appear to support each other and where do they conflict? For example, an espoused value may be that we want our middle school students to develop leadership qualities yet many of the artifacts of our school seem to clash with this value. The student council exists in name only, a dress code was recently imposed without student input, and the budget earmarked for student leadership activities (e.g. peer mediation) is almost nonexistent.

As group members share their observations in small groups and the large group, tacit assumptions will naturally begin to emerge. Ask the participants not to judge these assumptions but, instead, take note of them for later discussion. Using the example of student leadership, the tacit assumption might emerge that we want our students to be leaders but we really do not believe they are ready yet.

Step Six: List Assumptions and Identify Patterns

As the cultural assumptions emerge, have them written on chart paper and engage the group in a dialogue. What is the evidence that these are the assumptions that underlie our culture? Are there other assumptions that lie beneath these? How deeply embedded are these assumptions? Are they held throughout the system and how long have they shaped behavior? Are there any that seem to really drive the system in that they seem to be represented in many of the artifacts that are listed? Are there patterns that exist among these most powerful assumptions? Write down the responses to this last question on a separate page of chart paper.

If there does not seem to be clear patterns, a possible reason might be that there are different subcultures present. If that appears to be the case, you may decide to divide the group into smaller groups where at least some of the members represent their respective subcultures. Let each group process Step Six for the subculture and then report back in the large group.

Step Seven: Assess the Shared Assumptions

Looking at the set of powerful assumptions that are shared by the school community or subcultures, ask the group to explore the ways that these assumptions affect the problem or problems that were identified in Step One. In trying to solve the problem, how do these assumptions enhance or hinder the process? Focus the dialogue especially on those assumptions that are positive forces for change. List the ways that these assumptions can be used by the school community to enhance its central mission.

Step Eight: Celebrate the Exploration

The very process of uncovering the three levels of culture is a tremendous achievement and needs to be acknowledged and celebrated. There is also likely to be some anxiety resulting from the realization that our strongly espoused values may not always be consistent with what we actually practice. This cognitive dissonance may energize us to change our practices in the long run but is uncomfortable in the short run. For these reasons, adequate time and prior thought should be given to a closing activity that brings the group together.

This activity is modeled after a process described by Edgar Schein in two of his books:

- Schein, E. H. (1992). *Organizational culture and leadership* (2nd ed.). San Francisco: Jossey-Bass.
- Schein, E. H. (1999). *The corporate culture survival guide.* San Francisco: Jossey-Bass.

Pat Lopez is the principal of PS 12, an elementary school with 1300 students. PS 12's main building is one large structure broken up into two units joined together by corridors and a central courtyard. In addition, an annex is housed in a smaller building one block away. Two months ago, Pat met with teacher and parent representatives to problem solve how to create more of a sense of community despite the school's size. What came out of those meetings was a proposal to divide the school into three small "academies" each with a different theme. Pat gave the plan to Chris Wallace, the District Superintendent, who promised to read it right away. After several calls, Chris read the proposal and said that the proposal had to be shelved.

PAT'S POINT OF VIEW

I believe that my superintendent is a good person but politics came in to play here. There's a school in the district that has an academy for the gifted and Chris does not want any competition for this pet project. I know that I can make this proposal work and, in the long run, it will be better for my students, my teachers, my parents and me. Everybody is so stressed around here with all these tests and the size of this school makes planning, teamwork and communication so difficult. I have an appointment with Chris today and I'm feeling frustrated and exhausted.

ACTIVITY 8.5   CONFLICT ROLE-PLAY BETWEEN A PRINCIPAL AND A SUPERINTENDENT

Pat Lopez is the principal of PS 12, an elementary school with 1300 students. PS 12's main building is one large structure broken up into two units joined together by corridors and a central courtyard. In addition, there is an annex housed in a smaller building one block away. Two months ago, Pat met with teacher and parent representatives to problem solve how to create more of a sense of community despite the school's size. What came out of those meetings was a proposal to divide the school into three small "academies" each with a different theme. Pat gave the plan to Chris Wallace, the District Superintendent, who promised to read it right away. After several calls, Chris read the proposal and said that the proposal had to be shelved.

CHRIS' POINT OF VIEW

I like Pat. Pat has done an excellent job in the two years at the school. I think Pat needs more patience in terms of changing PS 12. There's a lot of pressure from the city and state regarding test scores and that's what I want Pat to concentrate on. To shake things up now, especially when PS 12 is one of the schools that scored poorly last year, is not wise. Neither one of us has tenure. What's the sense of taking on such a big project when I may not be here to support it. Pat is meeting with me today about a grant PS 12 received and I imagine Pat will bring up the proposal. I'm feeling annoyed that Pat does not try to understand my position.

Chapter Nine Skills Section

WEBQUEST: LEADING THE 21ST CENTURY SCHOOL

Introduction

This activity uses the Internet as part of a learning experience designed to help learners acquire, analyze, and synthesize information relating to educational leadership in a digital age. By actively engaging in this experience learners gain information and knowledge that can be applied to their efforts in schools and school districts.

The activity can be used in different ways. If you are an individual reader, skip the rest of this introduction and go to the WebQuest Activity. If you are teaching a course or facilitating professional development, it is suggested that you divide your participants into five teams of three to five persons. Tell them they will need to work collaboratively and this collaboration may be face to face (F2F) or virtual (e.g. email, video conferencing, etc.), depending on what is most conducive for teamwork. For example, you may have enough time and access to Web-connected computers that teams can work together in the same time and place. On the other hand, you and your group may need to work at times separated by time and distance and much of your collaboration will be asynchronous using virtual teamwork (some F2F is recommended).

In either case, the human relations aspects of collaboration do not change when IT is used to enhance learning. The dynamics of group process are still present and need to be guided. If collaboration is mainly virtual it is important that the facilitator be mindful that the social-emotional needs of teams and their individual members are harder to "read" in the faceless visage of the computer monitor. During F2F meetings, team members should have opportunities to share ideas and feelings, discuss process issues, and to assess their progress in working as a team as well as their progress in acquiring information. Samples of rubrics you can use are included.

Review the WebQuest Activity Sheet with your group. Teams can all work on the same topic or you can ask each team to work on a different topic and then come together to teach each other what they have learned. This jigsaw method is an excellent way to promote collaborative inquiry (for more information on the jigsaw method visit <http://www.jigsaw.org/chapter1.htm>.

A WebQuest is an inquiry-oriented activity developed in early 1995 at San Diego State University by Bernie Dodge with Tom March (see below for websites on WebQuests). Most or all of the information gathered by learners is acquired from the Web. WebQuests are designed to maximize learners' effective use of time on the Internet by supplying them with websites previously viewed by the instructor, thereby, focusing the learning more on using information rather than looking for it. Though there is often much to be gained by "surfing" (i.e. exploring without a prepared plan) the Internet, the focus of a WebQuest is not on surfing but on supporting learners' thinking at the levels of analysis, synthesis and evaluation.

If you are not familiar with WebQuests it is advised that, before you continue with this activity, you learn more at the following sites:

- <http://edweb.sdsu.edu/courses/edtec596/about_webquests.html>
  A San Diego State University site that gives you a broad overview on WebQuest.

- <http://www.education-world.com/a_tech/tech020.shtml>
  An Education World e-Interview with Bernie Dodge, the creator of the WebQuest design:

- <http://www.education-world.com/a_tech/tech011.shtml>
  An excellent article by Linda Starr in Education World on how to create a WebQuest.

WHAT HAPPENS IF YOU CANNOT FIND A LISTED SITE?

If you have spent time on the Internet, you know that sometimes you enter the Web address (i.e. URL) and it does not lead to the site you wanted. This may happen while you are on a WebQuest. There may be several reasons (and solutions) for this:

1. You accidentally typed the wrong address. Perhaps you added or left out a letter, number or slash mark. Check the address again and correct it if you find an error.
2. You typed the address correctly but you got an error message saying the site was not found or is no longer available. Web addresses do change so look to see if there is a link to another address where the needed information may be found. If there is no link, try the following:
   - *Trim the URL by deleting some of the information at the end.* For example, you may have entered the website below to no avail: <http://edweb.sdsu.edu/courses/edtec596/about_webquests.html> Try trimming your URL to <http://edweb.sdsu.edu> and click on your search or find button. This may bring you to the site of the organization that originally posted the original web address (in this case the education department at San Diego State University).
   - *If you are taken to a site after trimming, look for links to topics related to your search (e.g. WebQuest).* If there are none visible see if the site has a search option which you can use to find the information you are seeking.
3. If you have checked your address, trimmed your URL and are still greeted with a message that the site is unavailable you can do the following:
   - Try again later. The computer hosting the Web Site may either be malfunctioning or taken offline for some temporary reason.
   - Find the information on another website. Go to a search engine (e.g. <www.google.com>) and use the advanced search to find the information. Do

not do a general search. Take the advanced search tutorial if you are not sure how to conduct such a search.

TASK

In this activity, you collaborate in teams to plan and launch a WEBQUEST on a topic related to leading the 21st Century school. Your team's task is to find information from the Internet, analyze and evaluate that information, and present the most important information to the other teams.

PROCESS

Each team is responsible for completing these steps:

1. Decide on a topic from the list below. No topic can be selected by more than one team.
2. Teams must reach consensus on a few guiding questions and procedures that will maximize the effectiveness of the WebQuest. Decide on what "Big Questions" your team wants to answer regarding your team's topic. Also plan your search considering how you will divide the responsibilities, when each task will be completed and how you will communicate and give feedback to each other.
3. After you create your plan, it is advised that each member take on a different role so that the team receives, in a meaningful way, a variety of perspectives. For example, the team may want to role-play school planning team members (parent, classroom teacher, technology expert, principal, student representative) or people with different learning styles or attitudes about technology.
4. Follow your team's plan for team communication, using collected information, and developing a presentation for the other teams.
5. Assess your team's performance both as a team and as individuals using either sample rubrics described in the Assessment Section below or ones developed by your team.
6. Receive feedback from other teams and share your feedback on their efforts.
7. Celebrate everyone's learning.

TEAMS

1. Website Evaluation Team

Surfing the Internet can be fun and educational, but effective use of the Internet is often dependent on locating and using exemplary websites. Therefore, it is important that educators and older students be able to learn to evaluate websites. Pretend you are a website evaluation team and your responsibility is to find exemplary sites. First evaluate the websites below in these areas:

- Providing accurate and up to date information.
- Promoting higher order thinking.
- Giving students opportunities to interact.
- Being appealing to the senses.
- Being relatively easy to navigate.
- Sensitivity to needs of diverse learners.
- Offers excellent links to other learning sites.

Your next task is to select one or two of the best sites to be used to demonstrate the qualities that make up a great educational website to the rest of your school community. If your team does not think that any of the sites is excellent, your team's task is to find one that is. In your presentation to other teams, describe not only the results of your evaluation but the insights your team gained regarding the evaluation and decision-making processes you used. Websites:

- Traveling through the Solar System http://wizard.hprtec.org/builder/ worksheet.php3?ID=1141
- Women of the Century <http://www.education-world.com/a_lesson/lesson164.shtml>
- Searching for China <http://www.kn.pacbell.com/wired/China/ChinaQuest.html>
- Jan Brett's The Mitten <http://projects.edtech.sandi.net/grant/mitten/>
- The India-Pakistan Conflict <http://www.angelfire.com/wy/peacequest/index.html>

2. Digital Equity Team

Your team's challenge is to learn more about the problem of equity in this digital age and the possible solutions to the problem. Visit these websites, dialogue with team members about what you find and develop some creative ideas to foster digital equity at the societal, district or school level. Present your ideas to the other teams in a way that encourages open dialogue. Websites:

- More than a Matter of Equity <http://access.ncsa.uiuc.edu/Stories/diversity/index.html>
- The Digital Divide Network <http://www.digitaldividenetwork.org/content/sections/index.cfm>
  <http://www.digitaldividenetwork.org/content/sections/index.cfm?key=2>
- Thinking about people with disabilities <http://www.wired.com/news/culture/0,1284,40646,00.html>
- eSchool news article <http://www.eschoolnews.com/news/showStory.cfm?ArticleID=3584>
- Pew Research Center 2000 report <http://www.pewinternet.org/reports/toc.asp?Report=21>
- Pew Research Center 2002 report <http://www.pewinternet.org/reports/toc.asp?Report=67>
- The Digital Equity Toolkit <http://www.nici-mc2.org/de_toolkit/pages/toolkit.htm>
- Cornerstones for children who are hard of hearing <http://pbskids.org/lions/cornerstones/>
- Making education available for children with disabilities <http://ncam.wgbh.org/cdrom/guideline/>
- Training teachers to bridge the divide <http://www.pt3.org/stories/equity.html>

3. Training and Professional Development Team

Your team is responsible for the adult learning in a district or school. Using the information at the websites below, discuss the advantages and disadvantages of using technology to promote adult learning. Also discuss what strategies could be used to make best use of technology for professional development while being mindful of costs and the principles of how people learn best. Present your ideas to the other teams in such a way that demonstrates the technology and the best practices of adult learning. Websites:

- Preparing Tomorrow's Teachers <http://www.pt3.org/stories/faculty.html>
- K-12 curriculum on Internet safety <http://www.cybersmartcurriculum.org/home/>
- Professional development for teachers interested in international collaboration <http://www.iearn.org/professional/workshop.html>

- Montgomery County (MD) professional development website <http://www.mcps.k12.md.us/departments/dsd/plc.htm>
- Project learning (click on More Fun Than a Barrel of . . . Worms?!)

<http://glef.org/principals.html>

4. Learning From Other Schools Team

It is time to go back to school. Your team is responsible for exploring different visions of the twenty-first century school. Visit these real and virtual schools on the Internet and discuss with your fellow team members your observations, questions and feelings about these schools. Compare and contrast them with each other and with schools that you have worked in. Think about what your team can do to separate hype from true performance. In your presentation to other teams, give them a picture of what other schools are doing and what lessons can be learned from these schools. Websites:

- Hunterdon Central Regional High School in New Jersey <http://www.scholastic.com/administrator/backtoschool/articles.asp?article=school_spotlight#>
- Bluff Ridge Elementary School in Syracuse, Utah, using cross-grade collaboration (elementary and HS) to study democracy <http://ali.apple.com/ali_sites/ali/exhibits/1000003/>
- California's New Technology High School <http://www.edweek.org/ew/ewstory.cfm?slug=38newtechhigh.h21&keywords=technology>
- Virtual high schools (Concord Consortium) <http://www.principals.org/news/bltn_web_rural_hs1101.html>
- Redesigned school environments from George Lucas Educational Foundation <http://www.glef.org/redesigning/home.html>
- Preview mini-documentaries on technology integration. <http://store.yahoo.com/glef/teacindigage.html#>
- Brookvale Public School in New South Wales, Australia.(look for its technology plan) <http://www.brookvaleps.nsw.edu.au/Menu.html>

5. New Technology Team

Your team's task is to think about various kinds of technologies and what a school would need to do to effectively implement them. New technology is only important if it is used to further learning in a spirit of community. In your discussion, think about the different issues that schools might have depending on if they were private or public, elementary or secondary, small or large, urban or rural, etc. Visit the websites below (substitute if newer technologies are introduced) in order to develop ideas on how new technology can or cannot be used to improve a school's learning climate. Drawing on your conclusions, develop a short guide (in eform or in print) to new technology giving examples from two or more websites to support your findings. Give your guide and present your ideas to other teams. Websites:

- Using handheld computers <http://aa.uncwil.edu/numina/tech%20web%20page/web/>
- National standards for technology for students, teachers and administrators from the International Society for Technology in Education. <http://cnets.iste.org/index.shtml>
- 2020 Schools <http://www.ta.doc.gov/reports/TechPolicy/2020Visions.pdf>
- Using technology to collaborate <http://www-personal.ksu.edu/~slg2537/websitepages/Communication.html>
- Ementoring <http://www.serviceleader.org/schools/telem.html>
- Reducing school violence <http://www.kn.pacbell.com/wired/nonviolence/index.html>

EVALUATION

On the next two pages are sample rubrics that can be used to assess both individual and team performance. They also can be used for self-assessment.

Rubric for Teams

RUBRIC	Novice	Practitioner	Expert
Initial Planning	Team members communicate with each other F2F and/or electronically. They agree on a sharing of responsibilities and a schedule.	Team members communicate with each other F2F and/or electronically. They explore each other's strengths and interests. They use this knowledge to agree on a sharing of responsibilities and a schedule.	Team members communicate with each other F2F and/or electronically. They explore strengths and interests. They use this knowledge to agree on a sharing of responsibilities and a schedule. As a team they develop a plan for ongoing support and feedback.
Research	Members complete their respective searches and share information at the end. Team makes sure that each person has an understanding of the "whole picture".	Members complete their respective searches and share information during the search and at the end. Each member has an understanding of the "whole picture" and gives help to one another.	Members complete their respective searches and share information during the search and at the end. Each member has an understanding of the "whole picture" and gives help and ongoing feedback to one another.
Learning Outcomes	Team presents some information to the class that reflects new learning. Each member contributes an equal share.	Team presents a good deal of information to the class that reflects new learning. Each member contributes an equal share. Presentation includes some media.	Team presents a good deal of information to the class that reflects new learning and critical thinking. Each member contributes an equal share with smooth transitions throughout. Presentation includes some media and audience interaction.

Rubric for Individual Team Members

RUBRIC	Novice	Practitioner	Expert
Initial Planning	Individual prepares to begin web search after communicating with other team members. Has taken on an equal share of the team's responsibilities but has not generated any guiding questions to serve as a framework for web exploration.	Individual has prepared for the search and taken on an equal share of responsibilities. Additionally, person has generated some guiding questions that will elicit useful facts.	Individual has prepared for the search and taken on an equal share of responsibilities. Additionally, person has generated some guiding questions that will elicit useful facts and some self-reflection as the WebQuest progresses.
Research	Individual either remains at the assigned links or explores a succession of other links with little prior thought about where to go ("surfing").	A thoughtful step-by-step procedure is used to move the research forward.	Research begins with a clear purpose and searching continually reflects that purpose. However, the student is able and willing to change if new information necessitates a different purpose (consult with other teammates first).
Learning Outcomes	Individual's contribution to team presentation reflects some increased knowledge on the topic.	Individual's contribution to presentation reflects increased knowledge and how this applies in practice. Examples are given.	Individual's contribution to presentation reflects an in-depth understanding of the topic. Higher order thinking is evidenced in the individual's analysis of different perspectives.

CONCLUDING QUESTIONS

Based on what you learned in this WebQuest activity, ask yourself these questions:

1. Do you believe that new technologies will significantly enhance learning and, if so, how? If not, why?
2. How has your opinion about technology use changed as the result of this WebQuest?
3. Would you encourage teachers to use WebQuests? Why or why not?
4. How can you prepare for the changes in education brought on by new technologies?
5. Which of your leadership skills would you primarily draw upon in promoting technology integration in your school or school district?
6. What is the most important thing you learned from all the WebQuests?

READINGS

The following thirteen readings are contributions from colleagues and experts in the field of education leadership and social and emotional learning. Recognizing that the school leader is the critical link in assuring that theory becomes practice in schools, these authors contributed their readings with the purpose of assisting these leaders. Their writings provide the reader with an extension of, or another point of view on, the topics presented in this book.

The Readings may be utilized as desired by individuals or groups. To assist you in using this book for a university course, institute, or seminar, we have listed suggested places where the Readings would add a contextual frame to the chapters in *SMART SCHOOL LEADERS*.

ADVERSITY AS A ROUTE TO LEADERSHIP

Carmella B'Hahn

Adversity levels us all. It can make or break us and its potential as a binding force across the generations and cultural divides is awesome. Why then do we not use it more often as a teaching tool, share our stories of struggle and harness the inherent gifts? As educational leaders, particularly during traumatic world and local events, we hear the painful stories of many adults and children and are challenged to support them so they can continue to teach and learn in schools. But rarely do we, as leaders, receive the strategies and gifts to help us in this crucial role we play. This article suggests that we have much to learn from adversity that can be helpful in our roles as school leaders. Perhaps in our painful places lies the most effective fuel for transformation, the raw material for the inner strength and resilience required in wise leaders.

The impact of all that we have experienced travels with us wherever we go. It all enters the classroom door and creates what Carl Jung would call a "collective consciousness." We cannot put our wounds on a shelf and collect them at the end of the day. Our creative plans and visions rest on foundations created by the way that we have tended our wounds and faced the challenges of our lives. Poet Mark Nepo says, "That which is not ex-pressed is de-pressed. The more we give voice to our pain in living, the less build-up we have between our soul and our way in the world."[1] In other words, if we want to model being truly authentic as we seek to educate the hearts and minds of the young people we serve, unveiling our pain is vital.

As leaders and teachers we are expected to be a tower of strength and to have the tools to deal with all that walks through our doors. Of course what we do to ourselves, we will do to our students. If we are in charge of guiding a group and have put a protection around our own pain and what we perceive as our unacceptable selves, there will be no container of safety for others to share and tap the valuable lessons offered by their life challenges. So first, we have to acknowledge our own hidden painful experiences that hold the potential to craft and strengthen our leadership qualities still further. Then we have to facilitate the growth of others. In speaking to a number of teachers and leaders who held families together post 9/11, this need was evident. The very teachers and administrators who were so strong for the children and parents in their schools did so almost without thinking. This was what they were *supposed* to do, protect the children above all else. But as I listened to the stories of these courageous leaders, I recognized that they had not found the space to share their own stories. They carried their pain within and were in need of an opportunity to release it and to honor the steps they took during these horrific challenges.

How then do we begin to foster positive transformation from our places of pain and inspire others to do likewise? This has been my quest for over a decade. Severe adversity was my personal catalyst into an inner strength that I had hitherto merely glimpsed. In 1992, my life was shattered in an instant when my five-year-old son, Benjaya, fell down a riverbank while playing with friends. He drowned. There one minute, gone the next. I was faced with the most challenging task of my life. Initially the task was survival—living through the nightmare without losing my sanity. Later the task matured with the question, "Now that I have survived, how can I thrive and use my learning to help others?"

I began a five-year research and writing project, a quest to discover if those who face the biggest challenges in life have the greatest opportunity to wake up from automatic pilot and discover their innate resilience. By interviewing people who have experienced and healed from the effects of major adversity I sought to discover what *keys* help us break through instead of breaking down. In this paper I will share in some depth three of the more prominent keys: *Share Your Pain, Find the Hidden Gifts, and Reclaim Your Heart and Spirit.*

First, however, let me set the cultural container in which most of us must wrestle to free the resource of our pain. Unfortunately, most of us have been conditioned with the pattern of trying to protect our soft spots by avoiding subjects of pain at all costs. Our role models have taught us to deny the depth of our vulnerability, even to ourselves. The infrastructure to share pain and so prevent the pressure cooker build-up of our emotions has generally broken down in the west. Separation, fragmentation, and isolation are the sad side effects of our modern quest for freedom and individual expression. No longer do our family and social networks receive our daily woes, or even our pleasures. In our nuclear family and single parent culture many of us are starved of an effective outlet, or the time to integrate our minor daily experiences, let alone the bigger issues of our lives.

Separation from the sources of wisdom in a community—especially the wisdom of our elders—has increased our sense of vulnerability and loneliness. And if there is no one to hear our pain we can become desperate and do anything to get attention, to be heard and noticed. As leaders, we need to know that this impacts adults and young people alike in our schools. There is an urgent need in our society to be heard, and perhaps for young people that place could be in their educational communities where most of their days are spent.

Teachers, school counselors and other support personnel are often privy to children's stories, which could be a wonderful resource for healing in our school communities. However, as adults, we must remember and remind each other that we too need our safe place to be heard. We are often not aware of the human consequences of knowing, caring and facing the reality of trauma. When we empathetically engage with others and open our hearts to someone else's story of devastation, we, as the helper, experience "vicarious traumatization" an occupational hazard that is an inescapable effect of our work.

The first key, *Share Your Pain,* is one of the major keys to healing that emerged from the stories of my interviewees. It is essential to find a constant ally to listen to our story. During the weeks after the 9/11 tragedy, some schools set up grieving rooms where adults could take time out when they needed respite, but generally most of the attention went to helping young people cope because the need was so great. Yet, school leaders also needed to understand their own vulnerabilities in order to restore their own sense of hope and resilience. It was precisely because of this need that two women—Linda Lantieri of Educators for Social Responsibility and Cheri Lovre of Crisis Management Institute—combined their expertise to create a handbook for school personnel to encourage them to give space to their grief and to work with others in the process of releasing it. This guide was given to 2,000 teachers in the Ground Zero area at the end of the school year 2002 when there would be time in busy schedules to use it well. There was interest from many other school systems, and from this beginning Project Renewal was born, a project specifically to support New York City school leaders with their recovery process.[2] Among other services, Project Renewal created retreats where at last the pain could be shared and truly heard.

Some schools, P.S. 150 being one, chose to create an inclusive creative event to mark the first anniversary of September 11. Parents, teachers, and students shared breakfast together at school, supporting each other that intense windy morning. Close to the time that the planes hit the towers, all eyes were lifted together to the sky, this time at the sight of many big colorful butterflies flying free from the boxes held by children representing each class. It was the togetherness, the mutual sharing of such a poignant day, as well as the amazing symbology of transformation, that created a deeply healing impression for that school community.

There are many ways we can encourage the sharing of students' pain. A middle school assistant principal told of the way in which the school set up a lunchtime counseling center to help young people cope with the loss of a well-loved fellow student who had been run over and killed by a man with impaired vision. The school arranged for individual counseling at lunchtime as well as group counseling and a number of after school grieving ceremonies to allow the young people to cope with their loss. Moments of silence were incorporated into the school days as appropriate.

It is important to recognize the stories that young people may be holding inside and unable to reveal. It is also important to recognize how we can help our young people to turn this adversity into leadership in service for others. Our nation's schools are replete with immigrants from all over the world. Many of these have left their troubled countries and arrived on our shores to try and heal the pain of the past and to build a new future. Those young people sit silently in our classrooms . . . along with young people who are traumatized by domestic violence, physical and sexual abuse, and neglect.

Arn Chorn-Pond, a child of war in Cambodia, is one of those young people. He believes that being heard was his saving grace. Arn was forced from his home by the Khmer Rouge at nine years old, separated from his family, and made to work in a child labor camp where children were dying of starvation and overwork all around him. Here is a snippet of his story:

> *One time it was raining hard and I was looking out the window. The Khmer Rouge were having a good time punishing people in the rain. There was one guy who they punished every day until he became weak, hitting him with a screwdriver in his knees. Finally they brought him close by my window. One guy was so angry, he found a stick on the ground and hit him in the neck until he was dead. They put him in a tree right outside my window, sitting there wearing an American helmet with a cigarette in his mouth. His eye was still open. These are the things I remember from childhood . . ."*

Arn was put on the front line of the war when the Vietnamese invaded Cambodia and given a gun to kill "the enemy". When he could take no more, he escaped into the jungle to live with the monkeys. Many months later he was found close to death, nursed to health and eventually brought to the U.S. by an American aid worker who became his foster father. He attended school where he was bullied mercilessly because the students knew nothing of his past.

> *Finally, I began more and more to heal myself and was encouraged to go out and talk . . . I didn't want to talk about it because I thought nobody cares about my life. First I learned from my heart a few words, 'My name is Arn. I'm from Cambodia. I live in the camp. My family die.' People listened and then they made a line to hug me and cry too. For the first time I felt cared for and I felt powerful . . . I began to work for Amnesty International and I was asked to speak at St. John the Divine Church to 10,000 people. It was about peace and disarmament in New York. Halfway through my speech I couldn't take it and I cried uncontrollably. Then there were 10,000 people crying. They asked me if I want to stop and I said, 'No, I want to finish it. This is a turning point for me.' When I finished I felt I was on the top of a mountain.*

> *I think I am alive today because I had the courage to speak out my story and I learned how to love again and how to feel the pain of others as well as my own.*

Arn's story epitomizes the potential of adversity as a route to leadership. Having successfully motivated himself through his trauma and shared his story repeatedly over the years, he felt enthused and compelled to assist others to do likewise. Much of his sharing was done in schools he visited accompanied by other children of war. These young people encouraged their listeners to become good citizens and help prevent conflict, thus empowering themselves and others. Arn has also masterminded many inspirational projects including working with street gangs to help them understand the effects of violence, and assisting the survival of his cultural heritage by discovering the few remaining Cambodian master musicians and performers and helping them pass on their "treasures" before they die. He now lives in Cambodia and runs "Cambodian Volunteers for Community Development" which has 50,000 young members—traumatized children and orphans from the war. They are rebuilding their country, planting trees, learning English and trying to heal themselves. *"I was saved and others were not,"* said Arn, *"so I'm wanting to do something good before I die. I want to grow up to be a good adult and hopefully be a role model for other kids."*

Arn's story is an extreme example, but even minor challenge offers wisdom that can be harnessed for the good of oneself and others. When a group leader believes and trusts that the sharing of pain can be transformational, a safe container will be created for healing and bonding to occur, which in turn will allow a more fertile ground for learning. It does not require the "leader" to be fully healed, only to be willing to be honest with emotions that are passing through in the moment. Real life stories are riveting teachers and faster healing and deeper connections are two rich rewards of sharing stories in a group. As school leaders, it would serve us well to create safe places for our school community to tell their stories, and to remember to find a place for us to tell ours as well.

A second key—*Find the Hidden Gifts*—holds an approach that is central to the discovery of our resilience. The French word for wounded is blessé, which is from the same root as blessing. The discovery and constructive use of the blessing/opportunity inherent in life's challenges results from asking the simple, down-to-earth questions—What can I learn from this? What is the gift?

More often than not we try to wriggle free from the discomfort of pain and yearn for the joy we believe we don't have, as if joy is an illusive quality outside of ourselves, far away from the sorrow we feel. The two qualities usually remain separated in our minds, perceived as mutually exclusive. In the paradigm held by those I interviewed for my book, *Mourning Has Broken,* nothing could be further from the truth. I, for one, found big, fat pearls of joy and wisdom at the same source as my anguish and became convinced that the further we fall, the higher we can climb.

The idea is not to escape or suppress the pain by looking for positives to take its place. It is to accept the cloud of pain while opening our eyes to the silver lining that *already exists.* To hold the pain and joy, the bitter and the sweet, side-by-side is the aim— the two halves making a whole and providing us with a feeling of our own fullness.

Karen Proctor, a young African American, is another example of how adversity can strengthen leadership qualities. Karen became determined to succeed in spite of being a "triple minority"—not white, male or Catholic—at her Notre Dame University. She became super controlled, describing herself as "a rock-like woman of control." Then, age 34, she found herself in a horrific car crash. Rendered helpless in the hospital she said, *"my lesson was to let go of control and soften my heart. The car crash told me I can't always be in control. I hated dependency because my mother was dependent, but I found myself in a situation where I was totally dependent on others, including degrading things for someone so proud and haughty. I am so grateful that life gave me the opportunity to break down my pride and become more humble. I could have died. Now I see the beauty in people and my eyes are wide open. Life is such a gift. Why we forget that is astounding to me."*

Finding this gift from her excruciating pain positively transformed Karen's attitude to life. She is quick to admit she needed a big shakeup to stop her in her tracks and is convinced that trauma such as hers offers the opportunity to build strength of character that then can be used to help others. During her rehabilitation at the hospital she was able to inspire many others who had been badly injured to find enough inner strength to go on. Her doctors called her "the miracle girl" because, after she grasped an understanding of the inherent gift the crash was offering her, the speed of her healing began to surpass all their predictions. At one point the doctors had all expected her to die. Karen, now physically whole again, uses her newfound qualities in her position as Vice President of Community Affairs and Government Relations at Scholastic Inc., the global children's publishing and media company where she directs Scholastic's corporate citizenship initiatives.

Our children need to see these examples. These stories of those who have not only survived, but who have overcome diversity are central to their own development of resiliency and self-efficacy. In your school communities there are many heroes and sheroes who could share their stories including the learning they have gained from their most painful experiences. The challenge for you as leaders is to create the culture that supports this sharing, and also encourages and honors it.

The third key I'd like to share is: *Reclaim Your Heart and Spirit.* We live in a society where consumerism is the name of the game: the size of our bank balance, the level of our IQ and where we stand on the career ladder are paramount. Reason and logic are deified in this drive for material success, leaving our hearts, spirits and emotional lives to fight for space on the back seat. Severe adversity, however, has the knack of purging the unnecessary things of life by questioning what really matters. And if status, reputation, possessions and money were high on our list before the challenge hit, we may find ourselves struggling to find resources and strength in the foundations of who we are. This key is about discovering the power of our inner world—finding out who we are behind what we do and what we have. It is about reinforcing our hearts and spirits and making a shift toward consulting the heart as well as the head and toward valuing emotional and spiritual intelligence.

In 1992, Mary Manti was assistant principal to Patrick Daly at P.S.15 in Brooklyn and had 25 years teaching experience. Then, in a horrifying incident, Mr. Daly was shot dead in the crossfire of a drug deal gone sour and Mary, catapulted into the job of acting principal, found herself applying this key to the shocking situation before her. She focused primarily on using love and harnessing the natural human spirit in helping herself and her school community. She told me:

In difficult times, people have to fall back on the inner qualities that are developed throughout life such as faith, hope, love, kindness, patience, and courage. These traits connect you with your heart and spirit.

It took a leap of faith by a lot of members of the school community to believe that things could move on in the school in a positive way. I've heard such a leap compared to a trapeze artist who must let go of the bar with one hand while reaching toward the next with the other hand. There's that second in between when it appears you aren't holding onto anything. We were called on to take that leap, having faith that whatever we needed to sustain us would be there . . . a belief that everything works toward the ultimate good.

The entire staff joined me in reminding the children of how much Mr. Daly loved them and of how he knew they loved him in return. We spoke of how we were all going to be sad for a long time, and the children knew tissues were available all over the building. If we felt like crying we did. We also told 'Mr. Daly stories' to the children that would bring smiles to their faces. We encouraged them to speak of Mr. Daly, draw pictures, write letters and remember positive things.

We didn't hang Pat's picture on every wall. Rather we tried to make the spirit of what he stood for come alive in order that we could emulate that spirit. All I could do was what was placed in front of me, a step at a time, and the big picture would be taken care of by the Director of Life.

Mary was role-modeling, staying in touch with her heart and spirit throughout the experience of external loss—perhaps the ideal scenario. She was so rock solid in her own inner resources that this created a safe container for all those around her to grieve in their own way. It is essential when working with people experiencing trauma to help them find their innate resources, and of course necessary that the "helper" is deeply resourced before beginning his/her work. When we look to Mary's resources we see that from the beginning she was using the qualities she already had.

Identifying resources is a simple activity. We all have them waiting to be claimed and used. The problem is that we tend to be on automatic pilot and suffer from resource amnesia when in shock. I suggest that you spend time making a list of your resources and then, as you go about your day leading others, use this strategy to help others identify the resources they already have and see how they can be applied to whatever the challenge is at hand.

There are inner and outer resources we can draw from for ourselves and the young people we are developing.[3] *Inner resources* include spiritual beliefs, connections to one's essential self, good physical health, creative thinking, communication skills, an ability to feel a full range of emotion, a sense of feeling safe in the world, the ability to be in contact with others and maintaining a sense of self. *External resources* include access to community groups and workshops, spiritual practice, friends, family, having a home, emotional support, access to transport, to the natural world, and to cultural educational and creative community resources.

In conclusion, we have seen that the challenge to school leaders is to both model and encourage a culture of safety and learning that is more transparent. Leadership qualities in both children and adults is created and enhanced when we succeed in:

a) Opening fully to our pain, using the resources we already have to support us.
b) Recognizing our pain as a source of strength as opposed to a sign of weakness.
c) Sharing our story and encouraging deep listening.
d) Seeking out the wisdom and gifts within our challenges.
e) Deepening our connection to heart and spirit.

Twenty-first century administrators must extend beyond the current focus of teaching our children to read, write and problem solve mathematically. The call is to create the cultural context for children to feel safe enough to also learn by using the rich yet painful challenges of life to heal, inspire and help them become the leaders of tomorrow.

NOTES

1. Nepo, M. 2000. *The Book of Awakening,* Berkeley, Ca : Conari Press, p. 52.
2. Project Renewal is an initiative of Educators for Social Responsibility National (www.esrnational.org) and is supported in part by The September 11 Fund.

3. From an article by Pat Ogden in the Hakomi Somatics Training Manual (Hakomi Somatics Institute, P.O. Box 19438, Boulder, Colorado 90308 www.hakomisomatics.com).

Carmella B'Hahn, who also co-authored Benjaya's Gifts, co-founded the holistic teaching center, MetaCentre, in 1984 and later spent a decade pioneering waterbirth in Britain through her company BirthWorks. Carmella lives in southwest England with her son, and now runs workshops in the U.K. and U.S. on transformation through trauma. She can be contacted at carmella@macunlimited.net. Website: www.carmellaB.freeuk.com

Mourning Has Broken (Crucible Publishers, England, 2002) is available on-line at www.reclaiming.com or by calling toll free 1-888-647-2532 to place an order.

MULTICULTURAL EDUCATION: DIVERSITY, EQUITY, AND SOCIAL JUSTICE

Yvonne De Gaetano

INTRODUCTION

Cultural diversity today is no longer a topic relevant only to our nation's urban areas. Groups different from the mainstream are found in almost every area of the United States and their numbers are growing. Demographic changes have occurred in the last 20 years as a result of the largest immigration in the United States since the early 1900s. This new wave of immigration represents many diverse groups, including Africans, Asians, Latinos, and Europeans. It is important to note that the majority of the newest immigrant groups are vastly different in cultures and languages from the mainstream North American population. Their presence has provoked alarmed reaction from a significant portion of the mainstream population precisely because of their cultural and linguistic differences and increasingly large numbers. In addition, the shock of the 9/11 tragedies has added to the sense of distrust and alienation of people who are different.

As in the past when large numbers of immigrants came to these shores, schools once again have been challenged with the task of providing services to the children of the newest immigrants. Principals and school personnel are faced with the moral and practical dilemmas of providing these children with high-quality, equitable schools—the kind of schooling that all children deserve. This article will address the role of school administrators in establishing and providing schools that are equitable and responsive to issues of diversity and social justice.

CULTURAL DIVERSITY

As we continue to become a more complex and diverse nation, there are questions that we need to ask about how we will address diversity in our society in general, and in our schools specifically. What can school administrators do to create schools that affirm diversity and promote social justice for *all* students? Even more fundamental, how do we view diversity?

There are many school administrators who understand that how one handles cultural diversity is central to academic, social, and emotional learning for everyone, and particularly to school reform efforts. There are, however, administrators who may perceive cultural diversity in their schools as a problematic issue. Other administrators may view diversity as a topic that teachers need to address in classrooms in response to mandates from their district or the State Education Department. How cultural diversity is viewed is critical to how well or poorly a school functions and how poorly students, teachers and parents interact in school.

The administrator benefits greatly from a deep and broad understanding of how to embrace cultural diversity as a core value reflected in the culture and climate of the school. It is important to note that cultural diversity is not simply about different ethnic or racial groups; it is a broader, more inclusive idea that includes social class issues, gender, gender orientation, disability, language diversity and age differences.

MULTICULTURAL EDUCATION

The field of study that best addresses cultural diversity in schools is multicultural education, but the concept of multicultural education is often misunderstood. Multicultural education is often viewed as the "feel good" superficiality of lessons about our similarities while ignoring our differences, or as an add-on to the "regular" curriculum or lessons in schools, or as the festivals of "ethnic" holidays. Multicultural education, however, is not a simple process that is implemented on a particular day or in a specific month of the year.

Fundamentally, multicultural education is about increasing the academic outcomes for *all* students. This means that multicultural education is about striving for equity in school in terms of gender, cultural, racial, linguistic, and exceptional groups. Implicit in the concept of *multi*cultural education is the idea that teaching and learning through the perspective of only one group—monoculture education—is not an equitable education for anyone. Ultimately, multicultural education is about preparing students to be active participants in a democracy.

CHARACTERISTICS, APPROACHES AND IMPLEMENTATION OF MULTICULTURAL EDUCATION

The work of Sonia Nieto and James Banks, two major multicultural education theorists, is critical in our understanding of the essence of multicultural education. Nieto (2000) defines multicultural education as a whole school approach that has the following seven characteristics:

1. *Antiracist education*—This means being anti-discriminatory in the ways in which the school functions, not favoring one group of students over another. For example, one must be aware of who is being represented in the curriculum and learning materials and how teachers and administrators interact with particular students and their families.
2. *Basic education*—In addition to reading, writing and mathematics, the basics of schooling must include multicultural education, which presents more perspectives and more than one reality. Multicultural education is basic to becoming an educated person.
3. *Important for all students*—Multicultural education is not just for minority students; it includes all students—minority and majority—because all students need to be afforded a complete and unbiased education.
4. *Pervasive*—Multicultural education is not the culture corner or the celebration of specific ethnic holidays—it must be included as an integral part of the everyday teaching and as part of how the school as a whole functions.
5. *Education for social justice*—Thinking and learning are the vehicles to take action for social justice, a necessity for living in a true democracy. In a social justice environment, teachers help students analyze and critique events that occur to them and others in the broader world context to foster a sense of justice. And administrators make sure that they model social justice for the students, parents and teachers by the way they interact with others and how they lead, guide, and direct the business of the school.
6. *A process*—There is no recipe for the implementation of multicultural education; it is a never ending practice in which we are always increasing our understanding and our awareness of ourselves and of our students and their lives.
7. *Critical pedagogy*—Children and their lives are at the core of the curriculum. Multiple perspectives become the way of thinking about issues and events. The many

facets of diversity are valued and critical thinking, reflection and action are integral to the outcomes of the learning process and to the school as a whole. To respond to all of these points, school leaders need to insist that multicultural education be part of the very fabric of what occurs in schools.

How, then, do teachers and administrators implement multicultural education in their classrooms and in the school as a whole? To support multicultural education, it is important that administrators know about and understand how teachers implement it in their classrooms. James Banks (2003; 1996) has described different approaches to the implementation of multicultural education in the classroom. He describes the first approach as the *Contributions Approach*. At this level, teachers focus primarily on heroes and holidays and the "culture corner." This approach reduces multiculturalism to celebrations of certain ethnic holidays, to famous people, and to the objects of a culture. With the *Additive Approach*, teachers add a unit or read books that are culturally relevant to the "regular" curriculum. The basic structure of how and what is taught, however, as well as the assumptions about what needs to be taught remain unchanged.

With a third approach, *the Transformational Approach*, teachers fundamentally change the way the curriculum is thought about and taught. Students are presented with different perspectives on important issues so that they may think critically and develop analytical skills. Teachers ask students to consider the perspectives of different peoples regarding historical events. Literature, for example, is selected not only for pleasure, or to increase knowledge, but also with the purpose of developing empathy and caring, qualities that are critical in living and participating in a just democracy. At the fourth level, the *Social Action Approach*, teachers extend the transformational approach to add social action. For example, teachers help students identify, study and analyze important issues in their communities or in the broader world and then take action to participate in the solution of problems related to the issues. Although these implementation approaches involve teachers and their classrooms directly, administrators are critically involved in the implementation of these approaches in their schools as a whole by supporting and affirming them.

Another way of thinking about the implementation of approaches to multicultural education in the classroom and school is by addressing the various components that are integral to schooling. De Gaetano, Williams and Volk (1998) have conceptualized the process of implementing multicultural education as one that is circular rather than linear because the process is never ending (see Figure 1). It is continually deepened and refined as teachers consciously pay attention to infusing multicultural education into their classrooms.

The metaphor of the circle begins with defining goals for the kind of, or approach to, multicultural education to be implemented in the school, and in the classrooms specifically. As a school leader, ask yourself, "How do I want my school to function? Where do I want my school to be in three years, in five years?"

When Ruth became the principal of a failing elementary school, she asked herself those very questions. She knew that ultimately multicultural education is about providing all children with equality of educational opportunity so that they may develop their cognitive, social, emotional and physical abilities to the fullest level possible. She began by setting a course of action so that faculty, staff, students and families knew what would be expected of them. She provided the best possible staff development based on teachers' needs. She was visible in the classrooms, giving feedback to teachers and encouraging them to set high goals for their students. And she always made sure that teachers and parents had a voice in important decisions that affected the children and school as a whole.

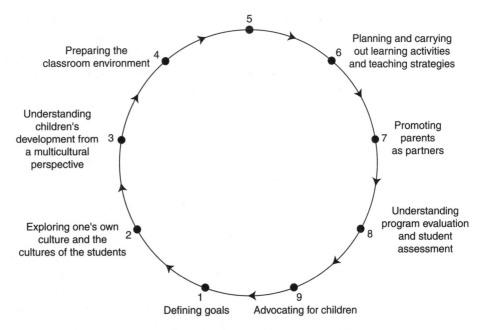

FIGURE 1   Understanding first and second language development.
(From: De Gaetano, Y.; Williams, L.R. & Volk, D. (1998). *Kaleidoscope: A multicultural approach for the primary school classroom.* Upper Saddle River, NJ: Merrill, Prentice Hall)

In the most developed levels of multicultural education, teachers strive to promote a strong sense of democratic ideals and social action in their students (Banks, 2003; Bennet, 2003; De Gaetano, Williams & Volk, 1998; Nieto, 2000).

The next consideration is that of exploring and knowing about one's own culture and beliefs. It is important to understand that everyone has a culture and that one's culture has a strong influence in the ways in which one approaches learning. Whether we are aware of it or not, culture is an integral part of every one of us. We, therefore, need to become more consciously sensitive to how we have been influenced by the culture of our family and our environment. By becoming more aware of the power and influence of our own culture, we begin to appreciate and understand the power of the culture of others. For example, as educators we need to know that the culture—the values, beliefs, and experiences—of the students is critical in the implementation of multicultural education. That does not mean that educators have to be experts about the various ethnicities of each student, but it does mean that we need to know about the way of life of the students and their families.

> *When Charles became principal, he made it his business to learn as much as possible about the families in his school. He personally met and talked with the families as they picked up their children from school. He called them when their children behaved well or when they improved or excelled in their schoolwork. He listened to their stories and became acutely aware that many families had different experiences from one another. Some had come from rural areas, others from large cities. Some families were newly arrived immigrants, others were second generation, and others still, were born and raised in the community. They were different families with different views of the world. By making the school environment an encouraging one that builds on what the child brings to school, the possibilities for continued development and growth are enhanced. Charles knew this and encouraged the teachers to get to know their students in new ways.*

This is cultural information that forms the vital threads that educators need to connect to what must be learned to make learning relevant to students.

The school environment and what goes on in classrooms that implement multicultural education is one that reflects who and what the students are. In classrooms this means that careful attention is given to the physical set up, and to the books and other learning materials in the classroom. The subtle and not so subtle messages about race, gender, class, disability and religious differences to what is in the classroom need to be examined. How children are grouped for learning is also critical. Tracking is an insidious practice that harms children by the messages they get from separating them by their assumed cognitive abilities as "smart" or "dumb."

> *Upon entering Lourdes' school, one is treated to a visual feast. Colorful signs in a variety of languages welcome the visitor. Mounted on bright paper, children's work is displayed everywhere. The implicit messages are that this is a school where a lot of learning is taking place, and multilingualism is valued. The classrooms confirm this first impression. Children are busy exploring ideas in small groups, reading individually, or conferring with teachers. The children are in heterogeneous classrooms and the climate of each is one of cooperation and caring. Lourdes worked hard at encouraging and enabling the teachers to work in such an atmosphere.*

The next consideration for implementing multicultural education is that of understanding the development of children's language. Teachers need to know the stages of language development in order to help children expand and enrich their language repertoire. For children whose first language may not be English, it is important to understand that the greater the level of development of the first language, the greater the potential for the development of the second language. This is no easy task, especially when bilingual education programs across the nation have been criticized and schools and districts have been forced to return to the "English only" approach. As a leader, how will you prepare the children entrusted to you? What do you know and believe about second language learning? What are your beliefs about bilingualism? These are critical questions that you must ask yourself.

The next area of focus is that of integrating into the learning process what has been learned about the students and their culture and experiences. When a student learns about graphing, teachers can use information about students' families or children's places of birth. Analogies can be made about the movements of people in history and students' immigration or migration patterns. In addition, the children's communities are wonderful sources from which to develop curriculum. It is in this dimension of implementation where issues of race and power are dealt with openly and sensitively, and teachers focus specifically on helping children think about equity and social justice in their learning. Administrators, too, must be open to addressing these important topics. How equitably they behave toward the students, teachers, staff and parents, sends a strong message and sets a powerful tone in the school.

Promoting parents as partners in the education of their children is one of the critical aspects of schooling. Teachers and administrators must make every effort to communicate effectively with the parents of their students. Understanding that parents may also be partners with teachers in different ways—at home as well as in the classroom—is also important. The attitudes of teachers and administrators toward parents, however, is probably the single most significant factor in promoting parents' comfort level toward the schools that their children attend.

> *Upon seeing the school where he would be principal, Charles noticed the graffiti that marred the walls. The streets surrounding the school were littered with wrappers,*

garbage, and broken bottles. One of the first things he did, therefore, was to organize a meeting of the parents of the school and other community members to address these issues as well as to learn about their concerns. He made phone calls to the parents, talked to the shop owners, and put up fliers around the neighborhood. At the meeting, he heard the concerns of the parents and other community members, and of their fear of the neighborhood. Soon after, he formed groups of parents and others in the community who would join him in painting over the graffiti on the school walls and cleaning up the area surrounding the school. With the help of the police in the area, he developed a "hot line" so that when parents saw anyone putting graffiti back on the walls, they called the precinct, which quickly sent police out to the area. In a few months, the area around the school was clean, the walls of the school were free of graffiti, and parents reported feeling safe. By listening to the parents' concerns and working alongside them, Charles gained their trust. It was only the beginning of a close relationship between the parents and the school administration.

Assessment is essential in the implementation of multicultural education. Assessment measures that help teachers discover what students *can* do, instead of what they cannot, help teachers know what to build upon for children's learning. Children will be tested many times throughout their lifetime. They, therefore, need to learn how to take standardized tests and do well on them. Educators, however, must make sure that they also assess students in diverse ways with a variety of assessment tools. Even in this climate of high stakes tests, administrators who value multicultural education know that assessment does not shape the curriculum; rather, assessment tools indicate the degree to which the goals of the curriculum have been met and how much learning has taken place.

Finally, teachers must become advocates for the students that they teach, and school administrators must become advocates not only for the students, but also for their families and the teachers in their school. Teachers and administrators together have the obligation to speak out against injustices and inequities that may exist in their school systems.

THE ADMINISTRATOR AND MULTICULTURAL EDUCATION IN PRACTICE

The process of implementing multicultural education in schools is deepened and enhanced as we continue to think about and practice as multicultural educators. By knowing and understanding the often complex process of implementing multicultural education in their schools, administrators can support and facilitate what happens in them. Although there are no recipes for implementing multicultural education, administrators need to consider the following:

1. *The cultural composition of the teachers and school staff*—Make sure that diversity is represented and affirmed in the hiring practices of the school. When the teaching staff is white and racial or ethnic minorities hold the nonprofessional jobs in a school, a strong message of status and inequality is made. Become creative in searching for an ethnically, linguistically, and racially representative group of professionals and non-professionals in your schools.
2. *The curriculum*—Ask yourself if the curriculum is connected to, and infused with, issues of diversity. Help teachers focus on the children and their families as points of references for teaching content. Knowledge about the lives, backgrounds, and experiences of the children enable teachers to connect what children must learn to

who and what they are. Help teachers to deal with the "hard" topics of race, discrimination, oppression, and power issues within the curriculum.

3. *Pedagogy*—Encourage teachers to use a variety of approaches in their teaching. Remember that quiet classrooms do not always translate into classrooms where children are learning. Many students learn best when they are engaged in active learning where they are exploring, experimenting, researching, and discussing. Some students work well on their own while others learn best working in groups. Help teachers understand that children already come with knowledge, and that teaching and learning are a reciprocal process.

4. *Professional Development/Growth*—Support teachers with continuous professional development that goes beyond the superficial aspects of multicultural education. Teachers need help in teaching for social justice even as they teach the mandated curriculum. And professional development is important in maintaining the kinds of interactions that must take place in schools that implement multicultural education.

5. *Interactions in the School*—The quality of interaction that takes place in schools is one of the most critical factors in schools that value multiculturalism. You must interact with children, adults, and the community with respect and caring. Your school needs to prepare students to become productive, active, caring members of a democratic society. And finally, you set the tone and thrust for schools to do this through the practice of education that is multicultural.

When schools become places of academic learning where issues of equity and social justice are central, students are prepared for living in a democracy that fosters peace and justice.

REFERENCES

Banks, J. A. (2002). *An introduction to multicultural education* (3rd ed.), Boston: Allyn & Bacon.

De Gaetano, Y; Williams, L. R. & Volk, D. (1998). *Kaleidoscope: A multicultural approach to the primary school classroom.* Upper Saddle River, NJ: Merrill, Prentice Hall.

Nieto, S. (2000). *Affirming diversity* (3rd. ed.), New York: Longman.

HOW LEADERS CAN INSPIRE AND STRUCTURE SOCIAL AND EMOTIONAL LEARNING TO SET A NEW STANDARD FOR EDUCATION IN THE 21ST CENTURY

Maurice J. Elias, Ph.D.

At your next "Back to School Night" for parents and your next Opening of Year or other faculty meeting for staff, ask these questions. Encourage people to answer honestly and to share their responses among themselves before having an overall discussion:

—Do you want the children you teach, as well as your own children, to become knowledgeable?

—How about responsible? Nonviolent? Drug free? Caring?

—If I were to tell you that the curriculum is too crowded to provide all of these for children—to be knowledgeable, responsible, nonviolent, drug-free and caring—which would you want to give up?

When teachers and parents around the United States and in other countries have been asked this question, they recognize that the choice is a difficult one. Actually, it is an impossible one. We cannot prepare children to assume their adult roles and the mantle of civic leadership unless they emerge from their school years with ALL of these attributes.

Indeed, with all the efforts at school reform, with all the expenditure of time, talent, and money on education, we know we have not yet achieved what we believe, what we *know,* our education system can produce. Visionary leaders in our schools know that there is a piece missing. What is "The Missing Piece"? The missing piece in the process of civilizing and humanizing our children, without doubt, is social and emotional learning (SEL). Any protest that this is outside of the province of the school is inaccurate and dooms us to continued frustration and Herculean efforts at damage control and repair. The roster of social casualties will grow ever larger (Elias, 2001).

In Chapter Five of *SMART* School Leaders, Janet Patti cast a revealing light on what social and emotional learning looks like in schools. In this chapter, the focus is on how to communicate about it to staff, parents and other key stakeholders, and also the kinds of structures that enable SEL to be lived in schools. First, it helps to mention that the current movement for emotional intelligence, catalyzed by Daniel Goleman's (1995) book of that name, is not the first work of this kind to reflect advances in research on the brain, learning, and emotion. Howard Gardner's Multiple Intelligences model, with which most educators are familiar professionally and most parents know intuitively, clearly addresses the value of interpersonal and intrapersonal intelligence. Gardner and Goleman make the case for what we all know as "The Other Side of the Report Card." This is the side where we learn about children's work habit, character and life skills. It is a clear complement to academic abilities and something schools have been attending to for decades, albeit not systematically. Now, however, research shows clearly that both sides of the report card are essential for success in school and in life (Elias, Zins, Weissberg, & Associates, 1997).

Parents and educators resonate to discussions about "The other side of the report card." They know that this is the side that reflects how we live with one another and whether we are inclined toward peace or war and the skills needed to avoid problems of violence and alcohol and drug abuse. The interpersonal life of schools, classrooms, hallways, recess, lunchrooms, buses, study halls, school athletic and non-athletic teams, clubs and performance groups and formal and informal gatherings of students, staff and parents rests on the character of the people involved and the skills they need to enact their tasks effectively. Sometimes, the pressure of high stakes testing and perceived admissions standards to the "finest" schools lead people to act as if the skills and attributes of character are not as important as academic grades (Elias, 2001). But consider: In life, does it matter who shows up, who works well with others, who can solve problems, who is prepared for what they must do, who can function as part of a team and who is an ethical person? Are these any less important than algebra, geometry, chemistry and spelling? The dialogue to bring SEL into schools must be a dialogue of leadership, not followership. It tends to succeed when presented along the lines shared here.

SKILLS ESSENTIAL FOR SOCIAL, ACADEMIC, AND LIFE SUCCESS

Another key aspect of SEL is its basis in skills. Some educators and parents have bad tastes in their mouths from prior movements in values clarification, affective education, and even overly preachy character education. The SEL that is being presented in schools now has a solid empirical base and that base keeps pointing to our children's needs to walk away from our educational system with a wide array of skills. Relevant research conducted by the Collaborative for Academic, Social, and Emotional Learning (CASEL, an international group of educators, researchers, practitioners, and policymakers concerned with preparing teachers for the challenges of education in the 21st century) is summarized in numerous publications at www.CASEL.org and elaborated in a forthcoming book by Zins, Weissberg, Wang, and Walberg, "Building Student Success on Social and Emotional Learning" (NY: Teachers College Press). It yields a clearer picture of the skills and competencies students need for both academic and life success. The research indicates that social and emotional factors reflected on "The other side of the report card" correlate positively with academic grades and school performance. Furthermore, enhancing social-emotional competencies in combination with a positive, supportive classroom and school climate can improve academic performance (Pasi, 2001). CASEL has identified the following teachable skills as underlying positive youth development and academic performance. These findings are based on converging evidence from research, site visits to schools that excel in addressing students' academic, social, and emotional development and analysis of exemplary programs for social and emotional learning. Think of them as literacy skills—the skills of social-emotional and interpersonal, vocational, family, and community literacy (Elias et al., 1997).

- knowing and managing emotions
- recognizing strengths and areas of need
- showing ethical and social responsibility
- taking others' perspectives and sensing their emotions
- respecting others and self
- appreciating diversity
- setting adaptive goals
- problem solving
- clear listening and communication
- social approach and relationship-building
- cooperating, negotiating, and managing conflict nonviolently, and
- help-seeking and help-giving.

SCHOOL CONDITIONS ESSENTIAL FOR STUDENT SUCCESS

The research also strongly suggests that schools must organize themselves effectively if students are to develop sound character and see themselves and their learning as positive resources for their families, schools, workplaces, and communities. Skills and knowledge must be imparted in contexts that reinforce and exemplify these behaviors (skills) if they are to be internalized in ways that will help students learn to participate actively in the institutions that allow for a free and democratic society.

Schools of social, emotional, character, and academic excellence generally share five main characteristics (Novick, Kress, & Elias, 2002):

1. A school climate articulating specific themes, character elements, and/or values such as respect, responsibility, fairness and honesty.
2. Explicit instruction and practice in SEL skills.
3. Developmentally appropriate instruction in health-promotion and problem-prevention skills.
4. Services and systems to enhance coping skills and social support for transitions, crises, and resolving conflicts.
5. Widespread, systematic opportunities for positive, contributory service.

Leaders of many schools with such climates have incorporated social-emotional learning or character education into their overall mission statements or board policies. They have ongoing, coordinated, high-quality, empirically supported programs to teach skills for social and emotional learning and to infuse character into various aspects of the school routine and environment. These schools also devote specific time toward preventing problems such as bullying and other forms of violence, alcohol, tobacco and other drug use, and pregnancy.

The most forward-looking of these schools organize student support and guidance services to be anticipatory, rather than only reactive. They provide assistance for children as they and their families face life crises and challenges, rather than wait until academic or behavioral deterioration becomes manifest. In that same vein, these schools also emphasize teaching ALL students conflict resolution skills, since all will experience many, many conflicts in the interpersonal environment of schools and the community. Finally, there is a strong emphasis on high quality service learning experiences, certainly at the high school but also (in many cases) at the middle school and elementary levels.

IMPLICATIONS FOR SCHOOL GOVERNANCE AND POLICY

Findings from recent research have clear implications for those concerned with educational policy and school governance. For educational leaders who believe that excellence in education can and must include both sides of the report card, here is what can and must be asked of our schools:

- Sound classroom structure and function is based on a foundation of caring relationships and such relationships must be nurtured among all school staff, students, and parents.
- Students function better and learn more effectively when they are encouraged to have clear, positive goals and values, to manage their emotions and make responsible decisions, and to engage in setting goals for their own learning while also pursuing the academic goals that must be reached to function well in our society.
- Students behave more responsibly and respectfully when given opportunities for moral action and community service.

- Students and staff respond well, and discipline problems are minimized, when there is a challenging academic curriculum that respects all learners and is organized to motivate them and help them succeed.
- The school staff must be a caring, moral community of learners, and must model as well as teach caring and moral behavior for students.
- The opportunities for a child to achieve moral probity and to reach social, emotional, and academic goals are enhanced to the extent to which the school, parents, and the community collaborate.
- The concerns of students with special needs must be fully integrated into the mainstream functioning of the school as much as possible.

A NEW STANDARD FOR 21ST CENTURY EDUCATION

Educational leaders know that business as usual will not meet the challenges facing our students, and our schools, today or tomorrow. The evidence is in place to support bold recognition that students' success in school and preparation for their life roles in families, workplaces, communities, and as citizens in a complex, participatory democracy needs their active engagement. Nurturing *The Other Side of the Report Card* is incumbent upon visionary leaders who organize schools so that they promote both academic and social-emotional excellence. We must bring emotional intelligence into every classroom, if we want students to leave schools and display emotional intelligence wherever they go. Indeed, the important message of recent research is that enhancing children's social, emotional, ethical, and academic development is one inseparable goal, rather than a set of competing priorities. This defines the educational standard for the 21st Century.

REFERENCES

Elias, M. J. (2001). Prepare children for the tests of life, not a life of tests. *Education Week,* September 26, pp. 40.

Elias, M. J., Zins, J. E., Weissberg, R. P., Frey, K. S., Greenberg, M. T., Haynes, N. M., Kessler, R., Schwab-Stone, M. E., & Shriver, T. P. (1997). *Promoting social and emotional learning: Guidelines for educators.* Alexandria, VA: Association for Supervision and Curriculum Development.

Goleman, D. (1995). Emotional intelligence. New York: Bantam.

Novick, B., Kress, J. S., & Elias, M. J. (2002). *Building learning communities with character: How to integrate academic, social, and emotional learning.* Alexandria, VA: Association for Supervision and Curriculum Development.

Pasi, R. (2001). *Higher Expectations: Promoting Social Emotional Learning and Academic Achievement in Your School.* New York: Teachers College Press.

WHAT MAKES A LEADER?

Daniel Goleman

IQ and technical skills are important, but emotional intelligence is the sine qua non of leadership.

Every businessperson knows a story about a highly intelligent, highly skilled executive who was promoted into a leadership position only to fail at the job. And they also know a story about someone with solid—but not extraordinary—intellectual abilities and technical skills who was promoted into a similar position and then soared.

Such anecdotes support the widespread belief that identifying individuals with the "right stuff" to be leaders is more art than science. After all, the personal styles of superb leaders vary: some leaders are subdued and analytical; others shout their manifestos from the mountaintops. And just as important, different situations call for different types of leadership. Most mergers need a sensitive negotiator at the helm, whereas many turnarounds require a more forceful authority.

I have found, however, that the most effective leaders are alike in one crucial way: they all have a high degree of what has come to be known as *emotional intelligence*. It's not that IQ and technical skills are irrelevant. They do matter, but mainly as "threshold capabilities;" that is, they are the entry-level requirements for executive positions. But my research, along with other recent studies, clearly shows that emotional intelligence is the sine qua non of leadership. Without it, a person can have the best training in the world, an incisive, analytical mind, and an endless supply of smart ideas, but he still won't make a great leader.

In the course of the past year, my colleagues and I have focused on how emotional intelligence operates at work. We have examined the relationship between emotional intelligence and effective performance, especially in leaders. And we have observed how emotional intelligence shows itself on the job. How can you tell if someone has high emotional intelligence, for example, and how can you recognize it in yourself? In the following pages, we'll explore these questions, taking each of the components of emotional intelligence—self-awareness, self-regulation, motivation, empathy, and social skill—in turn.

EVALUATING EMOTIONAL INTELLIGENCE

Most large companies today have employed trained psychologists to develop what are known as "competence models" to aid them in identifying, training, and promoting likely stars in the leadership firmament. The psychologists have also developed such models for lower-level positions. And in recent years, I have analyzed competency models from 188 companies, most of which were large and global and included the likes of Lucent Technologies, British Airways, and Credit Suisse.

Source: *From* Harvard Business Review, *November, December 1998. Copyright © 1998 by Harvard Business School Publishing Corporation. All rights reserved.*

In carrying out this work, my objective was to determine which personal capabilities drove outstanding performance within these organizations, and to what degree they did so. I grouped capabilities into three categories: purely technical skills like accounting and business planning; cognitive abilities like analytical reasoning; and competencies demonstrating emotional intelligence such as the ability to work with others and effectiveness in leading change.

To create some of the competency models, psychologists asked senior managers at the companies to identify the capabilities that typified the organization's most outstanding leaders. To create other models, the psychologists used objective criteria such as a division's profitability to differentiate the star performers at senior levels within their organizations from the average ones. Those individuals were then extensively interviewed and tested, and their capabilities were compared. This process resulted in the creation of lists of ingredients for highly effective leaders. The lists ranged in length from 7 to 15 items and included such ingredients as initiative and strategic vision.

When I analyzed all this data, I found dramatic results. To be sure, intellect was a driver of outstanding performance. Cognitive skills such as big-picture thinking and long-term vision were particularly important. But when I calculated the ratio of technical skills, IQ, and emotional intelligence as ingredients of excellent performance, emotional intelligence proved to be twice as important as the others for jobs at all levels.

Moreover, my analysis showed that emotional intelligence played an increasingly important role at the highest levels of the company, where differences in technical skills are of negligible importance. In other words, the higher the rank of a person considered to be a star performer, the more emotional intelligence capabilities showed up as the reason for his or her effectiveness. When I compared star performers with average ones in senior leadership positions, nearly 90% of the difference in their profiles was attributable to emotional intelligence factors rather than cognitive abilities.

Other researchers have confirmed that emotional intelligence not only distinguishes outstanding leaders but can also be linked to strong performance. The findings of the late David McClelland, the renowned researcher in human and organizational behavior, are a good example. In a 1996 study of a global food and beverage company, McClelland found that when senior managers had a critical mass of emotional intelligence capabilities, their divisions outperformed yearly earnings goals of 20 percent. Meanwhile, division leaders without that critical mass underperformed by almost the same amount. McClelland's findings, interestingly, held as true in he company's U.S. divisions as in its divisions in Asia and Europe.

In short, the numbers are beginning to tell us a persuasive story about the link between a company's success and the emotional intelligence of its leaders. And just as important, research is also demonstrating that people can, if they take the right approach, develop their emotional intelligence. (See the insert "Can Emotional Intelligence Be Learned?")

SELF-AWARENESS

Self-awareness is the first component of emotional intelligence—which makes sense when one considers that the Delphic oracle gave the advice to "know thyself" thousands of years ago. Self-awareness means having a deep understanding of one's emotions, strengths, weaknesses, needs, and drives. People with strong self-awareness are neither overly critical nor unrealistically hopeful. Rather, they are honest—with themselves and with others.

The Five Components of Emotional Intelligence at Work

	Definition	Hallmarks
Self-Awareness	the ability to recognize and understand your moods, emotions, and drives, as well as their effect on others	self-confidence realistic self-assessment self-deprecating sense of humor
Self-Regulation	the ability to control or redirect disruptive impulses and moods the propensity to suspend judgment—to think before acting	trustworthiness and integrity comfort with ambiguity openness to change
Motivation	a passion to work for reasons that go beyond money or status a propensity to pursue goals with energy and persistence	strong drive to achieve optimism, even in the face of failure organizational commitment
Empathy	the ability to understand the emotional makeup of other people skill in treating people according to their emotional reactions	expertise in building and retaining talent cross-cultural sensitivity service to clients and customers
Social Skill	proficiency in managing relationships and building networks an ability to find common ground and build rapport	effectiveness in leading change persuasiveness expertise in building and leading teams

People who have a high degree of self-awareness recognize how their feelings affect them, other people and their job performance. Thus a self-aware person who knows that tight deadlines bring out the worst in him plans his time carefully and gets his work done well in advance. Another person with high self-awareness will be able to work with a demanding client. She will understand the client's impact on her moods and the deeper reasons for her frustration. "Their trivial demands take us away from the real work that needs to be done," she might explain. And she will go one step further and turn her anger into something constructive.

Self-awareness extends to a person's understanding of his or her values and goals. Someone who is highly self-aware knows where he is headed and why; so, for example, he will be able to be firm in turning down a job offer that is tempting financially but does not fit with his principles or long-term goals. A person who lacks self-awareness is apt to make decisions that bring on inner turmoil by treading on buried values. "The money looked good so I signed on," someone might say two years into a job, "but the work means so little to me that I'm constantly bored." The decisions of self-aware people mesh with their values. Consequently, they often find work to be energizing.

How can one recognize self-awareness? First and foremost, it shows itself as candor and an ability to assess oneself realistically. People with high self-awareness are able to speak accurately and openly—although not necessarily effusively or confessionally—about their emotions and the impact they have on their work. For instance, one manager I know was skeptical about a new personal-shopper service that her company, a major department-store chain, was about to introduce. Without prompting from her team or her boss, she offered them an explanation. "It's hard for me to get behind the rollout of this service," she admitted, "because I really wanted to run the project, but I wasn't selected. Bear with me while I deal with that." The manager did indeed examine her feelings. A week later, she was supporting the project fully.

Such self-knowledge often shows itself in the hiring process. Ask a candidate to describe a time he got carried away by his feelings and did something he later regretted. Self-aware candidates will be frank in admitting to failure—and will often tell their tales with a smile. One of the hallmarks of self-awareness is a self-deprecating sense of humor.

Self-awareness can also be identified during performance reviews. Self-aware people know—and are comfortable talking about—their limitations and strengths, and they often demonstrate a thirst for constructive criticism. By contrast, people with low self-awareness interpret the message that they need to improve as a threat or a sign of failure.

Self-aware people can also be recognized by their self-confidence. They have a firm grasp of their capabilities and are less likely to set themselves up to fail by, for example, overstretching on assignments. They know, too, when to ask for help. And the risks they take on the job are calculated. They won't ask for a challenge that they know they can't handle alone. They'll play to their strengths.

Consider the actions of a mid-level employee who was invited to sit in on a strategy meeting with her company's top executives. Although she was the most junior person in the room, she did not sit there quietly, listening in awestruck or fearful silence. She knew she had a head for clear logic and the skill to present ideas persuasively, and she offered cogent suggestions about the company's strategy. At the same time, her self-awareness stopped her from wandering into territory where she knew she was weak.

Despite the value of having self-aware people in the workplace, my research indicates that senior executives don't often give self-awareness the credit it deserves when they look for potential leaders. Many executives mistake candor about feelings for "wimpiness" and fail to give due respect to employees who openly acknowledge their shortcomings. Such people are too readily dismissed as "not tough enough" to lead others.

In fact, the opposite is true. In the first place, people generally admire and respect candor. Further, leaders are constantly required to make judgment calls that require a candid assessment of capabilities—their own and those of others. Do we have the management expertise to acquire a competitor?
Can we launch a new product within six months? People who assess themselves honestly—that is, self-aware people—are well suited to do the same for the organizations they run.

SELF-REGULATION

Biological impulses drive our emotions. We cannot do away with them, but we can do much to manage them. Self-regulation, which is like an ongoing inner conversation, is the component of emotional intelligence that frees us from being prisoners of our feelings. People engaged in such a conversation feel bad moods and emotional impulses just as everyone else does, but they find ways to control them and even to channel them in useful ways.

Imagine an executive who has just watched a team of his employees present a botched analysis to the company's board of directors. In the gloom that follows, the executive might find himself tempted to pound on the table in anger or kick over a chair. He could leap up and scream at the group. Or he might maintain a grim silence, glaring at everyone before stalking off.

But if he had a gift for self-regulation, he would choose a different approach. He would pick his words carefully, acknowledging the team's poor performance without rushing to any hasty judgment. He would then step back to consider the reasons for the

Can Emotional Intelligence Be Learned?

For ages, people have debated if leaders are born or made. So too goes the debate about emotional intelligence. Are people born with certain levels of empathy, for example, or do they acquire empathy as a result of life's experiences? The answer is both. Scientific inquiry strongly suggests that there is a genetic component to emotional intelligence. Psychological and developmental research indicates that nurture plays a role as well. How much of each perhaps will never be known, but research and practice clearly demonstrate that emotional intelligence can be learned.

One thing is certain: emotional intelligence increases with age. There is an old-fashioned word for the phenomenon: maturity. Yet even with maturity, some people still need training to enhance their emotional intelligence. Unfortunately, far too many training programs that intend to build leadership skills—including emotional intelligence—are a waste of time and money. The problem is simple: they focus on the wrong part of the brain.

Emotional intelligence is born largely in the neurotransmitters of the brain's limbic system, which governs feelings, impulses, and drives. Research indicates that the limbic system learns best through motivation, extended practice, and feedback. Compare this with the kind of learning that goes on in the neocortex, which governs analytical and technical ability. The neocortex grasps concepts and logic. It is the part of the brain that figures out how to use a computer or make a sales call by reading a book. Not surprisingly—but mistakenly—it is also the part of the brain targeted by most training programs aimed at enhancing emotional intelligence. When such programs take, in effect, a neocortical approach, my research with the Consortium for Research on Emotional Intelligence in Organizations has shown they can even have a *negative* impact on people's job performance.

To enhance emotional intelligence, organizations must refocus their training to include the limbic system. They must help people break old behavioral habits and establish new ones. That not only takes much more time than conventional training programs, it also requires an individualized approach.

Imagine an executive who is thought to be low on empathy by her colleagues. Part of that deficit shows itself as an inability to listen. She interrupts people and doesn't pay close attention to what they're saying. To fix the problem, the executive needs to be motivated to change and then she needs practice and feedback from others in the company. A colleague or coach could be tapped to let the executive know when she has been observed failing to listen. She would then have to replay the incident and give a better response; that is, demonstrate her ability to absorb what others are saying. And the executive could be directed to observe certain executives who listen well and to mimic their behavior.

With persistence and practice, such a process can lead to lasting results. I know one Wall Street executive who sought to improve his empathy—specifically his ability to read people's reactions and see their perspectives. Before beginning his quest, the executive's subordinates were terrified of working with him. People even went so far as to hide bad news from him. Naturally, he was shocked when finally confronted with these facts. He went home and told his family, but they only confirmed what he had heard at work. When their opinions on any given subject did not mesh with his, they, too, were frightened of him.

Enlisting the help of a coach, the executive went to work to heighten his empathy through practice and feedback. His first step was to take a vacation to a foreign country where he did not speak the language. While there, he monitored his reactions to the unfamiliar and his openness to people who were different from him. When he returned home, humbled by his week abroad, the executive asked his coach to shadow him for parts of the day, several times a week, in order to critique how he treated people with new or different perspectives. At the same time, he consciously used on-the-job interactions as opportunities to practice "hearing" ideas that differed from his. Finally, the executive had himself videotaped in meetings and asked those who worked for and with him to critique his ability to acknowledge and understand the feelings of others. It took several months, but the executive's emotional intelligence did ultimately rise, and the improvement was reflected in his overall performance on the job.

It's important to emphasize that building one's emotional intelligence cannot—will not—happen without sincere desire and concerted effort. A brief seminar won't help; nor can one buy a how-to manual. It is much harder to learn to empathize—to internalize empathy as a natural response to people—than it is to become adept to regression analysis. But it can be done. "Nothing great was ever achieved without enthusiasm," wrote Ralph Waldo Emerson. If your goal is to become a real leader, these words can serve as a guidepost in your efforts to develop high emotional intelligence.

failure. Are they personal—a lack of effort? Are there any mitigating factors? What was his role in the debacle? After considering these questions, he would call the team together, lay out the incident's consequences, and offer his feelings about it. He would then present his analysis of the problem and a well-considered solution.

Why does self-regulation matter so much for leaders? First of all, people who are in control of their feelings and impulses—that is, people who are reasonable—are able to create an environment of trust and fairness. In such an environment, politics and infighting are sharply reduced and productivity is high. Talented people flock to the organization and aren't tempted to leave. And self-regulation has a trickle-down effect. No one wants to be known as a hothead when the boss is known for her calm approach. Fewer bad moods at the top mean fewer throughout the organization.

Second, self-regulation is important for competitive reasons. Everyone knows that business today is rife with ambiguity and change. Companies merge and break apart regularly. Technology transforms work at a dizzying pace. People who have mastered their emotions are able to roll with the changes. When a new change program is announced, they don't panic. Instead, they are able to suspend judgment, seek out information and listen to executives explain the new program. As the initiative moves forward, they are able to move with it.

Sometimes they even lead the way. Consider the case of a manager at a large manufacturing company. Like her colleagues, she had used a certain software program for five years. The program drove how she collected and reported data and how she thought about the company's strategy. One day, senior executives announced that a new program was to be installed that would radically change how information was gathered and assessed within the organization. While many people in the company complained bitterly about how disruptive the change would be, the manager mulled over the reasons for the new program and was convinced of its potential to improve performances. She eagerly attended training sessions—some of her colleagues refused to do so—and was eventually promoted to run several divisions, in part because she used the new technology so effectively.

I want to push the importance of self-regulation to leadership even further and make the case that it enhances integrity, which is not only a personal virtue but also an organizational strength. Many of the bad things that happen in companies are a function of impulsive behavior. People rarely plan to exaggerate profits, pad expense accounts, dip into the till or abuse power for selfish ends. Instead, an opportunity presents itself and people with low impulse control just say yes.

By contrast, consider the behavior of the senior executive at a large food company. The executive was scrupulously honest in his negotiations with local distributors. He would routinely lay out his cost structure in detail, thereby giving the distributors a realistic understanding of the company's pricing. This approach meant the executive couldn't always drive a hard bargain. Now, on occasion, he felt the urge to increase profits by withholding information about the company's costs. But he challenged that impulse. He saw that it made more sense in the long run to counteract it. His emotional self-regulation paid off in strong, lasting relationships with distributors that benefited the company more than any short-term financial gains would have.

The signs of emotional self-regulation, therefore, are not hard to miss: a propensity for reflection and thoughtfulness; comfort with ambiguity and change and integrity—an ability to say no to impulsive urges.

Like self-awareness, self-regulation often does not get its due. People who can master their emotions are sometimes seen as cold fish—their considered responses are taken as a lack of passion. People with fiery temperaments are frequently thought of as "classic" leaders—their outbursts are considered hallmarks of charisma and power. But when such people make it to the top, their impulsiveness often works against them. In my research, extreme displays of negative emotion have never emerged as a driver of good leadership.

MOTIVATION

If there is one trait that virtually all effective leaders have, it is motivation. They are driven to achieve beyond expectations—their own and everyone else's. The key word here is *achieve*. Plenty of people are motivated by external factors such as a big salary or the status that comes from having an impressive title or being part of a prestigious company. By contrast, those with leadership potential are motivated by a deeply embedded desire to achieve for the sake of achievement.

If you are looking for leaders, how can you identify people who are motivated by the drive to achieve rather than by external rewards? The first sign is a passion for the work itself. Such people seek out creative challenges, love to learn and take great pride in a job well done. They also display an unflagging energy to do things better. People with such energy often seem restless with the status quo. They are persistent with their questions about why things are done one way rather than another. They are eager to explore new approaches to their work.

A cosmetics company manager, for example, was frustrated that he had to wait two weeks to get sales results from people in the field. He finally tracked down an automated phone system that would beep each of his salespeople at 5 P.M. every day. An automated message then prompted them to punch in their numbers—how many calls and sales they had made that day. The system shortened the feedback time on sales results from weeks to hours.

That story illustrates two other common traits of people who are driven to achieve. They are forever raising the performance bar and they like to keep score. Take the performance bar first. During performance reviews, people with high levels of motivation might ask to be "stretched" by their superiors. Of course, an employee who combines self-awareness with internal motivation will recognize her limits, but she won't settle for objectives that seem too easy to fulfill.

And it follows naturally that people who are driven to do better also want a way of tracking progress—their own, their team's, and their company's. Whereas people with low achievement motivation are often fuzzy about results, those with high achievement motivation often keep score by tracking such hard measures as profitability or market share. I know of a money manager who starts and ends his day on the Internet, gauging the performance of his stock fund against four industry-set benchmarks.

Interestingly, people with high motivation remain optimistic even when the score is against them. In such cases, self-regulation combines with achievement motivation to overcome the frustration and depression that come after a setback or failure. Take the case of an another portfolio manager at a large investment company. After several successful years, her fund tumbled for three consecutive quarters, leading three large institutional clients to shift their business elsewhere.

Some executives would have blamed the nosedive on circumstances outside their control. Others might have seen the setback as evidence of personal failure. This portfolio manager, however, saw an opportunity to prove she could lead a turn-around. Two years later, when she was promoted to a very senior level in the company, she described the experience as "the best thing that ever happened to me. I learned so much from it."

Executives trying to recognize high levels of achievement motivation in their people can look for one last piece of evidence: commitment to the organization. When people love their job for the work itself, they often feel committed to the organizations that make that work possible. Committed employees are likely to stay with an organization even when they are pursued by headhunters waving money.

It's not difficult to understand how and why a motivation to achieve translates into strong leadership. If you set the performance bar high for yourself, you will do the same for the organization when you are in a position to do so. Likewise, a drive to surpass goals and an interest in keeping score can be contagious. Leaders with these traits can often build a team of managers around them with the same traits. And of course, optimism and organizational commitment are fundamental to leadership—just try to imagine running a company without them.

EMPATHY

The very word empathy seems unbusinesslike, out of place amid the tough realities of the marketplace.

Of all the dimensions of emotional intelligence, empathy is the most easily recognized. We have all felt the empathy of a sensitive teacher or friend; we have all been struck by its absence in an unfeeling coach or boss. But when it comes to business, we rarely hear people praised, let alone rewarded, for their empathy. The very word seems unbusinesslike, out of place amid the tough realities of the marketplace.

But empathy doesn't mean a kind of "I'm okay, you're okay" mushiness. For a leader, that is, it doesn't mean adopting other people's emotions as one's own and trying to please everybody. That would be a nightmare—it would make action impossible. Rather, empathy means thoughtfully considering employees' feelings—along with other factors—in the process of making intelligent decisions.

For an example of empathy in action, consider what happened when two giant brokerage companies merged, creating redundant jobs in all their divisions. One division manager called his people together and gave a gloomy speech that emphasized the number of people who would soon be fired. The manager of another division gave his people a different kind of speech. He was upfront about his own worry and confusion, and he promised to keep people informed and to treat everyone fairly.

The difference between these two managers was empathy. The first manager was too worried about this own fate to consider the feelings of his anxiety-stricken colleagues. The second knew intuitively what his people were feeling, and he acknowledged their fears with his words. Is it any surprise that the first manager saw his division sink as many demoralized people, especially the most talented, departed? By contrast, the second manager continued to be a strong leader, his best people stayed and his division remained as productive as ever.

Empathy is particularly important today as a component of leadership for at least three reasons: the increasing use of teams; the rapid pace of globalization; and the growing need to retain talent.

Consider the challenge of leading a team. As anyone who has ever been a part of one can attest, teams are cauldrons of bubbling emotions. They are often charged with reaching a consensus—hard enough with two people and much more difficult as the numbers increase. Even in groups with as few as four or five members, alliances form and clashing agendas get set. A team's leader must be able to sense and understand the viewpoints of everyone around the table.

That's exactly what a marketing manager at a large information technology company was able to do when she was appointed to lead a troubled team. The group was in turmoil, overloaded by work and missing deadlines. Tensions were high among the members. Tinkering with procedures was not enough to bring the group together and make it an effective part of the company.

So the manager took several steps. In a series of one-on-one sessions, she took the time to listen to everyone in the group—what was frustrating them, how they rated their colleagues, whether they felt they had been ignored. And then she directed the team in a way that brought it together: she encouraged people to speak more openly about their frustrations and she helped people raise constructive complaints during meetings. In short, her empathy allowed her to understand her team's emotional makeup. The result was not just heightened collaboration among members but also added business, as the team was called on for help by a wider range of internal clients.

Globalization is another reason for the rising importance of empathy for business leaders. Cross-cultural dialogue can easily lead to miscues and misunderstandings. Empathy is an antidote. People who have it are attuned to subtleties in body language; they can hear the message beneath the words being spoken. Beyond that, they have a deep understanding of the existence and importance of cultural and ethnic differences.

Consider the case of an American consultant whose team had just pitched a project to a potential Japanese client. In its dealings with Americans, the team was accustomed to being bombarded with questions after such a proposal, but this time it was greeted with a long silence. Other members of the team, taking the silence as disapproval, were ready to pack and leave. The lead consultant gestured them to stop. Although he was not particularly familiar with Japanese culture, he read the client's face and posture and sensed not rejection but interest—even deep consideration. He was right: when the client finally spoke, it was to give the consulting firm the job.

Finally, empathy plays a key role in the retention of talent, particularly in today's information economy. Leaders have always needed empathy to develop and keep good people, but today the stakes are higher. When good people leave, they take the company's knowledge with them.

That's where coaching and mentoring come in. It has repeatedly been shown that coaching and mentoring pay off not just in better performance but also in increased job satisfaction and decreased turnover. But what makes coaching and mentoring work best is the nature of the relationship. Outstanding coaches and mentors get inside the heads of the people they are helping. They sense how to give effective feedback. They know when to push for better performance and when to hold back. In the way they motivate their protégés, they demonstrate empathy in action.

In what is probably sounding like a refrain, let me repeat that empathy doesn't get much respect in business. People wonder how leaders can make hard decisions if they are "feeling" for all the people who will be affected. But leaders with empathy do more than sympathize with people around them: they use their knowledge to improve their companies in subtle but important ways.

SOCIAL SKILL

Social skill is friendliness with a purpose: moving people in the direction you desire.

The first three components of emotional intelligence are all self-management skills. The last two, empathy and social skill, concern a person's ability to manage relationships with others. As a component of emotional intelligence, social skill is not as simple as it sounds. It's not just a matter of friendliness, although people with high levels of social skill are rarely mean-spirited. Social skill, rather, is friendliness with a purpose: moving people in the direction you desire, whether that's agreement on a new marketing strategy or enthusiasm about a new product.

Socially skilled people tend to have a wide circle of acquaintances, and they have a knack for finding common ground with people of all kinds—a knack for building rapport. That doesn't mean they socialize continually; it means they work according to the assumption that nothing important gets done alone. Such people have a network in place when the time for action comes.

Social skill is the culmination of the other dimensions of emotional intelligence. People tend to be very effective at managing relationships when they can understand and control their own emotions and can empathize with the feelings of others. Even motivation contributes to social skill. Remember that people who are driven to achieve tend to be optimistic, even in the face of setbacks or failure. When people are upbeat, their "glow" is cast upon conversations and other social encounters. They are popular, and for good reason.

Because it is the outcome of the other dimensions of emotional intelligence, social skill is recognizable on the job in many ways that will by now sound familiar. Socially skilled people, for instance, are adept at managing teams—that's their empathy at work. Likewise, they are expert persuaders—a manifestation of self-awareness, self-regulation, and empathy combined. Given those skills, good persuaders know when to make an emotional plea, for instance, and when an appeal to reason will work better. And motivation, when publicly visible, makes such people excellent collaborators; their passion for the work spreads to others, and they are driven to find solutions.

But sometimes social skill shows itself in ways the other emotional intelligence components do not. For instance, socially skilled people may at times appear not to be working while at work. They seem to be idly schmoozing—chatting in the hallways with colleagues or joking around with people who are not even connected to their "real" jobs. Socially skilled people, however, don't think it makes sense to arbitrarily limit the scope of their relationships. They build bonds widely because they know that in these fluid times, they many need help someday from people they are just getting to know today.

For example, consider the case of an executive in the strategy department of a global computer manufacturer. By 1993, he was convinced that the company's future lay with the Internet. Over the course of the next year, he found kindred spirits and used his social skill to stitch together a virtual community that cut across levels, divisions, and nations. He then used this de facto team to put up a corporate Web site, among the first by a major company. And, on his own initiative, with no budget or formal status, he signed up the company to participate in an annual Internet industry convention. Calling on his allies and persuading various divisions to donate funds, he recruited more than 50 people from a dozen different units to represent the company at the convention.

Management took notice: within a year of the conference, the executive's team formed the basis for the company's first Internet division, and he was formally put in charge of it. To get there, the executive had ignored conventional boundaries, forging and maintaining connections with people in every corner of the organization.

Is social skill considered a key leadership capability in most companies? The answer is yes, especially when compared with the other components of emotional intelligence. People seem to know intuitively that leaders need to manage relationships effectively; no leader is an island. After all, the leader's task is to get work done through other people, and social skill makes that possible. A leader who cannot express her empathy may as well not have it at all. And a leader's motivation will be useless if he cannot communicate his passion to the organization. Social skill allows leaders to put their emotional intelligence to work.

It would be foolish to assert that good-old-fashioned IQ and technical ability are not important ingredients in strong leadership. But the recipe would not be complete without emotional intelligence. It was once thought that the components of emotional intelligence were "nice to have" in business leaders. But now we know that, for the sake of performance, these are ingredients that leaders "need to have."

It is fortunate, then, that emotional intelligence can be learned. The process is not easy. It takes time and, most of all, commitment. But the benefits that come from having a well-developed emotional intelligence, both for the individual and for the organization, make it worth the effort.

Daniel Goleman is the author of Emotional Intelligence *(Bantam, 1995) and* Working with Emotional Intelligence *(Bantam, 1998). He is cochairman of the Consortium for Research on Emotional Intelligence in Organizations, which is based at Rutgers University's Graduate School of Applied and Professional Psychology in Piscataway, New Jersey. He can be reached at Goleman@javanet.com.*

SCHOOLS OF POSSIBILITY: BECOMING A RELATIONSHIP-CENTERED LEARNING COMMUNITY

Sue Keister

If we take time to reflect together on who we are and who we could choose to become, we will be led into the territory where change originates. We will be led to explore our agreements of belonging, the principles and values we display in our behaviors, the purposes that have called us together, the worlds we created.

—Margaret Wheatley and Myron Kellnor-Rogers, *A Simpler Way*[1]

In my work with schools as both a teacher and a developer of social and emotional learning programs and training over the past 25 years, I have noticed that in times of intense change, there is a habitual impulse for schools to sprint into action before reflecting deeply upon who they are, what they collectively value and believe, where they want to go together and how they want to get there. I believe that the quality of education that we truly seek, the quality that calls forth and reveals the potential of all participants in our schools, does not depend upon "doing" something differently so much as "being" different with one another. What does that mean for leadership in times of change?

Research and experiences over the years convince me that a school's potential for thriving in times of change is revealed when we choose to be a learning community of reciprocal relationships. A *learning community* is a unified group of individuals who share a common purpose and construct knowledge together, calling forth the creativity and resources each individual brings to the group as well as the resources from families, communities, school disciplines, and the world around us. *Reciprocal relationships* are those mutual relationships with people, nature, things, and ideas that create growth and genuine transformation by valuing, revealing, and supporting the unique qualities and potential of all participants. A *learning community of reciprocal relationships* is a group of individuals who share a common purpose and a set of values and beliefs about teaching and learning within a culture of reciprocity. Within this culture, all members participate and learn with and from each other, recognizing that everyone has something of great value to contribute to the whole. Reciprocal relationships allow a learning community to discover together what they want their school to be.

For years, I have pondered several questions about the potential of relationship-centered learning communities characterized by reciprocity: When is school a learning community of reciprocal relationships in pursuit of every participant's potential? What are the essential elements? Does a relationship-centered learning community have the potential to liberate the collective intelligence and imagination of its members? If so, how?

THE RELATIONSHIP—CENTERED LEARNING COMMUNITY

These questions led me to wonder about *relationship-centered leadership.* Who is the relationship-centered leader and what are his/her qualities and characteristics? We often think of leadership in terms of the qualities, roles, and responsibilities of an individual who will lead the way, keep us safe, take the risks and accept the responsibility when things go awry. A relationship-centered perspective views leadership as a reciprocal process that cultivates genuine mutual respect and shared responsibility and accountability among all participants for the collective success of the common vision. Within this definition, all participants become leaders and stewards of the shared vision and core values of the learning community. How can this be accomplished?

This line of inquiry led me to a three-year school transformation process called *In Pursuit of Possibilities* that was supported by a Fetzer Institute Fellowship grant, Quest International, and the Surdna Foundation and included a fieldguide for school communities.[2] Salt Lake City Public Schools adopted it as part of the district's Eccles-Annenberg initiative and brought together seven-member, multi-site teams of administrators, educators, and community members from each of the five middle schools over a period of two years to engage in ongoing dialogues about what it means to become a relationship-centered learning community that advocates for its students. We undertook a similar process as a school-wide initiative at Glendale Middle School in Salt Lake City, Utah; Worthingway Middle School in Worthington, Ohio; and Summit Elementary School in Summit Station, Ohio, where young people were also included in the process. Through ongoing dialogue, district-wide and school-wide teams addressed and reflected upon four essential elements that characterize the process of becoming a relationship-centered learning community:

- *Developing a <u>Shared Purpose</u>: What is the overarching intention of our learning community's work?*
- *Creating <u>Guiding Principles</u>: What are our shared beliefs and values about young people, teaching, and learning?*
- *Designing <u>Supporting Structures</u>: What are the resources and internal structures needed to support both the creation of guiding principles and the practice that honors them?*
- *Engaging in <u>Dynamic Practice</u>: What is the ever-emerging work of the school that brings the purpose and principles to life in the classroom and school?*

In the case of the Salt Lake City School District, the original impetus for this work grew out of the research conducted by a Middle Level Task Force (MLTF) about how to best address the emerging needs of a rapidly changing and diverse student population of middle level students during their transition years. In this research, the task force discovered some troubling trends: 1) declining academic scores; 2) increasing levels of truancy and misconduct; 3) negative perceptions of school climate reported by students, parents, and teachers; and 4) serious gaps in meeting the unique needs of a changing and increasingly diverse student population between ages 10–15.

The task force used these trends to develop a set of recommendations that helped shape the Middle Level Initiative within Salt Lake City's district-wide school improvement plan. The mission statement for the Salt Lake City Schools' middle level initiative was "to create the best possible learning environment for the middle level students in Salt Lake City Schools." With the five Middle Level Site Teams and Glendale Middle School, we set out to establish a relationship-centered learning community and develop a vital student advocacy initiative. The three-year project allowed us to collectively discover and explore key elements and outcomes of relationship-centered learning communities and relationship-centered leadership. Similar stories accompany the participation of the two Ohio schools. The results were truly transformational for the school community as a whole, as well as the administrators, teachers, students and community members.

THE JOURNEY OF BECOMING A RELATIONSHIP-CENTERED LEARNING COMMUNITY

We met as multi-site teams and as the full staff of Glendale Middle School, Worthingway Middle School and Summit Elementary School approximately six times per year for three years of their participation in the process. We started both the district-wide and school-wide processes with an annual retreat that opened with the "big questions," i.e.; *Why do we need community? What is a learning community and why is it important? How do we build genuine trust, respect, and a sense of bonding? How do we engage and unleash the collective intelligence and imagination of the entire community? What will sustain us?*

During the retreat, we explored the image of the educator with questions such as; *What brings me to my current work? What parts of myself do I offer to my students? Where do I find identity and integrity as a teacher? How are my values and beliefs reflected in my work?* From there we explored schools as living systems to better understand their organic and self-organizing nature that thrive on the participation, shared vision, caring, authentic communication, and contribution of every member. We then worked on the practices that nourish our inner values and beliefs and help us align them with our outer lives of service and action. These practices cultivated self-awareness, shared agreements, genuine dialogue, and deep reflection and inquiry regarding our assumptions about young people, teaching, and learning. After the opening retreats, we were ready to begin our work of creating guiding principles, designing supporting structures, and engaging in the teaching and learning practices that would honor the principles in the daily life of the school community.

For both the district teams and schools participating in the process, we documented the process from the perspective of an *outer journey* (ways the school community collaborated and reflected together) and an *inner journey* (ways each participant reflected on the personal meaning of the process). The outer journey consisted of staff and small group dialogues about the four elements of vision, principles, structures, and practices; individual and group projects around dynamic teaching and learning practices that honor the vision and principles; and the development of project portfolios. The inner journey involved ongoing dialogues onsite in which participants reflected on questions such as, *How do I live my core beliefs and values? How do I contribute? How do I support others? What am I learning about myself? What surprises me, challenges me, opens me, and nourishes me?* Together, we gathered over 100 hours of dialogue and interview transcripts and videos that reveal what administrators and teachers discovered as they looked within themselves; uncovered their assumptions about young adolescents, teaching and learning; created more trusting relationships; and grew into a genuine learning community. What follows are the key tenets for leading and implementing successful district-wide and school-wide transformation that the seven school leadership teams and I discovered and experienced together during our *In Pursuit of Possibilities* journey.

KEY TENETS FOR LEADING SCHOOL TRANSFORMATION THROUGH RELATIONSHIP-CENTERED LEADERSHIP

First and foremost, *the school district needs to place an emphasis on creating relationship-centered learning communities as part of the district mission and plan.* The ideal scenario is a district-wide commitment to developing relationship-centered learning communities as part of the district's overall mission and plan. Middle Level Coordinator Kathleen Christy and I co-developed and facilitated that process among all the middle schools in the Salt Lake City School District between 1999–2001. We were able to integrate the process into the school district's Eccles-Annenberg Plan for improving literacy and student advocacy among middle level students.

> **The educational leaders create their own learning community.** District leaders and principals need a learning community of their own in which to discuss, debate, and reflect upon the ideas and possibilities for change that are emerging at their sites.

In Salt Lake City, we created Middle Level Site Teams from each of the five middle schools who created their own community in addition to their school communities. Kathleen Christy remarked, *"The vision of our Middle Level Initiative is to create the best possible learning environment for young adolescents. Our monthly cluster team dialogues really breathed life into the middle level philosophy for everyone. I understood it intellectually, but the dialogues around mission, guiding principles, what they look like in action, and the sharing from staff helped me understand what it really means to be an advocate for young adolescents."*

Rosemary Baron, Principal of Northwest Middle School in Salt Lake City commented, *"We're proud of the fact that we took the time to dialogue as middle school teams to focus on what we are about—a rare luxury in public schools. It had such a unifying effect and opened the door for conversations among the principals and between school faculties that wouldn't have happened if we had stayed in our buildings. We got so many new ideas, and we have been enriched immeasurably."*

Cherrie Brinlee, Principal of Clayton Middle School in Salt Lake City stated, *"I loved working together with other schools on our district-wide Literacy and Student Advocacy plans. I enjoyed sharing our structures and practices—Clayton's Student Advocacy questionnaire, Glendale's school-wide reading and advocacy program, Bryant's principal signing every student's report card, Hillside's student-driven character education curriculum, Northwest's supportive team structure. . . . Learning together was an exhilarating experience."*

> **The principal believes that a relationship-centered learning community creates the optimal learning environment and engages the school community in an exploration of its possibilities.** The key to the success of the process is the principal's belief in the educational value of a relationship-centered learning community and the ability to convey that vision to the staff. That vision is rooted in an understanding that relationships are essential to optimize student learning, teacher satisfaction, and positive community engagement.

Principal Larry Peterson of Glendale Middle School in Salt Lake City led his school to a remarkable turnaround in two years by "relentlessly" engaging his entire staff in a two-year process of personal and collective reflection and action regarding the school's mission, beliefs, organizational structure, and teaching and learning practices to meet the needs of a diverse and highly challenged student population and community. In that time frame, the school went from 50 percent staff turnover, the lowest academic scores in the district, no business partners, and a declining enrollment to 100 percent staff retention, an innovative and integrated literacy and student advocacy curriculum, significant increases in reading and math scores, team instruction, 20 business partners, and engaged staff, students, and community. As a result, Larry Peterson went on to become the sole winner of the coveted 2001 Huntsman Award for leadership excellence in secondary education for the state of Utah.

> **The principal embodies a relationship-centered leadership style in which all members of the school community have leadership responsibilities in developing guiding principles, support structures, and teaching and learning practices.** A relationship-centered leader guides administrators, teachers, community members, and students in creating a shared vision and taking actions that support the guiding principles. Leadership actions are motivated by a deep commitment to serve others and to be accountable to something larger than ourselves without the need to control or demand compliance from others.

Principal Jim Wightman of Worthingway Middle School in Worthington, Ohio remarked, "*In Pursuit of Possibilities gave us a structure to enter into real meaningful dialogue about what our purpose is and what we believe 100 percent about education. Discussion at this level had never taken place before. We also interviewed all staff and students about what it meant to go to school here. We discovered that relationships and academic excellence are our major commitments. When we faced financial difficulties, our purpose and principles gave us tools to say, "This is what we are committed to; this is what we will and will not do.*"

Clearly, the relationship-centered leader embodies a participatory, collaborative, and democratic leadership style and establishes a shared leadership infrastructure characterized by reciprocal relationships and imbued with trust and respect. In successful schools where the relationship-centered learning community takes root, staff, parents, community members, and students engage in ongoing dialogue and conversation about the kind of school they want to create together. In successful schools, staff, parents, community members, and students participate in this process through both large and small group conversation circles, written communications, questionnaires, participatory conferences, telephone calls, and other creative means.

> **The school community brings its vision and guiding principles to life by giving all members a meaningful role in their enactment.** In the schools where this process is successful, there is a deep respect for the contributions of everyone in the school community and a genuine desire to learn from everyone in the learning community—students, families, community members, elders, support staff, and so on. Dialogue is the essential skill in this process and must be taught and practiced among all members of the school community participating in the process.

Principal Jim Wightman engaged his entire staff, all students, and parents and community members in an "Appreciative Inquiry" process of mutual interviewing. All the teachers interviewed each other on a series of questions about the purpose of the school, their beliefs about teaching and learning, their hopes and aspirations for their students, their personal satisfaction, and their ideas for making the school an ideal learning environment for their students. Students were made aware of the process and interviewed each other as a school-wide class lesson about the same questions from a student perspective. Parents were sent a questionnaire to return and teachers randomly called parents for a telephone interview. Parents were also invited to a dialogue at the school to help revise and refine the purpose statement and vision statement. The results were synthesized and circulated for all participants to review. Then the conversations began about shaping the purpose statement and guiding principles. When they were articulated to everyone's satisfaction, the art department put them on creatively designed posters to be displayed throughout the school. Everyone felt ownership of the process and proud of the collective effort.

> **The relationship-centered learning community provokes and evokes a living ecology of student-centered teaching and learning.** As this process unfolds, students and adults become partners in learning in a self-organizing way. Because everyone feels seen, heard, known, and valued, the collective intelligence and imagination of the entire learning community is revealed, and people come forward from every sector with creative ideas and solutions.

Principal Jane Larson of Hillside Middle School in Salt Lake City tells about a curriculum that emerged at her school and became a district model for character education. She shared, "*We met as a school staff to discuss how to hear the voice of every student and discover how each one feels about Hillside. We created a safe space within classrooms for dialogue between students and teachers. To hear students articulate their thoughts was astounding. We tallied the top five responses in each classroom and, in the students' own writing, posted them in the hallways. We created together a curriculum that would address the students' concerns. It was a school-wide effort that focused every person at Hillside on the needs of our students. We are all student advocates now.*"

> **A relationship-centered learning community is sustained when the staff is engaged in collective leadership of the process of dialogue and reflection about vision, principles, and practices.**

Kathy Erhard, Principal of Summit Elementary School in Ohio, reflected, "*It's meaningless to have belief statements posted on the wall. They must be the center of ongoing dialogue and integral to the day-to-day life of the school. At Summit, we demonstrated them in our daily practice, illustrated them, journalled about them, made them topics of staff meetings and expressed them through every aspect of our learning community. We lived our beliefs. We became a family, our students loved school, test scores improved in all areas, and the community became much more involved. The effort transformed out school.*"

AWAKENING COLLECTIVE INTELLIGENCE AND IMAGINATION IN LEARNING COMMUNITIES

After three years of participating and reflecting on these central questions, I am now convinced that a powerful "field" of collective intelligence and imagination emerges when schools become learning communities of reciprocal relationships that gather together for ongoing conversation and reflection about their common vision, their shared guiding principles, the supporting structures, and the daily teaching and learning practices. With shared agreements governing the way they treat one another, all participants feel safe and valued to speak their truth to the learning community. Trust emerges, bringing out the best in every participant and inviting a heightened level of participation and commitment. When people feel safe and valued, they develop a state of relaxed alertness that optimizes learning and participation. This creates a unified and fertile ground upon which a leader can inspire, facilitate, manage, and sustain the creative and deep engagement of the entire learning community in the change process.

Such a process requires *relationship-centered leadership*—a reciprocal process in which all participants take on leadership responsibilities as they strive toward a shared vision with a deep commitment to service rather than self-interest. Relationship-centered leadership becomes stewardship motivated by the deep desire to invite, reveal, ignite, and cultivate the potential of young people and the adults who support them. Over time, schools become "communities of truth," so engaged and invested with each other and their common purpose that nothing the world throws at them can break their bonds of community or distract them from their commitment—to create a learning environment that is bursting with the passion, creativity, leadership, and cohesive vision of all its members. The conscious and intentional cultivation of the whole human being within a relationship-centered learning community can then expand from our schools into our culture, institutions, society and global community, fostering recognition that we are all one relationship-centered and interdependent human family.

Susan Carroll Keister is President of Integral Vision Consulting and an educational consultant specializing in school transformation, international curriculum and training development, and group facilitation. Ms. Keister has over 20 years of experience as an author, speaker, trainer and executive in positive youth development, including her role as Vice President for Program Development at Quest International, an educational not-for-profit dedicated to providing high quality programs and training to adults and young people in social and emotional learning, positive prevention, character education, and service-learning. Susan lead the development of the acclaimed K–12 Lions-Quest programs and is currently developing, training, and supporting positive youth development efforts for Lions-Quest International and others educational organizations throughout the world. She has collaborated with leaders from over 14 countries, advises several major educational organizations, and is a Fellow of the Fetzer Institute in Kalamazoo, Michigan, which helped fund the In Pursuit of Possibilities pilot initiative in schools throughout the U.S.

NOTES

1. Wheatley, Margaret., and Myron Kellnor-Rogers, *A Simpler Way*. San Francisco: Berrett-Koehler Publishers, 1996, p. 100.
2. Graves, Judy, and Susan Keister, *In Pursuit of Possibilities*. Newark, Ohio: Quest International, 1999
   [All quotations in this article are taken from this book].

MOVING FROM COLLABORATIVE DECISION MAKING TO COMMUNITY

Kimberly Kinsler

Collaborative or shared decision-making is often proposed as a way to improve our nation's public schools. School teams are given responsibility for many planning and decision-making tasks formerly held by school principals and district superintendents. A key component in many successful improvement programs (e.g. James Comer's School Development Program; Henry Levin's Accelerated School Program), such teams are increasingly mandated by states attempting to improve student performance. However, research is finding that the mere existence of these teams may do little to achieve these ends. Often missing are two essential ingredients, emotional commitment and a sense of true community, neither of which can be legislated or mandated into being. To help improve the functioning of shared decision-making teams (SDMT), this reading will provide a context for understanding the institution of these teams, note common obstacles that often hamper their successful functioning, and offer advice to principals interested in empowering them.

SITE-BASED MANAGEMENT AND SHARED DECISION MAKING

The concept of site-based management teams (SBMT) is not new. In the 1960s and 1970s, some states adopted *decentralization* and *school-site budgeting* as ways to give parents and local communities the political power to offset state authority or administrative inefficiency (David, 1989). In the 1990s, the calls for SBMTs began again. Prestigious commissions and groups (e.g., the Carnegie Commission on Teaching as a Profession (1986) and the National Governors' Association (1986)) supported these changes. Based on organizational and cultural features of effective schools (Edmonds, 1976), public education systems were encouraged to shift responsibility for primary critical decision-making and problem solving activities to their local schools. These second wave reforms sought, through restructuring, to "flatten" administrative hierarchy to give teachers and parents a greater voice (Smith & Purkey, 1985; David, 1989:46).

Many states embraced this reasoning and hastily mandated the creation of local SBMTs and SDMTs. With the former, groups are given aegis over critical bureaucratic matters such as budgeting, hiring and curriculum. Through these committees, schools gain greater autonomy over these matters in exchange for assuming responsibility for results (Garms, et al, 1978; Cohen, 1988). SDMTs, on the other hand, are groups of local individuals whose member's function collaboratively to fact find, problem solve and advise management teams.

Research found a large disparity between the potential versus the actuality of this reform. Ideally, SBM/SDMTs have the potential to tailor aid to the unique characteristics and needs of schools. These efforts can also expand the management capacity and instructional decision-making skill of local stakeholders. However, in practice, SBM/SDMTs were often unable to win the inspired and committed involvement of local stakeholders. They frequently encountered obstacles, both large and small, that compromised both their operation and success. The most prominent of these challenges were the lack of power given to these teams by states and local administrators, the unwillingness of stakeholders to participate, and the validity of the organizational model used in the process.

FACTORS MITIGATING SBM/SDMT SUCCESS

Power and Authority.   Matters of power are often far more complex than they seem, and the empowerment of SBM/SDMTs is no exception. States, local educational agencies (LEAs) and local schools vary greatly in the amount of responsibility and purview given to these teams. Ideally, LEAs should cede to SBMTs control over their local school budget, curriculum, and personnel decisions. According to David (1989), SBMTs or school councils should receive either a lump-sum budget or some portion of their budget for equipment, materials, supplies, and sometimes staff development. However, their actual authority over these areas is affected by a number of factors including the amount of money SBMTs receive (teams may only be given aegis over discretionary funds, with staffing, building repairs and textbooks removed) and the degree to which they are freed from spending restrictions. Similarly teams' influence over curriculum may be severely affected by the extent these functions are centralized at state and district levels, e.g., where SEAs and LEAs prescribe required textbooks, curricula (via standards and curriculum frameworks) and standardized testing. Their power over staffing can likewise be restricted to the use of limited "residual dollars" or acting in an advisory capacity (David, 1989).

At the school level, the most significant factor determining a team's real power is the principal and how much she cedes power to and validates the team's activities. Principals vary widely in the amount and types of responsibilities they give teams. Currently, high stakes testing makes principals even more reluctant to relinquish control. Many principals feel threatened by the progressively negative consequences to administrative personnel for poor school performance (see Kinsler & Gamble, 2000). Doubtful of their teams' effectiveness, they may create teams in name only. They may micromanage their operations and decisions. Teams may be given aegis over only the most insignificant tasks. They may even be asked to rubber-stamp plans previously made by the administration. When superintendents and principals fail to share authority, SBMTs have no real power. More importantly, such actions send strong messages to the school community about the degree to which participatory governance and other reforms are welcome.

Teacher Willingness to Participate.   Teachers' willingness to participate greatly varies. Despite the potential of SBM/SDMTs to *break down* the walls of teacher isolationism, facilitate the sharing of ideas and problem solving efforts, and grant teachers a say in determining school policies and practices, many teachers are reluctant to become team members. A teacher's willingness is heavily influenced by a number of factors. These include the additional workload; the types of tasks and responsibilities asked of participants; teachers previous experience with school innovation; their life stage in the profession; and administrator facilitation.

In light of what Lortie (1975) calls the "presentism" of their already full and hectic day, some teachers may not want to, or feel able, to add team responsibilities to their workloads. Moreover, even where teachers have committed themselves to these collaborative teams, after several years of active participation, they can become "burned out" by the additional demands. One teacher who worked at a school where I was the consultant complained that he was just "meetinged out."

Weighed against these heavy costs are the relevance and impact of team activities. Teachers are most willing to participate in teams when they can make a difference and the decisions made are relevant to their work in the classroom or as professionals (Smylie, 1992:55). Teachers, thus, tend to be more willing to participate on SBM/SDMTs that focus on instructional matters, such as curriculum development, text and related materials selection, and staff development. Conversely, they are reluctant to participate on committees that deal with administrative and managerial decisions (Conley, 1991;

Smylie, 1992:60). Miller (1995) found that many teachers voiced reluctance when asked to devise curriculum or other plans for their schools. He found that many teachers anticipated that their laboriously wrought plans would not be supported and may have even be overturned at the principal or district level.

Veteran teachers may be particularly hesitant to participate. Having lived through a long series of previously failed school innovation efforts, they tend to be more skeptical than novice teachers about their systems' ability to change and more doubtful about student outcomes. Moreover, they have acquired a battery of instructional and interpersonal strategies with proven survival value which they may not want to abandon for new and often unproven ones (House, 1998).

Interestingly, veteran teachers who were former school activists and in the vanguard of earlier innovation efforts were found to be particularly reluctant to participate. Having experienced a series of educational start-ups, implementations and abandonments, they may be cynical about school reform. According to Huberman (1988), such teachers may enter later career stages with attitudes characterized by either "defensive focusing" or "disenchantment." In schools with a large percentage of such teachers, the creation of successful SBM/SDMs is impeded.

The Challenge of Traditional School Culture.   The school's traditional culture is third obstacle to change. Characteristically, an organization's culture serves to perpetuate the status quo. Consider for a moment that most individuals educated in North American public schools have surprisingly similar images of what good and "proper" schooling looks like. One common image is a hierarchical structure. Administrators' lead, teachers' teach and are led. According to Servioganni (1994: xix), learning together makes sense to us, but leading together defies many of the norms of leadership we have been taught and have come to accept. This view is as true for school administrators as it is for teachers and parents. Thus, acting in contrary ways can engender doubt, hesitancy and reluctance. Malen and Agawa (1988) found that teacher willingness to participate in SBM/SDMTs is negatively influenced by their reluctance to challenge traditional patterns of principal authority. Johnson (1990) similarly argues that teachers may be unwilling to violate implicitly negotiated treaties between teachers and principals that acknowledge and enforce each other's authority and autonomy (in Smylie, 1992:55). Teachers, therefore, look for cues from administrators to determine their willingness to support collaborative efforts. When these signals are not forthcoming, due to a mutual reluctance to violate traditional mores, teachers and parents will tend not to challenge the status quo.

Teachers' culture may also exert a negative force on SBM/SDMT efforts. Research has revealed many unspoken norms that define and govern teachers' working relationships with other teachers. One norm is that individual teachers should not stand out or receive differential status that challenges the notion of professional equality (see Kinsler & Gamble, 2000:264). While creating a SBM/SDMT, the process may further balkanize the school by isolating, ignoring and further alienating those faculty not willing to embrace the effort. According to Elkind (1995:17), this dynamic creates social and emotional barriers between involved and uninvolved teacher groups that virtually guarantee that the former will not grow in number. In addition, these teams are commonly asked to evaluate the effects of curricular and instructional programs and these efforts to judge other teachers' knowledge and practice can be perceived as violating norms of teacher autonomy and privacy (Smylie, 1992:56). Teachers resist responsibilities that require them to tell other teachers what they should do in their classrooms (Miller, 1995:3)

Mandated Affect.   Negative emotions are often a by-product of personal change. Change can shake one's confidence and can make individuals doubt their abilities, especially their ability to adapt to new requirements (Evans: 1996:32). People are likely to fear and resist these new behaviors and beliefs and to cling more tenaciously to old familiar patterns. Even under the best of circumstances, change challenges people's sense of competence, frustrates their wish to feel effective and valuable, and causes conflict and confusion (Evans, 1996). This is particularly true in the current atmosphere of high stakes accountability. Very intense pressure is being exerted on school staffs to change long-established practices and beliefs under threat of increasingly punitive consequences. This pressure creates the very conditions most likely to elicit negative emotions.

Curiously, the literature of school reform is relatively silent on the issue of negative affect and the emotions that commonly accompany change. Where affect is addressed, the feelings, emotions and dispositions most likely discussed are the "safer" ones needed in the effort, e.g., supportiveness, trust, and collegiality. Characteristically omitted are discussions of the more volatile emotions that naturally accompany change. So rare are discussions of these more intense emotions that Hargreaves (1997:14) posits a "fear of the furies" in the school reform literature. This omission not only invalidates the legitimacy of these emotions, but also downplays both their significance and prevalence, thereby handicapping implementers' ability to anticipate, accept, engage and address this very real challenge.

The reason for this omission is simple. Negative affect is inconsistent with a traditional rational-structural approach to organizational change. This approach assumes that mandating changes in institutional structures and shifting responsibility for critical decision-making will get poorly performing schools to duplicate the structures and functions of effective schools. This model asserts that logic and leverage (i.e., explanations, mandates, and ultimately the threat of punitive consequences) will get people in schools to relinquish old practices for new ones. However, commitment and dedication are aspects of the change process that cannot be legislated or mandated (Fullan, 1997:35).

According to Hargreaves (1994:80), the likely result of these mandated changes is "contrived collegiality," i.e., groups formed by external administrative dictates and forced to engage in activities devoid of spirit, commitment and inspiration. To the extent that schools are primarily institutions for socialization, second only to the family, the nature of the ties that bond individuals need consideration. Schools appear to be less influenced by objective logic and mechanistic procedures for leveraging change than business organizations. For cultural change to occur in schools, an analogical model may be needed that addresses the affective side of the change process.

SCHOOL AS ORGANIZATIONAL COMMUNITIES

A more appropriate model may be the analogy of school as community. A community is a collection of individuals bound together by natural will and who are together bound to a set of shared ideas and ideals (Sergiovanni, 1994:xvi). The quality of the relationships between individuals is particular, characterized by the kinds of personalized, authentic, caring and unconditionally accepting emotions found in families, extended families, neighborhoods and other social organizations. Change within communities, of necessity, brings to the fore consideration for the quality of relationships that exist between individuals—the very issues and dynamics characteristically omitted in traditional school change efforts.

Another critical characteristic of communities is the expectation and acceptance of a degree of chaos, i.e., spontaneity, unpredictability and destabilization. American schools exist and operate destabilized not only by recent mandates for structural and cultural change, but also by changing social, demographic, and economic forces. As change invariably elicits many deep emotions, both positive and negative, school staffs' reactions to these destabilizing forces will have a strong emotional component. Despite its unavoidable presence in everyone's lives, most of us dislike and tend to resist change in practice. This resistance often results in reactions that are unpredictable, irrational, inconsistent and unresponsive to mandates and traditional managerial mechanisms for leveraging change in organizations. For change efforts to succeed, particularly those focused on culture-based reform, change agents must come to understand and embrace feelings as essential elements in the transformation process. Continued emphasize on the linear, rational, and formal structures of schools will doom many, if not most, change efforts to failure.

How individuals cope with change depends as much on how it is presented, as on the nature of the change and the type of organization undergoing change. Perceptions and feelings can rarely be altered by rational explanations alone. While people must discover their own meaning in change before they can accept it, the development of meaning can often be facilitated in a context of specific relationships (with parents, friends, teachers or other significant beings) and circumstances (Evans, 1996).

MOVING FROM SHARED DECISION MAKING TO COMMUNITY

How then should schools move from the mere form of shared decision making to create the substance of true community? First, there are no recipes and each school community must find their own path for this transition process (Sergiovanni, 1994). Crucial to the successful implementation of this innovation is the ability of school administrators to help staff and parents care about their subjective reality and achieve a more productive understanding and interpretation of the change effort.

A critical step in this transformation is by "disconfirming" stakeholders' readings of the situation and their satisfaction with current practices. This does not mean castigating and blaming people, but challenging them to face realities they have avoided. Simultaneously needed is a reduction in the anxiety surrounding the change—the fear of trying. Needed to reduce this fear of trying is clear evidence of the caring and support of change agents. As change agents work with the implementers of change to take the difficult steps toward new learning, they build relationships in schools. Their efforts will determine if implementers make meaning of, and learn to accept and embrace innovations (Evans, 1996).

The Role of the Principal.   The principal is probably the most pivotal individual in this change process. It is the principal's responsibility to make clear that the meaning of school and cultural reform for teachers and parents takes precedence over roles and new structures. It is essential, therefore, for principals to understand how all stakeholders understand the change effort, how it affects interaction patterns and beliefs, and how best to fit these understandings and the change effort into the community's sense of the world (Evans, 1996:17). A necessary part of this effort is acknowledging the reality of change by publicly voicing the feelings of loss, risk, and anxiety, and what the change means for the entire community. Coming to grips with these feelings is crucial to motivation, for few will accept the loss and discontinuities of change unless these feeling can be understood, accepted, and contextualized. The signals principals give will determine the seriousness with which staff will regard the innovation.

For most innovations to flourish staff must adopt them actively, becoming vigorous, engaged participants. Thus, principals' second task is to help the implementers of change move from loss to commitment, from a letting go of the old to a true acceptance of their new functions and roles (Evans, 1996:58). This transition period may be full of distress and ambivalence as people try to grasp the full extent of what is being lost and gained, and try to modify their pattern of meaning to incorporate the new (Evans, 1996:60). Helping teachers and parents better manage the fear of the unknown is the healthiest thing administrators can do (Fullan, 1996:226)

The impulse for rejection is natural at this phase. But conflict at this point does not automatically signify that something is wrong or to be avoided. As conflict is both natural and inevitable, it is ill advised for principals to work only with like-minded individuals. The innovation stands more of a chance of success if differences are confronted early in the process. It is best to work through the discomfort of diversity caused by the reform rather than to attempt to keep it in sealed-off communities (Fullan; 1996:230). All staff and parents must be assured that they are valued and that the principal will help them get the school where it needs to go while preserving their psychological safety. The principal straddles a fault line between pressure and support, change and continuity—confirming her commitment to the people who must accomplish change. (Evans, 1996). In turn, their commitment will have as its base a sympathetic principal who acknowledges their distress while confirming the promise of change.

Ultimately, commitment must be translated into the day-to-day work of SBM/SDMTs in the years ahead. This is a long and arduous process, and helping staff in this effort will require sustained, regular support and contact by the principal. Fellowship building (i.e. the active, engaged, self-managing commitment to change among those who must implement it) should be an essential feature of this phase. Change implementers need to know what will be expected of them and what they can expect from others. They need continuous opportunities to reflect upon, discuss, argue about, and work through changes in their assumptions (Evans; 1996: 65-67). Principals should acknowledge and reward good faith efforts, and help teams understand temporary setbacks. Personal contact, focused on task performance and emotional adjustment rather than just one or the other, will help sustain staff. Principals must also continue to make clear their caring and their commitment to working with people as they take the difficult steps necessary to transform their school. By setting high expectations, constant caring, and support of the sort found in communities, principals can help SBM/SDMTs acquire the skills and confidence needed for the present reforms.

In summary, principals are critical to their schools becoming communities. Unless they make serious efforts to move their schools from traditional, current benefits of shared decision-making will not be achieved. Ultimately, this effort will require what Goleman (1995) calls "emotional intelligence". As there is no thought without emotion and no emotion without thought, principals must develop and use their understanding of this relationship to add the missing ingredient to their schools. If they fail in these efforts, they risk the maintenance of the traditional culture of the schools, teachers' disbelief in the genuineness of these efforts, and ultimately, a rejection of empowerment in this form (Evans, 1996:67).

REFERENCES

Carnegie Commission on Teaching as a Profession (1986). *A nation prepared: Teachers for the 21st century.* Hyattsville, MD: Carnegie Forum on Education and the Economy.

Conley, S. (1991). Review of research on teacher participation in school decision making. *Review of Research in Education.* 17, 225–265.

David, J.L. (1989). Synthesis of research on school-based management. *Educational Leadership.* May. Pp. 45–53.

Evans, R. (1996). *The human side of school change: Reform, resistance, and the real-life problems of innovation.* San Francisco, CA: Jossey-Bass Publishers

Fullan, M. (1997) The complexity of the change process. In Michael Fullan (Ed.) *The challenge of school change.* Arlington Hts, Il: Skylight Publishers.

Fullan, M. (1996). Emotion and hope: Constructive concepts for complex times. In A. Hargreaves (Ed.) *Rethinking educational change with heart and mind.* Alexandria, VA: Association for Supervision and Curriculum Development.

Hargreaves, A. (1996). *Rethinking educational change with heart and mind.* Alexandria, VA: Association for Supervision and Curriculum Development.

Hargreaves, A. (1994). *Changing teachers, changing times: Teachers work and culture in the post-modern age.* New York: Teachers College Press

House, E.R. (1998). *Schools for sale: Why free market policy won't improve America's schools and what will.* New York: Teacher College Press.

Miller, E. (1995) Shared decision-making by itself doesn't make for better decisions. *Harvard Educational Letter.* Vol. VI, no. 6. pp. 1–4.

National Governor's Associations (1986) *Time for results: The governor's 1991 report on education.* Washington, DC: Author.

Sergiovanni, T.J. (1994). *Building community in schools.* San Francisco, CA: Jossey-Bass Publishers.

Smylie, M.A. (1992, Spring). Teacher participation in decision-making: Assessing willingness to participate. *Educational Evaluation and Policy Analysis.* Vol. 14, No. 1. pp. 53–67.

NURTURING FACILITATIVE LEADERSHIP

Kimberly Kinsler

In the field of educational administration, facilitative leadership is increasingly assuming the title and regard as "best practice" and is being advocated by many "reform gurus." Echoed in recent top-down mandates and initiatives, current and future school administrators are being prodded to adopt this approach (e.g., N.Y. State's Department of Education's 2002 guidelines for school leaders). This is a very difficult task, as any major behavioral or attitudinal change is fraught with doubt, setbacks and resistance. Few administrators can casually abandon long and deeply-held beliefs about chains of authority, routinized ways of interacting with subordinates and the power and privilege earned at significant personal and monetary costs spent in study and time in the "trenches." Similarly, few administrators can not be but negatively affected by our public school systems' history of reform failure, trendy adoption patterns, poor follow-through and the paucity of research proof on the effectiveness of each new panacea (Kinsler & Gamble, 2000). Particularly in this current era of accountability, a more likely result is for administrators to hunker down and fiercely implement familiar and predictable practices. More than mandates, top-down directives and abstract promises, current and future administrators need evidence and real world assurances that the loss, uncertainty and sacrifice accompanying change are worth the effort. They need to believe that what they lose will more than be offset by what they gain for themselves, their staffs and their students.

To provide some of this much-needed proof, this reading offers a case study of one principal's change effort. His fears, missteps and struggles are reported, for to omit them would devalue and invalidate the difficulty administrators face in making this transition. Hopefully, this study illustrates that, like any commitment to personal growth, adopting a new leadership style is a long hard process, prone to setbacks, optimally aided and supported by others, but more important, possible and worthy of pursuit.

In 1998, Mr. V was given the principalship of a poorly performing elementary school in East Harlem. The previous year, the New York State Education Department had labeled the school as a School Under Registration and Review (SURR) for its students' history of declining achievement scores. Under these guidelines, the school had three years to make significant improvement or risk further punitive action, i.e., the more restrictive categorization of "Corrective Action" and increasingly greater control by the State. The school's designation as SURR led to a number of changes in the school. Among them were the adoption of a nationally known, comprehensive school improvement model and my involvement to aid in its implementation; the retirement of the school's long-time principal at the end of its first SURR year; and the District Superintendent's decision to offer the school's stewardship to Mr. V.

As an individual, Mr. V was a warm and charismatic man. He had previously been the director of a middle school in the same district and openly admitted that he knew little about running an elementary school. Mr. V was also an avowed practitioner and advocate of a well-known top-down leadership model. This posed a potential problem, as the school's chosen model of excellence required the creation of a site-based management (SBM)/shared decision making (SDM) governance structure, which conflicted with Mr. V's leadership approach. Moreover, as Mr. V largely attributed his past success to his use of this top-down model, he immediately began to apply this traditional approach with school staff. I was asked to stay on to aid the school in meeting NYSED SURR school governance requirements, in form if not in substance.

In Mr. V's first year, all were trying to feel their way, as they got to know each other and worked to improve students' scores. The principal set new rules for classroom procedures. I encouraged staff to construct needs assessments, analyze student test data and explore the school's capacity for instructional problem solving. Staff complied differentially with both Mr. V's and my efforts to improve the functioning of the school. Some teachers, who preferred the more personal style of the previous principal, objected to what they regarded as the more in-trusive, formal climate created by several of Mr. V's changes. By late spring, they had asked to be transferred to other schools. Except for these few, most staff and Mr. V sought a work-ing relationship that clearly placed removal from the SURR list as their greatest priority. Con-sistent with Mr. V's top-down management approach, by year's end, the school's leadership (i.e., the Principal, its SED representative, its staff developers and I) had developed an in-structional plan for the school's third, and deciding year on the SURR list. As we readied our-selves for this challenge, to everyone's surprise, New York City's School Chancellor preemptively seized control of the school, and moved its aegis to his own district. Now under the guidelines of the "Chancellor's District," the school's instructional plans were set aside, replaced by the Chancellor's prescribed curricula and texts for literacy and mathematics. Dis-trict schools also were required to create and utilize a site-based governance structure.

Compliance in form if not in substance became the order of the day. My work with the staff over the previous two years had resulted in the creation of a School Leadership Team (SLT) and several problem-solving subcommittees (SDMTs). My efforts to establish and ad-vance these teams led to my continued affiliation with the school. Despite doubts as to the willingness of the administration to share responsibility in key areas like budget, staff hir-ing, and instructional planning, some of the school's best and most veteran teachers joined in this effort. Superficially, all went well. The principal attended SLT meetings, SDMTs met to identify needs in the implementation of the newly mandated curricula, and teams devel-oped plans to address these and school climate issues. As the work of these SDMTs pro-gressed and more plans were implemented throughout the school, problems arose. Team members complained that the administration, while offering "lip service," seldom supported their efforts by following through on the administrative components and had been overheard speaking with disdain about both the need for these teams and the quality of their products. It was not uncommon for the principal benignly to countermand team plans by creating poli-cies and engaging in practices that conflicted with those of the teams. When I brought the concerns of team members to his attention, Mr. V defended the administration's practices by the need to keep things moving in this period of crisis. When the time came to write the school's instructional plan for the upcoming year, the principal unilaterally created one with the help of the school's staff developers. This act was a severe blow to team members who had worked hard to develop supplementary curricular programs, causing several veteran teachers to doubt the principal's commitment to site-based management and the value of con-tinued team membership.

Despite these problems, the whole school staff strove to improve instruction and student performance. Staff learned and tried to apply the new mandated curricula in reading and mathematics, and team members assumed greater responsibility for instructional planning and problem solving with non-mandated curricular instruction. Their good faith efforts had positive results, and by end of the third SURR year, there was significant improvement in stu-dent achievement. The school's progress was publicly noted and rewarded by a visit from then President, Bill Clinton. School staff's reactions to these accolades were noteworthy. To many staff members, the principal appeared to regard the school's progress as a personal achieve-ment and further validation of his top-down managerial style. Conversely, staff felt that the students' progress had been a team effort and that their hard work deserved greater ac-knowledgement.

By the start of Mr. V's third year, his honeymoon with the staff was over. They had worked hard to earn his respect and regard. He, on the other hand, seemed blind to their efforts. As a result, staff morale plummeted. Teachers who had served on problem-solving subcommittees resigned in frustration and disappointment. As the change in staff attitudes became more disgruntled, Mr. V felt forced to acknowledge and comment on it. Initially, he downplayed its significance by attributing the shift to teachers he characterized as slackers and troublemakers, and vowed to come down hard on them. I pointed out that the most disgruntled staff was actually some of his best and hardest working teachers. I told him that team members did not feel supported in their work, and that one or two staff developers were typically given the responsibility of unilaterally developing the school's instructional plan, often disregarding teacher input. Acknowledging the truth in these claims, he defended his actions, again justifying their necessity by the exigencies created by current accountability measures. He, personally, was being held responsible for the school's student performance— not teacher teams! He was the one being pressured to move the school, and the individual who would pay the penalties for failure. As he was being held accountable, it was only correct that he pay for decisions that he made! Despite these justifications, Mr. V worried that teachers' increasing dissatisfaction would have a negative impact on student performance. He felt at a crossroads. His old practices were not working and, in fact, increasingly alienating his faculty. On the other hand, he had little understanding of and faith in shared governance. When students' test scores declined that year, Mr. V was forced to question the effectiveness of his old leadership style with this staff, and to consider his possible adoption of a facilitative leadership approach.

Still, change was more easily said than done. Mr. V had no models of what facilitative leadership looked liked or how it operated. Seeking help, Mr. V sought my advice, as the person responsible for the establishment and maintenance of his school's site-based management. My first recommendation was that the school's educational plan for the 2001–2002 academic year incorporate the instructional plans developed by his SLT subcommittees— which he did. At the start of the academic year, I advised Mr. V to support the subcommittees work in monitoring the implementation and effectiveness of these plans, attend more SLT meetings and regard his SLT, rather than his administrative cabinet, as his central planning committee. He worried over this latter change, but when reminded of the success of a plan devised and implemented by the literacy subcommittee to tutor the school's lowest achieving students, he agreed. Gradually, the school's site-based governance teams and their work became increasingly regarded as critical problem-solving sites where teacher opinion and input was sought, valued and acted upon. This transition was slow, volatile and fraught with setbacks. At varying times, all the school's APs and staff developers balked at sharing power, attempted to reassert their control over particular activities and complained to the principal. When Mr. V gave into their complaints, teachers became upset. Mr. V felt torn by lower level administrators who wanted him to return to the old ways of doing things and his teaching staff who were emerging as his instructional partners. When he was most in doubt, I reassured him by noting the new energy in the school created by increasing teacher and parent involvement in these teams.

When it came time to write the school's educational plan for 2002–2003, Mr. V asked me to lead the process! I, in turn, assigned responsibility for the development of the instruction plans to the various SDMTs. With a heightened sense of purpose, these subcommittees gathered and analyzed data, identified instructional need areas and developed consensual plans, discussed throughout the school in grade level meetings. Those who had previously controlled this process began to realize that if they were to have any input, they had to work in and with these teams. Purchasing and staff development, for the first time, became a logical support and follow through of these instructional plans. Teachers volunteered to come in during their spring vacation to type up and make final edits on the plan along with Mr. V. When the document was completed, Mr. V commented that he, personally, had contributed less yet felt more confident and pleased with this plan than with any previous plan.

A final stage in the plan's ratification process was for the school's staff to defend their proposed activities before a panel of district administrators. Usually, principals bring those administrative staff who typically write the document, i.e., their APs, the union representative, and the staff developers. That year, Mr. V took no APs, one staff developer, the school's union representative (who also co-chaired the SLT) and teachers! His teachers, who had chaired the various subject specific SLT subcommittees, spoke eloquently on the development and rationale for their respective action plans. The plan passed the panel's review with recommendations for only superficial modifications. All felt a sense of reward and accomplishment.

In Mr. V's four years as principal, both he and his staff have been transformed. Privately, Mr. V told me that for the first time he understood the potential of facilitative leadership. He saw how sharing power could lead to his greater empowerment as a leader. He also learned of the benefits of nurturing leadership capability in his staff. In particular, he noted the work of one teacher, who despite setbacks had constantly rallied school staff to believe in the SLT and the work of the subcommittees. When the school's long time AP retired with no funds immediately available to restaff the position, Mr. V asked this teacher to assume some administrative responsibilities while she completed coursework on her administration license. In this capacity, she continues to be a driving force in facilitating and nurturing leadership potential in other staff and continues to guide and advance the operation of the school's SLT and its subcommittees. At the end of the 2001–2002 school year, the school's achievement rate improved sufficient to warrant its exit from both the Chancellor's District and the State's SURR list.

As this short case study illustrates, becoming a facilitative leader is not an easy process and, for many individuals, it is a lonely and anxiety-ridden endeavor. Change, however, is possible and, if leaders are to win and build upon the support and expertise of staff, it is also necessary. Mr. V's journey provides lessons for those who lead the way.

SUPERVISOR AS COACH

Marcia Knoll

If student achievement is the goal of everything we do in schools, then the question is how can the supervisor's work with members of the instructional staff effectively reach that goal? The response requires a change in the way supervision is conducted. The supervisor must become a coach with all of the actions and behaviors that it encompasses.

ADULT LEARNERS

Consider first, how adults learn. Adults are very different from children and their learning needs reflect these differences. Supervision frequently places adults in the role of children with disastrous results. Adults seek to control the situation to feel comfortable about how they will be impacted. They do not wish to appear foolish or incompetent. It is, therefore, important to treat adults as adults by involving them in planning activities, giving choices when possible, and encouraging them to be self-directed in their efforts.

Adults have a wealth of prior knowledge and experience that should be both capitalized on and respected. When supervisors ignore this and become a directing parent, adults build walls around themselves and resist suggestions no matter how well intended. Adults will feel more comfortable when they are able to link a new idea, strategy or procedure to something that they know and have been successful with. This enables them to find an area of comfort in what might otherwise be overwhelming.

Adults are motivated by need. It isn't so much what they should do, but rather what they can do to make their situation better. They respond quickly and strongly to something that will benefit them or relieve a situation with which they are not comfortable. New strategies or procedures should be clearly related to how they will be of benefit or how an existing concern or problem may be resolved.

Adults are performance-centered. They do not wait to act on something they believe will be of help. A delay may cause a lack of enthusiasm or diminished interest in the idea. It is therefore important to start a new strategy immediately, even if it is not complete so that results can be viewed and discussed.

Adults hold points of view, beliefs and ideas that have evolved from their experience. New ideas may conflict with these long-held beliefs. At times, it may be important to target how new ideas may be viewed in light of long-held beliefs. For example, if a teacher resists the use of graphic organizers because she believes that students should take their own notes, point out the benefits of using organizers to assure that students have the correct information with which to study for tests. At the very least, encourage questions and dialogue on the subject.

When I became a principal in New York City, I found that the instructional staff was a mixture of creative and dynamic teachers, as well as those who had become stuck in the past. All of them meant well but only some of them were doing the job of helping students achieve. The dilemma, of course, was how to move those stuck teachers and show respect for them at the same time? I decided that the way to respect everybody and expose them to new and exciting ideas at the same time was to provide an opportunity for each teacher to demonstrate his/her best practice to the staff. I used the monthly faculty meetings for this project. Each teacher selected the month for the presentation of a best practice. All teachers presented a best practice and, within a few months, many of the best practices had spread into classrooms across the grades, even those who had been stuck in the past. Many teachers told me that this was the first time in their careers that anyone had given them recognition for their work.

BUILDING TRUST

Next, consider how important trust-building is to the supervisor as coach. When you are trusted, people are far more likely to believe what you say and respond to what you ask. They believe that they will benefit rather than be harmed by the experience. It is important, however, to remember that trust requires taking the risk of being betrayed. When that happens trust is almost impossible to restore.

In working with hundreds of teachers over the past five years, three distinct elements of trust have surfaced as important indicators:

- Being open rather than closed to ideas, suggestions and varied points of view.
- Being supportive rather than controlling by believing that others truly want to be successful and do try their best.
- Being dependable so that people can rely on the confidentiality and consistency of your actions.

But words are easy. It takes actions to make people believe you have these attributes.

The first behavior that trusted leaders exhibit is that of being open. These leaders ask questions rather than make assumptions that may be off target. Open leaders are flexible. They invite honest feedback about ideas and make decisions based on that input as they consider alternatives. They build consensus to solve problems asking for the involvement of others. Open leaders take calculated risks as they initiate new ideas or act on needs. They make expectations clear verbally and/or in writing so that there are no surprises and they followup on ideas and promises. They are accessible and a visible presence always in the heart of the action. On a personal note, open leaders practice active listening including positive body language by smiling, nodding and making eye contact. They exhibit a sense of humor and share personal anecdotes. Open leaders accept criticism and vulnerability as they reveal their feelings.

Trusted leaders are supportive. They are non-judgmental and avoid public embarrassment of professionals. They listen and respond appropriately. They are always willing to step in and give a hand when necessary, even if it involves taking over a class or relieving a teacher's duty assignment. I remember very clearly a hectic morning in my school when the office received a call asking that the principal come immediately to kindergarten room 4. It was an emergency. I went at once. I found Shelly, the teacher, in a state of panic. She had received a call on her cell phone saying that one of her twin boys had been knocked unconscious at school. She had to take him to the emergency room. I had about a million things to do that day but, without a moment's hesitation, I told her to go to her son and I would take her class. I asked her to call us as soon as she knew how he was. That teacher never forgot my willingness to help her in a time of need. Supportive leaders are action-oriented. They provide needed resources, make personal contacts, write notes and letters and make verbal comments of recognition. Supportive leaders share accomplishments of others and self with everyone. They are even willing to take the flack when necessary.

Lastly, trusted leaders are dependable. They do what they say and say what they do. They follow up on promises and statements. They can be relied upon to be punctual, keep a commitment, and pay attention to deadlines. If you ask for a phone call from them, you will receive one. Dependable leaders provide needed or requested help and demonstrate their knowledge and skills. You can be sure they will maintain confidentiality. So honest interchanges are far more likely to occur.

LISTENING

We all know how important listening can be, but how many of us are really good listeners? Of all of the communication skills, listening is the most poorly-developed. Most people listen to respond, rather than listen to understand. We would much rather talk than listen. But there are large differences between listening just long enough to frame a response and listening to truly understand what the other person is saying. Most misunderstandings and miscommunications are caused by a lack of listening to what the other person is saying.

Being a good listener is a powerful tool that contributes to making the supervisor as coach effective. It requires that we put ourselves on hold. That means that we suspend a quick retort, a suggestion and making a judgment. The three listening tools of attending, seeking to understand and deferring evaluation can help you to become a better listener.

By attending, you focus on the speaker and communicate your interest in him or her and the message. The speaker can see you attending by observing your body language. Imagine how you feel when you are trying to explain something to someone who is sorting papers, reading a note or looking for something in a desk. Those distractions communicate many things, none of which are of interest to the speaker. Sustain attention even though a message is not of interest and do not allow yourself to change your focus to other, perhaps more pressing matters. Take notes if that is helpful to you and most of all, be patient.

Seek to understand even when it becomes difficult to do so. The brain naturally selects and organizes information as it listens, viewing the data being input through the listener's perception. Sometimes the message is confused or unclear because it is coded with feelings and apprehensions and lack of confidence on the part of the speaker about how to word the message. The listener must decode the message to understand. Recording questions to ask may be helpful.

Each of us has an internal belief system formed early in life and confirmed, modified or denied by life experiences. Our beliefs and attitudes filter communications and cause emotional reactions to what we hear that may distort, block, create suspicion or enhance the message. It is important to remember to keep your emotions in check as you carefully listen to the intent of what is being expressed. One of my teachers told me about her concern for a child in her second grade class. The little girl came to school in the same outfit, that was now very soiled, for about a week. The teacher was particularly distressed and angry when the child wore the outfit on the day when class photographs were taken. I thanked the teacher for her concern and said that the first step was to speak with the parents. A meeting was scheduled for the next morning. Both parents and the teacher were at the meeting. The teacher expressed her concern about the child's welfare. The parents thanked the teacher and said that they too were concerned. Grandmother was ill and the little girl was convinced that if she wore her lucky outfit, grandmother would get well. I asked the guidance counselor to join us. We developed a plan to work with the child at school and home to help her to accept that her good thoughts and wishes for grandmother were more powerful than the outfit she was wearing.

THE LANGUAGE OF COMMUNICATION

Oral communication is the single most valuable tool for the supervisor as coach to provide the support, challenge and opportunity needed for teacher growth. Active listening provides support through communications that express caring, interest, understanding, empathy, validation, and encouragement. Reflection targets challenge and opportunity through communications that empower teachers by requiring them to extend their thinking.

When the supervisor as coach uses the three elements of active listening, teachers feel comfortable, accepted and understood. This climate of validation and encouragement sets the stage for teachers to think about and act on the teaching and learning process without fear of criticism and judgment.

NONVERBAL ACTIVE LISTENING

Our nonverbal language sends powerful messages. Sometimes how we look communicates more than what we say. For example, when a person maintains eye contact with you do you feel that they are interested in you? As another example, it is almost impossible not to return a smile. The purpose of nonverbal active listening is to express caring and interest. I care about you, you're important and I'm interested in you are the messages that are communicated. Nonverbal active listening involves your body, arms, hands, face and voice in delivering those messages. Here are some of the actions that confirm the messages. Sit next to or across from the other person with a relaxed body posture. Turn to face the other person and lean forward moving slowly and infrequently. Keep your arms and your hands relaxed and open with the palms facing up. Use your hands to gesture. Show expression on your face and smile and nod frequently. Look directly at the other person and maintain eye contact. Maintain silence except for an occasional meaningful "uh huh."

The purpose of active listening is to express understanding. I seek to understand and I am sensitive to your needs are the messages that are communicated. There are two actions that communicate the messages of active listening. Paraphrasing restates or summarizes what the speaker has said. It informs the speaker that you have heard what they said. It also expresses a desire to understand by reflecting back for clarification. For example, statements such as, "So you are saying . . ." "I hear you saying . . ." Statements that express recognition of emotions are the second actions. These statements communicate that you recognize how the speaker feels. For example, statements such as, "You are feeling . . ." "I can feel how hurt you were when . . ."

INTERACTIVE LISTENING

Problem solving is the purpose of interactive listening so necessary to the coaching experience. "Your ideas are valid" and "You have the power and the ability" are the messages communicated. Two actions communicate these messages. Statements that validate the actions proposed express confidence in the speaker and show support for the ideas proposed. For example, statements such as, "You really know how to . . . That sounds like a great solution." Statements that encourage action express the belief that the speaker has the ability to be successful. For example, statements such as, "You have some good experience with . . . You have the organizational skills to . . ."

REFLECTION THAT FOSTERS TEACHER GROWTH

The tools of active listening establish a climate of trust and acceptance that helps teachers to feel comfortable and encourages them to speak openly and professionally about instructional practices. This sets the stage for change and growth. Reflection moves beyond building confidence and validating effort. It focuses on teacher growth through the process of reflection. The purpose of reflection is to help teachers to extract meaning from their teaching experiences as they examine the results of their planned lessons. When one considers the amount of time that teachers are alone in their classrooms, developing the habit of reflecting on their instructional practice is essential if teachers are to be continuously growing, self-directed professionals.

The supervisor as coach can help teachers to develop reflection as a natural outcome of every teaching experience through asking questions. The rule is ASK, DON'T TELL. Authentic and sustained growth demands commitment, responsibility and ownership and it must, therefore, be in the hands and minds of the teacher. Teachers must own it. The supervisor as coach, however, is the agent of the change process by guiding the teacher through questions to examine instructional practices, reflect on their effectiveness and seek ways to help every student to be successful. Three types of questions guide the reflective process. They are questions that focus on instruction, probe for information and seek clarification. The total involvement of the teacher in this effort is critical if change is to occur.

QUESTIONS THAT FOCUS ON INSTRUCTION

These questions ask the teacher to analyze and reflect on specific aspects of instruction. Teachers are invited to discuss their impressions and assessments of the lesson. In this process, teachers are asked to recall specific pieces of information that support their impressions and assessments. Teachers are encouraged to demonstrate student understanding and achievement of lesson objectives through examples of student behavior and products. For example, questions such as, "What about the lesson particularly pleased you? Did you achieve the objective you set? How do you know the students understand the concept?" I recall observing a particularly deadly lesson that began with a lecture and ended with a debate that fell apart because the sixth grade students had no idea about how to participate in a debate. I wanted to encourage the teacher to use strategies that involved the students in active participation rather than lecturing. It was essential for the teacher to reflect on the debate and come to his own solution rather than my suggestions, which he would not own. I began by saying that I was delighted to see him try debating as a strategy. He smiled and nodded. I then asked him if he was satisfied with how the students conducted the debate. The teacher opened up and talked about how difficult it had been for the students. I asked him how he could prepare students for a debating activity. Together, we came up with a plan.

QUESTIONS THAT PROBE FOR INFORMATION

These questions ask the teacher to fill in gaps in statements. Teachers are asked to extend what they have said or done to provide more information and explore reasons for their decisions and actions and resulting outcomes. For example, questions such as, "Can you explain your thinking in forming the student groups? Say more about the instructional strategy you selected. Why do you believe that would lead to chaos?"

Probing takes a skilled questioner. The art of probing is to help the person being coached identify weaknesses or limitations without feeling coerced.

QUESTIONS THAT SEEK CLARIFICATION

These questions ask the teacher to explain statements or actions that are not clearly understood. Teachers may be asked to clarify generalizations or vague statements by using more precise language. In this process, teachers are asked to think deeply beyond the obvious statements to clarify their real meaning. For example, questions such as, "Are you saying that none of the students are ready for this topic? What do you mean when you say these students are hard to teach? Do you mean that this problem cannot be solved?"

Active listening and reflection are used interactively throughout communications with teachers. The skillful communicator knows when active listening is needed to convey the messages of understanding situations or confidence in ability. The skillful communicator also knows that questions that stimulate reflection should be used in every communication with teachers to help them to focus on instruction, explain decisions and clarify and articulate problems so that they can be solved.

CLOSING

Changing the behaviors and actions of a supervisor to those of a coach may be a most challenging undertaking for those who are practiced in traditional models of supervision, as well as those who are new to the role of supervisor. We tend to supervise the way we were supervised just as we tend to parent as we were parented. Becoming a supervisor as coach shifts the focus of responsibility for instructional effectives from you, the supervisor, to the entire staff as individuals and as a collective. Consider how rewarding your work can become when your behaviors and actions as a coach result in an entire instructional staff being committed to professional growth and instructional effectiveness as their on-going individual and collective responsibility.

WARRIORS TO ADVANCE EQUITY: AN ARGUMENT FOR DISTRIBUTING LEADERSHIP

Larry Leverett

You can't mandate things that matter most!! Equity matters most to many in our schools and society and the charge of changing schools and districts to achieve equitable outcomes is certainly something that we have not been able to successfully mandate. Equity is hard work and requires the collective commitment and energy of the entire school or district education community.

Achieving equitable outcomes for all learners is beyond the capacity of individual, highly talented leaders and requires the knowledge and expertise of others in the school or district organization working with a shared sense of purpose. "Equity warriors" are needed at every level of the organization in equity-focused schools and districts. Leaders must build capacity and provide support to multiply the force of contributors prepared to advance the equity mission.

Who are these "equity warriors" and what are their roles? Equity warriors are people who, regardless of their role in a school or district, passionately lead and embrace the mission of high levels of achievement for all students, regardless of race, social class, ethnicity, culture, disability or language proficiency. They view themselves as having the power to influence the teaching and learning agendas in meaningful ways. Equity warriors often act outside their formally assigned roles, communicate effectively and persistently with diverse publics to influence the core business of schools and districts, participate successfully in cross-functional teams, work to improve their knowledge, skills and disposition, engage in risk-taking and model the values, beliefs and behaviors for others to emulate in the quest for higher levels of learning for all groups of children and youth.

Equity warriors occupy a variety of roles, including but not limited to, coaches, mentors, curriculum leaders, classroom teachers, school management team leaders and members, community leaders, parent education specialists, technology coordinators, library media specialists and guidance counselors. They are found laboring in nearly all other roles commonly found in schools and districts. Typically, equity warriors are driven by personal values and beliefs, have an area of knowledge or expertise about which they are passionate, contribute freely to equity work beyond their assigned role and are willing to grow and learn to become more effective in advancing the equity agenda in their school, district or community.

Those involved in education know through experience, research and documented best practice that school or district leadership models that solely rely upon principals, superintendents or other appointed, formal leaders to change systems are often unsuccessful in developing the needed critical mass to force the abandonment of old paradigm approaches to improve the core business of schools and districts—teaching and learning. The elimination of bad practice in classrooms, schools and districts is more attainable when leadership is spread across the school or district horizontally and vertically and when people in the organization share the zeal and commitment to make meaningful change happen.

> *"An organization cannot flourish—at least, not for long—on the actions of the top leader alone. Schools and districts need many leaders at many levels" (Fullan, 2002).*

Educators are all too familiar with short-lived change efforts led by highly capable, charismatic school and district leaders. It is clear that person-dependent change strategies are not likely to result in sustained support of long-term equity agendas. The frequent turnover of principals and superintendents and the rapid-fire introduction of multiple poorly supported improvement efforts continually result in fragile reforms with short life spans. The "equity war" calls for many leaders in many different roles who join in sustained demonstrations of collective will and internally driven systems of collective responsibility that can be continued even when the principals or superintendents leave. Formal leaders, no matter how talented, cannot make the equity agenda thrive without leadership coming from others in the school or district.

> *"The days of the principal as the lone instructional leader are over. We no longer believe that one administrator can serve as the instructional leader for an entire school without the substantial participation of other educators"* (Lambert, 2002).

School and district administrators committed to equity must make growing leaders throughout the organization an important priority. They must invest in building capacity, consistently model attitudes, behaviors and practices supportive of creating "leaderfull" organizations, and demonstrate a commitment to learning to lead in ways that support others having access to leadership roles. Leaders for equity-focused schools provide staff with the resources they need to grow as equity warriors.

Professional learning communities and high performance organizations support the wisdom of distributing leadership to achieve organizational goals. Roles in these organizations are not bound by rigid, narrowly defined job descriptions that constrain staff to working in the education version of silos. Schools and districts that embrace theories of action based on the distribution of leadership have abandoned overly top-down, reactive, hierarchical, highly centralized approaches that have historically concentrated leadership among a few, mostly those in appointed administrative positions. Appointed leaders in equity-focused organizations embrace a commitment to building learning organizations and providing opportunities for all who share the equity mission to give their gifts, to develop their skills and to have access to leadership that is not dependent on one's "place" in the hierarchy or formal organizational chart.

> *"The basic idea of distributed leadership is not very complicated. In any organized system, people typically specialize, or develop particular competencies, [which] are related to their predispositions, interests, prior knowledge, skills, and specialized roles . . . It is the "glue" of a common task or goal—improvement of instruction— and a common frame of values for how to approach that task—culture—that keeps distributing leadership from becoming another version of loose coupling"* (Elmore, 2000).

Creating conditions that are conducive to growing an army of people willing to engage in a sustained effort to achieve equity is the challenge for leaders in today's schools. Leadership that embraces collective effort, promotes a shared sense of purpose and mission, engages many in collaboration across roles and develops organizational cultures that set high expectations for adults and children, is leadership that results in a more fertile environment for meaningful changes in the teaching and learning environment.

Driving an equity agenda in our schools and districts requires new thinking about the roles of leaders—a shift from the power and control paradigm to one that concentrates on aligning the culture around a set of normative beliefs, attitudes, expectations and actions.

As school or district leaders in appointed positions, we have choices. We can continue status quo-oriented leadership and management styles that limit the expectation for leadership to a small group of formal leaders, *or* we can commit to the development of school or district cultures that expand the base of leaders. The decisions we make as appointed leaders influence the depth of support within our organizations for the challenging work of fostering equity. Leaders who grow equity warriors are leaders who are most likely to have the support needed to advance the important work of improving teaching and learning.

There are literally hundreds of schools across America's landscape that are successfully making progress towards equity. Equity warriors are at work as leaders in these schools and districts. Improved teaching and learning and more equitable outcomes for the learners are occurring. The reality is that schools can make a difference in the quality of a child's experience as a learner. It takes leadership from across the school or district to increase the probability of making needed changes happen. Distributed leadership provides fertile ground for sustaining long-term commitments to the desired goals of equity. The important work of achieving equitable outcomes for all learners cannot be mandated nor can it be accomplished without the support and expertise of school staff at all levels.

REFERENCES

Elmore, R. F. (Winter 2000). *Building a New Structure for School Leadership.* Washington, D.C., The Albert Shanker Institute.

Fullan, M. (May 2002). *The Change Leader.* Educational Leadership, 59 (8): 16-20.

Lambert, L. (May 2002). *A Framework for Shared Leadership.* Educational Leadership, 59 (8): 37-40.

DEMOCRACY AND SCHOOLS

Nicholas M. Michelli

It was Jefferson who wrote, "Those who hope to live in a state that is both ignorant and free ask for what never was, nor never will be."[1] Benjamin Barber, the distinguished Rutgers political scientist who writes about democracy and education concludes that "Democracy is not a natural form of association; it is an extraordinarily rare contrivance of cultivated imagination." He goes on to make the case for the role of education in a democracy. "Empower the merely ignorant and endow the uneducated with a right to make collective decisions and what results is not democracy but, at best, mob rule: The government of private prejudice and the tyranny of opinion—all those perversions that liberty's enemies like to pretend (and its friends fear) constitute democracy. . . . Democratic education mediates the ancient quarrel between the rule of opinion and the rule of excellence by informing opinion and, through universal education in excellence, creating an aristocracy for everyone."[2]

Taken together, these two conceptions of the relationship between education and democracy make the case that the single most important institution for the maintenance of education is the American public school. Now, we all know that most schools will say something in their statements prepared for regional accreditation about teaching for democracy, but, in practice, I would argue that it is getting harder and harder to find concrete evidence of how such schools act on their statements. We take democracy for granted. We assume that it is something that can be handled in social studies instruction. We also often assume that teaching for democracy stops with civics—teaching students how to register to vote, about the structure of government, and about the mechanics of democracy. It isn't. Rather, teaching for democracy must be ingrained in all aspects of education, and be the responsibility of all teachers and, perhaps most critically, all administrators.

Allow me to explore this assertion through three dimensions: the obligation of classroom teachers to teach for critical thinking, the obligation of classroom teachers to teach for democratic personal relationships, and the obligation of administrators to be supportive and get out of the way.

TEACHING FOR CRITICAL THINKING

Central to Barber's assertion about the role of education in democracy is his concern for overcoming the tyranny of opinion. It is the same concern Jefferson asserts, we cannot be ignorant and free. And yet increasingly, with the pressure of standardized testing, classroom teachers are focusing more and more on what is likely to be on the test and less and less on the critical analysis of content. There are many definitions of critical thinking. The one that is closest to my concern for democratic practice comes from Matthew Lipman, who asserts that critical thinking is thinking that leads to good judgments because it is based on criteria, sensitive to content and self correcting.

This definition requires us to examine our judgments, whatever form they might take, through a critical lens. Judgments can be assertions of support for political candidates, a belief that a scientific hypothesis is the best one to explain observed phenomenon, or an assertion about the quality of a play. The important thing is that opinion does not stand without reason. With Lipman's approach, students are asked "why?" whenever they make an assertion. They are asked about the criteria that led to their judgment or conclusion. For example, in discussing the war in Iraq, we ask students, "Why did you support the President's call for war in Iraq? What were your criteria?" Then one must consider the context. "What is the context in which such a judgment is asserted?" Of course, for many, it is a judgment made after September 11, 2001. There is no question that this is a context that is very different from the context that proceeded it. So, the first two aspects of Lipman's conception of critical thinking has students seek the criteria they use in making assertions—as we all should—and think about the context. The third part of his definition has to do with self-correction. That is, an assertion, a judgment, must be open to consideration by others through a community of inquiry. In such communities—which we would hope all classrooms could become—students ask questions of the assertions each may make. "Why do you believe that? What were your criteria? Did you consider X? Are you taking into account the good of all, or are you selfish?" In such a community of inquiry, students are expected to change their perspectives and judgments, if persuaded by others. This, I would argue, is an essential quality of democracy. We need classrooms where all important judgments are subject to critical thinking of this kind. Where students learn to argue for their perspectives. Where they learn to question the perspectives of others. Where they learn to adjust their views based on the arguments they hear. Imagine citizens in a democracy making the case for particular policy decisions, particular candidates, and listening to the reactions of others.

Robert Putnam, Dean of the Kennedy School of Government at the University of Massachusetts, argues that social capital has weakened in the past generation in the United States. By "social capital," Putnam means the trust, norms and networks outside of the family that allow people to work together in a democratic order. Membership in voluntary groups like fraternal organizations, women's clubs, labor unions—and bowling leagues—has declined dramatically in the United States. In one of his most widely-cited works—*Making Democracy Work: Civic Traditions in Modern Italy*, sometimes compared with Tocqueville in its influence on our understanding of democracy—Putnam explores democracy in Northern and Southern Italy.[3] He points out that, in the North, democracy is strong and citizen participation wide. In the South, democracy is weak, with an almost feudal structure. The difference, he argues, lies in the absence of broad associations and networks in the South and the presence of extensive networks in the North. From these networks—choral societies and football clubs, reading groups and rotary clubs—evolved a dense network of civic engagement and social capital and a sense of general reciprocity. People think, "I'll do this for you now without expecting anything immediate in return, because down the road you'll do something for me and I'll do something for you." Reciprocity forms a high level of social trustworthiness and trust; that social connectedness makes all institutions in such communities more productive. It is these rich networks that Putnam argues have disappeared in the United States in recent decades, leading among other things, to a marked decline in voting—down 25 percent in the last 30 years, a decline in trust in our institutions and a decline of 40 percent in the last 25 years of participation by citizens in town or school meetings in which discussion occurs. He argues they are gone for many reasons, in part because television viewing has removed the opportunity for volunteerism, but also because we no longer value these networks. Putnam has, of course, expanded these views in *Bowling Alone,* a work in which he explores the implications of recreating communities in the United States.[4] Communities that I argue must begin in the classrooms of our public schools.

TEACHING FOR DEMOCRATIC PERSONAL RELATIONSHIPS

An important adjunct to teaching for critical thinking is helping young people learn the appropriate interactions between human beings in a democratic context. As Gary

Fenstermacher argues, "We must attend to our manner as human beings as well as our method as pedagogues. It is the manner in which we communicate our disciplines that conveys our beliefs and understandings of democratic community. The promotion of our discipline, our content, is the occasion for the display of manner. It is the occasion to communicate to learners the best of what it means to be human, using what John Goodlad calls "nurturing pedagogies."[5] What is the manner in which we communicate with children? Do we show respect, empathy, concern, and openness to the ideas of others? All of these are critical democratic characteristics that cannot be left to chance. Teachers must learn to model the qualities of democratic life. Increasingly, tools are becoming available to allow for this kind of work to go forward. I think, for example, of The *Don't Laugh at Me* curriculum developed by Peter Yarrow and his associates. It is designed to prevent the cruel taunting and bully-like behavior often found in children and adolescents, and antithetical to democratic practice.[6]

THE ROLE OF ADMINISTRATORS

So, if we accept these assertions: that democracy must be recreated with each new generation, that public schools must be the places where democratic practice is learned and perfected, that critical thinking applied to all disciplines and all judgments leads to better democratic life, that this is the responsibility of all teachers, and that democratic behavior must be modeled and taught by teachers, where does that leave administrators? As in all significant educational changes that come about intentionally, the role of school leaders is central. We need principals who accept these views, who believe as I do that teaching for critical thinking will in fact raise the scores of children on the tests that increasingly govern our lives, and are willing to take some risks in encouraging more reflective teaching. We need principals who understand the importance of their support for this kind of education. The reward systems in public schools for teachers are very rigid and limited. There are few extrinsic rewards that can be made available to teachers who do excellent work. Principals need to engage in providing intrinsic motivation through acknowledgement of the work and through support by every means possible.

Finally, we need administrators who run schools as communities of inquiry, as places where teachers learn to talk about important professional issues in a supportive and nurturing environment. For many teachers, a bad teaching day is a personal event that destroys emotional health. Instead, it should be the sort of event that can be analyzed so that the teaching judgments are transparent and all can learn from the experience. This takes an administrator who values human interaction and learning among teachers.

American democracy is at risk. There is no more important venue for its continuation than our public schools.

NOTES

[1] This is the most common form of the quotation. See *Perspectives: The Newsletter of the Colorado Partnership for Educational Renewal* 5, no. 2 (1995): 3. The actual quotation from Jefferson is, "If a nation expects to be ignorant and free in a state of civilization, it expects something that never was and never will be." This is from a letter to Colonel Charles Yancey, January 6, 1816.

[2] Benjamin Barber, *An Aristocracy of Everyone: The Politics of Education and the Future of America* (New York: Ballantine Books, 1992), p. 5.

[3]Robert D. Putnam. *Making Democracy Work: Civic Traditions in Modern Italy* (Princeton: Princeton University Press, 1993).

[4]Robert D. Putnam, Bowling Alone (Boston: Simon and Shuster, 2001)

[5]See Donna H. Kerr, "Voicing Democracy in an Imperfect World: Toward a Public Pedagogy of Nurture," in Wilma F. Smith and Gary D. Fenstermacher (eds.) *Leadership for Educational Renewal* (San Francisco: Jossey Bass, 1999).

[6]The Don't Laugh At Me Program is an antibullying program for grades 2-8. Information regarding this program can be obtained at *www.operationrespect.org*

SHADOWS AND SPIRITUALITY

Parker J. Palmer

A leader is someone with the power to project either shadow or light onto some part of the world and onto the lives of the people who dwell there. A leader shapes the ethos in which others must live, an ethos as light-filled as heaven or as shadowy as hell. A *good* leader is intensely aware of the interplay of inner shadow and light, lest the act of leadership do more harm than good.

I think, for example, of teachers who create the conditions under which young people must spend so many hours: some shine a light that allows new growth to flourish, while others cast a shadow under which seedlings die. I think of parents who generate similar effects in the lives of their families or of clergy who do the same to entire congregations. I think of corporate CEOs whose daily decisions are driven by inner dynamics but who rarely reflect on those motives or even believe they are real.

We have a long tradition of approaching leadership via the "power of positive thinking." I want to counterbalance that approach by paying special attention to the tendency we have as leaders to project more shadow than light. Leadership is hard work for which one is regularly criticized and rarely rewarded, so it is understandable that we need to bolster ourselves with positive thoughts. But by failing to look at our shadows, we feed a dangerous delusion that leaders too often indulge: that our efforts are always well intended, our power is always benign, and the problem is always in those difficult people whom we are trying to lead!

Those of us who readily embrace leadership, especially public leadership, tend toward extroversion, which often means ignoring what is happening inside ourselves. If we have any sort of inner life, we "compartmentalize" it, walling it off from our public work. This, of course, allows the shadow to grow unchecked until it emerges, larger than life, in the public realm, a problem we are well acquainted with in our own domestic politics. Leaders need not only the technical skills to manage the external world but also the spiritual skills to journey toward the source of both shadow and light.

Spirituality, like leadership, is a hard thing to define. But Annie Dillard has given us a vivid image of what authentic spirituality is about: "In the deeps are the violence and terror of which psychology has warned us. But if you ride these monsters down, if you drop with them farther over the world's rim, you find what our sciences cannot locate or name, the substrate, the ocean or matrix or ether which buoys the rest, which gives goodness its power for good, and evil its power for evil, the unified field: our complex and inexplicable caring for each other, and for our life together here. This is given. It is not learned."[1]

Here Dillard names two crucial features of any spiritual journey. One is that it will take us inward and downward, toward the hardest realities of our lives, rather than outward and upward toward abstraction, idealization, and exhortation. The spiritual journey runs counter to the power of positive thinking.

Why must we go in and down? Because as we do so, we will meet the darkness that we carry within ourselves—the ultimate source of the shadows that we project onto other people. If we do not understand that the enemy is within, we will find a thousand ways of making someone "out there" into the enemy, becoming leaders who oppress rather than liberate others.

Source: *Excerpted from Chapter V, Leading from Within of* Let your life Speak *by Parker J. Palmer,* © 2000 *by Jossey-Bass. This material used by permission of John Wiley & Sons, Inc. pp 78-85.*

But, says Annie Dillard, it we ride those monsters all the way down, we break through to something precious—to "the unified field, our complex and inexplicable caring for each other," to the community we share beneath the broken surface of our lives. Good leadership comes from people who have penetrated their own inner darkness and arrived at the place where we are at one with one another, people who can lead the rest of us to a place of "hidden wholeness" because they have been there and know the way.

Václav Havel would be familiar with the journey Annie Dillard describes, because downward is where you go when you spend years "pinned under a boulder." That image suggests not only the political oppression under which all Czechs were forced to live but also the psychological depression Havel fell into as he struggled to survive under the communistic regime.

In 1975, that depression compelled Havel to write an open letter of protest to Gustav Husak, head of the Czechoslovakian Communist party. His letter—which got Havel thrown in jail and became the text of an underground movement that fomented the "Velvet Revolution" of 1989—was, in Havel's own words, an act of "autotherapy," an alternative to suicide, his expression of the decision to live divided no more. As Vincent and Jane Kavaloski have written, Havel "felt that he could remain silent only at the risk of 'living a lie,' and destroying himself from within."[2]

That is the choice before us when we are "pinned under a boulder" of any sort, the same choice Nelson Mandela made by using twenty-eight years in prison to prepare inwardly for leadership instead of drowning in despair. Under the most oppressive circumstances, people like Mandela, Havel, and uncounted others go all the way down, travel through their inner darkness—and emerge with the capacity to lead the rest of us toward community, toward "our complex and inexplicable caring for each other."

Annie Dillard offers a powerful image of the inner journey and tells us what might happen if we were to take it. But why would anybody want to take a journey of that sort, with its multiple difficulties and dangers? Everything in us cries out against it—which is why we externalize everything. It is so much easier to deal with the external world, to spend our lives manipulating material and institutions and other people instead of dealing with our own souls. We like to talk about the outer world as if it were infinitely complex and demanding, but it is a cakewalk compared to the labyrinth of our inner lives!

Here is a small story from my life about why one might want to take the inner journey. In my early forties, I decided to go on the program called Outward Bound. I was on the edge of my first depression, a fact I knew only dimly at the time, and I thought Outward Bound might be a place to shake up my life and learn some things I needed to know.

I chose the weeklong course at Hurricane Island, off the coast of Maine. I should have known from that name what was in store for me; next time I will sign up for the course at Happy Gardens or Pleasant Valley! Though it was a week of great teaching, deep community, and genuine growth, it was also a week of fear and loathing.

In the middle of that week, I faced the challenge I feared most. One of our instructors backed me up to the edge of a cliff 110 feet above solid ground. He tied a very thin rope to my waist—a rope that looked ill-kempt to me and seemed to be starting to unravel—and told me to start "rappelling that cliff.

"Do what?" I said.

"Just go!" the instructor explained, in typical Outward Bound fashion.

So I went—and immediately slammed into a ledge four feet down from the edge of the cliff, with bone-jarring, brain-jarring force.

The instructor looked down at me: "I don't think you quite got it."

"Right," said I, being in no position to disagree. "So what am I supposed to do?"

"The only way to do this," he said, "is to lean back as far as you can. You have to get your body at right angles to the cliff so that your weight will be on your feet. Its' counterint but it's the only way that works."

I knew that he was wrong, of course. I knew that the trick was to hug the mountain, to stay as close to the rock face as I could. So I tried it again, my way—and slammed into the ledge, another four feet down.

"You still don't have it," the instructor said helpfully.

"OK," I said, "tell me again what I am supposed to do."

"Lean way back," said he, "and take the next step."

The next step was a very big one, but I took it—and, wonder of wonders, it worked. I leaned back into empty space, eyes fixed on the heavens in prayer, made tiny, tiny moves with my feet, and started descending down the rock face, gaining confidence with every step.

I was about halfway down when the second instructor called up from below: "Parker, I think you'd better stop and see what's just below your feet." I lowered my eyes very slowly—so as not to shift my weight—and saw that I was approaching a deep hole in the face of the rock.

To get down, I would have to get around that hole, which meant I could not maintain the straight line of descent I had started to get comfortable with. I would need to change course and swing myself around that hole, to the left or to the right. I knew for a certainty that attempting to do so would lead directly to my death—so I froze, paralyzed with fear.

The second instructor let me hang there, trembling, in silence, for what seemed like a very long time. Finally, she shouted up these helpful words: "Parker, is anything wrong?"

To this day, I do not know where my words came from, though I have twelve witnesses to the fact that I spoke them. In a high, squeaky voice, I said, "I don't want to talk about it."

"Then," said the second instructor, "it's time that you learned the Outward Bound motto."

"Oh, keen," I thought. "I'm about to die, and she's going to give me a motto!"

But then she shouted ten words I hope never to forget, words whose impact and meaning I can still feel: "If you can't get out of it, get into it!"

I had long believed in the concept of "the word become flesh," but until that moment, I had not experienced it. My teacher spoke words so compelling that they bypassed my mind, went into my flesh, and animated my legs and feet. No helicopter would come to rescue me; the instructor on the cliff would not pull me up with the rope; there was no parachute in my backpack to float me to the ground. There was no way out of my dilemma except to get into it—so my feet started to move, and in a few minutes I made it safely down.

Why would anyone want to embark on the daunting inner journey about which Annie Dillard writes? Because there is no way out of one's inner life, so one had better get into it. On the inward and downward spiritual journey, the only way out is in and through.

Notes

[1.] Annie Dillard, Teaching a Stone to Talk. (N.Y.: Harper-Collins, 1982), pp. 94-95.

[2.] Vincent Kavaloski and Jane Kavaloski, "Moral Power and the Czech Revolution," Fellowship, Jan-Feb, 1992, p. 9.

THE INTERNET: SOCIAL ISSUES AND THE YOUNG

Anthony G. Picciano

The Internet effects the social and psychological lives of people in ways that its architects could never have imagined. Not only has the Internet been embraced by hundreds of millions of adults but also it is quickly evolving into the mass media and communications technology of choice among young people. In the United States, according to data collected by netwatch.org (2002), more than half of all households or approximately 171 million people are connected to the Internet. Young people in these households are often the most frequent users. In a survey conducted by The Pew Internet & American Life Project (2002), sixty percent of children under the age of eighteen—and more than seventy-eight percent of children between the ages of twelve and seventeen—go online on a regular basis. People under the age of twenty-one are becoming so proficient that there is a growing concern that a "digital disconnect" is occurring between technology-savvy students and their less savvy teachers and parents. As a result, school leaders now face a number of decisions which as little as ten years ago or prior to the Internet, were non-existent. In the not too distant future, school leaders will have to provide for a fully electronic education system that extends the classroom activity into homes, places of business, and onto portable appliances so that students and educators can engage in that activity at any time and any place.

THE INFLUENCE OF THE INTERNET AND WORLD WIDE WEB

Perhaps the most important issue is the influence that Internet technology may be having on the *social maturation and development* of young people. Concerns exist about the ease of their communication and interaction with known and unknown people and about the uncensored images of violence and obscenity they see. In addition, there are concerns about young people's ability to establish fictional identities and share fantasies with like-minded individuals in the anonymous recesses of Web pages, chat rooms and discussion boards. As an extreme example, in 1999, after the Littleton killings at Columbine High School, Eric Harris and Dylan Klebold, the high school students and gunmen, were described in one publication (McCullagh, 1999) as "Doom-playing, AOL-subscribing, Web-site publishers . . ." The two teenagers had posted violent images and slogans on the Internet and Harris' Web site included instructions for making bombs. In response to the tragedy, President Bill Clinton blamed the violence on TV, the movies, and the Internet as influencing our American society and especially the minds of young people. Yet within hours of the shootings, Ron Dries, Internet manager for the Colorado's Jefferson County Public Schools, set up a Web page where parents could get information about their children (Walsh, 1999). People from around the country started sending email messages expressing their sympathy and condolences. A Columbine Memorial Web site was subsequently set up which has had more than 10 million visitors. Paradoxically, the Internet was partially blamed for the violence at Columbine while at the same time used as the main communications vehicle for people to express their feelings and sorrow.

What is it about the Internet that enables it to captivate millions of people? Is it a form of mass media? Is it a communications tool? Is it a virtual electronic library? Is it an entertainment system? The answer to all of the above is yes and herein lies its ability to entice young people.

JUST ANOTHER MEDIUM—SOME CAUTIONS

While it might be easy to dismiss the Internet/WWW as just another medium, this severely underestimates its power and potential. Never before has there been a medium that combines multimedia capability, hyperlinked information retrieval, synchronous and asynchronous communications, and interactivity in a loosely organized structure that transcends governmental oversight and authority. Other media (e.g., television, books and magazines, and radio) and communication tools (e.g. telephone) pale in comparison. Television and radio are passive, one-way communication mediums, which while rich in video and audio, do not allow individuals to interact with each other. The telephone is strictly a synchronous communications tool with little capacity for imaging or information retrieval. The Internet/WWW represents the convergence of several media, information retrieval, and communications technologies into one technology. Furthermore, once an investment has been made in a computer workstation, the incremental costs for using the Internet/WWW are negligible. For example, it costs no more to send an email to a neighbor a few houses away than it does to send one to a colleague in Japan.

Because of its communications capabilities and its growing acceptance into people's homes and businesses, the Internet/WWW has spawned a number of enterprises designed to duplicate corporate operations (e.g. amazon.com, travelocity.com, e-bay.com) as well as governmental services including education. Internet-based distance learning is increasingly being viewed as an important instructional component for students who by necessity or by choice are being educated in their homes. Major distance learning initiatives such as the United States Department of Education's *Star Schools* created in 1988, have been established for primary and secondary school populations. More than 1.6 million students annually enroll in *Star Schools*. Many states have also begun to establish "virtual" schools using the Internet for course delivery.

The purposes of virtual primary and high schools vary from school to school, but essentially they are designed to provide on-line alternatives to traditional primary and high schools. The Kentucky Virtual High School is aimed in large part at students in small, rural school districts that suffer from a shortage of teachers qualified to teach upper-level math, science and foreign language courses. The Florida High School hires teachers who design and teach Internet courses, many of them central to a basic high school curriculum, like algebra and English. In the near future, the Florida High School expects to offer all the courses necessary for a student to earn a high school diploma. While most of the students enrolled are public high school students attending regular in-class courses, about thirty percent are home-schooled students. The most extensive virtual venture may be *The Virtual High School,* financed in part through a U.S. Department of Education grant and operated by the nonprofit Concord Consortium in Concord, Massachusetts. It is operated as a cooperative, with schools in 26 states and a number of countries agreeing to design and teach Internet-based courses in exchange for their students being able to participate. In addition to government and school district funded programs, for-profit ventures are also targeting distance learning students. Companies such as Kaplan Education Inc., Apex Learning Inc., and former US Education Secretary William Bennett's K-12 venture are aggressively pursuing students for specialized courses and educational needs.

Given its extraordinary media and communications benefits, why the concerns with young people spending a good deal of time using the Internet/WWW? First, content is completely unregulated. The Internet/WWW is a global, voluntary organization with little oversight beyond address naming conventions. The address naming convention is essential to prevent the confusion that would result if users had the same names and/or addresses for email or URLs. Nationally-based government agencies have little jurisdiction over a global entity. Even the United Nations has no jurisdiction over voluntary electronic communities. Therefore, Web sites can contain and depict almost any type of violence, hatred, or pornography without censorship. Television, films, and other media attempt to regulate and warn through rating systems when material may be questionable for viewing by young people. These attempts at regulation have been modestly successful. Practically no attempts have been made to regulate questionable material on the Internet/WWW beyond the posting of individual warnings on some Web sites. Prurient interests, whether commercial or not, rarely will be aggressive in this regard. To the contrary, young people who read, see, and interact with their material are frequently seen as future consumers or converts. School administrators have begun to feel the need to protect students from accessing questionable material by implementing filtering or blocking procedures in their schools. Furthermore, the Children's Internet Protection Act (HR 4577 - FY 2001) requires schools using federal funds for Internet use or connections to have filtering systems in place or risk losing federal education aid.

Second, one can use the Internet/WWW easily and privately. While a boon to the serious researcher, any topic is readily available by searching *Yahoo, Google,* or any other search engine. In the privacy of his or her bedroom, a young person can view, download, and interact electronically without having to keep and hide a book, videotape, or other "hard copy" of something that others such as their parents might see and find questionable. Unless a parent is particularly proficient, it is extremely difficult and time-consuming to find objectionable material by searching billions of bytes of disk files on someone else's computer. Furthermore, many young people are more proficient in using computer technology than their parents and would have no problem deliberately hiding material they did not want their parents to see on their disk files. School administrators can provide a great service to their communities by initiating programs to educate both children and parents in the positive ways the Internet can be used for learning, entertainment, and social activities in which the entire family can participate.

Third, the Internet/WWW was originally developed to function as an international vehicle for the free exchange of information and data. While a good deal of commercial or fee-based material is available, most of the material on the Internet/WWW is free. Indeed, the most dangerous materials, those related to hatred, bigotry, and calls for violence are available free of charge. Young people do not have to ask Mom and Dad for extra allowance or work a few hours longer after school in order to purchase these materials.

Fourth, although the amount of time young people are spending on the Internet/WWW is difficult to gauge, in many instances, it is many hours per day. Would it not be better if this time were spent socializing, studying or playing with others? For example, on an average Monday through Friday, a K-12 student sleeps eight to ten hours, is in school (including travel time) for another eight to nine hours, and perhaps has five to eight hours for other activities. If the child is replacing socializing with friends, participating in an after school activity, or studying in a library, time spent on the Internet/WWW may be problematic. On the other hand, if the time spent on the Internet/WWW replaces watching situation comedies on television, listening to music alone on a walkman, or conversing on the telephone with friends, time spent on the Internet/WWW may be at least as valuable. Aside from access to questionable content, the Internet/WWW requires active participation, and it may be a better way to spend time than as a passive "couch potato" or in other solitary pursuits. Here educators can take advantage of the time and energy that students are expending on the Internet by initiating electronic group and community activities. The history of a neighborhood or community, environmental issues, reporting on school events and sports, and charity drives are examples of activities that can easily be supported and enhanced by Internet technology.

Fifth, because of its interactivity, the Internet/WWW entices young people to act out fantasies. Fantasizing is not problematic unless one spends too much time or starts losing a sense of what is real. During play, children have always acted out fantasies as heroes and heroines, mommies and daddies, cowboys, or glamour queens. In the past, children shared their fantasies with a handful of playmates, many of whom adopted roles that helped a child play out his or her fantasies - I'll be the mommy and you be the daddy or I'll be the doctor and you be the patient. Because of the need to come together in a common physical space, fantasy play activities occurred for a limited time, usually until suppertime. On the Internet/WWW, people can adopt personae and engage others over extended periods of time. There actually is no need to end a fantasy on the Internet/WWW. Using synchronous chat rooms and asynchronous discussion boards, young and old adopt completely fantasized personae and use them for months and years on end with others who also adopt fantasized personae. Is this problematic? There is not a concrete answer but it might be for some individuals. To understand this better, a brief discussion of the power of interaction on a computer network is appropriate.

YOUTH INTERACTION AND THE INTERNET/WWW

Interaction is highly desirable. This is one of the important facilities of the Internet/WWW that has attracted so many users. The ability to ask a question, to respond, to follow up with another question is the basis of much teaching and learning theory, and is usually considered beneficial. Interaction may also include persuading others to a point of view, suggesting certain behavior, or seducing a person to a particular activity. This may or may not be beneficial depending on the point of view, the behavior, or the activity. The ability to screen or stop questionable interactions is a sign of maturity. Young people may not know when is the time to stop. Furthermore, interacting with others in the privacy of their rooms when chats and discussions seem to have no end, where mom or dad or other adults cannot see or hear the interaction, might surely test a young person's ability to stop an activity. The social and psychological effects of the Internet/WWW, as well as how the interactive nature of the new media effects the behavior of participants, are areas in which a good deal of study is needed.

In an extensive review of the literature, Ebersole (1999) identified a number of theories in several disciplines that could be applied to the study of this phenomenon including: critical mass, uses and gratifications, social presence and media richness, diffusion of innovations, social information processing, and media dependency. What is clear is that the Internet/WWW and other forms of new electronic media are surely effecting the way people, especially the young, are socially interacting and developing. What is not known is whether this is positive or negative or both. It may depend on the inclinations of the individual. What is also clear is that educators need to interface with this world in their classrooms, through their assignments, homework, and online discussion groups of topics that are important to young developing minds.

WHAT ARE EDUCATORS TO DO?

Educators need to understand better how their students are using the Internet/WWW and to provide guidance and assistance so that its use is beneficial. The Pew Internet and American Life Project (2002) survey mentioned earlier was conducted of gender-balanced, racially diverse groups of students from 36 different schools around the United States. The survey identified five major uses of the Internet/WWW:

1. Students use it for research and homework as they would use books, articles, and a reference library to find primary and secondary source material for reports, presentations, and projects.
2. Students use it to find tutoring when they have difficulty with some material. For example, *America Online* offers free tutoring services from certified teachers to all its subscribers.
3. Students use it for study group activities, to collaborate with classmates on projects, to study for tests and to trade class notes.
4. Students use it to supplement guidance counseling activities. This is especially important to high school students making choices about a college or a career.
5. Students use it to gather and store information and data on their computers as they would in a notebook. With laptop computers and portable digital appliances, students electronically keep notes, calendars, syllabi, assignments, address and telephone books.

Educators, especially school building administrators, should try to understand how their students are using the Internet/WWW and also:

a) *Proactively encourage its proper uses both in the school and in the home.* A starting point is to have a plan on how this technology is to be used for school-related activities. Surveying households in the school district especially those with children as to whether or not they have access to the Internet/WWW is basic information that should be collected with other school census data. A major school responsibility is to reduce or eliminate the "digital divide" between students who have and do not have access to technology. Equipping technology centers and making them available before and after normal school hours is desirable. Collaborating with libraries that increasingly are providing technology centers/services is another possibility.

b) *Provide guidance on how to use the Internet/WWW as a tool.* It can help them with their homework, doing papers and seeking advice. By the same token, children should be cautioned about the "dark side" of the Web where less than scrupulous adults are looking to take advantage of them. Children need adult guidance to distinguish between what is good and what is not only bad but also potentially harmful.

c) *Include and involve parents in planning Internet/WWW activities.* Two days after leaving office, Harold Levy, former Chancellor of the New York City public schools, wrote a New York Times op-ed piece entitled "What a Chancellor Needs Most." He identified the accomplishments of his administration and, among them was the creation of a new Board of Education Web site, which provides "information and analysis about everything from student performance to teacher certification." He also praised the benefits to parents of technology beyond the classroom especially informative school Web sites that celebrate student work, provide important information about school events or make available electronic forums for discussing community issues. Levy recommended that parents be involved with the development of information resources including school Web sites. Parents may provide the first alerts when their children need guidance in Internet/WWW usage. The school should be ready and able to assist parents in this regard in a confidential and supporting manner. Developing a support program for parents will be most successful if parents are involved with its design. Providing "good practices" information on Internet/WWW use to parents in the form of a pamphlet or on a school homepage is a relatively simple task. For example, the decision where a computer workstation for children's use should be situated in a house - in a family room where parents can visually monitor a child's activity or in the privacy of bedroom where they cannot - is an important one. Having information from the school regarding the pluses and minuses of such a decision would help parents determine the best location. The fact that many young people are proficient users of the Internet/WWW requires adults to assure that their children beneficially use it. The schools need to be proactive in helping parents with this responsibility.

d) *Model behavior for the entire school community by becoming proficient in using Internet technology.* Where teachers, students, parents, and other administrators see a school principal actively using the technology in pedagogically or administratively appropriate ways, a powerful and positive message is sent throughout the community. Unfortunately, the opposite is also true. School administrators who appear technologically illiterate send a negative message.

Lastly, the Internet/WWW is in its nascent stage. Over the next ten years or so, the Internet/WWW will continue to evolve and become more of an influence on our society and the development of young people. It will make major advances when higher speed or broadband communications become more generally available at an affordable price in people's homes. Two-way video, for instance, which presently is sparingly used, will be commonplace. The Internet/WWW will challenge and surpass commercial television and radio as the dominant mass medium in American households. School leaders would be wise to see its potential and plan now for how it will be best used for students, teachers, parents, and the larger community.

REFERENCES

Netwatch.org (August 2, 2002). *http://www.net-watch.org/*

Levin, D. & Arafeh, S. (August 14, 2002). *The Digital Disconnect: The widening gap between Internet-savvy students and their schools.* The Pew Internet & American Life Project. *http://www.pewinternet.org/reports/toc.asp?Report=67*

McCullagh, D. (April 27, 1999). Washington: The Net Must Pay. *Wired News.* *http://www.wired.com/news/politics/0,1283,19359,00.html*

Walsh, T. (May 3, 1999.). Colorado school reaches out through the Internet. *Government Computer News. http://www.gcn.com/archives/gcn/1999/May3/1c.htm*

Ebersole, S.E (1999). *Adolescents' use of the World-Wide Web in ten public schools: A uses and gratifications approach.* Doctoral dissertation for Regent University College of Communication and the Arts In Partial Fulfillment of the Requirements for the Doctor of Philosophy in Communication. http://faculty.uscolo.edu/ebersole/diss/

Levy, Harold (August 21, 2002). What a chancellor needs most. *The New York Times,* p. A17.

DIGITAL TECHNOLOGIES ENTER THE SCHOOL

Robin Stern, J. Theodore Repa, and Frank Moretti

Welcome to digital technology! With computers and wireless devices rapidly making their way into homes and schools, with children and teachers alike more facile, with email, with the proliferation of individual websites and asynchronous conversations—it is a natural next step for the this medium to be used in constructivist ways for students. We want the technology to be invisible. We don't want to think technology; we want to think content. We want to think collaboration. This is a call for the teachers to get on board where the students are and are going. They are growing up *digital*. For example, our children don't think about technology when they send a message to a friend. They just send email. Children don't think about using technology when they forget their homework, they just get online and visit the class web site. We now can build on a significantly different educational platform than ever before, more powerful and more complex therefore offering more opportunities for imaginative learning to take place. We as educators are learning it and applying it, at the same time, to the task at hand—teaching our children.

With the advent of computers in the classroom, teachers no longer need to shepherd the entire class through the material being taught but, rather, can adjust the pacing of the material so that students move at their own pace. The teacher's role can shift to educational facilitator and the students can take more responsibility for individual learning needs. Teachers, in turn, can pay more attention to the total experience of the child—including the affective and physical as well as the cognitive dimensions of learning. The teacher can teach social - emotional skills that will ultimately help children both enhance their academic performance and feel a greater sense of well being. Teachers can act as facilitators for small groups of students working on a particular problem. Teachers can work with students individually, for example, on frustration tolerance and motivation—leaving the content delivery to the digital environment. Teachers can initiate and follow the kind of conversations and patterns of interactions that students are engaged in online as part of the normal educational experience.

Social–emotional learning for students and teachers is already changed as a result of the emerging technologies. Many students have gone from communicating with each other during school hours by passing notes and brief conversations, to phone calls to emailing each other to constant instant messaging. Many teachers have gone from giving out homework orally (thereby requiring students to jot it down) to posting it on the school web. In addition, communication with parents is being relocated to email - replacing the familiar and frequent backpack notes.

Children, nowadays, often talk to two or three friends at a time without even picking up the phone—they are receiving multiple incoming messages (IMs). Children have access to primary resources and can even visit museums without ever leaving their home. Teachers share information about their students without the normal constraints of time or space. Teachers share resources online, communicate with students who have been absent, and develop virtual support groups. All these are possible now as the digital world, and the possibilities it brings, expands and increases daily.

In the following pages we will describe three different uses of new technologies that can promote social - emotional learning in schools. The first is an experiment that was done in an independent school in Manhattan where email and asynchronous conversations were used as extensions of the classroom. The second focuses on how middle and high school teachers can integrate resources on the Internet into their current teaching and curriculum while supporting social and emotional learning. The third is the use of stand-alone products to enhance social and emotional skills in the classroom. These games/environments provide students with the opportunity to "try out" choices and see consequences, to explore sensitive issues and have the opportunity for self-reflection and increased social interaction around these applications

USING TECHNOLOGY TO IMPROVE COMMUNICATIONS AND INTERACTIONS AMONG STUDENTS, ADULTS AND PARENTS IN SCHOOLS

Improving communications in schools using technology means breaking out of the proverbial "box". One of the essential lessons of Plato's Allegory of the Cave, the important and classic story, pertains to the fact that we, prisoners of our own perceptions and circumstances, perceive choice and possibility only within their confines. Only when released from these confines can we begin our exploration of new uncharted landscape, and can we see the past as having been confining. Only recently have the *constraint and the confines* of the traditional classroom on social-emotional learning become apparent, as powerful digital communications have superceded more conventional methods of discourse and of teaching and learning. This is the story of the Dalton School's sortie into the world of electronic, networked-based communications and the effects it had, particularly on social-emotional learning as the students "climbed" out of the cave of print and into the light of the digital universe.

Helped by technologically and politically savvy allies, and before Internet use was commonplace, the Dalton School had the opportunity to build one of the first high-speed, local area networks located in a school. Using First Class as the mail system and providing a bank of modems for home users, the faculty and students created a range of conferences emanating from both curricular and non -curricular entities (e.g. clubs, special interest groups). At first, the "Forum" was perceived as an additional encumbrance, but it quickly grew to become an assumed and essential part of the communications system of the school. Well over a hundred asynchronous conferences became a significant part of the discursive life of the school. Often the community forums addressed important matters too difficult to discuss face to face, such as race and socioeconomic disparities.

The Forum's power and centrality in the community became evident in the third year. A student prank on the student network caused the network to be shut down. The response of most people was what can only be described as cyber-culture shock. *People became disoriented and experienced feelings of separation and real anger.* Some described the school as experiencing a kind of death. Altogether this reaction produced such a sense of community pressure that the responsible students confessed their "crimes." The network was restored much to everyone's relief. Many expressed the kind of euphoric feelings than only reunions occasion. Indeed the return of the Forum was a reunion, but of a kind of community that we only understand in its fullness when deprived of it. The incident opened the authors' eyes to the fact that we were living at a time when the nature of community, social interaction, and personal means of identification were changing in the invisible but compelling grip of networked-based, digital technologies. The world was surrounding and embracing itself with invisible ligatures and lines of connectivity that were aggressively changing the world of interaction forever. Students became denizens of the Forum from daylight to the early hours of the next day. We were living in the matrix of our own making, one that made possible profound communications and *relationships* in which people populated each *others'* minds, but did so at no place or time.

What does this all mean in practice for social-emotional intelligence and education? The authors observed many incipient possibilities. One important premise is that at Dalton, the observations are premised on an electronic communications environment in which all the users know one another, or easily can get to know one another, as members of the same community. (these relationships contrast for example with Sherry Turkle's work (1997) in exploring the social and psychological effects of individuals interacting anonymously. A second premise is that electronic, asynchronous discourse represents the creation of a third medium of personal experience lodged between the face-to-face universe of public interaction and the private conversations within the mind. When students respond in the open environment of a classroom or in the public space of a school they are both aware of the pressure of their peers and of the fact that what they say will evanesce, literally disappear, except for minimal memory traces. They are constrained both by the pressure of the moment and relieved by the sense that their remarks will not linger. The existence of the third medium relieves a student of that pressure of the moment, thus increasing the possibility of less encumbered response, a response both true to the student held view as well as more considered because of the process of objectification involved in the writing process. The continued existence of the response as part of the cyber environment of the school creates an interesting and benign pressure akin to but different from the traditional peer pressure students live with daily. Students have to live with the words they write and be willing to defend or represent them in public discourse. Pressure becomes less psychological and more related to the content of the culture of discourse. Even if students are never queried on one of their online responses, those students still imagine that their comments are part of what the participating group thinks they think. Their comments become their badges of identification and over time representative of a position they hold or are believed to hold. This process represents a new merging of conversation, considered written expression, intellectual content, and personal development.

When an affirmative action discussion raged in the online Forum at Dalton, tens participated and hundreds read regularly. The participants were defining themselves, to themselves and to their community, in respect to an important issue in the context of a written medium. This definitional voyage seems to meet what most educational theorists, from Plato on, wanted to achieve—character development in the context of serious and relevant content, development of the skills of analysis and expression in the grip of real interests, and contention with issues of value and substance. Before educators seek to cure the problems of contemporary education though global connections we should explore the power of digital technologies in revitalizing those communities in which we have a 150 year investment—our schools—still the most important single institution for the education of our children.

INTEGRATING INTERNET RESOURCES INTO CURRENT MIDDLE AND HIGH SCHOOL TEACHING WHILE SUPPORTING SOCIAL–EMOTIONAL LEARNING

The many middle and high school teachers we have worked with on integrating technology in the classroom have conflicting thoughts about the value of the Internet. On the one hand, they recognize the value of the many resources that students have available to them at a click of the mouse, and the ease of access. Students are no longer confined to finding information in a textbook or library. On the other hand, teachers are concerned about students spending excessive amounts of time either finding appropriate resources on the web or examining inappropriate sites. The freedom to access information from around the world can be both a benefit and a curse, particularly in this litigious society. Another issue of concern to teachers is how they can help students evaluate the accuracy and usefulness of web material. Not all material on the web is equally valuable or even accurate. Lastly, teachers are concerned that the technology and the net may actually support social isolation of students and retard their social and emotional learning. In *short,* how can middle and high school teachers model and control choosing appropriate web materials in the context of the normal classroom that supports the cognitive as well as the affective learning of children?

It is clear that computers and other forms of digital technology, *alone,* currently do little to enhance cognitive and social and emotional learning. Students can use computers to write, compute, or interact, but they can accomplish all of this without the use of computers. Learning of any kind depends on the culture of the learning environment (Mercer, 1993); currently at the middle and high school level the creation of the learning environment is primarily the responsibility of the teacher. Teacher-student and student-student interactions, not digital technology itself become keys to successful cognitive and social-emotional learning experiences. For digital technology to be successfully implemented into the teacher created learning environment, teachers have to view it as helpful for their teaching and the learning environment (Cuban, 1986 and Cohen, 1987). Teachers see the use of digital technology in the classroom as supplemental to what they do (Cuban, 1993), requiring answering the question "why use digital technology?" not how.

Presentation software packages, used creatively with assignments that use technology to enhance communication and interaction, can fit into teachers' view of the learning process and offer practical answers to their concerns about appropriate and inappropriate student use of the Internet. A part of the normal activity of middle and high school teachers is structuring materials for students in ways that allow them to more easily master the content. They often prepare the material in outline format or in sequential steps in order to assist students in organizing complex materials. They create ever-changing communication and interaction patterns that students and teachers can use to support each other in mastering the content. Presentation software can aid teachers in producing materials in this manner using the template option. For example, a middle school teacher might organize material on the structure of a simple paragraph on the following presentation software template slide.

WRITING A PARAGRAPH

- Select Topic
- Opening or Topic Sentence
- Description of Topic Sentences
- Concluding Sentence

| *Previous slide* | *Next slide* | *Back to first slide* | *View graphic version* |

This slide could be saved on a disk that students could later load onto a computer and examine it at their leisure, assuming they had the appropriate presentation software on their computer. Better yet, the slide could be placed on the teacher's class web site and be accessed by any student at any time via their web browser. The advantage of the web browser approach is that students do not have to have the presentation software on their computer and the web browser is platform independent.

Obviously, the presentation software offers many bells and whistles, like changing colors and font sizes as well as importing clip art, audio, and video images, to make the material more attractive to students. One of those bells and whistles is of particular interest to the teacher who wants to model using information on the web to enhance learning while maintaining reasonable control of where the student searches. It is called hyperlinking.

Hyperlinking web material to the slide template allows the student to click on the word or phase in the content on the slide and immediately be transported to a web site that enhances students' understanding of the material being studied. This transformation again assumes students have access on their computer to the web.

Hyperlinking web material using presentation software is a relatively easy task. Basically, after the slide has been created, the teacher goes to the web to select appropriate links that will supplement student learning of the topic. By having the teacher identify the appropriate links, the teacher is modeling how to select links and can even conduct a mini-lesson on evaluating the quality of web sources. Next, the teacher copies the web address to the link and pastes it to the word or phase in the slide presentation. This procedure controls the web sites students should explore on the topic being studied. Finally, the teacher saves the hyper-linked slide presentation on a disk or the class web page. A sample of a hyperlink slide presentation follows. The underlined words following the bullets indicate hyperlinks to the web and would appear in a light blue color on the computer screen.

Elementary School Story Sites

- *Sample lesson plans*
- *Children's literature sites*
- *Children's literature webguide*
- *Another Children's literature webguide*
- *Children's literature links*
- *Preschool choices*
- *Bedtime stories (need password)*

The teachers can hyperlink and save a slide in about eight clicks of the mouse. Details of the hyperlinking and saving processes are provided in the help section of presentation software packages or you can contact any of the authors at *theodore.repa@nyu.edu* if you have questions.

This example of developing hyperlink slides for the computer provides a simple way for teachers to use technology in an invisible, yet helpful way to both student and teacher, to enhance cognitive and social and emotional teaching and learning for the individual pupil or groups of pupils. It incorporates some constructivist strategies by enabling students to explore the learning of the material at their own pace following guided leads from the teacher (Koschmann, 1996). It requires, however, that the teacher be familiar with both how to actively engage students in their own learning and the "how to" of digital technology. By using hyperlinked slides in conjunction with teacher-designed instructional technology strategies that promote communication, the teacher can model how students can responsibly use resources on the web while supporting social and emotional learning.

EMOTIONALLY INTELLIGENT DIGITAL PRODUCTS

When the concept of emotional intelligence hit the ground running in 1995 there were several compact disc products that parents and teachers could buy for their children to introduce concepts of social - emotional learning. Products, such as *FIN FIN* by Fujitsu and *PURPLE MOON: ADVENTURES IN FRIENDSHIP* created by Brenda Laurel, were pioneering efforts in developing relationship skills through the use of interactive digital simulation. The effectiveness of teaching and learning with these products and others, depends, to a great extent, on the creative exploration and contextualization by the teaches and parents. The sky is the limit as far as using stand alone digital products as jumping off points for conversation and deepening dialogues with children about important social-emotional issues.

More recently, RELATE FOR TEENS by Ripple Effects has proven to be the most complex, rich and engaging software available on the market for social-emotional learning. Developer Alice Ray tells us about her product and how to use it in the classroom: "The goal of the program is to make best practices in social learning available to youth and the adults who work with them, providing them just what they need, when they want it, in the way they most like to learn. It is not a substitute for human interaction, but a catalyst for more satisfying and productive interaction. Within the program there is the opportunity to engage in systematic skill training focusing on the key "building blocks" of social-emotional health—empathy, assertiveness, impulse control, management of feelings, decision making, self-understanding and connection to community." Students report having fun while learning "cool" things about how to interact better with others. One teen told us that the interface really "rocks." In today's world you can't get any better than that!

In addition to the award-winning *Relate for Teens,* Alice Ray and her partner, Sara Berg have developed a similar product for younger children, called *Relate for Kids.* We are very excited about this product because we know, as educators, that the earlier we begin teaching social-emotional learning lessons, the more they will become part of the child's development and the better equipped they will be with social/emotional lessons learned. *Relate for Kids* and *Relate for Teens* have won more than two dozen national and international awards. Two other products, new to market are equally powerful learning tools: *Right Now,* developed in the wake of Sept. 11 and an uncertain world, builds skill for diversity and managing trauma, among other things. The other, *Teaching Coach,* is a groundbreaking training program for teachers to help them be more effective working with students in the classroom.

WEB-BASED APPLICATIONS

Today, the Web is the popular development environment. Once Web applications are created; they are ubiquitously available and completed integrated with the communications capacity of the web. Furthermore, unlike CD-ROMs you can't lose the applications! The SIMS ONLINE CHARTER EDITION offers the user his/her own piece of land to create any atmosphere or environment of his/her choice (e.g. coffee bar, dance club, museum, etc.). In addition to a physical environment, the user is encouraged to build a network of friends to enhance his or her power, wealth, reputation and social standing. The user can be a peacemaker, pest or recluse; he/she can choose his role, his/her attitude, personality and destiny. ACTIVEWORLDS and ATMOSPHERE are two other fascinating programs that allow users to create virtual worlds, in which they can interact. Children and teachers can use all of these applications, and others, as part of existing curriculum lessons or as learning tools for SEL skills, for role playing opportunities and as conversation starters. In addition, in the classroom or afterschool context, these applications are a beginning in developing SEL skills in the "real" world.

CONCLUSION

Technology is new to us grownups. To the children we are teaching, it is already background. They are growing up and learning with very different technical underpinnings in educational practice. Technology can afford us a new, more complex and comprehensive way to deliver quality education in both process and content. Ultimately, the educational process is about people—people learning how to deal with themselves and with each other. The current and future technologies offer new opportunities for all of us to become more socially and emotionally competent. And this is only the beginning.

REFERENCES

Cohen, D.K. (1987). Educational Technology, Policy and Practice. *Educational Evaluation and Policy Analysis.* 9, (2), p. 153-170.

Cuban, L. (1986). *Teachers and Machines: The Classroom Use of Technology since 1920.* New York: Teachers College Press.

Cuban, L. (1993). *How Teachers Taught: Constancy and Change in American Classrooms 1890–1990.* New York: Teachers College Press.

Koschmann, T. (1996). Paradigm Shifts and Instructional Technology: An Introduction. In T. Koschmann (red), *CSCL: Theory and Practice of an Emerging Paradigm.* New Jersey: Lawrence Erlbaum Associates Inc.

Cassell, J. and Jenkins, H. eds: *From Barbie to Mortal Combat* (1999), MIT PRESS, Cambridge, Mass,

Turkle, S. (1997). *Life on the Screen: Identity in the Age of the Internet.* New York: Simon & Schuster.

NOTE FROM AUTHORS

At Teacher's College, Columbia University, the Robin Stern's course in Social -Emotional Learning and Digital Technology (co-developed by Ted Repa) is now part of the core curriculum in the Program of Communication, Education and Technology. The George Lucas Educational Foundation has taken a serious interest in the subject of SEL—please check out their website at GLEF.org. Researchers at major universities such as MIT and NYU are investigating the relation between emotion and technology. Maurice Elias and Linda Bruene at UMDNJ and Rutgers University are using digital technology to inform and expand their existing SEL programs and, in collaboration with Robin Stern and Frank Moretti at Columbia University, are working on further applications and environments for the teaching and learning of SEL. For more information about these projects and courses you can contact the authors at RBin@aol.com.

EMOTIONAL INTELLIGENCE

LEADERSHIP COMPETENCIES

SELF-AWARENESS

- *Emotional self-awareness.* Leaders high in emotional self-awareness are attuned to their inner signals, recognizing how their feelings affect them and their job performance. They are attuned to their guiding values and can often intuit the best course of action, seeing the big picture in a complex situation. Emotionally self-aware leaders can be candid and authentic, able to speak openly about their emotions or with conviction about their guiding vision.
- *Accurate self-assessment.* Leaders with high self-awareness typically know their limitations and strengths, and exhibit a sense of humor about themselves. They exhibit a gracefulness in learning where they need to improve, and welcome constructive criticism and feedback. Accurate self-assessment lets a leader know when to ask for help and where to focus in cultivating new leadership strengths.
- *Self-confidence.* Knowing their abilities with accuracy allows leaders to play to their strengths. Self-confident leaders can welcome a difficult assignment. Such leaders often have a sense of presence, a self-assurance that lets them stand out in a group.

SELF-MANAGEMENT

- *Self-control.* Leaders with emotional self-control find ways to manage their disturbing emotions and impulses, and even to channel them in useful ways. A hallmark of self-control is the leader who stays calm and clear-headed under high stress or during a crisis—or who remains unflappable even when confronted by a trying situation.
- *Transparency.* Leaders who are transparent live their values. Transparency—an authentic openness to others about one's feelings, beliefs, and actions—allows integrity. Such leaders openly admit mistakes or faults, and confront unethical behavior in others rather than turn a blind eye.
- *Adaptability.* Leaders who are adaptable can juggle multiple demands without losing their focus or energy, and are comfortable with the inevitable ambiguities of organizational life. Such leaders can be flexible in adapting to new challenges, nimble in adjusting to fluid change, and limber in their thinking in the face of new data or realities.
- *Achievement.* Leaders with strength in achievement have high personal standards that drive them to constantly seek performance improvements—both for themselves and those they lead. They are pragmatic, setting measurable but challenging goals, and are able to calculate risk so that their goals are worthy but attainable. A hallmark of achievement is in continually learning—and teaching—ways to do better.
- *Initiative.* Leaders who have a sense of efficacy—that they have what it takes to control their own destiny—excel in initiative. They seize opportunities—or create them—rather than simply waiting. Such a leader does not hesitate to cut through red tape, or even bend the rules, when necessary to create better possibilities for the future.
- *Optimism.* A leader who is optimistic can roll with the punches, seeing an opportunity rather than a threat in a setback. Such leaders see others positively, expecting

the best of them. And their "glass half-full" outlook leads them to expect that changes in the future will be for the better.

SOCIAL AWARENESS

- *Empathy.* Leaders with empathy are able to attune to a wide range of emotional signals, letting them sense the felt, but unspoken, emotions in a person or group. Such leaders listen attentively and can grasp the other person's perspective. Empathy makes a leader able to get along well with people of diverse backgrounds or from other cultures.
- *Organizational awareness.* A leader with a keen social awareness can be politically astute, able to detect crucial social networks and read key power relationships. Such leaders can understand the political forces at work in an organization, as well as the guiding values and unspoken rules that operate among people there.
- *Service.* Leaders high in the service competence foster an emotional climate so that people directly in touch with the customer or client will keep the relationship on the right track. Such leaders monitor customer or client satisfaction carefully to ensure they are getting what they need. They also make themselves available as needed.

RELATIONSHIP MANAGEMENT

- *Inspiration.* Leaders who inspire both create resonance and move people with a compelling vision or shared mission. Such leaders embody what they ask of others, and are able to articulate a shared mission in a way that inspires others to follow. They offer a sense of common purpose beyond the day-to-day tasks, making work exciting.
- *Influence.* Indicators of a leader's powers of influence range from finding just the right appeal for a given listener to knowing how to build buy-in from key people and a network of support for an initiative. Leaders adept in influence are persuasive and engaging when they address a group.
- *Developing others.* Leaders who are adept at cultivating people's abilities show a genuine interest in those they are helping along, understanding their goals, strengths, and weaknesses. Such leaders can give timely and constructive feedback and are natural mentors or coaches.
- *Change catalyst.* Leaders who can catalyze change are able to recognize the need for the change, challenge the status quo, and champion the new order. They can be strong advocates for the change even in the face of opposition, making the argument for it compellingly. They also find practical ways to overcome barriers to change.
- *Conflict management.* Leaders who manage conflicts best are able to draw out all parties, understand the differing perspectives, and then find a common ideal that everyone can endorse. They surface the conflict, acknowledge the feelings and views of all sides, and then redirect the energy toward a shared ideal.
- *Teamwork and collaboration.* Leaders who are able team players generate an atmosphere of friendly collegiality and are themselves models of respect, helpfulness, and cooperation. They draw others into active, enthusiastic commitment to the collective effort, and build spirit and identity. They spend time forging and cementing close relationships beyond mere work obligations.

List of Contributors

Maurice J. Elias, Ph.D. is Professor of Psychology and Coordinator of the Internship Program in Applied School and Community Psychology at Rutgers University. He is the Coordinator of the Leadership team for the Collaborative for Academic, Social and Emotional Learning (CASEL). He is the author of numerous books in the field of social and emotional learning including *Building Learning Communities with Character* (2003), EQ + IQ = Best Leadership Practices for Caring and Successful Schools (2003) and *Promoting Social and Emotional Learning: Guidelines for Educators* (1997).

Daniel Goleman, Ph.D. is the Co-director of the Consortium for Research on Emotional Intelligence in Organizations, Graduate School of Professional Psychology at Rutgers University. He is also the author of New York Times best-sellers *Emotional Intelligence* (1995) and *Working with Emotional Intelligence* (1998). His 2002 book *Primal Leadership,* co-written with Richard Boyatzis and Annie McKee, demonstrates that a leader's emotional intelligence has an enormous impact on group performance and on an organization's bottom line. Dr. Goleman's article, "What Makes a Leader?" which is included in this volume, received the highest reader ratings ever in the Harvard Business Review (1998), becoming the best-selling reprint in the journal's history.

Marcia Kalb Knoll, Ed.D. began her career in education as a teacher, and then administrator in the New York City Public Schools, serving as assistant principal and then principal of P.S. 220 and Director of Curriculum and Instruction for District 28 schools in Queens, New York. In 1988 she became Assistant Superintendent of the Valley Stream Central High School District on Long Island, New York. Dr. Knoll is currently a Professor of Educational Administration and Supervision at Hunter College of the City University of New York. A past president of The Association for Supervision and Curriculum Development, her latest book is *The Administrator's Guide to Student Achievement and Higher Test Scores* (Prentice Hall, 2002).

Larry Leverett, Ph.D. is presently the Superintendent of Greenwich Connecticut Public Schools and the former superintendent of Plainfield New Jersey Public School District. Dr. Leverett has also worked as New Jersey Assistant Commissioner for Urban Education and in various leadership positions in K-12 education and community development. He has had extensive experience reforming schools and consulting in school districts across the country. He is a graduate of the Urban Superintendent's Doctoral program at Harvard University and a sought after speaker.

Carmella B'Hahn has worked with holistic approaches to life, transitions, and death for over twenty years. In 1984, she cofounded MetaCentre, a teaching and retreat center in England. She has written on the topics of birth and death for professional journals as well as the popular press. She co-authored *Benjaya's Gifts* (1996) in which she shares what she learned from her son's birth and sudden drowning at five years old. Her second book, *Mourning Has Broken* (2002) draws on in-depth interviews with a variety of people from different backgrounds who have used the traumatic shadows in their lives to propel them on a journey of transformation toward greater resiliency.

Yvonne De Gaetano, Ph.D. is an Associate Professor in the Department of Curriculum and Teaching in the School of Education at Hunter College. She is the Coordinator of the Childhood Education and Early Childhood Education Bilingual Extension Programs. Dr. De Gaetano's interests include multicultural education, teacher preparation, and school reform. She has presented at numerous conferences, nationally and internationally, on these topics. Currently, she directs two federally funded grants that focus on bilingual teacher preparation and the improvement of instruction for English Language Learners through the arts. Dr. De Gaetano is the co-author of two books: *ALERTA: A multicultural bilingual approach to teaching young children* and *Kaleidoscope: A multicultural approach for the primary school classroom.*

Susan Keister is President of Integral Vision, an educational consulting and coaching organization specializing in school transformation, social and emotional competencies, character education, service-learning, and positive prevention. Ms. Keister has over 27 years of experience as an executive, author, speaker, teacher, and trainer for Quest International, leading the development of the acclaimed Lions-Quest K–12 programs. These positive youth development programs have been translated into 17 languages in 33 countries and are used by more than 350,000 educators throughout the world. She is a Fellow of the Fetzer Institute.

Kimberly Kinsler, Ph.D. is a professor of Education Foundations at Hunter College of the City University of New York. Dr. Kinsler is Co-Director of the Inquiry Based School Improvement Project, a New York State Department of Education funded program to help public schools establish Site Based Management/Shared Decision Making teams. She has a long history of work in the area of school improvement, having served as a school improvement coach for both James Comer's *School Improvement Project* and Henry Levin's *Accelerated School Program.* Her experiences in helping to improve public schools became the basis for a co-authored book, *Reforming Schools* (2000).

Nicholas Michelli, Ed.D. is University Dean for Teacher Education for the City University of New York and Professor in the University's Ph.D. program in Urban Education. He oversees programs for educators at the nation's largest public urban university. He served as Dean of the College of Education and Human Services at Montclair State University for twenty years where he was professor and dean emeritus. He is the co-author of *Centers of Pedagogy* (1999) and has contributed articles and book chapters focusing on education for democracy and urban education. Peter Lang Publishers will publish Dr. Michelli's next book on excellence in teacher education in 2004.

Frank Moretti, Ph.D. is the Executive Director of the Columbia Center for New Media Teaching and Learning and Professor of Communications at Teachers College, Columbia University. As Associate Headmaster of the Dalton School and Founder and Executive Director of the New Laboratory and Learning, Moretti has 15 years of experience in school-based leadership in technology development and is recognized as a leading theorist and practitioner in the use of digital technology in education. He founded the software company, Learn Technologies Interactive/Voyager. He contributes extensively to national conferences and seminars on technology and education and has written extensively on the role of technology in education.

Parker J. Palmer, Ph.D is a writer and traveling teacher who works on issues in education, community, spirituality and social change. Palmer is senior associate of the American Association for Higher Education and senior adviser to the Fetzer Institute. In 1998 he was named one of the thirty most influential senior leaders in higher education. He is best known for his book *The Courage to Teach, to Know As We Are Known.* The selection in this book was taken from *Let Your Life Speak, Listening for the Voice of Vocation.*

Anthony Picciano, Ph.D. is a professor in the graduate program in Education Administration and Supervision at Hunter College of The City of New York. Dr. Picciano is involved in urban school systemic reform initiatives especially in the design and implementation of technology, the teaching of mathematics, science and technology, and staff development. His latest book, *Educational Leadership and Planning for Technology,* 3rd Edition (2001), is a revision of an earlier work, *Computers in the Schools: A Guide to Planning and Administration* (1994). He is also the author of *Distance Learning* (Prentice-Hall-Merrill, 2000) which looks at the growing field of Web-based distance learning. He has also published numerous articles and papers.

J. Theodore Repa, Ph.D. recently retired professor and Chair of the Department of Administration, Leadership, and Technology at the Steinhardt School of Education at New York University, enjoys a 38-year-career focusing on issues of leadership and equity in education. He maintains his 23-year affiliation with NYU through the Metropolitan Center for Urban Education, an institution that focuses on improving high poverty, low achieving schools. Formerly deputy director of Metro Center, Dr. Repa, a graduate of Stanford University, has expanded his interest in equity in education to include developing one's leadership potential by strengthening one's social and emotional competence.

Robin Stern, Ph.D. is an educator, psychotherapist and psychological consultant who has developed and implemented programs to promote personal and professional growth through self-awareness in schools and businesses. Currently, she is an adjunct associate professor at Teachers College, Columbia University, and a member of the Board of Directors of both The Woodhull Institute for Ethical Leadership and Educators for Social Responsibility. Robin teaches and consults about social-emotional learning and digital technologies, as well as the psychology of leadership and the development of emotional competence. Robin regularly writes and speaks about ethical leadership, emotional intelligence, and communication.

Endnotes

Chapter One

[1]Kotter, J. 2002.

[2]Goleman, D. 1995.

[3]SEL programs exist in school districts across our country. They include but are not limited to character education, service learning, conflict resolutions, violence prevention, decision making and empathy building. Programs that address these skills are working within hundreds and thousands of schools on a daily basis. Some of the best program efforts can be reviewed in CASEL's Safe and Sound (2003): An Educational Leader's Guide to Evidence-Based Social and Emotional Learning (SEL) Programs, along with the CD-Rom is available for $10.00, plus postage and handling from the Laboratory for Student Success (LSS) at www.temple.edu/LSS. You can obtain a PDF version of the guide at the CASEL website, www.casel.org.

[4]Goleman, D. 1998, p. 12.

[5]Ibid, p.19. Daniel Goleman tells us that when IQ tests are correlated with how well people perform in their careers the highest estimate of how much difference IQ accounts for is about 25%. In *The Emotionally Intelligent Workplace,* Goleman tells us that when we distinguish successful people within a job category, EI is a strong predictor of stellar performance, p.24.

[6]Goleman, D., Boyatzis, R. and McKee, A. 2002. p. 38.

[7]Ibid, p. 113.

[8]Just about any educational journal or newspaper today addresses the serious national principal shortage. Both the National Association of Secondary School Principals and The National Association of Elementary School Principal websites have a series of articles that address this critical national shortage. www.naesp.org and www.nassp.org. The article titled *The principal shortage: Crisis or opportunity* by Leslie Fenwick and Mildrid C. Pierce addresses specific shortage factors based on diversity factors.

[9]Interview with Mary Butz, Executive Director of the Office of Leadership Development of the New York City Department of Education in October, 2002.

[10]ECI Accreditation Training Manual: Driving Personal and Professional Development obtained during a training with the Hay Group on May 7-8, 2002.

Chapter Two

[1]The principals' stories in this chapter are taken from a three year qualitative research study conducted by the authors of this text (Patti & Tobin, 2001a and 2001b). The research explored the school principal's role in implementing the RCCP program. To protect the research participants' anonymity, their names and school identifiers have been changed.

[2]Barth, 1990, p. 68. Roland Barth is the founding director of the Principals Center at Harvard University. This book is well-written with excellent insights for educators who are trying to create change within their schools.

[3]Patti, J. & Tobin, J. 2001a. Other writers have reported on the death of support for principals and described some support networks that have filled the void (Barth, 1980; Mohr, 1991, & Senge et al., 2000).

[4]Palmer, 1998.

[5]Salovey & Mayer, 1990.

[6]Goleman, 1998.

[7]Goleman, D., Boyatzis, R., & McKee. The authors' viewpoints (Patti and Tobin) on applying findings from research in business settings to education reflect a wary pragmatism. Many past and present efforts at making schools run more like businesses have actually harmed education. Schools and businesses exist for different purposes and are aligned with different core values that can clash with each other (e.g. cutting costs vs. educating special needs children). That said, both kinds of organizations can benefit from studying the best practices of the other and adapting them for their own purposes. Leaders who are emotionally competent are needed in both schools and businesses.

[8]LeDoux, J., 1996. For a further look at the relationship of the cognitive and emotional processes of the brain, view The Secret Life of the Brain, Episode Four: The Adult Brain: To Think by Feeling. PBS Video Series ©2001 Thirteen/WNET New York. Its visual effects and human stories expertly illustrate the importance of our emotions.

[9]This tour derives from a number of resources that integrate brain research with education. See Berninger & Richards (2002); Caine & Caine (1994), and Sylvester (1995).

[10]The new technologies that have informed neuroscientists are positronic emission tomography [PET] scans, functional magnetic resonance imagery [FMR] and magnetoencephalography [MEG].

[11]LeDoux, J., 1996.

[12]This principal was part of our research (Patti & Tobin, 2001). Shortly before this book was finished, this principal left his school to head up a new school that was designed with his input. As part of his leave-taking from his old school, he was very cognizant of the emotional work that he and his school community needed to do to ease the transition. His leadership in this emotional journey enabled him, his staff, his students and their families to adapt to the change.

[13]Saarni, C. 1999.

[14]Many teachers in schools we have visited complain that principals are often unaware of problems because the lines of communication are top-down and because their principals rarely spend time in classrooms.

[15]In Chapters Two and Three we will discuss some of these processes and strategies.

[16]Sergiovanni, T. 1993.

[17]In this era of relying on standardized testing as an "objective" measure of school success, it is useful to keep in mind this quote from systems writer, Daniel Kim: "We tend to think that we believe what we measure but it's more likely that we measure what we believe." Quote taken from Senge et al, 2000, p. 358.

[18]It is useful to begin with questions. Ackerman et al. in Chapter Nine of their book, Making Sense as the School Leader, suggest a thoughtful beginning approach.

[19]Goleman, 1998, p. 70.

[20]Bandura, A. 1997.

[21]Eisenberg, N. & Zhou, Q. 2000, page 166.

[22]Saarni points out that there is considerable variability in emotional elicitors between and within cultures. Children learn how to appraise their emotions based on many social factors. Very different things may trigger joy or anger, depending on whether you grow up in Tokyo or Baton Rouge. Even in the same family, children are likely to respond to different triggers. How might your five-year-old and your fourteen-year-old respond differently if you rubbed their heads?

[23]The phrase "emotionally hijacked" (also amygdala hijack) has been used by Daniel Goleman to describe what happens to the brain when it goes into emergency mode. Read Chapter Five of Goleman's *Working with Emotional Intelligence* (1998) to see how the performances of a guest speaker, a champion boxer and an automobile driver were all affected by hijacks.

[24]See McKay, M.; Davis, M. & Fanning, P. 1997 for an in-depth description of cognitive behavioral techniques for regulating emotions.

Chapter Three

[1]The World Trade Center was located in District 2 and several schools in the immediate area had to be evacuated because of the danger of either physical destruction or poisonous air. Many students witnessed horrifying sights. Afterwards, thousands of students had to attend school in different sites while their schools were cleaned and detoxified or new spaces were prepared. Many of these students, and students from around the city, later experienced symptoms related to post traumatic stress syndrome. PS 51 is located about three miles from the scene of the attack. At the time of the attack, Nancy was an assistant principal at PS 40 in District Two.

[2]Barth, R. S. 1980; Deal, T. & Peterson, K.D., 1991.; DuFour, R. & Eaker, R., 1992.; Patti, J & Tobin, J. 2001a., and Sergiovanni, T. 1993.

[3]This school leader saw this emotional situation as a "teachable moment" for the teacher. Modeling an assertive and respectful way to handle an emotional situation, he first listened to the teacher, lessened the emotional intensity, and then asked her to think of another way she could handle the problem. This took only a few minutes. Later, he might speak to the teacher alone. Only if the teacher continued to be abusive would he invoke the power of his authority.

[4]Blase, J. & Blase, J. R. 1994; Stein, S. J. & Book, H. E., 2000.

[5]Seligman, M., 1991.

[6]Goleman, D. 1998. p. 129. How optimism is expressed depends on cultural norms. A person in Japan and a person in the United States may display optimism in very different ways.

[7]Interestingly, the word community also comes from these same root words as Peter Senge and his coauthors point out in their book, Schools That Learn (2000). This book is an excellent source of ideas on how to improve schools using systems thinking. For a good method of using dialogue to open up communication in large groups see pages 75-77 in their book.

[8]Griffin, E. 1997.

[9]Gardner, H. 1983. A person high in interpersonal intelligence would probably learn communication and other social skills much easier and quicker than the rest of us. We all know some people who just seem to have a "knack" of knowing how to relate to others.

[10]Blum, D. 1998; Ekman, P. 1999; Ekman, P. & Friesen, W. V. 1975; Ekman, P. & Rosenberg, E. (Eds.), 1997.

[11]Meharabian, A. 1971. Meharabian's research findings are often misrepresented as applying to all communication. In contexts which are relatively emotion-free (i.e. asking a clerk for stamps) a much lower percentage of meaning would be conveyed by body language (unless I suddenly realized that this clerk was the one who had laughed at my tie the last time I bought stamps).

[12]Blum, D. 1998; Carter, R. 1998.

[13]Ekman, P. & Friesen, W. V. 1975.

[14]Sax, L., 2002.; Tannen, D., 2001.

[15]Ekman, P. & Friesen, W. V. 1975; The research on "reading" facial expressions has received much more attention among law enforcement officials and intelligence officers since the events of September 11, 2001 (see Kaufman, M.T. 2002.)

[16]Bolton, R. 1979.

[17]Goleman, D. 1998.

[18]See Stone, D., Patton, B., & Heen, S. 1999, pages 189-200 for an excellent discussion of the ways that humans distort their messages.

[19]Gordon, T. 1977.

[20]Goleman, D.; Boyatzis, R.; McKee, A. 2002., p. 47.

[21]Blase, J. Blase, J. R. 1994.

[22]Goleman, D.; Boyatzis, R.; McKee, A. 2002., p. 109.

[23]Boyatzis, R. E., 2002.

[24]Berra, Y. 2001. *When you come to a fork in the road, take it!* New York: Hyperion, p. 3. While Yogi Berra's verbal miscues are famous and many may interpret Yogi's mistakes as a sign of poor intelligence, I believe that he is probably gifted in the area of emotional intelligence. Not only has his Hall of Fame success been matched by his success as a husband, father, grandfather and friend, but listen to how he describes his life: "I've always done things that *feel* right" (page 3). An intuitive thinker to say the least!

[25]Goleman, D.; Boyatzis, R.; McKee, A. 2002. The key in getting accurate feedback is to develop trustworthiness. Your staff members will give you honest feedback if they can trust that you will accept it, use it for self-learning, and not retaliate against them.

Chapter Four

[1]Folger, Poole & Stutman 1997. p. 4.

[2]Costatino, C.A. & Merchant, C.S. 1996. p. xiii.

[3]Deutsch, M. 2002. p. 30. Deutsch's chapter is in *The Handbook of Conflict Resolution* (see references). For those readers who would like to learn more about the theoretical and practical underpinnings of the field of conflict resolution, this volume provides a great deal of in-depth information.

[4]Thomas, K.W. 2002.

[5]Goleman, D., Boyatzis, R. & McKee, A. 2002.

[6]National Center for Education Statistics. 2002.

[7]Toppo, G. 2003.

[8]Tyler, K. 2002 and Whitemyer, D. 2002. These estimates are based on studies of various organizations and not specifically schools. Based on self-reports and observations of school principals I have worked with, however, I would estimate that these estimates are not too far off. If that was the case, imagine the cost savings of an effective conflict resolution system for the whole school.

[9]In this context, we are defining power as using force and control to decrease or contain destructive conflict. Power can also be thought of as the ability to accomplish one's goals in which case a power-based or interest-based approach could both be described as potentially powerful.

[10]Fisher, R. & Ury, W. 1991.

[11]Based on personal experience in negotiating and mediating disputes, I believe that it is this initial stage of problem definition that people have the least skill at doing and they are usually unaware that they are not doing it well. They are certain they know what the problem is even before they speak to the other party.

[12]These steps are an adaptation of five steps described in Chapter Eight of *The Courageous Messenger* by Ryan, Oesttreich, and Orr III, 1996. The book is an excellent resource for anyone who sometimes finds it difficult to speak up at work. In using the steps in my own workplace and in coaching others in theirs, I have adapted the steps to include the emotional assessment because emotions can inform or impede the process.

[13]Ury, W. 1991.

[14]McCarthy, W. 1991.

[15]Freund, J. C. 1992.

[16]Ury, W., Brett, J.M., & Goldberg, S.B. 1991.

[17]Glickman, C. et al 2001. In their book for school leaders, the authors discuss a variety of ways leaders can deal effectively with conflict in school groups.

[18]These values come from Roger Schwartz's book, *The Skilled facilitator*, p. 8. Schwartz adapted the earlier work of Argyris & Schon, 1974.

[19]Schwartz, R. 1994. p. 75.

[20]Schwartz, R. 1994.

[21]Stone, D; Patton, B., & Heen, S. 1999. These colleagues at the Harvard Negotiation Project call these difficult conversations "learning conversations." They suggest that you reframe the way you approach the conversation either in individual or group settings as a way to promote mutual learning. I found this book to be a very useful guide to help me think through how I might bring up an undiscussable issue in a group I had been involved with for a long time. I was carrying the book one day while waiting for the subway and a man approached me carrying the same book. "It's a great book, isn't it?" the man said and then added, "It helped me not only with my clients but also my personal life." He was feeling the power of competency.

[22]These stages are described in some detail in Slaikeu, K. 1996.

[23]Milner, N. 1994. p. 413.

[24]Deutsch, M. 2002.

[25]Aber, J.L.,; Jones, S.M.; Brown, J.L.; Chaudry, N.; Supples, F. 1998, and Stevahn, L.; Johnson, D.W.; Johnson, R. T.; Schultz, R. 2002, pp. 305–332 The Stevahn study found that students who spent time learning conflict resolution *and* social studies content in integrated lessons learned more content than students who only learned content. This deeper learning occurred despite the fact that the integrated lessons took no more time than the content only lessons.

[26]Frederickson, L. 2003.

[27]Rooney, J. 2003. Rooney calls these kinds of leaders "castle builders" because they purposively design organizational structures to defend their teachers and students. Roland Barth, in his book *Run School Run* (1980), describes these leaders as *conductors* and *insulators* of information, respectively making sure that people in their schools get the information they need to excel while being insulated from all unnecessary information that would produce anxiety, fear and confusion. He believes that a key task of principals is to reduce fear in their schools.

[28]Lynch, J. 2003.

[29]George, J. 2000. Watching some principals and school superintendents work is like watching the Peking Acrobats perform. You ask, "How do they do that?" The answer is simple. They have the skills and the knowledge that makes it look easy.

Chapter 5

[1]Comer, J. 2003. p. 11.

[2]Black, S. 2002. This article can be obtained at http://www.asbj.com/current/research.html. For further information visit the Civil Rights Project at Harvard University's Graduate School of Education and Achieve, Inc.

[3]Roderick, T. 1987. Educators for Social Responsibility Metro Newsletter. For more information about New York City Educators for Social Responsibility, please visit the website at www.esrmetro.org.

[4]Brandt, R. 2003. pp. 57-70.

[5]Schaps, E.; Schaeffer, F. and McDonell, S. 2001, pp. 1-6.

[6]Weissberg, R.; Resnik, H.; Payton, J. and Utne O'Brien, M., March, 2003, pp. 46–50.

[7]Copies of the Safe and Sound report can be downloaded free from the CASEL website at www.casel.org, or ordered in hardcopy with CD-ROM from www.temple.edu.LSS.

[8]Haynes, N. and Marans, S. 1999, pp. 165-66.

[9]J. Wallender, R. Weissberg, M. Rubin and P. Salovey. (2003). This manuscript has been submitted for publication. The research was supported by a grant from the Fetzer Institute, p. 9. The most recent research on the ink between SEL and academic achievement can be found in Zins, J. E., Weissberg, R. P., Wang, M. L., & Walberg, H. J. (Eds.) (in press). Also,

see Elias, M. (2003) Academic and social–emotional learning. International Academy of Education.

[10]A few exemplary leaders who have been working intently with SEL are Jerry Tarnoff, Superintendent of West Orange Public Schools; Richard Warren, Superintendent of Franklin Public Schools, Massachusetts; Paula Papponi, Superintendent of Jemez Valley Schools, New Mexico; Larry Leverett, former Superintendent of Plainfield, NJ schools and now Superintendent of Greenwich Public Schools in Connecticut; Evelyn Castro former Superintendent of Community School District 4 in New York City and Sheldon Berman, Superintendent of the Hudson Public Schools in Massachusetts.

[11]Information for this section was taken from an interview with Dr. Berman and available information at the Hudson Public Schools' website: www.hudson.k12.ma.us/schools_district/administration/nsoc.htm The Don't Laugh at Me Program referred to in this chapter is a project of Operation Respect. See note 26 for more details. Information about The Responsive Classroom can be found at their website www.responsiveclass.org. Recently Dr. Berman's work was highlighted at the George Lucas website www.gclef.org

[12]The Resolving Conflict Creatively Program is a key initiative of Educators for Social Responsibility. It is a research-based, school-wide comprehensive SEL program that builds upon the six themes of the peaceable school discussed in this chapter. You can get more information about this initiative at the Educators for Social Responsibility website, www.esrnational.org. The stories of the three principals in this chapter were adapted from a 1999-2001 study we conducted with seven New York City school principals. The full study can be obtained from the CUNY Dispute Resolution Consortium.

[13]The late William Kreidler, of ESR, an internationally renowned conflict resolution expert coined the term peaceable, a view of the peaceful resolution of conflict as a dynamic process.

[14]Refer to the CASEL *Safe and Sound* guide described in note 7 above.

[15]Lantieri, L. and Patti, J. 1996, pp. 26-27.

[16]The work with the Young Ambassadors took place at the Roosevelt Middle School in Vista, California in the early 90's. This work continues today at Roosevelt and other schools. Read Chapter Seven for a longer version of how this work was implemented.

[17]Boleman, L. and Deal, T. 2001. *Washington Post,* April 25, 2001.

[18]Renato Taguiri in Owens, R. 1998, p. 162.

[19]Debra Viadero's story paints a complex portrait of students who pick on others. pp. 24-27.

[20]R. Skiba, R. Peterson, K. Boone and Fontanini. 2000, p. 61.

[21]Benedetto Saraceno, M.D., 2001. In Mrazek, P. and Hosman, C. Eds. Report from the Inaugural World Conference on the Promotion of Mental Health and Prevention of Mental and Behavioral Disorders. (Alexandria, VA: World Federation for Mental Health, 2002).

[22]Stories of bullying permeate Shaw's book. On p. 111 you will find the DOJ citation. Refer to Note 19 for the reference to Harris, Williams and teens who committed the school shootings.

[23]Garbarino, J. 1999. p. 142 and back cover.

[24]Weiler, J. 1999.

[25]The Mickey Mantle School, formerly P811M is located at 466 West End Avenue in New York City. For more information see http://www.nycenet.edu/d75/schools/P811M/default.htm

[26]Don't Laugh at Me is an outstanding program made possible through a collaboration between Operation Respect and Educators for Social Responsibility. It was conceived and produced by Peter Yarrow of Peter, Paul and Mary with Educators for Social Responsibility. The teachers guide, video and CD have been made available, free of charge, to over 10,000 teachers across the country. For more information go to www.operationrespect.org: Arnold Goldsteins, *The Prepare Curriculum: Teaching Pro-social competencies* provides a very helpful, structured, sequential skill-building focus (Illinois: Research press, 1999); Nicholas Long, Mary Wood and Frank Fescer, *Life Space Crisis Intervention, Second Edition* (Texas: Pro-Ed, 2001).

[27]Lieber, C.M. 2002, p. 259.

Chapter 6

[1]The No Child Left Behind legislation is the major piece of legislation driving public education at the time of this book. To learn more about this Act, please visit www.nochildleftbehind.gov.

[2]Goleman, D. 2001, p. 195.

[3]Hall, G. & Hord, S. 2001, p. 4. In Chapter 3 of this book there is a lengthy discussion about the use of innovation configurations to plan for the change process. See p. 36–54. The IC map is a visual representation of what the innovation will look like from initiation to full implementation.

[4]Fullan, M., 1999, p. 21

[5]Kotter, J. 2002.

[6]To learn more about the implementation of The Resolving Conflict Creatively Program at The Roosevelt Middle School in Vista, California see L. Lantieri and J. Patti, 1996.

[7]Senge, P. 1990.

[8]See N. 3

[9]Fullan, M., 2001.

[10]See note 8, p.193. Hall and Hord equate this implementation dip with their level of Management within the Stages of Concern of the Concerns-Based Adoption Model. (CBAM).

[11]Fullan, M. Note 9, p. 44

[12]Rybeck, D. *Putting Emotional Intelligence to Work: Successful Leadership is More than IQ.* (Mass: Butterworth-Heinemann, 1998). p. 66

[13]Lieber, C. 2002, p. 145

[14]Owens, R. (1998). Owen traditionally does a wonderful review of organizational behavior related to education. This text was the source for all references made in this paragraph.

[15]Byram, A. 1986. The classic Lewin, Lippit and White's studies (1930; 1960) often referred to as the Iowa Child Studies series found that while authoritarian leaders tended to have more productive groups in quantitative terms, democratic leaders' groups had greater work motivation. Groups under democratic leadership tended to have friendlier environments, to be more group-minded and less submissive to the leader. The boys observed in the study exhibited a preference for democratic leaders.

[16]Hersey, P. & Blanchard, K. 1982

[17]Goleman, D., Boyatzis, R. & Annie McKee. 2002. Chapter 4.

[18]You can obtain the LEAD 360 Self and Other instruments from *The Center for Leadership Studies* in Escondido, California. Scoring software is available for analyzing results. Visit the website: www.situational.com.

[19]Ibid, n.18. Information regarding the analysis of the situational leadership styles is available to researchers who use the LEAD 360 self and other.

[20]Senge, P. et al. 1994.

[21]Interview with Arthur Foresta at New Visions, 1998.

[22]Abraham Maslow (1954) synthesized a large body of research related to human motivation. His hierarchy of human needs is based on two human needs, deficiency and growth needs. Each lower need is met by moving to the higher need. You can read about Maslow in almost any psychology textbook. Chapters 2 through 4 in Paul Hersey and Ken Blanchard's, *Management of Organizational Behavior* does a wonderful job of reviewing Maslow's work.

[23]Herzberg, F. January, 2003, p. 87-96.

[24]Bodine, R. & Crawford, D. *The Quality School.*

[25]Thomas, K.W. 2002.

[26]The reference to McClelland's work was obtained from the Hay group.

[27]Cherniss, C. and Adler, M. p. 102

[28]Cherniss, C. and Goleman, D. 2001.

[29]The American Psychological Association's 14 principles can be obtained at their website www.apa.org

[30]Albert Bandura (1994). In V.S. Ramachaudran (Ed.). 1998. Available on line at http://www.emory.edu/EDUCATION/mfp/BanEncy.html, p. 1-14.

[31]Goleman, D. 2001. p. 183

[32]Ibid, p. 185

[33]Meier, D. 1994.

[34]Fullan, Michael .See note 4

[35]Wheatley, Margaret. 2002, p. 4

Chapter Seven

[1]Facing History and Ourselves is a non profit organization dedicated to the education of social justice issues in secondary education. Facing History's national headquarters is in Brookline, Massachusetts. FHAO provides teachers with staff development in the form of workshops and institutes. They also provide access to an assortment of materials for classroom use as well as ongoing research in 20th century history. You can visit their website at www.facinghistory.org or call 617-232-1595.

[2]The term ethnic cleansing is widely reviewed in the Drazen Petrovic article, p. 342

[3]Kinsler, K. & Gamble, M. 2001.

[4]The 2002 Phi Delta Kappa Census can be read in the March 2003 edition of Phi Delta Kappan. This can also be accessed at the www.pdkintl.org website.

[5]Taken from the Facing History and Ourselves Resource Book, p. 129.

[6]Gary Marx, Mar 2002 p. 68. Obtained online through EBSCO, ISSN No. 0161-7389. Also, ASCD Annual Conference online, "Ten Trends: Educating Children for a Profoundly Different Future." www.simulconference.com/ASCD/2003/scs/1273a.shtml.

[7]The National Research Council (NRC) revealed over 20 years ago that minority children were over represented in special education classes. In January 2002, The National Academy of Sciences (NAS) released its report that also addresses the under-representation of minority children in gifted education. The National Association of Black School Educator's report *Addressing over-representation of African-American students in Special Education*, is another great source addressing this topic. Please go to http://www.ideapractices.org to read more.

[8]Meier, D. 1995, p. 6-7.

[9]Kohn, A. March 2003, Volume 60, no.6, p 29.

[10]Dee Brown wrote *Bury my Heart at Wounded Knee: An Indian History of the American West:* (Henry Holt and Company,1970). I remember when this book hit the shelves. It was an incredible eye opener for many of us who were not aware of the tragic events that happened at Pine Ridge, South Dakota in the mid 1800's. There are a number of informative websites to visit, but one in particular that I used was http://www.dickshovel.com.

[11]Sheldon Berman's book, *Children's Social Consciousness and the Development of Social Responsibility* (N.Y: State University Press) is one of the best reviews of the literature done in this area. The Berkowitz and Gibbs study, p.95, is just one of the many that Berman has reviewed to expand our understanding of moral reasoning, development and action. Chapter five on Educational Interventions and Social Responsibility provides rich background on practices that are effective.

[12]Taken from Peter Elbow's speech "Critical Thinking is Not Enough," at the Reninger Lecture at the University of Northern Iowa in April, 1983.

[13]I have taught in the Lesley College program and found it to extend my own thinking and learning as well as that of its students. For more information please visit the Educators for Social Responsibility website, www.esrnational.org.

[14]Meier, D. p. 22.

[15]Carl Glickman's article, p. 41 can be obtained online from EBSCO, Host, ISSN 0013-1784. Carl Glickman is Chair of School Improvement at Southwest Texas State University and President of the Institute for Schools, Education and Democracy.

[16]Ibid, p. 4

[17]Christine E. Sleeter, 2001.

[18]The controversial Coleman Report prompted the legislative request to explain the lack of equal education opportunity that existed in the South. It indicated that SES was the major factor for inequities in the educational system. This report sparked the research that led to the Effective Schools research. Educators needed to explain the factors that were making a difference in schools for all children, especially children of color.

[19]Christine Sleeter, See Note 17.

[21]Fischer, L. 2001.

[22]Facing History Resource book, (See note 1) p. 385.

[23]Lickona, T. Winter 2001, p. 239–251.

[24]Service Learning Policy Deliberation, A set of resources to advance service-learning through policy alignment development and support by Terry Pickeral presented at AACTE, 2003.

[25]Lantieri and Patti, 1996.

[26]Thomas, G. November, 2002, p. 13

[27]Sheldon Berman, same as Note 11, p. 202

[28]See Note 3, Preface xv.

Chapter Eight

[1]This fictional account is based on a hypothetical case described in Tony Wagner's excellent 1998 article, *Change as collaborative inquiry: A constructivist methodology for reinventing schools*. We have elaborated on the case and created the fictitious name for our principal.

[2]Conley & Goldman, 1994.

[3]Hord, S.M. *Facilitative leadership: The imperative for change*, 1992. This monograph extensively reviews the literature on facilitative leadership as it relates to school change. Noteworthy is the fact that the author describes ways superintendents, leadership teams and principals can facilitate change using a six component model of intervention. For other descriptions of research on facilitative leadership, see Blase & Blase, 1994.

[4]Hord. See note 3.

[5]Cartwright, D. & Zander, A., 1960.

[6]Cartwright & Zander.

[7]Tuckman, B. 1965.

[8]The act of breaking a school norm is often most vividly felt by persons new to a school. As a new teacher many years ago, I was transferred from a very open bohemian school to one of the most traditional schools in the same district. At first, I could not understand why the administrators and the staff kept looking at me in a peculiar way. People were polite but most seemed to avoid eye contact. Instead, they stared at my chin. After a few days of this, I finally discovered that I was breaking a norm when the assistant principal followed me into the men's bathroom and, while I went about my business, solemnly informed me that the school "expects male teachers to wear ties here." I had broken a norm and, though I had no major objections to wearing ties, the norm and the way I was informed of it, gave me a distinctly unpleasant taste of the organizational culture.

[9]Katzenbach, J. R. and Smith, D.K. 1993.

[10]Folkerts, K. 1999.

[11]Griggs, L. 1995.

[12]Janis, I. 1983.

[13]Odden, E. & Wohlstetter, P. 1995.

[14]Holloway, J. H. 2000.

[15]Schlechty, P. C. 1997.

[16]DuFour, R. & Eaker, R., 1992.

[17]Odden & Wohlstetter.

[18]Schein, E. H. 1992. Edgar Schein has written extensively about organizational culture. Another useful book by the same author is *The Corporate Culture Survival Guide*, 1999.

[19]Schein, 1992, p. 382

[20]Lambert, M. D. & Gardner, M. E. 1995.

[21]Houston, P. 2001, p. 428. The author of this article captures the dilemmas that creative school superintendents face when confronted by impossible demands. School principals and other educators would also benefit from stepping in the shoes of the district leader and getting a different point of view.

[22]Lashway, L. 2000.

[23]Conley & Goldman.

[24]This question was posed by Thomas Gordon in his excellent book, *Leadership Effectiveness Training*, 1977. Gordon's ideas have proven to be extremely helpful in my work with principals especially in the areas of dealing with conflict and effective decision making. In my observations of school leaders, it is clear that there are times when a leader needs to make important decisions without a group's input especially when an urgent problem must be handled immediately. However, I also observed how many principals use this reasoning to justify many of their decisions. In most cases, these urgent problems would have been better solved if principals had taken some time to gather more information from involved parties and to involve them in decision-making. Principals who view most of their problems as emergency fires to be put out quickly by them alone wind up receiving little information and less help from others. As one principal confessed, "All day long I just run around putting out fires.!"

[25]Lashway. See note 22.

[26]Richard, A. 2000. In Richard's article, Alvarez states that the accountability burden, added to all of the other responsibilities that principals face, make potential leaders reluctant to apply for open positions. In addition to shared accountability, she suggested that some school districts might hire business managers to lessen the burdens of instructional leaders.

[27]Schools have had a long history of being the center of societal struggles. The issues of school governance and school accountability can be seen as the latest extension of that history. While a deep understanding of this history is essential for anyone interested in school leadership, it is beyond the scope of this book. For further resources on accountability issues, search for The National Accountability Network at <www.annenberginstitute.org>.

[28]For portraits of some of these efforts in schools see: 1. Apple, M. & Beane, J. 1995; 2. Quellmaslz, E., Shields, P. & Knapp, M.S. 1995.

[29]Crow, G.M., 1998.

[30]Cloke, K. & Goldsmith, J., 2002.

[31]Cloke & Goldsmith.

[32]In the hierarchical culture that exists in most schools it is difficult to discover, much less utilize, the leadership skills of people not in positions of authority. For an interesting commentary on discovering teacher leadership outside of school see Roland Barth, 2001.

[33]Schwartz, R. M. 1994.

[34]Goleman, D., Boyatzis, R. & McKee, A., 2002.

[35]Apple, M. & Beane, J.; Blasé & Blasé, 1994. For a non-USA model, read the article, *The remarkable impact of creating a school community* in *American Educator,* Spring 1988, p. 10-17 & 38-43. In this fascinating interview of a headmistress of a German secondary school, a collaborative school model that had been implemented in over two hundred schools is described. This model has had measurable success dealing with academic and human relations issues when compared to traditional German schools. Another wonderful European example of a collaborative school model can be found in a 1993 book about Reggio Emilia by Caroline Edwards, Lella Gandini and George Forman entitled, *The Hundred Languages of Children*.

[36]Quote taken from Cloke & Goldsmith, p. 3.

Chapter Nine

[1]The story of Gutenberg and what the effects of a new technology can have on social beliefs, norms and practices makes fascinating reading. It also gives us insights into how slow the process of change is. For a better sense of this story see Man, J. 2002; Cameron, E. 1999, and the website <http://www.digitalcentury.com/encyclo/update/print.html>.

[2]Jones, G. R. 2002.

[3]United States Census Bureau, 2002.

[4]Solomon, G. 2002.

[5]Schlechty, P. 1997. Phillip Schlechty, founder of the Center for Leadership in School Reform, describes how the printing press took many years before it's potential was realized but that, eventually, the institutions that did not adapt to the changes it brought were made obsolete. Schlechty warns that schools also face obsolescence if they do not eventually adapt to IT.

[6]Hird, A. 2000. Hird sees students as an untapped resource for helping a school become cyber-savvy. She found that students in a Rhode Island high school much more knowledgeable about the potential of IT than their teachers. Hird suggests that school leaders might use students to teach teachers how to use technology to enhance learning.

[7]There are some writers who would dispute my contention that books are essentially linear (Robbie McClintock at Columbia's Institute for Learning Technologies <www.ilt.columbia.edu> is one).

[8]Sousa, D. A. 2001.

[9]Drucker, P. F. 2002.

[10]These characteristics were gleaned from several sources: Center for Education 2002; Caldwell, B. J. 1999, and two issues of *Educational Leadership* (Volume 53, issue 2 and Volume 54, issue 3).

[11]Fullan, M. 1997. p. 223. The staff meeting described in the following paragraphs is an elaboration on a process presented in Fullan's book. The ability to suspend one's beliefs in order to understand the perspective of another is a key skill in the conflict resolution strategies described in Chapter Three of our book. It is also a useful skill for students to learn when exploring character motivation in literature or analyzing the actions of historical figures.

[12]Goleman, D., Boyatzis, R., & McKee, A. 2002. p. 219.

[13]Naisbitt, J. 2000.

[14]Fiske, E. B. 1995. Fiske's chapter is in the book, *Designing Places for Learning*, edited by Anne Meek. Anyone interested in learning more about schools that have incorporated innovative designs would find many excellent ideas in this volume.

[15]In one school I consulted with, I mentioned the name of a first year teacher in the school to two teachers and these teachers informed me that they had never met the woman.

[16]Anne Taylor (1995), a professor of architecture, says that school design often transmits cultural values and we need to look at what the physical environment of our schools say to children. She thinks that the designs of schools and prisons bear disturbing similarities. She sees merit in Howard Gardner's idea of a school as museum to accommodate diverse learning styles.

[17]Becker, F. & Steele, F. 1995. Becker and Steele's book provides the "Big Picture" of how organizational ecology affects collaboration and effectiveness. Unfortunately, the examples the authors give to illustrate these concepts come from the business world and may not be very useful to educators.

[18]Taylor, A. 1997.

[19]Fiske. See note 14.

[20]School or district leaders who are either helping to plan a new school or restructuring a large school into smaller units will find valuable resources at the web site, <www.smallschoolsworkshop.org> developed by the University of Illinois at Chicago.

[21]Dan Bodette, Principal of SES, sent these photos. The school was built on the grounds of one of its community partners, the Minnesota Zoo, which the students use for learning laboratories. The winner of a 1999 American High Schools Award from the U.S. Department of Education, the school was opened in 1995 with the mission of developing active citizen leaders who are environmentally informed, self-perpetuating learners, and connected to the local and global community. For more information visit SES website: <http://www.district196.org/ses/Visitor/index.html>

[22]<http://aa.uncwil.edu/numina/tech%20web%20page/web.html> This site has excellent links to how wireless handhelds can enhance learning and collaboration. Also read Shotsberger, P.G. & Vetter, R. 2002.

[23]United States Department of Education, 2000.

[24]Drucker, P. F. 2000. Another thought-provoking piece of writing on this topic is presented by John Wilinsky (2002), a professor of literacy and technology at the University of British Columbia. He believes that it is still too early to tell if the Internet will rival the printing press' impact and offers the dissenting opinion of Larry Cuban. However, he thinks the analogy of the printing press can inspire us in trying to make sense of the new technologies and sees the Internet as a means of furthering John Dewey's vision.

[25]Tanner, D. & Tanner, L. 1995. The authors provide an excellent account of the battles over the curriculum that have shaped what is learned in schools in the past and today.

[26]For a thoughtful article on the interplay between social emotional learning and IT, see the reading by Stern, Repa and Moretti at the back of this book.

[27]Ellmore, Olson, and Smith, 1995.

[28]I purposely chose this description of a student because it is descriptive of my son. Except for a few exceptions, most of my son's teachers have attempted to have him fit into the curriculum rather than have the curriculum fit him. He has learned how to do it and now gets high honors in his middle school by figuring out what teachers want. Unfortunately, the consequence of this "fitting in" is a boring school day and a real loss of wonder that still marks his learning when he is not in school. Sadly, many principals are sent the "problem" kids when many of these students would not be problems if they were in a learning environment that "fit" their interests and learning styles.

[29]This innovation is not far off and less powerful electronic paper is already being produced by Xerox as this book is written. Technological change is occurring so rapidly that this chapter will likely be somewhat outdated before it gets printed. If you had this book on electronic paper, rather than on "real" paper, you or I could update this information very quickly.

[30]A teacher at Dzantik'i Heeni Middle School in Juneau, Alaska involved his students in a project to dispel myths about their state. The project evolved and led to the creation of an award-winning web site as described in Burness, P. & Snider, W. 1995, p. 218.

[31]Michael Dertouzos (1997) calls this ability to customize learning materials to individual learners "automated tutors" (p. 183). Based on his work as the Director of MIT's Laboratory of Computer Sciences, Dertouzos sees these tutors as slowly evolving as computers become more intelligent. These tutors would create a map of your strengths and weaknesses as you construct meaning in learning situations. As you continue to learn, they would then customize your learning in such a way to scaffold you with questions and interactions much like a real tutor does. They would not replace, only augment, the one-on-one interactions between a student and a master teacher. In some cases (e.g. dyslexic adults, or students who have had traumatic experiences) there may be distinct psychological advantages to having a tutor that is not a person because the learner may feel safer in that context. Theoretically, automated tutors could also customize learning for small groups working together. For fascinating imaginative tours into the possibilities and dangers of a future digital world read Dertouzos' book, and *Being Digital* by Nicholas Negroponte (1996).

[32]Read Yee's 1998 article in *Educational Leadership* for a fuller description of her efforts to reshaper her leadership to meet her school's needs. The whole issue (Volume 55, issue 7) is dedicated to new leadership.

[33]Cummins & Sayers, 1997.

[34]Mann, J. 2002.

Chapter 10

[1]Bryk, A.S. and Schneider, B. March 2003, 60, No.6, p. 40-45.

[2]Merriam Webster's Collegiate Dictionary, Tenth Edition. (Springfield: Ma. 1996)

[3]Covey, Stephen. 1989, p. 287.

[4]Covey, S. 1999, Unnumbered 2nd page.

[5]The reference to the Lakota tribal wisdom called the Circle of Courage is adapted from the description of the four dimensions of the medicine wheel from Larry K. Brendtro,

Martin Brokenleg and Steve Van Bockern. *Reclaiming Youth at Risk*. Indiana: National Educational Service, 1990) p. 37-46. Also, please see Brendtro and Brokenleg's chapter, The Circle of Courage, Children as Sacred Beings in Linda Lantieri, (Ed.) *Schools with Spirit*. p. 39-52. For more information about this wonderful work done with Native American youth please visit the website at www.reclaiming.com.

[6]Brendtro and Brokenleg, 2002, p. 43

[7]The National Association of Elementary School Principals Fact Sheet on the Principal Shortage can be obtained on line at www.naesp.org/misc/prin_shrtg_facts.htm.

[8]This reference is found on page 25 of the chapter titled Between Mind and Body: Stress, Emotions and Health by Kenneth R. Pelletier, Ph.D. of Stanford University's School of Medicine found in Daniel Goleman, and Joel Gurin, (Eds.) 1993.

[9]This reference is found on page 40 of the same volume in note 8. The chapter is titled "Mind and Immunity," by Janice K. Kiecolt-Glaser, Ph.D. and Ronald Glaser, Ph.D. The husband and wife team, one a psychologist and the other an immunologist do a superb job of explaining the stress-immune system connection.

[10]Gary Bloom, p. 14-18.

[11]Michael H. Antoni, Ph.D. is associate professor of psychology and psychiatry at the University of Miami and an investigator at the Center for the Biopsychosocial Study of AIDS at the University of Miami School of Medicine. His chapter is titled Stress Management: Strategies That Work. See note 8 for full reference.

[12]Ram Dass and Paul Gorman, 1985, p. 211

[13]Boyatzis, McKee, and Goleman, Passion at Work, p. 88

[14]Robert Greenleaf published his essay, "Servant as Leader," in 1970. He began consulting on this topic after he retired from 38 years in management research development and education at AT&T. For more information about servant leadership and Greenleaf's work, visit the website of The Greenleaf Center at www.greenleaf.org.

[15]Sergiovanni, T. 1990, p. 139

[16]The Franklin Covey website is a wonderful site for reading some of Stephen Covey's articles (www.franklincovey.com). This reference is taken from an article called Centering on Principles, 1994.

[17]See note 12.

[18]Rachael Kessler, September 2002, www.aasa.org/publications/sa/2002_09/kessler.htm.

[19]The Harvard Principal Center in Cambridge, Massachusetts began its Principal Center in the 1980's. Since that time they have served as a major site of renewal for principals across the world. For information about the Center, visit the website at www.gse.harvard.edu/principals/

[20]Boleman and Deal. 2001, revised edition.

[21]Note 19 addresses the Harvard Principals Center. The Center for Creative Leadership is in North Carolina. Go to www.ccl.org. For more information about the Courage to Lead program, read Parker Palmer's article in Lantieri, L. (Ed.) 2002. Exciting work with school administrators is presently in progress.

[22]Journal entry taken from Principal Mae Fong's annual Principal Performance Review self assessment, 2002.

[23]Thich Nahat Hahn, 1987.

References

Aber, J.L.; Jones, S.M.; Brown, J.L.; Chaudry, N.; & Supples, F. 1998. Resolving Conflict Creatively: Evaluating the developmental effects of a school-based violence prevention program in neighborhood and classroom context. *Development and Psychopathology,*10, 187–213.

Ackerman, R.H.; Donaldson. G. A. & Van Der Bogert, R. 1996. *Making sense as a school leader.* San Francisco: Jossey-Bass.

American Psychological Association (Nov. 1997) Learner-Centered psychological principles. A framework for school redesign and reform. Washington D.C.: ADA.

Apple, M. & Beane, J. (Eds.) 1995. *Democratic schools,* Alexandria, VA: Association for Supervision and Curriculum Development.

Bandura, A. *Self-efficacy: The exercise of control.* New York: Freeman.

Bandura, A. 1997. Self-efficacy: Toward a unifying theory of behavioral change, *Psychology Review,* 84, 191–215.

Bandura, A. 1994. Self-efficacy. In V.S. Ramachaudran (Ed.). *Encyclopedia of Human Behavior,* Vol.4, pp. 71–81. New York: *Academic Press.*

Barth, R.S. 2001. Teachers at the helm, *Education Week,* 20, 24, 48 & 32–33.

Barth, R.S. 1990. *Improving schools from within: Teachers, parents and principals can make a difference.* San Francisco: Jossey-Bass.

Barth, R.S. 1980. *Run school run.* Cambridge, MA: Harvard University Press.

Becker, F. & Steele, F. 1995. *Workplace by design: Mapping the high-performance workscape.* San Francisco: Jossey-Bass.

Berninger, V.W. & Richards, T.L. 2002. *Brain literacy for educators and psychologists.* San Diego, CA: *Academic Press.*

Berman, S. 2001. *Hudson High School: Community by design, Safe Learning,* 1,1, 22–25.

Berman, S. 1997. *Children's Social Consciousness and the Development of Social Responsibility.* NY: State University Press.

Blase. J. & Blase, J.R. 1994. *Empowering teachers: What successful principals do.* Thousand Oaks, CA: Corwin Press.

Black, S. 2002. (Dec.) Keeping kids in school. In <*http://www.asbj.com/current/research.html.*>

Bloom, G. 1999 (Sept/Oct). Sink or swim no more. *Thrust for Educational Leadership,* 99, Vol. 29.

Blum, D. 1998 (October). Face it!, *Psychology Today,* 32–39\67–70.

Bodine, R. & Crawford, D. & Hoglund. P. 1993. *The Quality School.* Illinois: Research Press.

Bolman, L.G. & Deal, T. 1997. *Reframing organizations: Artistry, choice and leadership.* San Francisco: Jossey-Bass.

Boleman, L.G. & Deal, T. 2nd Edition (2001) *Leading with soul.* San Francisco: Jossey-Bass.

Bolton, R. 1979. *People skills: How to assert yourself, listen to others and resolve conflicts.* New York: Simon & Schuster.

Boyatzis, R.E., 2002.(April 24). Positive resonance: Educational leadership through emotional intelligence, *Education Week.*

Boyatzis, R. McKee, A. & Goleman, D. 2002. Passion for Work, *Harvard Business School Press.*

Brandt, R. 2003. How new knowledge about the brain applies to social and emotional learning, In (Eds.) Elias, M., Arnold, H. & Steiger-Hussey, C. *EQ + IQ=Best leadership practices for caring and successful schools.* CA: Corwin Press.

Brendtro, L. Brokenleg, M. and Van Bockern, S. 1990. *Reclaiming Youth at Risk.* Indiana: National Educational Service, 1990.

Brendtro, L. and Brokenleg, M. 2002. The Circle of Courage, Children as sacred beings, In (Ed.) Lantieri, & *Schools with Spirit,* Boston: Beacon Press.

Burness, P. & Snider, W. 1995. *Learn & live.* San Rafael, CA: George Lucas Foundation.

Brandt, R. 2003. How new knowledge about the brain applies to social and emotional learning, in Elias, M., Arnold, H. and Steiger Hussey, C. (Eds.) *EQ + IQ,=Best leadership practices for caring and successful schools.* Corwin Press.

Bryman A. (1986). *Leadership and Organizations,* London: Routledge & Kegan Paul.

Bryk, A.S. and Schneider, B. (March, 2003). Trust in Schools: A core resource for school reform. *Educational Leadership.* Volume 60, No. 6.

Caine, R.N. & Caine, G.C. 1994. *Making connections: Teaching and the human brain.* Menlo Park, Ca: Addison-Wesley.

Carter, R. 1998. *Mapping the mind.* Los Angeles: University of California Press.

Cartwright, D. & Zander, A. 1960. *Group dynamics: Research and theory* (2nd ed.). Evanston, Ill.: Row, Peterson.

Cherniss, C. 1998. *Social and emotional learning for leaders. Educational Leadership,* 55, 7, 26–28.

Cherniss, C. and Adler, M. 2000. *Promoting Emotional Intelligence in Organizations: Making Training in Emotional Intelligence Effective,* (Alexandria, Virginia: American Training Society for Training and Development.

Cherniss, C. and Goleman, D. 2001. *The Emotionally Intelligent Workplace: How to Select for, Measure, and Improve Emotional Intelligence in Individuals, Groups, and Organizations* (San Francisco: Jossey Bass).

Cialdini, R.B., 1984. *Influence: How and why people agree to do things.* New York: William Morrow.

Cloke, K. & Goldsmith, J. 2002. *The end of management and the rise of organizational democracy.* San Francisco: Jossey Bass.

Comer, J. 2003. Transforming the lives of children. In (Eds.) Maurice Elias, Harriet Arnold and Cynthia Steiger Hussey, *EQ + IQ=Best Leadership practices for caring and successful schools.* California: Corwin Press.

Conley, D.T. & Goldman, P. 1994. *Facilitative leadership: How principals lead without dominating.* Eugene, OR: University of Oregon. (ED 379 728). Available from Oregon School Study Council.

Cooper, R.K. & Sawf, A., 1997. *Executive EQ: Emotional intelligence in leadership and organizations.* New York: Grosset\Putnam.

Costatino, C.A. & Merchant, C.S. 1996. *Designing conflict management systems: A guide to creating productive and healthy organizations.* San Francisco: Jossey-Bass.

Covey, S. 1989. *The 7 Habits of Highly Effective People, Powerful Lessons In Personal Change.* New York: Simon and Schuster.

Covey, S. 1999. *Living the 7 Habits, The Courage to Change.* New York: Simon and Schuster.

Crow, G.M. 1998. Implications for leadership in collaborative schools. In Diana Pounder (Ed.) *Restructuring schools for collaboration: Promises and pitfalls.* Albany: State University of New York Press.

Cummins, J. & Sayers, D. 1997. *Brave new schools: Challenging cultural illiteracy through global networks.* New York: St. Martin's Press.

Dass, R. and Gorman, P. 1991. *How can I help? Stories and reflections on service.* New York: Alfred A. Knopf, Inc.

Deal, T. & Peterson, K.D., 1991. *Reframing organizations.* San Francisco: Jossey-Bass.

Dertouzos, M. 1997. *What will be: How the new world of information will change our lives.* San Francisco: HarperCollins.

Deutsch, M. & Coleman, P.T. 2000. *The handbook of conflict resolution: Theory and practice.* San Francisco: Jossey-Bass.

Deutsch, M. 2000. Cooperation and competition. In Morton Deutsch & Peter Coleman (Eds.) *The handbook of conflict resolution: Theory and practice.* San Francisco: Jossey-Bass.

Drucker, P.F. 2002. Managing in the next society. New York: St. Martin's Press (Truman Talley).

DuFour, R. & Eaker, R., 1992. *Creating the new American school: A principal's guide to school improvement.* Bloomington, IN: National Education Service.

Earl, L.M. 1997. Rethinking assessment and accountability. In Andy Hargreaves (Ed.) *Rethinking educational change with the heart in mind.* Alexandria, VA: Association for Supervision and Curriculum Development.

Edwards C.; Gandini, L.; & Forman, G. (Eds.) 1993. *The hundred languages of children.* Norwood, NJ: Ablex.

Eisenberg, N. & Zhou, Q. 2000. Regulation from a developmental perspective. *Psychological Inquiry,* 11, 3, 166–171.

Ekman, P., 1999. Basic emotions. In T. Dalgleish and M. Power (Eds.) *Handbook of cognition and emotion.* Sussex, UK: John Wiley & Sons.

Ekman, P. 1992. An argument for basic emotions. *Cognition and Emotions,* 6, 161–168.

Ekman, P. & Friesan, W.V., 1975. *Unmasking the face: A guide to recognizing emotions from facial expressions.* Englewood Cliffs, N.J.: Prentice-Hall.

Ekman, P. & Friesan, W.V. 1971. Constants across cultures in the face and emotion. *Journal of Personality and Social Psychology,* 17, 124–129.

Ekman, P. & Rosenberg, E. (Eds.), 1997. *What the face reveals: Basic and applied studies of spontaneous expression using the Facial Action Coding System (FAS)* New York: Oxford University Press.

Elbow, P. 1983. (April) *Critical thinking is not enough.* Speech presented at the Reninger Lecture at the University of Northern Iowa.

Elias, M. 2003. *Academic and social-emotional learning.* International Academy of Education.

Elias, M., Arnold, H. and Steiger Hussey, C. (Eds.) 2003. *EQ + IQ =Best leadership practices for caring and successful schools.* Corwin Press.

Ellmore, D.A., Olson, S.E., & Smith, P.M. 1995. *Reinventing schools: The technology is now!* (available at *www.nap.edu*).

Facing History and Ourselves resource book: Holocaust and human behavior, 1994. Facing History and Ourselves National Foundation, Inc.

Fisher, K. & Fisher, M.D. 1998. *The distributed mind: Achieving high performance through the collective intelligence of knowledge work teams.* New York: AMACOM.

Fischer, L. 2002. *The dance of power within: identity, pedagogy, curriculum.* Lesley College: masters thesis.

Fisher, R. & Ury, W. 1991 (2nd ed.) *Getting to yes: Negotiating agreement without giving in.* New York: Penguin.

Fiske, E.B. 1995. Systemic school reform: Implications for architecture. In Anne Meek (Ed.) *Designing places for learning.* Alexandria, VA: Association for Supervision and Curriculum Development.

Folger, J.P., Poole, M.S., & Stutman, R.K. 1997. *Working through conflict: Strategies for relationships, groups and organizations.* New York: Addison Wesley Longman.

Folkerts, K. 1999. *The emotionally intelligent team.* Denton, TX: Center for Study of Work Teams, University of North Texas (CSWT paper available at <*www.workteams.unt.edu)*>.

Frederickson, L. 2003. Social emotional learning, service learning & educational leadership. Available at <*www.casel.org*>.

Freund, J.C. 1992. *Smart negotiating: How to make good deals in the real world.* New York: Simon & Schuster.

Fullan, M. 1997. Emotion and hope: Constructive concepts for complex times. In Andy Hargreaves (Ed.) *ASCD Yearbook 1997: Rethinking educational change with heart and mind.* Alexandria, VA.: Association for Supervision and Curriculum Development.

Fullan, M. 2001. *Leading in a culture of change.* San Francisco: Jossey Bass.

Fullan, M. 1999. *Change forces: The sequel.* Falmers Press.

Fullan, M. & Hargreaves, A. 1996. *What's worth fighting for in your school?* New York: Teachers College Press.

Garbarino, J. 1999. *Lost boys: Why our sons turn violent and how we can save them.* The Free Press.

George, J. 2000. Emotions and leadership: The role of emotional intelligence. *Human Relations,* 53, 8, 1027–1055.

Glickman, C. 2002. *Leadership for learning: How to help teachers succeed.* Alexandria, VA: Association for Supervision and Curriculum Development.

Glickman, C., Gordon, S.P. & Ross-Gordan, J.M. 2001. *Supervision and instructional leadership: A developmental approach* (5th Ed.). Boston: Allyn & Bacon.

Glickman, C. May 2002. The courage to lead. *Education Leadership,* Vol. 59 Issue 8.

Goleman,D.; Boyatzis, R.; McKee, A. 2002. *Primal leadership: Realizing the power of emotional intelligence.* Cambridge, MA: Harvard Business School Press.

Goleman, D. 1995. *Emotional Intelligence.* New York, Bantam Doubleday Dell.

Goleman, D. 1998. *Working with emotional intelligence.* New York: Bantam Doubleday Dell.

Goleman, D. & Cherniss, C. *The Emotionally intelligent workplace.* San Francisco, Jossey Bass.

Goleman, D. & Gurin, J. (Eds.) 1993. *Mind body medicine, How to use your mind for better health.* Spectrum America.

Goleman, D.; Boyatzis, R.; McKee, A. 2002. *Primal leadership: Realizing the power of emotional intelligence.* Cambridge, MA: Harvard Business School Press.

Gordon, T. 1977. *Leadership effectiveness training,* New York: Bantam Books, 1977.

Greenleaf, R. 1970. Servant as leader. Obtained at *www.greenleaf.org.*

Griffin, E. 1997. *A first look at communication theory.* New York: McGraw-Hill.

Griggs, L. 1995. Diverse teams: Breakdown or breakthrough, *Training and development,* 49, 10, 22–29.

Hall, G. and Hord, S. 2001. *Implementing change: Patterns, principles and potholes.* Allyn & Bacon.

Hahn, T.N. 1987. *Being peace.* Berkeley, CA: Parallax Press.

Haynes N. & Marans, S. 1999. The cognitive, emotional, and behavioral (CEB) framework for promoting acceptance of diversity. In Cohen, J. (Ed.) *Educating minds and hearts* (1999) New York: Teachers College Press.

Hersey, P. and Blanchard, K. 1982. *Management of organizational behavior,* fourth edition. New Jersey: Prentice Hall.

Herzberg, F. 2003 (January). One more time: How do you motivate employees? In The *Harvard Business Review: Special Issue on Motivating People.*

Hird, A. 2000. *Learning from Cyber-savvy students: How internet-age kids impact classroom teaching.* Sterling Virginia: Stylus.

Holloway, J.H. 2000. The promise and pitfalls of site-based management. *Educational Leadership,* Vol. 57, No. 7.

Hord, S.M. 2002. *Facilitative leadership: The imperative to change.* Austin, TX: Southwest Educational Laboratory (ED370 217). Available at *www.sedl.org.*

Houston, P. 2001. Superintendents for the 21st Century: It's not just a job, it's a calling, *Phi Delta Kappan,* 82, 6, 428–433.

Janis, I. 1983. *Groupthink: Psychological studies of policy decisions and fiascoes* (2nd ed. rev.). Boston: Houghton Mifflin.

Jones, G.R. 2002. *Cyber schools: An education renaissance.* New York: ibooks.

Kahrs, J.R. 1996. Principals who support teacher leadership. In Gayle Moller and Marilyn Katzenmeyer (Eds.) *Every teacher as a leader: Realizing the potential of teacher leadership.* San Francisco: Jossey-Bass.

Katzenbach, J.R. & Smith, D.K. 1993. *The wisdom of teams: Creating the high-performance organization.* Boston: Harvard Business School Press.

Kaufman, M.T., 2002. Face it: Your looks are revealing, *New York Times,* September 8, Week In Review, 13.

Kessler, R. 2002 (September). *Five principles for welcoming soul into school leadership.* School Administrator.

Kinsler, K. & Gamble, M. 2001. *Reforming schools.* London/New York: Continuum.

Kohn, A. 2003 (March). Almost there but not quite. *Educational Leadership,* Volume 60, no.6, p. 29.

Kotter, J. 2002. *The heart of change: Real life stories of how people change their organizations,* MA: Harvard Business School Press.

Lambert, L. 2002. A framework for shared leadership, *Educational Leadership,* 59, 8, 37–40.

Lambert, L. 1998. How to build leadership capacity, *Educational Leadership,* 55, 7, 17–19.

Lambert, M.D. 1995. Reciprocal team coaching, *Thrust for Educational Leadership,* 24, 5, 20–22.

Lambert, M.D. &. Garner, M.E. 1995. The school district as interdependent learning community. In Lambert et al. (Eds.) *The constructivist leader.* New York: Teachers College Press.

Lantieri, L. and Patti, J. 1996. *Waging peace in our schools.* MA: Beacon Press, 1996.

Lantieri, L. 2002. (Ed.) *Schools with Spirit.* Boston: Beacon Press.

Lashway, L. 2000. Who's in charge? The accountability challenge, *Principal Leadership,* Vol 1, No.3 (available at *www.principals.org*).

Lashway, L. 1995. *Facilitative leadership.* Eugene, OR: ERIC Clearinghouse on Educational Management (ED381 851).

LeDoux, J. 1996. *The emotional brain.* New York: Simon & Schuster.

Lieber, C. 2002. *Partners in learning: From conflict to collaboration in secondary classrooms.* MA: Educators for Social Responsibility.

Lickona, T.T. 2001 (Winter). What is good character and how can we develop it in our children? In *Reclaiming Children and Youth.*

Lynch, J. 2003. *Are your organization's conflict management practices an integrated conflict management system? In <http://www.mediate.com/articles/systemsedit3.cfm?nl=18* Parent URL:

Man, J. 2002. *Gutenberg: How one man remade the world with words.* New York: John Wiley & Sons.

Manstead, A.S. & Fischer, A.H. 2000. Emotional regulation in full. *Psychological Inquiry,* 11, 3, 188–191.

Manz. C.C. & Sims, H.P. 1989. *Super leadership: Leading others to lead themselves.* New York: Prentice Hall.

Marx, G. 2002 (March). Preparing students and schools for a radically different future in *USA Today Magazine,* Vol. 130 Issue 268.

Matthews, J. 1998. Implications for collaborative educator preparation and development: A sample educational approach. In Diana Pounder (Ed.) *Restructuring schools for collaboration: Promises and pitfalls.* Albany: State University of New York Press.

Mayer, J.D., Salovey, P. & Caruso, D. 2000. Models of emotional intelligence. In Robert J. Sternberg (Ed.) *The handbook of intelligence.* Cambridge, UK: Cambridge University Press.

McCarthy, W. 1991. The role of power and principle in getting to yes. In J. William Breslin and Jeffery Z. Rubin (Eds.), *Negotiation Theory and Practice,* Cambridge MA: The Program on Negotiation at Harvard Law School.

McKay, M.; Davis, M. & Fanning, P. 1997. *Thoughts and feelings: Taking control of your moods and your life.* Oakland, CA: New Harbinger.

Meharabian, A. 1971. *Silent messages.* Belmont, CA: Wadsworth.

Meier, D. 1994. *The power of their ideas: Lessons for America from a small school in Harlem.* MA: Beacon Press.

Meier, D. & Schwarz, P. 1995. Central Park East Secondary School: The hard part is making it happen. In Michael W. Apple (Ed.) *Democratic schools.* Alexandria, VA: Association for Supervision and Curriculum Development.

Milner, N. 1994. Linda Colburn: On-the-spot-mediation in a public housing project. In Deborah M. Kolb (Ed.), *When talk works: Profiles of mediators.* San Francisco: Jossey-Bass.

Mohr, N. 1998. Creating effective study groups for principals. *Educational Leadership,* 55, 7, pp. 41–44.

Naisbitt, J. 2000. *High tech/High touch: Technology and our search for meaning.* New York: Broadway Books.

National Center for Education Statistics. 2002. *Indicators of school crime and safety.* Available at URL: *http://nces.ed.gov.*

Negroponte, N. 1996. *Being digital.* New York: Vintage Books.

Neuman, M. 2000. Leadership for student learning, *Phi Delta Kappan,* 82, 1, 9–12.

Novick, B.; Kress, J. S. & Elias, M.J.(2003). *Building learning communities with character: How to integrate academic, social and emotional learning.* Va: Association for Supervision and Curriculum Development.

Odden, E. & Wohlsetter, P. 1995. Making school-based management work, *Educational Leadership,* 52, 5, 32–36.

Olson, L. 2000. Principals try new styles as instructional leaders, *Education Week,* 20, 9, 1 & 15–17.

O'Toole, J. 1995. *Leading change: Overcoming the ideology of comfort and the tyranny of custom.* San Francisco: Jossey-Bass.

Owens, R. 1998. *Organizational Behavior in Education, 6th edition,* MA: Allyn and Bacon.

Palmer, P. 1998. *The courage to teach: Exploring the inner landscapes of a teacher's life.* San Francisco: Jossey-Bass.

Patterson, J.L. 1993. *Leadership for tomorrow's schools.* Alexandria, VA: Association for Supervision and Curriculum.

Patti, J & Tobin, J. 2001a. *Leading the way: Reflections on creating Peaceable Schools. Reclaiming Children and Youth,* 10, 1, Spring 2001, 41–46.

Patti, J & Tobin, J. 2001b. *The principal's leadership style, behaviors and leadership strategies used to implement the Resolving Conflict Creatively Program in their schools: A three-year study of the factors that inhibit and enhance this process.* Report presented to the Dispute Resolution Center at the City University of New York June 6, 2001.

Petrovic, D. 1994. Ethnic cleansing-An attempt at methodology. *European Journal of International Law,* Volume 5, No.3.

Phi Delta Kappa. March, 2003. The 2002 Phi Delta Kappa Census.

Pickeral, T. 2003. *Service learning policy deliberation:* A set of resources to advance service-learning through policy alignment development and support. Presented at American Association of Colleges for Teacher Education national conference.

Purser, R.E. & Cabana, S. 1998. *The self managing organization: How leading companies are transforming the work of teams for real impact.* New York: The Free Press.

Quellmaslz, E., Shields, P. & Knapp, M.S. 1995. *School-based reform: Lessons from a national study.* Washington, D.C.: U.S. Department of Education.

Ramsay, M. 1999. *Leadership in teams.* Denton, TX: Center for Study of Work Teams, University of North Texas (CSWT paper available at www.workteams.unt.edu).

Rallis, S.F. 1990. Professional teachers and restructured schools: Leadership challenges. In Brad Mitchell & Luvern L. Cunningham (Eds.) *Educational leadership and changing contexts of families, communities and schools.* Chicago : University of Chicago Press.

Rees, F. 2001. *How to lead work teams.* San Francisco: Jossey-Bass.

Richard, A. 2000. Panel calls for fresh look at duties facing principals, *Education Week,* 20, 9, 5.

Robbins, H.A. & Finley, M. 2000. *The new why teams don't work: What goes wrong and how to make it right.* San Francisco: Berrett-Koehler.

Roderick, T. 1987/1988 (Dec.) Johnny can learn to negotiate. *Education Leadership.*

Ruble, T.L. & Thomas, K.W. 1976. Support for a two-dimensional model of conflict behavior. *Organizational Behavior and Human Performance,* 16, 143–155.

Ryan, K. D., Oestreich, D.K., & Orr III, G.A. 1996. *The courageous messenger: How to successfully speak up at work.* San Francisco: Jossey-Bass.

Rybeck, D. 1998. *Putting emotional intelligence to work: Successful leadership is more than IQ.* Mass: Butterworth-Heinemann.

Saarni, C. 1999. *The development of emotional competence.* New York: Guilford.

Salovey, P. & Mayer, J. 1990. *Emotional intelligence. Imagination, cognition, and personality,* 9(3), 185–211.

Saraceno, B. M.D. 2002. WHO mental health activities, in Mrazek, P.J. & Hosman, C. M.H. (Eds). *Toward a strategy for worldwide action to promote mental health and prevent mental and behavioral disorders.* Report from the Inaugural World Conference on the Promotion of Mental Health and Prevention of Mental and Behavioral Disorders. Alexandria, VA: World Federation for Mental Health.

Sax, L., 2002. Maybe men and women are different, *American Psychologist.* 57, 6\7, 444.

Schaps, E. Schaeffer, E. & McDonell, S.N. 2001(Sept 12) What's Right and Wrong in Character Education Today? *Education Week.*

Shaw, J. (2000). *Jack and Jill why they kill: Saving our children, saving ourselves.* Seattle: Onjin-jinkta Publishing.

Schein, E.H. 1992. *Organizational culture and leadership* (2nd ed.). San Francisco: Jossey-Bass.

Schein, E.H. 1999. *The corporate culture survival guide.* San Francisco: Jossey-Bass.

Schlechty, P. 1997. Inventing better schools: *An action plan for educational reform.* San Francisco: Jossey-Bass.

Schwartz, R.M. 1994. *The skilled facilitator: Practical wisdom for developing effective groups.* San Francisco: Jossey-Bass.

Seligmanm M., 1991. *Learned optimism.* New York: Alfred A. Knopf.

Senge, P. 1990. *The Fifth Discipline: The art and practice of the learning organization.* New York: Doubleday.

Senge, P; Cambron-McCabe, N.; Lucas, T.; Smith, B.; Dutton, J. & Kleiner, A. 2000. *Schools that learn: A fifth discipline fieldbook for educators, parents and everyone who cares about education.* New York: Doubleday.

Sergiovanni, T. 1996. *Leadership in the schoolhouse: How is it different? Why is it important?* San Francisco: Jossey-Bass.

Sergiovanni, T. 1993. *Building community in schools.* San Francisco: Jossey-Bass.

Sergiovanni, T. 1990. *Moral leadership.* San Francisco: Jossey Bass.

Shaw, L. 2000. Jack and Jill why they kill: Saving our children, saving ourselves. Seattle: Onjin-jinkta Publishing.

Shotsberger, P.G. & Vetter, R. 2002. The handheld web: How mobile wireless technologies will change web-based instruction and training. In Allison Rossett, A. (Ed.). *The ASTD E-learning handbook: Best practices, strategies, and case studies for an emerging field.* New York: McGraw Hill.

R. Skiba, R. Peterson, K. Boone and Fontanini. 2000.(Fall). Reventing school violence with comprehensive planning. *Reaching Today's Youth.*

Slaikeu, K. 1996. *When push comes to shove: A practical guide for mediating disputes.* San Francisco: Jossey-Bass.

Sleeter, C. 2001. *Culture Difference and Power.* In Multicultural Education Series, James A. Banks (Ed.) New York: Teachers College Press.

Smith, D. 1996. The following part of leading. In Frances Hesselbein, Marshall Goldsmith and Richard Beckhard (Eds.). *Leader of the future.* San Francisco: Jossey-Bass.

Solomon, G. 2002. Digital equity: It's not just about access anymore, *Technology & Learning,* 22, 9.

Sosik, J.J. & Megerian, L.E. 1999. Understanding leader emotional intelligence and perform-ance. *Group and Organizational Management,* 24, 3, 367–390.

Sousa. D.A. 2001. *How the brain learns: A classroom teacher's guide.* Thousand Oaks, CA: Corwin Press.

Stein, S.J. & Book, H.E., 2000. *The EQ edge: Emotional intelligence and your success.* Toronto: Stoddart.

Stevahn, L.; Johnson, D.W.; Johnson, R.T.; Schultz, R. 2002. Effects of conflict resolution training integrated into a high school social studies curriculum. *Journal of Social Psychology,* 142, 3.

Stone, D., Patton, B., & Heen, S. 1999. *Difficult conversations: How to discuss what matters most.* New York: Penguin Books.

Suler, J. (2002).The basic psychological features of cyberspace. In *The psychology of cyberspace.* www.rider.edu/users/suler/psycyber/basicfeat.html (article orig. pub. 1996).

Sylwester, R. 1995. *A celebration of neurons: An educator's guide to the human brain.* Alexandria, VA: Association for Supervision and Curriculum.

Tannen. D., 2001. *You just don't understand: Women and men in conversation.* New York: William & Morrow.

Tanner, D. & Tanner, L. 1995. *Curriculum development: Theory into practice.* Englewood Cliffs, NJ: Prentice-Hall.

Taylor, A. 1997. Buildings that teach. In Burness, P. & Snider, W. (Eds.) *Learn & Live.* Nicasio, CA: The George Lucas Educational Foundation.

Taylor, A. 1995. How schools are redesigning their space. In Anne Meek (Ed.) *Designing places for learning.* Alexandria, VA: Association for Supervision and Curriculum Development.

Thomas, G. 2002 (Nov.) Involve students, then follow their lead, in *Community Links.*

Thomas, K.W. *Intrinsic motivation at work: Building energy and commitment.* (San Francisco: Berett-Koehler, 2002).

Tewel, K.J. 1995. Despair at the central office, *Educational Leadership,* 52, 7, 65–68.

Toppo, G. 2003. School violence hits lower grades, *USA Today,* 01/13/2003, p. 1.

Viadero, D. 2003 (January 15). Tormentors. *Education Week.*

Tyler, K. 2002. Extending the Olive Branch, *HR Magazine,* 47, 11, 85–87.

Tuckman, B. 1965. Developmental sequence in small groups. *Psychological Bulletin,* 63, 384–399.

United States Census Bureau, 2002. Statistical Abstract of the United States: 2001. (Available at *http://www.census.gov/prod/2002pubs/01statab/edu.pdf*).

United States Department of Education, 2000. *Schools as centers of community: A citizen's guide for planning and design.* Washington, D.C. : U.S. Dept. of Ed. (Available at *www.ed.gov/pubs/edpubs.html.*).

Ury, W. 1991. *Getting Past No: Negotiating your way from confrontation to cooperation.* New York: Bantam.

Ury, W., Brett, J.M., & Goldberg, S.B. 1991. Getting disputes resolved: Designing systems to cut the costs of conflict. Cambridge, MA: *The Program on Negotiation at Harvard Law School.*

Wagner, T. 1998. Change as collaborative inquiry: A 'constructivist' methodology for reinventing schools, *Phi Delta Kappan,* 80, 7, 378–383.

Wallender, J.; Weissberg, R.; Rubin, M. & Salovey, P. 2003. Can development of social–emotional competencies in childhood reduce risk for physical health problems across the life-span? (manuscript submitted for publication).

Weaver, R.G. & Farrell, J.D. 1997. *Managers as facilitators: A practical guide to getting work done in a changing workplace.* San Francisco: Berrett-Koehler.

Weissberg, R.P., Shriver, T.P., Bose, S., & DeFalco, K. 1997. Creating a districtwide social development project. *Educational Leadership,* 54, 37–39.

Weissberg, R., Resnik, H., Payton, J. and Utne O'Brien, M. 2003. (March) Evaluating Social and Emotional Learning Programs. *Education Leadership,* Volume 60, No. 6.

Weiler, J. 1999. An overview of research on girls and violence. In *Choices Brief,* Vol.1. Institute for Urban and Minority education, Teachers College, Columbia University.

Wellins, R.S.; Byham, W.C.; Dixon, G.R. 1994. *Inside teams: How 20 world-class organizations are winning through teamwork.* San Francisco: Jossey-Bass.

Whitemyer, D., 2002. Don't Just Do Something—Sit There, *Harvard Management Update,* 7, 12, 3.

Wheatley, M. 2002. The new science of leadership, an interview with Meg Wheatley from the radio series *Insight and Outlook* hosted by Scott London.

Willinsky, J. 2002. Democracy and Education: The missing link may be yours, *Harvard Educational Review,* 72, 3, 367–392.

Yang, O. & Shao, E.Y. 1996. Shared leadership in self-managed teams: A competing values approach, *Total Quality Management,* 7, 5, 521–534.

Yee, D.L. 1998. Chalk, chips, and children, *Educational Leadership,* 55, 7, 57–59.

Zins, J.E., Weissberg, R.P., Wang, M.L., & Walberg, H.J. (Eds.) (in press). *Building school success through social and emotional learning: Implications for practice and research.* New York: Teachers College Press.

Index